# THE QI BOOK OF THE DEAD

A Quite Interesting Book

# The QI Book of the Dead

John Lloyd and John Mitchinson

faber and faber

First published in 2009
by Faber and Faber Ltd
74–77 Great Russell Street
London WC1B 3DA

Typeset by Palindrome
Printed in England by CPI Mackays, Chatham

The right of QI Ltd to be identified as author of this work
has been asserted in accordance with Section 77
of the Copyright, Designs and Patents Act 1988

A CIP record for this book
is available from the British Library

ISBN 978-0-571-24490-4

2 4 6 8 10 9 7 5 3 1

# Contents

# Introduction

*This is a city of shifting light, of changing skies, of sudden vistas.*
*A city so beautiful it breaks the heart again and again.*

ALEXANDER McCALL SMITH

George Street in Edinburgh is one of the most elegant thoroughfares in one of the best-designed cities in the world. Wherever you stand along it, at one end can be seen the green copper dome of a Robert Adam church called St George's and, at the other, a massive stone column called the Melville Monument.

Loosely modelled on Trajan's Column in Rome, it is not quite as tall as Nelson's Column in London but it is equally striking and certainly more beautifully situated. The architect was William Burn (1789–1870) but he had more than a little help from Robert Stevenson (1772–1850), the great Scottish civil engineer, better known for his roads, harbours and bridges – and especially for his daring and spectacular lighthouses. According to the metal plaque near the base of the column, Stevenson 'finalised the dimensions and superintended the building of this 140-foot-high, 1,500-ton edifice utilising the world's first iron balance-crane, invented under his direction by Francis Watt in 1809–10 for erecting the Bell Rock lighthouse'.

The Melville Monument was constructed in 1823 in memory of Henry Dundas, 1st Viscount Melville (1742–1811) and it is his statue that glares nobly from the top down the length of George Street. As you might expect from all the trouble the good people of Edinburgh took to put him up there, Dundas was an extremely famous man in his lifetime. A dominant figure in British politics for over forty years, he was Treasurer to the Navy, Lord Advocate, Keeper of the Scottish Signet and (an interesting columnar coincidence, this) the First Lord of the Admiralty at the time of the Battle of Trafalgar. On the down side, he was a fierce opponent of the abolition of slavery (managing to successfully prevent it for several years) and has the distinction of being the last person in Britain to be impeached.* And yet, unless you are a resident of the Scottish capital, or a naval historian specialising in the Napoleonic wars, it is my guess that you have never even heard of him.

Life – what's it all about, eh?

In Edinburgh, early one sunny morning last August, I was standing at the east end of George Street looking into St Andrew Square where Dundas's memorial stands. The huge fluted edifice rose, dark against the recently risen sun, into the watercolour sky. As I watched, across the grass still bright with dew, ran a small girl, no more than four years old. She was alone, wearing a pink top and white jeans, with blonde Shirley Temple curls. She rushed towards the immense column and, when she was a few yards away, she stopped. She looked slowly up its gigantic length

---

* Impeachment is the process of putting a public official on trial for improper conduct (in this case corruption and misappropriation of public funds) with the intent of removing him or her from office. The House of Lords acquitted Dundas (and offered him an Earldom by way of apology) but he never held office again.

till the angle of her head told me she was staring at the blackened figure on the top. Her back to was to me – I never saw her face – but from the whole attitude of her body it was obvious that she was awestruck. It was the perfect photograph. Though I didn't have a camera with me, I can still see it in my mind's eye as clearly as if it were on the screen in front of me now. It also seemed to be the perfect metaphor. Here were the two bookends of human life. Far up in the sky, long dead, a great stone man whose name very few of us now know; below, still earthbound, still with everything to live for, a tiny real human being whose name is completely unknown to all of us (including me) but who has the potential, if she but knew it, to become the most famous woman in history.

Perhaps in those few moments, staring at the forbidding personage in the sky, something turned over in the tumblers of her brain, opening a hidden lock and inspiring her to future greatness. Or, perhaps, at some subconscious level, she suddenly came to the same conclusion as the Greek philosopher Epictetus: that fame is 'the noise of madmen'. After all, it is not necessary for the world to know who you are to live a good and worthwhile life.

John Mitchinson and I hope that you may be inspired to greatness by the journeys of the three score and eight extraordinary human beings here within, or at least draw some comfort from knowing your life is nowhere near as bad as it could be.

JOHN LLOYD

# Prologue

*I don't think anybody should write his autobiography until after he is dead.*
SAMUEL GOLDWYN

The first thing that strikes you about the Dead is just how may of them there are. The idea you hear bandied about that there are more people living now than have ever lived in the past is plain wrong – by a factor of thirteen. The number of *Homo sapiens sapiens* that have ever lived, fought, loved, fussed pottered and finally died over the last 100,000 years is around ninety billion.

Ninety billion is a big number, especially when you're trying to write a book with a title that implies it covers all of them. But it all depends how you look at things. Ninety billion is big, but also small. You could bury everyone who has ever lived, side by side, in an area the size of England and Scotland combined. Or Uruguay. Or Oklahoma. That's just 0.1 per cent of the land area of the Earth. And if you piled all the dead people who have ever lived on to an enormous set of scales they would be comfortably outweighed by the ants that are out there right now, plotting who knows what. It's all a question of perspective.

*Prologue*

The Dead are, literally, our family. Not just the ones we know we are related to: our two parents, four grandparents and eight great-grandparents. Go back ten generations and each of us has a thousand direct relatives, go back fifteen and the number soars to more than 35,000 (and that's not counting aunts and uncles). In fact, we only need to go back to the year 1250 to have more direct ancestors than the number of human beings who have ever lived. The solution to this apparent paradox is that we're all inter-related: the further back you go, the more ancestors we are likely to share. The earliest common ancestor of everyone living in Europe only lived about 600 years ago, and everyone alive on the planet today is related both to Confucius (551–479 BC) and to Nefertiti (1370–1330 BC). So this is a book of family history for everyone.

Trying to organise relatives is always a challenge. The great film director Billy Wilder once pointed out that an actor entering through a door gives the audience nothing, 'but if he enters through the window, you've got a situation'. With this in mind, we've avoided the usual approach of organising the family get-together into professional groupings: scientists, kings, business people, murderers, etc. This is a perfectly reasonable system, except that, families being what they are, the actors and musicians will be tempted to flounce past the table labelled 'accountants' or 'psychologists' and vice versa. So we've started from a different premise, selecting themes that focus on the *quality* of lives rather than their *content*, qualities that are familiar to everyone: our relationship to our parents, our state of health, our sexual appetites, our attitude to work, our sense of what it all means. We also draw no distinction between people with universally familiar names and those who are virtually unheard of. The only criterion for inclusion is interestingness. The result is unexpected bedfellows: Sir Isaac Newton duetting with Salvador Dalì, for example, or Karl Marx singing bass to Emma Hamilton's soprano.

In E. M. Forster's novel *A Room with a View,* Mr Emerson remarks that getting through life is like 'a public performance on the violin, in which you must learn the instrument as you go along'. The major attraction of the Dead is that the violin has been put back in its case, and their lives – however, short, discordant or tuneless – have a definite beginning, middle and an end. That is their chief advantage over those of us who are still trying to spot the tunes in our own swirling cacophony: we can see or hear more clearly how one thing leads to another.

The original Egyptian and Tibetan Books of the Dead were kind of early self-help manuals, practical guides to getting the best out of the afterlife. Anyone hoping for the same in the pages that follow will be disappointed (as will those looking forward to ninety billion entries in the index). This is a book that is more interested in questions than answers, and in tapping into interesting connections rather than building a closed system of classification.

Above all, there's nothing like hanging out with the Dead to point up the sheer improbability of being alive. As the emphatically not-dead American writer Maya Angelou reminds us: 'Life loves to be taken by the lapel and told: "I am with you kid. Let's go." '

JOHN MITCHINSON

# The QI Book of the Dead

# CHAPTER ONE

# There's Nothing like a Bad Start in Life

*Whoever has not got a good father should procure one.*
FRIEDRICH NIETZSCHE

Our early experiences shape our character and the way our lives unfold, and a poor start can, of course, blight a person's prospects forever. But there is a more mysterious path that leads from truly dreadful beginnings to quite extraordinary achievement. As the Canadian novelist Robertson Davies put it: 'A happy childhood has spoiled many a promising life.'

Some of the most famous people in history had childhoods that were wrecked by a dead, absent or impossible father. We have chosen eight, but the list could have been twenty times as long: once you start to notice, they sprout up everywhere: Confucius, Augustus Caesar, Michelangelo, Peter the Great, John Donne, Handel, Balzac, Nietzsche, Darwin, Jung, Conan Doyle, Aleister Crowley – all of them victims of what psychologists would call 'inappropriate parenting'.

In the 500 years since his death, **Leonardo da Vinci** (1452–1519) has become our model for the solitary genius, the ultimate Renaissance man. The common wisdom is that, like Shakespeare, we know his work in great detail but next to nothing about his life. This is a myth. In fact, and again like Shakespeare, we know much more about Leonardo than we do about the vast majority of his contemporaries. We know he was illegitimate, the son of a notary in the small Italian hill town of Vinci, and that his mother, Caterina, was either a local peasant or an Arabic slave (recent analysis of the artist's inky fingerprints tends to suggest the latter). His father, Piero, quickly married off Caterina to a bad-tempered local lime-burner* and the young Leonardo found himself abandoned. His father went on to marry four times and sire another fifteen children; his mother also had new children of her own and refused to treat Leonardo as her son. Worse still, as a bastard, he was prevented from going to university or entering any of the respectable professions such as medicine or law.

Leonardo's response was to withdraw into a private world of observation and invention. The key to understanding his genius isn't in his paintings – extraordinary and groundbreaking though they are – but in his notebooks. In these 13,000 pages of notes, sketches, diagrams, philosophical observations and lists, we have one of the most complete records of the inner workings of a human mind ever committed to paper. Leonardo's curiosity was relentless. He literally took apart the world around him to see how it worked and left a paper trail of the process. This was first-hand research: he had to see things for himself, whatever that meant. He personally dissected more than thirty human corpses in his life-

---

* Lime-burners heated chalk in a kiln to 1,100 °C, to make quicklime, the main ingredient of mortar (the forerunner of cement) used in building.

It was an important but badly paid and dangerous job. The dust could cause blindness or spontaneously combust, producing hideous burns. On top of that, carbon monoxide released by the process made the lime-burners dizzy. It was an easy matter to fall into the kiln and be incinerated.

time, even though it was a serious criminal offence. This wasn't motivated by any medical agenda: he just wanted to improve the accuracy of his drawing and deepen his understanding of how the body worked (he ridiculed other artists' depictions of human flesh, saying they looked like 'sacks of nuts'). Out of the notebooks flowed a succession of inventions, some fantastical but others entirely practical: the first 'tank', the first parachute, a giant siege crossbow, a crane for emptying ditches, the very first mixer-tap for a bath, folding furniture, an aqualung, an automatic drum, automatically opening and closing doors, a sequin-maker and smaller devices for making spaghetti, sharpening knives, slicing eggs and pressing garlic. It was here, too, that Leonardo recorded his remarkable insights into the natural world: he was the first to notice how counting tree rings gave the age of the tree and he could explain why the sky was blue 300 years before Lord Rayleigh discovered molecular scattering.

Each page of the notebooks looks like an excerpt from a vast handwritten visual encyclopaedia. Paper was expensive so every inch was covered in Leonardo's neat script, all of it written back to front, which means you need a mirror to make it intelligible. No one knows why he chose to write this way. Perhaps as a left-hander he found it easier writing right to left; perhaps he didn't want people stealing his ideas. Whatever the reason, it's the perfect physical representation of his awkward genius. Leonardo didn't really care about fitting in or what others thought. He was a vegetarian when almost no one else was because he empathised with animals (one of his obsessions was setting free caged birds). Despite being commissioned by some of the most powerful grandees in Europe, he rarely finished any project he started. What mattered to him was to be free to do his own thing, to achieve the control over his life that had eluded him as an abandoned child:

> *It had long since come to my attention that people of accomplishment rarely sat back and let things happen to them. They went out and happened to things.*

Most of us picture him as he appears in the one authenticated self-portrait: a sixty-year-old, bald and bearded sage, a loner. But the young Leonardo was something quite different. His contemporary, the biographer Giorgio Vasari (1511–74), was unambiguous: he was a man 'of physical beauty beyond compare'. And that wasn't all, he was freakishly strong:

> *There is something supernatural in the accumulation in one individual of so much beauty, grace, and might. With his right hand he could twist an iron horseshoe as if it were made of lead.*

And a charmer:

> *In his liberality, he welcomed and gave food to any friend, rich or poor...his speech could bend in any direction the most obdurate of wills.*

But cross him and you'd have to deal with his 'terrible strength in argument, sustained by intelligence and memory'. This is Leonardo the gay Florentine about town, who was anonymously accused (and acquitted) of sodomy, whose teenage pupil and companion was known as Salai ('limb of Satan'), the precocious artist whose collection of pornographic drawings was eventually stolen from the Royal Collection in Windsor Castle, according to the art critic Brian Sewell, by a distinguished German art critic in a Sherlock Holmes cloak:

*There is no doubt that the drawings were a considerable embarrassment, and I think everyone was very relieved to find that they'd gone.*

The older sage and the racy young Adonis were both products of the same self-confidence. It was driven by study, by his attempt to come up with his own answers, the process he calls *saper vedere,* 'knowing how to see'. 'Learning', he once wrote 'never exhausts the mind.' It was what had sustained him as a child and there were times when it still gave him childlike pleasure. Once, in the Vatican, he made a set of wings and horns, painted them silver, and stuck them on a lizard to turn it into a small 'dragon' which he used to frighten the Pope's courtiers. On another occasion, he cleaned out a bullock's intestines, attached them to a blacksmith's bellows, and pumped them up into a vast malodorous balloon, which quickly filled the forge and drove his bewildered onlookers outside.

Leonardo was brilliant, but he was not infallible. He didn't invent scissors, the telescope, the helicopter or the telescope, as is frequently claimed. He was very bad at maths – he only ever mastered basic geometry and his arithmetic was often wrong. Many of his observations haven't stood the test of time: he thought the moon's surface was covered by water, which was why it reflected light from the sun; that the salamander had no digestive organs but survived by eating fire; and that it was a good idea to paint his most ambitious painting, *The Last Supper* directly on to dry plaster (it wasn't, what you see today is practically all the work of restorers). Also, because his fame in the years after his death was almost exclusively tied to a small body of thirty completed paintings, he was to have almost no impact on the progress of science. It wasn't until the nineteenth century that his notebooks – and their revolutionary contents – were fully deciphered.

Leonardo died in France at the age of sixty-seven. The legend has it that his new patron, King Francis I, sat by his bedside, cradling his head as he lay dying. It's tempting to see this symbolically as the abandoned child finally getting the parental love he never had as a child. But whatever he lacked, he had more than made up for it. As the king said: 'There had never been another man born in the world who knew as much as Leonardo.'

~

In theorising about the effects of a difficult childhood, **Sigmund Freud** (1856–1939) heads the field. He wrote a biography of Leonardo in 1910 based around a childhood memory Leonardo recounts in his notebooks:

> *While I was in my cradle a kite came down to me, and opened my mouth with its tail, and struck me many times with its tail against my lips.*

From this Freud spins an extraordinary tale of repressed memories of the maternal breast, ancient Egyptian symbolism and the enigmatic Mona Lisa smile – and reaches the conclusion that Leonardo was gay because he was secretly attracted to his mother. This is seems a tediously familiar interpretation now but was daringly original at the time. And, as always, Freud does make some good points. Moving on to Leonardo's relationship with his father, Freud suggests that, much as his father had abandoned him, Leonardo abandoned his 'intellectual children' – his paintings – in favour of pure scientific research. Leonardo's inability to finish anything and his childlike absorption in research is a way of insulating himself from the fear-inducing power of his father.

If Freud felt he had found the key to Leonardo, it's probably because it was a key issue in Freud's own life. Freud wasn't abandoned by his father, but he felt deeply betrayed by him. Jacob Freud was a wool merchant whose business failed when the young Sigmund was only a toddler. This plunged the family into poverty and meant they had to move from the relative comfort of Freiberg in Moravia, to an overcrowded Jewish enclave in Vienna. As the eldest of eight, Sigmund was exposed to the difficulties that poverty imposed on his parent's marriage. Young Sigmund resented his father's mediocrity, his inability to hold down a job, and the fact that he had been married twice before. A precocious reader, he soon found other heroes to act as surrogate fathers: Hannibal, Cromwell and Napoleon. At the age of ten he was permitted to name his younger brother, and chose Alexander, after Alexander the Great. Later, he would name one of his own sons Oliver, after Oliver Cromwell. In contrast, he adored (and was adored by) his mother, who called him her 'darling Sigi' even into his seventies. But this maternal devotion wasn't without its problems. When he was two and a half years old, 'his libido was awakened' by seeing her naked on a train. From this, Freud acquired a lifelong terror of travelling on trains. More importantly, he experienced at first hand the most notorious of all his theories – the Oedipus complex: the repressed desire to kill one's father and sleep with one's mother. For his final Greek exam at school, Freud chose to translate Sophocles' tragedy *Oedipus Rex*.

Sex was to dominate Freud's life, in one way or another, from then on. Studying medicine at the University of Vienna, his first major research project involved trying to untangle the sex life of the eel. Despite dissecting more than 400 specimens he was unable to find any evidence that male eels had testicles. Had he done so, psychoanalysis might never have happened. Frustrated by fish, he turned to neurology and began to formulate the theories that would make him famous. This was important to Freud. As a young medic, he was still preoccupied with the childhood idea of himself as a hero. He told his fiancée, Martha, that he had destroyed fourteen years' worth of notes, letters and manuscripts to obscure the details of his life, confound future biographers, and help establish his personal mythology.

It is often claimed, with some justification, that Freud reduced all human psychology to sex, so it is surprising to discover he didn't lose his virginity until he married at the age of thirty. By his own admission, his sexual activity after marriage was minimal (he was convinced it made him ill). His first crush, at thirty, was on the mother of a friend. He much preferred to keep women at a safe emotional distance: he was twenty-five before he had his first girlfriend. The closest he came to love during his first years of university was his friendship with another male student, Edward Silberstein. In fact, throughout his life, Freud had friendships with men, which look very much like infatuations or romances. Often, the intimacy would be followed by a dramatic falling-out and the breaking off of all communication. The most famous example of this is his relationship with Carl Jung. In the early days of their relationship they could spend up to thirteen hours a day walking and talking. But mutual paranoia started to creep in. Freud believed that Jung subconsciously wanted to kill him and take his place, and fainted on two separate occasions when Jung started talking about corpses. For his part, Jung suspected he had sexual feelings for Freud. In 1913 their relationship ended in an acrimonious split that left the 'brutal, sanctimonious' Jung floundering in a near-psychotic state for the next five years.

For a man who theorised endlessly about the family, Freud was a peculiar and far from attentive father. Rather than talk to his children at meals, he would place his newest archaeological curio in front of his plate and examine it. (He once claimed he read more archaeology than psychology, and his office was stuffed with Neolithic tools, Sumerian seals, Bronze Age goddesses, Egyptian mummy bandages inscribed with spells, erotic Roman charms, luxurious Persian carpets, and Chinese jade lions.) To educate his children about the facts of life, he sent them all to the family paediatrician. He believed so fervently that every son is driven towards deadly competition with his father that his own sons weren't even allowed even to study medicine, let alone psychoanalysis. In contrast, he exhaustively psychoanalysed his youngest daughter Anna, who shared with him her sexual fantasies and her forays into masturbation.

Freud suffered throughout his life from depression and paranoia. On the recommendation of his therapist friend Wilhelm Fleiss, he attempted to treat his mood swings with cocaine. Fleiss had elaborated a very dodgy theory that every illness, from sexual problems to disease, was determined by the bones and membranes of the nose and that cocaine could alleviate their symptoms. Freud was delighted with his early results, even encouraging his fiancée to take some 'to make her strong and give her cheeks a red colour'. After a close friend became seriously addicted, he reduced his consumption in favour of cigars, soon developing a twenty-a-day habit. It killed him eventually, but not before he'd suffered the agony of thirty operations for mouth cancer. Eventually, his entire upper jaw and palate on the right side were removed, and his mouth had to be fitted with a plate to allow him to eat and speak. Undeterred, he would lever his mouth open with a clothes pin to wedge a cigar in. He died three weeks after the start of the Second World War, his doctor easing his passage with massive overdoses of morphine.

In the end, Freud got what he'd craved since his childhood – heroic status and universal fame – but not quite in the way he envisaged. Just as he saw Leonardo's life as a movement away from the sensuousness of painting to the intellectual stimulus of science, so he was convinced that he was, in psychoanalysis, moving away from the neuroses of art in order to found a brave new science. In truth, while anyone who participates in therapy today owes a great deal to Freud's methods, his grand theories don't hold water. He is best read not as an experimental scientist but as a detective novelist who pieces together bits of evidence to come up with a cunning, all-consuming solution. As a psychological storyteller, he has few equals and it's hard not to regret his decision to turn down Sam Goldwyn's offer of $100,000 in 1925 to consult on a major Hollywood love story. But our real lives are rarely so neat as the stories we tell about them. As Voltaire once remarked: 'Men will always be mad, and those who think they can cure them are the maddest of all.'

∽

Unfortunately Freud never set down his thoughts on another great genius with a grisly childhood, **Isaac Newton** (1642–1727). Newton was the son of an illiterate Norfolk yeoman who could not even write his own name and who died four months before his son was born. At birth, according to his own memoirs, Newton was so small that he could fit into a two-pint pot and so weak he was forced 'to have a bolster all round his neck to keep it on his shoulders'. His mother married the Reverend Barnabas Smith when Isaac was three. Smith hated him on sight and refused to have him in the house, so he was sent to live with his grandmother. Like Leonardo, he became isolated and withdrew into his own world, building and inventing. In Grantham, he frightened the townspeople by flying a lantern with a kite attached. He also made a sundial by fixing pegs to the wall of his schoolmaster's house. It became known as 'Isaac's Dial'. He hated school, where he was bullied and usually came near the bottom of the class. Some measure of his unhappiness can be seen in the long list of sins he made as a teenager: 'Putting a pin in John Keys hat to prick him', 'Stealing cherry cobs from Edward Storey' and 'Denying that I did so', 'Peevishness at Master Clarks for a piece of bread and butter' and the revealing 'Threatening my father and mother Smith to burn them and the house over them'.

Reverend Smith died when Newton was seventeen and his mother responded by pulling him out of school so he could farm their land. He hated farming even more than school. It bored him. So, asked to watch the sheep, he would end up building a model of a waterwheel while the sheep wandered off and damaged the neighbours' fields. On one occasion he was walking a horse home when it slipped its bridle; Newton didn't notice and walked back with the bridle in his hands. All he wanted to do was study. His mother gave up and sent him back to school, where he astonished everyone by graduating with top marks.

From there he went to Trinity College, Cambridge. His Cambridge career, while not a disaster, was hardly a sparkling success – probably because he spent most of his time reading Descartes, Copernicus and Galileo, men whose radical ideas fell well outside the curriculum. When the university closed as a precaution against plague in 1665, Newton returned to his farmhouse in Lincolnshire. Over the next eighteen months, entirely on his own, he went on to discover the laws of gravity and motion and formulate theories of colour and calculus that changed the world forever. His discoveries in mechanics, mathematics, thermodynamics, astronomy, optics and acoustics make him at least twice as important as any other scientific figure who has ever lived, and the book that eventually contained all his most original work, *Principia Mathematica* (1687), is arguably the most important single book in the history of science. When he returned to Cambridge, still only twenty-six years old, he was elected the Lucasian Professor of Mathematics (a position now held by Stephen Hawking). Three years later, in 1672, he was elected Fellow of the Royal Society and acclaimed as one of the most brilliant men of the age.

Quite what happened to Newton over those two years staring out across the fens remains a mystery. His obsessiveness suggests he may have suffered from a mild form of autism, such as Asperger's Syndrome. Whether that's true or not, Newton was certainly *odd*. He often forgot to eat and, when he did, he did so standing at his desk. At times he would work in his laboratory for six weeks at a time, never letting the fire go out. Frequently, when entertaining guests, he would go into the study to get a bottle of wine, have a thought, sit down to record it, and become so preoccupied that he forgot all about the dinner party. He was obsessed with the colour crimson. An inventory of his possessions lists a crimson mohair bed with crimson curtains, crimson drapes, crimson wall hangings, a crimson settee with crimson chairs and crimson cushions. He was famously paranoid, keeping a box filled with guineas on his windowsill to test the honesty of those who worked for him. He had a nerdish dislike of the arts, calling poetry 'ingenious nonsense', and on the one occasion he went to the opera he left before the performance ended. Yet he was vain enough to sit for more than twenty portraits and his sense of his own uniqueness was never in doubt. He once constructed an anagram, *Jeova sanctus unus*, out of the Latin version of his name, Isaacus Neutonus. It means 'God's Holy One'.

There are obvious connections here with the confidence and self-absorption of Leonardo, and with the absent-mindedness of later thinkers like Einstein. All three took themselves very seriously; all three may have had neurological quirks; all three either missed out on or hated formal education. Significantly, of the three, Newton had the toughest childhood and he was also the one who found friendship hardest. All the contemporary accounts reveal a cold, austere and exasperating man. Even his servant only recalled him laughing once, when he was asked what was the use of studying Euclid. The slightest criticism of his work drove him into a furious rage, and his life was blighted by vicious feuds with other eminent mathematicians such as Leibniz and Robert Hooke. He had one love in his life – a young Swiss mathematician named Nicholas Fatio de Fuillier. The end of their affair caused Newton to have the first of a series of nervous breakdowns, and he almost certainly died a virgin.

Despite these personal failures, the public man was a notable success. He was the first natural philosopher to be knighted and was for many years President of the Royal Society despite achieving nothing of great scientific worth after 1696. In that year, he accepted the post of Warden of the Royal Mint. Instead of accepting this as the purely honorific position it was meant to be,

Newton took his new role very seriously and attacked it with his customary fanaticism. He spent his days reforming the currency to save the British economy from collapse. In the evenings he lurked in bars and brothels tracking down counterfeiters – whom he then personally arranged to have hanged, drawn and quartered. He was twice elected MP for Cambridge University but the job held no interest for him: the only comment he made during his entire political career was a request for someone to open the window.

But Newton also had a second, secret life. He was a practising alchemist. Of the 270 books in his library, more than half were about alchemy, mysticism and magic. In the seventeenth century, alchemy was considered heresy and a hanging offence. In conditions of utmost secrecy, he spent the bulk of his working life trying to calculate the date of the end of the world as encoded in the Book of Revelation, unravel the meaning of the prophecies of the Book of Daniel and relate the chronology of human history to the population cycle of the locust. Rather like Freud assuming he would be feted as a great scientist, Newton believed that it would be for his religious theories, rather than for his work on optics or motion, that he would be remembered. After his death, Newton's family discovered vast trunks of these religious and mystical writings containing over a thousand pages covered with one and a half million words of notes, as well as two completed books. They were so embarrassed about it that they either destroyed them or kept them hidden without admitting to their existence. A huge cache came to light as recently as 1936.

It would be easy to dismiss Newton's mystical writings as the ravings of a man who had lost his intellectual bearings. In fact, it was his belief in a creator-god that 'governs all things and knows all that is or can be done' that drove his scientific breakthroughs as well as his biblical and alchemical studies. Had he not been open to the notion of an unseen mystical force controlling the universe he might not have made his most famous discovery: the mathematical proof of the existence of gravity.

~

If Newton paid for his lonely, fatherless childhood with a debilitating social awkwardness, it also left him peculiarly equipped for intense, solitary work. The mathematician and engineer **Oliver Heaviside** (1850–1925) provides an even more extreme example of this. While not quite in the Newton league in terms of scientific achievement, without Heaviside we would have no long-distance telephones and a much less precise understanding of the behaviour of electrical and magnetic fields. Though he isn't a household name, Heaviside did for electromagnetism what Newton did for gravity: describing observable physical phenomena using mathematical equations.

Heaviside was born into poverty in Camden Town, London. His father was a gifted engraver, producing the woodcuts that illustrated the serialisation of Dickens's *Pickwick Papers* in the *Strand* magazine, but the house was poky, cold and dark, with most of the windows boarded up because of window tax. Thomas Heaviside was prone to violent outbursts, and tended to pick on Oliver, the youngest of his four sons, because he refused to behave like other children. Some of this was due to Oliver's partial deafness caused by catching scarlet fever as a toddler, but the following, heartbreakingly short school essay by the young Heaviside paints a dismal picture of life at home:

*The following story is true – There was a little boy, and his father said, 'Do try to be like other people, don't frown.' And he tried and tried but he could not. So his father beat him with a strap; and then he was eaten up by lions.*

His deafness also meant it was hard for him to play easily with other children, so he attended the all-girls school run by his mother. He disliked most academic subjects but was encouraged in a love of science by his uncle, Charles Wheatstone, one of the inventors of the telegraph. As a result, he regularly came top in the natural sciences but near the bottom in geometry, which he hated because it only involved learning proofs: there was no room for innovation. Even as a child, Heaviside preferred to work on his own and his faith in his ability to solve problems alone often appeared boastful to his classmates. This was to cost him dearly later in his life.

He left school at sixteen but continued to study hard, teaching himself Morse code, German and Danish. Through his uncle, he got a job at the newly formed Great Northern Telegraph Company based first in Denmark and then at Newcastle. It was to be the first and last paid job Heaviside ever had.

He started well enough, devising a clever system for locating the precise damage in a telegraph wire using mathematical formulae. But then he overdid it by asking for a huge pay rise. When this was refused, his response was to announce his retirement – at the age of just twenty-four. His family and colleagues were horrified, but this was to be the pattern of his life from now on: people admired his dazzling intellect, but found him touchy and hard to read. Just as Newton had retreated to the fens at the same age, Heaviside moved back to the family home in London, barricaded himself in a gloomy upstairs room and dedicated himself to private study. His subject was the brilliant but impenetrable work of the Scottish mathematician James Clerk Maxwell, whose *Treatise on Electricity and Magnetism* had just been published:

> *I saw that it was great, greater, and greatest, with prodigious possibilities in its power. I was determined to master the book. I was very ignorant. I had no knowledge of mathematical analysis (having learned only school algebra and trigonometry which I had largely forgotten) and thus my work was laid out for me. It took me several years before I could understand as much as I possibly could. Then I set Maxwell aside and followed my own course. And I progressed much more quickly.*

Heaviside emerged with something extraordinary. He had reduced the twenty equations in which Maxwell described how electric and magnetic fields behave down to just four. These, perhaps rather unfairly, are known as 'Maxwell's Equations' and are one of the cornerstones of modern physics. They inspired Einstein to call Maxwell the greatest physicist since Newton, but it was Heaviside's work that had made them intelligible.

Heaviside spent most of the next thirty years locked in his room, surfacing only for long solitary walks. His family would leave trays of food outside his door, but when he was deeply immersed in work he could survive for days on nothing more than bowls of milk. His deafness worsened and he suffered from a condition he called 'Hot and Cold Disease', in which a fear of hypothermia led him to wrap himself in several layers of blankets and wear a tea cosy on his head. He also kept the temperature of his room so high that most visitors started to feel faint after a few minutes in his company.

Despite these eccentricities, the work he produced continued to amaze and baffle. He devised a new form of calculus that is now considered one of three most important mathematical discoveries of the late nineteenth century. He solved the problem of how to send and receive messages down the same telegraph line, and how to transmit an electromagnetic signal over a long distance without distortion. This was patented in the USA by AT&T in 1904 and long-distance telephone calls became a reality. In an article for *Encyclopedia Britannica* in 1902, Heaviside predicted the existence of a conducting layer in the earth's atmosphere that would allow radio waves to follow the curve of the earth. It was eventually discovered in 1923 and named the Heaviside layer in his honour.

These breakthroughs brought Heaviside some fame but almost no money. The result was that he became more reclusive, even refusing to attend the ceremony for his election as a Fellow of the Royal Society in 1891. In 1897, aged forty-seven, he finally left home and moved to Newton Abbot in Devon. He didn't like country life much, complaining about his 'prying' neighbours who 'talk the language of the sewer and seem to glory in it'. By and by he gained a reputation as a grumpy loner who lived on tinned milk and biscuits. His one release was the new craze of cycling. He designed and built his own bicycle with foot-rests under the handlebars, so he could go 'scorching' down steep hills, folding his arms, sitting back and using the weight of his body to steer. He hospitalised himself twice, once after a close encounter with a chicken.

In 1909, increasingly disabled by gout and jaundice, and ostracised by his neighbours, Heaviside decided to move into a small cottage in Torquay to be nearer his brother, Charles. Mary Way, Charles's sister-in-law, joined him as his housekeeper.

Despite referring to it as his 'Torquay marriage', Heaviside insisted the couple kept a safe distance, only coming together to argue about what to eat or the temperature of the house. Over the next seven years, his controlling behaviour became intolerable. Mary was unable to leave the cottage and he forced her to sign a series of contracts that forbade her from even speaking to anyone else. In the end, she was rescued by her family, who found her in a near-catatonic state, a prisoner in her own home.

After Mary's departure, Heaviside went into a steep decline. His letters to friends and family were signed, inexplicably, W. O. R. M. He replaced all his furniture with large granite blocks, and lived in a kimono. He stopped washing himself and cleaning the house but spent a lot of time ensuring he had perfectly painted cherry-pink fingernails. The cussedness he had once reserved for other scientists he now visited on the local gas board, or 'the Gas Barbarians', as he called them. He stopped paying his (enormous) bills and was frequently cut off. He once attempted to restore the supply himself and ended up causing an explosion which left him with serious burns on his hands and face. In 1925 he died after falling off a ladder, and the walls of his cottage were found papered with unpaid bills.

It was a sad end for a man whose originality had earned him a place on the 1912 Nobel shortlist alongside Einstein and Max Planck. His unshakable belief in his own ideas was something he shared with Newton and Freud but Heaviside's withdrawal from the world was absolute and he does seem to have sunk into serious mental illness in his final years. It's impossible to judge whether this also damaged the quality of his work because the product of his neolithic furniture/pink nails period – the manu-script of the concluding part of his *Electromagnetic Theory* – was stolen by burglars shortly after his death. It's a tantalising prospect. Given his track record, the chances are it was stuffed with brilliant new insights. As his friend and fellow physicist G. F. C. Searle concluded, Oliver Heaviside was 'a first-rate oddity though never, at any time, a mental invalid'.

⌒

Madness was part of the birthright of a Byron. The one we all know about, the **6th Baron Byron, George Gordon** (1788–1824), was just one in a long line of rogues and rebels that stretched back to the Conquest. His great-uncle William – known as the 'Wicked Lord' – killed his cousin in an argument over the best way of hanging game. 'Foulweather Jack', his grandfather, was an admiral with a knack for sailing into storms, a talent that his son and grandson inherited. Byron's father 'Mad Jack' was a handsome libertine who had married his mother, Catherine Gordon, because he needed her money. He died when young George was four, leaving him nothing except debts and funeral expenses. The odds of the young aristocrat growing up to live a quiet and sober life were slim and he didn't disappoint, becoming in his turn a bisexual, an incestuous poet and the living embodiment of Romanticism.

Byron's father's death meant his mother was forced to return to Scotland and he spent his early years in Aberdeen. He was an only child and his relationship with his mother was not a happy one, as she suffered from terrible depressive mood swings. At the age of nine he was deflowered by his governess, who would visit his bed at night and 'play tricks with his person'. Far from enjoying the experience, it left him filled with feelings of 'melancholy' and she was later sacked for beating him. Like Freud – who was understandably fascinated by Byron – he grew up obsessed with Napoleon, and kept a bust of him on his desk at school. He amused himself by reading and claimed to have read 4,000 novels by the age of fifteen.

Byron's way of dealing with his difficult early life is in marked contrast to the solitariness of a Newton or a Heaviside. He flung himself into the world, shocking his fellow undergraduates at Cambridge by keeping a bear in his room, drinking burgundy from a human skull and consorting with choirboys. Immediately after college, he set off on a long, decadent, European Grand Tour, which got as far as Turkey and during which he and his friends wrote, drank, and slept with a large number of both boys and girls.

The publication of the first two cantos of *Childe Harold's Pilgrimage* meant Byron returned in 1812 to find himself famous. Rather like the young Leonardo, he cultivated his new-found celebrity by making sure he looked the part, insisting on white linen trousers, which he would wear only once, and order in batches of two-dozen at a time. He also ordered silk handkerchiefs in batches of 100, even though, at 9 guineas, each set cost the annual salary of the average domestic servant at the time.

The early poems created a new kind of hero, which we now call Byronic: moody, rebellious, smart, sophisticated and promiscuous, with a troubled past and a cynical view of life. Byron did his best to live up to it, although he wasn't particularly tall, had a club foot that gave him a pronounced limp, and found it difficult to control his weight, frequently putting himself on starvation diets:

> *I especially dread, in this world, two things, to which I have reason to believe I am equally predisposed – growing fat and growing mad.*

Despite this, Byron was irresistible to women. The archive of John Murray, his publisher, contains locks of hair posted to him from the heads and pubic regions of over a hundred women (including, most famously, Lady Caroline Lamb). Byron would sometimes reciprocate, although he was more likely to send a tuft cut from Boatswain, his Newfoundland dog. Lurking behind all his dealings with women is the feeling he didn't like them much – as one wag put it: 'He had to get off with women because he could not get on with them.' The one exception was his half-sister, Augusta Leigh. They had an affair and eventually a child together, and it seems likely that he decided soon afterwards to get married to someone else in order to reduce the risk of scandal.

This proved disastrous. For reasons that he was never able to properly explain, he decided to propose to Annabella Milbanke, the rather prim, maths-loving cousin of his former mistress, Lady Caroline Lamb. He claimed he was attracted to her because she didn't dance (Byron couldn't because of his deformed foot). The union was doomed from the start. He spent the journey to the church singing Albanian drinking songs, refused to kiss her during the service and later confessed he'd been fantasising about an old flame throughout the ceremony. They spent several weeks honeymooning at Seaham Hall, near Durham. The house was freezing cold and the only display of anything resembling affection Byron showed took place shortly after they'd arrived, when he roughly consummated the marriage on the drawing-room couch. Even the wedding cake was inedible: it had been a baked a month earlier and had gone stale. Soon after the honeymoon, just to rub things in, the newly-weds visited Augusta. During their stay, Byron banned his new wife from the drawing room and only slept in the marital bed when Augusta's period began. More humiliations followed, including his threatening her, while she was pregnant, with a loaded pistol. To no one's great surprise, Annabella left him on grounds of mental cruelty a year later. The subsequent court case, with its rumours of marital violence, incest and sodomy, destroyed Byron's social reputation and forced him into an exile on the Continent from which he never returned.

~

One of the patterns that links the group of lives in this chapter is how few of them went on to have children of their own. Leonardo and Newton were gay; Heaviside died a virgin. Freud did have six children, despite disliking sex, but was only really close – arguably too close – to his youngest, Anna. It is interesting to speculate what Byron would have been like as a father. Against the odds, Annabella did bear him a daughter, Augusta Ada Byron King, Countess of Lovelace, generally known as **Ada Lovelace** (1815–52), but he saw her only once, fleetingly. Thereafter, her mother did everything she could to protect the girl from her father's memory.

Annabella, after her divorce, became a cold and domineering control freak. She delegated the upbringing of her child to three female staff, whom Ada later called 'the Three Furies'. They were spies as well as teachers: Ada was allowed no freedom of thought or action and was brought up on an unvarying diet of logic, mathematics and science but '*not and never*' poetry. She was twenty before she even saw a portrait of her father.

The repressive parental regime backfired in an interesting way. Ada fulfilled her mother's hopes by developing exceptional gifts as a mathematician, but she also proved herself her father's daughter by bringing a poetic imagination to bear on mathematical problems. At thirteen, she was doing Leonardo-like calculations for a flying machine. By seventeen she had survived a debilitating bout of measles and run the full gamut of teenage rebellion from migraines and dramatic weight-loss to an attempted elopement. She entered society, keen on both dancing and intelligent conversation. As one of the few women at the time who could talk passionately about algebra, she soon had a group of admirers that included the most eminent scientists of the day.

One of these was the mathematician and engineer Charles Babbage, who was then trying to fund his Difference Engine, an 8-foot high, 15-ton, 25,000-part mechanical calculator which he had hoped would render obsolete the notoriously inaccurate books of tables on which the whole financial system depended. The reason such tables were unreliable was that they were compiled by people, known as 'computers'. (The first use of the word computer to mean any kind of calculating *machine* wasn't until 1897, a quarter of a century after Babbage's death.) Babbage failed to get his Difference Engine built, but he was very taken with Ada and over the next few years shared with her his plans for an even more ambitious project: the analytical engine, a larger, steam-driven calculator that could be programmed by adapting the punched cards recently used to automate French silk looms.

Babbage could see Ada's money and connections would be helpful, but he couldn't have anticipated how fully she would understand the machine's potential. Despite being married with three children under eight, she offered to translate a description of the engine produced by the Italian philosopher, Luigi Menebrea. Her work so impressed Babbage that he asked for her notes. They turned out to be three times the length of the original text. Published together, the book became an instant best-seller. It was, after all, by Byron's daughter on a subject women weren't supposed to understand. It is also a key text in the history of computing. Not only had Ada produced the very first computer programme – a plan to get the machine to produce the complex sequence known as Bernoulli numbers – she also allowed her imagination free rein, predicting that one day that such an engine might be used to compose music, reproduce graphics and become an invaluable tool for science, commerce and the arts. More even than Babbage himself, Ada Lovelace saw the awesome potential of what was one day to be known as the computer. In 1979, the US defence department named their software language 'Ada' in her honour, and her portrait is on the holographic stickers Microsoft use to authenticate their products.

Over the next decade, Babbage again tried and failed to get his engine built. Ada had other priorities. Her social status enhanced by her success, she was busy living up to her Byronic inheritance. Dosed on laudanum or cannabis to dull the pain of a slow-growing cancer, she fell out with her mother and her husband by plunging into a series of intense relationships. She had a brief affair with Dickens and then fell for John Crosse, a professional gambler who inspired her to devise a mathematical system to beat the bookies. There is no record of whether it worked, but her daughter Anne did go on to found the Crabbet stud, from which almost all the word's pure-bred Arabian horses now claim descent. Ada died at thirty-six, exactly the same age as Byron himself, and, for all her mother's attempts to keep them apart, she was buried with him.

Ada's story is an interesting variant on the absent-father scenario. Whether consciously or not, she established some kind of harmonic resonance with his memory during her short life, no doubt encouraged by her mother's hysterical attempts to suppress it. Who knows how the father–daughter bond might have evolved if he had lived? Byron's life and relationships were notoriously messy, full of betrayal and recrimination. Her story reminds us that sometimes a dead father, particularly an iconic one, might be more useful than a living one.

~

Hans, the father of **Hans Christian Andersen** (1805–75) died when his son was eleven, but by then the die was already cast. The Danish storyteller responsible for some of the most popular tales ever told endured a life of misery that bordered on the operatic. He was born in an Odense slum, the son of cobbler and a washer-woman (possibly the only thing he had in common with Stalin). The family lived in a one-room house and, even before his father's death, the young Hans had lived through enough trauma to fill a lifetime of therapy. Several biographers have suggested he may have suffered sexual abuse as a boy – in his mostly autobiographical first novel, *The Improvisatore,* a man called Federico lures a young boy into a cave – and an early teacher called Fedder Carstens, whom Anderson claimed was 'fond of me, gave me cakes and flowers and patted me on the cheeks' mysteriously left town within a year of Anderson's arrival at the school. As an adult, Andersen had a severe dislike of underground places.

They were a warm family, but his father became obsessed with the idea let slip by his grandmother that the family had once been rich and possibly even royal. This made an impression on the young Hans and fuelled his sense of being different from the other children in his neighbourhood. As soon as his father died, he was forced to work to support himself. It was a dismal experience.

While helping his grandmother at a hospital for the insane, he looked through a crack in a door and saw a naked woman in a room singing to herself. The woman noticed him and threw herself at the door in a murderous rage: the little trapdoor through which she received her food sprang open and she glared at him, her fingers scrabbling at his clothes. When an attendant at last arrived, Andersen was screaming in terror, 'half-dead with fear'.

His experience in a clothing mill was no better. His appearance was so effeminate that a group of his co-workers forced him to pull his trousers down in front of the rest of the workforce to see if he was a girl. Later, he signed up as a carpenter's apprentice but, on his first day at work, the previous episode still fresh in his mind, he could do nothing but stand trembling, blushing and upset. The other apprentices noticed his distress and taunted him until he fled.

Andersen wasn't an unprepossessing young man. Clumsy, pin-headed and perpetually dreamy, he walked around with his eyes half-closed: people would ask his mother if he was blind. Even his walk was unintentionally comic; one contemporary described it as 'a hopping along almost like a monkey'. This physical clumsiness meant he failed to fulfil the one dream that had sustained him since his early childhood: to become an actor. However, Jonas Collin, one of the directors of the Royal Theatre, took pity on him after his audition and offered to pay for him to return to school. The friendship with Collin and his family was one of the few relationships that Andersen managed to maintain through his life – but the return to school was a disaster. At the age of seventeen he was put in the lowest class with eleven- and twelve-year-olds, which, when added to his lanky frame and his dyslexia, made him an easy target for the sadistic bullying of the headmaster, who referred to him as an 'overgrown lump'.

Andersen emerged from this in worse shape than before. He was deeply neurotic, tormented by stress-induced toothaches, convinced his addiction to masturbation would lead to his penis falling off or send him mad. He was terrified of open spaces, of sailing, of being either burned or buried alive and of seeing a woman naked (the result his experience at the asylum as a child). He was so embarrassed about his skinny, concave chest that he built it up by stuffing newspaper in his shirt.

His love life was equally barren. Not one of his (usually gay) crushes was reciprocated. As his literary fame grew, he began to travel widely and struck up friendships with Mendelssohn and Dickens, and got to know Balzac, Victor Hugo, Alexandre Dumas and Heinrich Heine. But rather like Heaviside there was something about Andersen's manner that annoyed people. He could be both vain and ingratiating at the same time. After staying with his hero Dickens in 1857, his host stuck a card above the bed in the guest room saying: 'Hans Andersen slept in this room for five weeks which seemed to the family AGES.' Many think that the character of Uriah Heep was based on Andersen. Once he arrived unannounced to visit the other great contemporary master of the fairy tale, Jacob Grimm. Unfortunately, Grimm had never heard of Andersen and showed him the door.

His forays around Europe meeting the rich and famous did not go down well at home, and he was often abused on the streets of Copenhagen with shouts of: 'Look! There's our orang-utan who's so famous abroad!' Even his closest friends, the Collin family, would call him 'the show-off', and it was said that there was no man in Denmark about whom so many jokes were told.

Later in life, Andersen, rich but lonely, took to visiting brothels, paying the girls simply to talk to him. Like Newton and

Heaviside, he died a virgin but bad luck pursued him even beyond the grave. The man he had loved in vain since childhood, Edvard, the married son of Jonas Collin, was originally buried with Andersen (along with his wife), as the writer had requested, but the family later changed its mind and moved them, leaving Andersen to face eternity much as he had lived – alone.

In Denmark, Andersen's 'adult' plays and novels are still read, but it is the fairy tales that have made him famous internationally. Translated into 150 languages, inspiring countless adaptations and still selling by the millions each year, they are truly universal stories. It is impossible not to see Andersen – the gawky outsider whose love remained unrequited – in the tales of the Little Mermaid or the Ugly Duckling. Perhaps because the unhappiness of his childhood meant he was never able to 'grow up' properly in his personal life, his best and most powerful writing was always for children.

~

In most of the lives in this chapter the death or absence of a father operated subconsciously in shaping the pattern of the life. In the case of **Salvador Dalí** (1904–89), it was flamboyantly self-conscious. Dalí set out purposely to annoy and punish his father, who was a respectable lawyer and strict disciplinarian. The young Salvador deliberately wet his bed until he was eight, and developed a life-long scatological obsession, depositing faeces all over the house. To further infuriate his father, he also developed illegible handwriting – in reality, he could write perfectly well. At school, again, just to annoy his father, he pretended not to know things.

The generous interpretation is that this was a form of attention-seeking. The circumstances of his birth were unusual.

His parents had lost their first son – also called Salvador – only nine months and ten days earlier. He had been only two years old and the parents never fully recovered from the trauma. They talked continually of their lost 'genius', hung a photograph of him over their bed and regularly took the 'new' Salvador to visit the grave. It was all very disturbing for the young Dalí, who was made to feel he was somehow a reincarnation of his elder brother.

He grew up an unusually fearful child, plunging into fits of hysteria if he was touched, or saw a grasshopper or, like Andersen, a naked female body (this wasn't helped by his father keeping an illustrated medical textbook on venereal disease on the piano to terrify him). But like all the lives in this chapter he had an exaggerated sense of his own importance, dreaming, as Freud and Byron had done, of becoming a great hero:

*At the age of six I wanted to be a cook. At seven I wanted to be Napoleon. And my ambition has been growing steadily ever since.*

Dalí's grandiose self-assurance gathered pace during his teens. But, for all the posturing, he was prodigiously gifted, and was able to paint and draw with a classical precision that few of his contemporaries could match. As his mother remarked of his childhood sketches: 'When he says he'll draw a swan, he draws a swan, and when he says he'll do a duck, it's a duck.' At the Royal Academy in Madrid, he got himself expelled for refusing to take an oral exam. He wrote in explanation,

*I am very sorry but I am infinitely more intelligent than these three professors, and I therefore refuse to be examined by them. I know this subject much too well.'*

His relationship with his father, always strained, deteriorated further after his mother died when he was seventeen. Dalí would call this 'the greatest blow I had experienced in my life'. Eight years later, in 1929, things came to a head when his father was made aware of an early Surrealist sketch called *Sacred Heart* which contained an outline of Christ covered by the words: *Sometimes I Spit with Pleasure on the Portrait of My Mother.* His father asked him to renounce it publicly. Dalí refused and was physically thrown out of the family home and told never to return (although he claimed he came back soon afterwards with a condom containing his own sperm and handed it to his father saying, 'Take that. I owe you nothing any more!')

The year 1929 proved a turning point for other reasons. It was the year that Dalí joined the Surrealists and made, with Luis Buñuel, the first and best Surrealist film, *Un Chien Andalou.* The most shocking imagery in the film – an eyeball being sliced open with razor blade, the dead donkeys on the piano – leapt straight from Dalí's fertile dream life. This was also the year he first met Elena Diakonova, better known as Gala, the violent Russian nymphomaniac who became his muse, business manager and chief tormentor. Though she was married to the writer Paul Eluard at the time, Dalí immediately set out to seduce her. He concocted a malodorous paste from fish glue and cow dung, and daubed himself with it so that he smelt like the local ram. He then shaved his armpits, and stuck an orange geranium behind his ear. The strategy worked: they remained together as a couple until Gala's death in 1982.

The relationship probably wasn't ever consummated – at least not in the usual way. Dalí was (like Andersen) addicted to masturbation and much preferred to offer the oversexed Gala to other men (a practice known as candaulism, after the ancient Lydian king Candaules, who arranged to have his friend surreptitiously watch his wife undress). In return Gala looked after the practical side of their lives, as Dalí was incapable of even paying a taxi fare.

By 1936 Dalí had become an international sensation, even featuring on the cover of *Time* magazine. Fame only encouraged him to stage ever more ridiculous stunts. For Christmas, in 1936, he sent Harpo Marx a harp with barbed-wire strings as a present. (Harpo replied with a photograph of himself with bandaged fingers.) When he came to London to deliver a lecture, he wore a full diving suit with plastic hands strapped to the torso and a helmet topped with a Mercedes radiator cap. Sporting a jewelled dagger in his belt, he held two white Russian wolfhounds on a leash with one hand and a billiard cue in the other. He looked fantastic, but it nearly killed him. Dalí hadn't taken into account the fact that he couldn't breathe inside his helmet. He started the lecture but soon began to run out of oxygen. The audience didn't know he was suffocating and Gala had gone out for a coffee. He collapsed and his friends tried to hammer the bolts on the helmet, to no avail. Finally, when Dalí was nearly dead, a worker with a spanner was found who freed him.

This clownish side to Dalí annoyed the other Surrealists and, in the run up to war, his infantile fantasies quickly lost their charm: 'I often dreamed of Hitler as a woman. His flesh, which I had imagined whiter than white, ravished me.' When he declared his support for Franco in 1939 the other Surrealists expelled him. His response was typical: 'There is one difference between the Surrealists and me. I am a surrealist.'

The other thing that angered his colleagues was his (or rather,

Gala's) knack for making money. André Breton had already christened him 'Avida Dollars' (an anagram meaning 'I want dollars') and Dalí himself confessed to 'a pure, vertical, mystical, gothic love of cash'. The next two decades saw him transform himself into the first and biggest ever artist-celebrity, living in New York, working with Walt Disney and Hitchcock, designing the Chupa Chups lollipop wrapper and appearing on a host of TV adverts. He even created his own range of merchandise: artificial fingernails containing mirrors; bakelite furniture which could be moulded to fit the body; shoes fitted with springs to increase the pleasure of walking; and dresses with anatomical paddings to make women look more attractive. Outrageously he also signed sheets of blank artists' paper for $10 each (there may be as many as 50,000 still in circulation). By the mid-1960s, Dalí had achieved his dream of universal popularity: he was one of the most recognisable people in the world and about as far away from his father's modest ambition of turning him into an agricultural scientist as it was possible to imagine:

> *Every morning upon awakening, I experience a supreme pleasure: that of being Salvador Dalí, and I ask myself, wonderstruck, what prodigious thing will he do today, this Salvador Dalí.*

In 1958, when being interviewed by Mike Wallace for *60 Minutes*, Dalí had pronounced: 'Dalí is immortal and will not die.' It is a fascinating interview, despite the succession of preposterous statements (of which this is but one). What is revealing is not so much what he says but that fact that he refers to himself throughout in the third person. When he claims that 'Dalí himself' is his greatest work of art, for once, he isn't joking. The waxed moustache, the staring eyes, the cape and cane, the dramatic rolling of his 'r's: Dalí's whole life had become a performance.

The messianic braggadocio didn't last: Dalí's last years were tragic. He ended up in a stupor of clinical depression, ravaged by Parkinson's disease and cold-shouldered by Gala. To visit her in the castle he had restored and furnished for her, she insisted he apply in writing. When she died, he took to his bed, which in 1984 he managed set on fire by short-circuiting the button he used to call for his nurse. Eventually, he stopped eating, talking and drawing completely and finally died of heart failure, aged eighty-four. He is buried in the crypt of his own Teatre-Museu (Theatre-Museum) in Figueres, very close to where he was born.

In many ways, though, Dalí had never really left home at all. Despite the extravagance of his created 'Dalí' persona, he remained stuck in the pattern of his childhood: desperate to assert his identity, desperate to impress his father. For all the Freudian window-dressing of his art, Dalí didn't really develop as an artist or a human being. He is not an artist to turn to if you want insight. Interestingly, he once met Freud (whom he often referred to as his real 'father') in London in 1938. The eighty-two-year-old psychologist watched him draw. 'That boy looks like a fanatic,' he remarked to a colleague. Dalí was, of course, delighted: he didn't care what people said about him, only that they talked about him.

~

We can be certain Freud didn't intend it as a compliment. The best definition of fanatic as a psychological category comes from Aldous Huxley: 'a man who consciously over-compensates a secret doubt'. This is perfect for Dalí, the boy who never escaped the shadow cast by his older dead namesake, but it might apply equally well to Leonardo, Andersen, Ada Lovelace or even Freud himself. The relentless drive to succeed, the need to become famous, the emotional withdrawal, the sexual hang-ups, all are present and correct. What was their shared secret doubt? Obviously, it adapts itself to the particular circumstances, but all doubted they were good enough to please the angry, absent or inadequate father that had dominated their formative years. It is one of the great paradoxes, but without those individual acts of over-compensation we might be living in a world without the Mona Lisa, psychoanalysis, space travel, or the machine on which these words are written.

# CHAPTER TWO

# Happy-go-lucky

*I have tried too, in my time, to be a philosopher;*
*but I don't know how, cheerfulness was always breaking in.*
OLIVER EDWARDS in Boswell's *Life of Samuel Johnson* (1791)

History records surprisingly few cheerful people. Philosophers, in particular, have the reputation for being about as miserable as comedians, but Epicurus (341–270 BC) isn't one of them. His poor reputation is of a very different kind, as the high priest of high living and sensual pleasure, the philosopher of the debauchee and the gourmand.

Except that he wasn't. So far from indulging in orgies and banquets, Epicurus lived on barley bread and fruit, with cheese as a special treat only on feast days. Celibate himself, he discouraged sexual relations among his followers, and his students were allowed no more than a pint of wine a day.

But Epicurus had the misfortune to live in the highly competitive golden age of Greek philosophy, where he found himself up against the Academy founded by Plato, and the porch (*stoa*) of the Stoics: both articulate and well-organised opponents. The mud they slung at him over two millennia ago has stuck firm.

He was born into an Athenian family but grew up on the island of Samos, a mile off the coast of what is now Turkey. He was thirty-five before he arrived in Athens, taking a house with a large garden and setting up a school. He had brought his pupils with him and, unlike the Academicians and Stoics, with their very public disputations, the Epicureans kept themselves to themselves. Inscribed over the entrance arch were the alluring words: 'Stranger, here you will do well to tarry; here our highest good is pleasure.' You can see how the rumours started.

In fact, the Epicurean definition of pleasure is quite precise. It is simply 'the absence of pain in the body and of trouble in the soul', or *ataraxia*. This tranquil state is to be attained by 'sober reasoning' and most specifically *not* by 'an unbroken succession of drinking bouts and of revelry', 'sexual lust' and 'the enjoyment of fish and other delicacies'.

Epicurus' idea of 'the good life' was also not what you'd expect. 'It is impossible', he wrote, 'to live a pleasant life without living wisely and honourably and justly, and it is impossible to live wisely and honourably and justly without living pleasantly.' Decent behaviour depends on a decent standard of living. Asked to name the bare necessities, most of us would list food, water, warmth and shelter, but Epicurus insisted on a few more: freedom, thought and friendship. 'Of all the things', he wrote, 'which contribute to a blessed life, none is more important, more fruitful, than friendship.' Food and wine are pleasurable mainly because they are sociable. 'Eating or drinking without a friend is the life of a lion or a wolf.'

For a good meal with friends, something you can well do without ('fish and other delicacies' aside) is fear. 'It is better to be free of fear while lying upon a pallet, than to have a golden couch and a rich table and be full of trouble.' The German philosopher Friedrich Nietzsche observed: 'Wisdom hasn't come a step further since Epicurus, but has often gone many thousands of steps backwards.' One such backward step is to forget Epicurus' core idea: that freedom from pain depends on the absence of fear – fear of loss, fear of being found out, and, worst of all, fear of death. Epicurus solved the last one by dropping the whole idea of an afterlife – and with it the fear of eternal punishment. When you're gone, you're gone. What matters is a calm and contented life in the here and now. Ideally, sitting under a tree, talking philosophy with friends. But what Epicurus meant by 'philosophy' was different, too. 'Vain is the word of a philosopher', he said, 'which does not heal any suffering.'

This cheery benevolence makes Epicurus one of the sanest and most attractive of the major Greek philosophers. But there is much more to him than that. He was the first person to advocate equal rights for slaves and for women, and the first to offer free schooling. In teaching that we should believe only what we can test through observation, he laid the cornerstone of scientific method; and he was also one of the founders of atomic physics. Democritus of Abdera (460–570 BC) – known as the 'laughing philosopher' for finding life more comic than tragic – had guessed that the world was composed of *atomoi*: units of matter that were too small to be divided, but Epicurus took this further: 'Events in the world are ultimately based on the motions and interactions of atoms moving in empty space.' That implied no organising intelligence – any gods were made of atoms like the rest of us. These ideas – of fundamental randomness and the lack of a planned design for nature – anticipate both quantum mechanics and natural selection. Furthermore, Epicurus' dictum 'minimise harm; maximise happiness' was the first Greek version of the Golden Rule ('do as you would be done by'). It has inspired thinkers as diverse as Thomas Jefferson (the words 'the pursuit of happiness' in the US constitution are based on it) and Karl Marx (who gained his doctorate from a study of Epicurus). The humanist movement also claim him. The ancient sentence, engraved in Latin on the tombstones of his many Roman followers – *non fui, fui, non sum, non curo*, 'I was not; I have been; I am not; I do not mind' – is often used at humanist funerals. The philosophy of Epicurus is closer to Buddhism than any other Western philosopher's. Maxims such as: 'If you will make a man happy, add not to his riches, but take away from his desires' and 'A free life cannot acquire many possessions, because this is not easy to do without servility to mobs or monarchs' suggest he may have known of the teachings of Gautama Buddha (about 563–483 BC), who had died over a century earlier. Equally likely, Epicurus had simply come to the same conclusions from the same close observation of human life and suffering.

We don't know much about Epicurus the man. Perhaps because he advocated the 'hidden life': keeping the company of friends, not getting married, and refusing the limelight that other philosophers craved. But even his opponents praised him for his humane and genial temperament. His 300 books have survived only as quotations in the work of other writers. All we have by him are three letters. One was written to his friend and pupil Idomeneus as Epicurus was dying, painfully, from kidney stones:

*I have written this letter to you on a happy day to me, which is also the last day of my life. For I have been attacked by a painful inability to urinate, and also dysentery, so violent that nothing can be added to the violence of my sufferings. But the cheerfulness of my mind, which comes from the recollection of all my philosophical contemplation, counterbalances all these afflictions. And I beg you to take care of the children of Metrodorus, in a manner worthy of the devotion shown by the young man to me, and to philosophy.*

This mix of courage, humour and concern for others is the real Epicureanism. Weathering the unjust slurs, it became, with Stoicism, the most popular belief system in the classical world for over 800 years until the adoption of Christianity as the state religion of the Roman Empire in 312 AD. You can see why the Church suppressed it. Here is Epicurus' mantra, known as the *Tetrapharmakon*, or 'Four Cures'.

*Don't fear God,*
*Don't worry about death;*
*What is good is easy to get, and*
*What is terrible is easy to endure.*

It was almost 2,000 years before anything this simple and useful was produced again in the West: a kind of *How to be Cheerful in Four Easy Lessons.*

~

Vegetarianism, brotherly love and kidney stones also figure in the action-packed life of **Benjamin Franklin** (1706–90), 'the only President of the United States who was never President of the United States'.

Of all America's Founding Fathers, he best represents the excitement, energy and originality of the new colony. Born in Boston, the fifteenth of seventeen children and the youngest son of a youngest son, his parents were English Puritans. His father,

Josiah, was a candle-maker who had emigrated from North-ampton in 1683. The family wasn't rich and Ben left school at ten. By twelve, he was working as a printer, apprenticed to his elder brother James.

In 1721, James had established the *New-England Courant,* the American colonies' first independent newspaper. The following year, the paper ran a series of letters purporting to be from a Mrs Silence Dogood, a middle-aged widow. They caused a small sensation; not only were they were a fine political satire, aimed at embarrassing the Puritan establishment in the city, but the character of Mrs Dogood was so convincing that several gentlemen wrote in with proposals of marriage. When James discovered the letters were in fact the work of his younger brother, he was furious. But the sixteen-year-old Ben, flushed with his first literary success and tired of being bullied by James, responded by doing the unthinkable: he quit his job and ran away, first to New York and then to Philadelphia, where he found work in another printing house.

Mischievousness, courage and standing up to tyranny were to be the hallmarks of Ben Franklin's life, finding their ultimate expression in the Declaration of Independence. After an adventurous two-year interlude in London consorting with 'lewd women', impressing the British by swimming in the Thames, and learning the art of typesetting, he returned to Philadelphia where he set up his own printing firm and founded a society of like-minded tradesmen called the Junto – loosely derived from the Spanish for 'joined' – whose innovative thinking was to revolutionise the city.

Philadelphia was already an interesting place. Named after the Greek for 'brotherly love', unlike most of the Puritan enclaves (such as Boston) it embraced religious toleration. All the

Protestant denominations were represented – Moravians, Lutherans, Quakers, Calvinists – and there was even a Jewish community. Franklin, though always a believer, was no sectarian. He approved of the idea that all faiths should be allowed to flourish side by side. In a letter justifying his views to his hard-line Puritan parents he explained: 'I think vital religion has always suffered when orthodoxy is more regarded than virtue. And the Scripture assures me that at the last day we shall not be examined by what we thought, but what we did.'

As Franklin's business prospered, he was able to do an astonishing amount. In 1737, at the age of thirty, he was appointed as the city's postmaster and swiftly transformed the postal service. Along with his colleagues on the Junto, he helped finance America's first public library, started the first civic fire brigade and fire insurance scheme, opened the first public hospital, improved the city's street lightning, built pavements, set up a police force and founded the University of Pennsylvania. Some historians have argued that the close partnership between business, charities and civic institutions that is still such a feature of American cities today was Franklin's invention.

It was by no means the only thing he invented. As an eleven-year-old he devised a pair of wooden hand-flippers to help him swim faster. They didn't work particularly well, but he never looked back. He is credited with inventing the lightning conductor; the odometer (or milometer); the domestic log-burning stove (known still as a Franklin stove today); an extension arm for re-moving books from high shelves; a twenty-four-hour clock; a phonetic alphabet that did without the letters c, j, q, w, x, and y; a rocking chair with a built-in fan; the eerie-sounding glass armonica (Mozart and Beethoven both composed pieces for it); bi-focal lenses (he asked his optician to saw his existing lenses in two, grind the top halves more thinly and then set all four pieces back in the frame); and the notion of daylight-saving. He also produced the first flexible urinary catheter in America to help alleviate the agony of his brother John, who suffered from kidney stones. Nothing was beneath his curiosity: he once submitted a paper to the Royal Academy in Brussels recommending the search for a drug 'that shall render the natural discharges of wind from our bodies as perfume', believing this would do more for the common good than the works of Descartes, Aristotle and Newton put together.

He also made important contributions to science – the most famous being his daringly hands-on demonstration that lightning was electrical. This occurred in 1752, when, by flying a silken kite in a storm and touching a key tied to the string, he showed that electricity from the sky could be conducted through his body. Fortunately, the tingling sensation he experienced came from the latent charge in the thunderclouds rather than from a lightning strike on the kite. The latter would have resulted in not so much a tingling sensation as a 200 million-volt instant barbecue – as the Swedish physicist Georg Richmann found out less than a year later. In a fatal echo of Franklin's experiment, Richmann ran a metal wire from the roof of his house in St Petersburg. The wire ended with an iron bar hanging above a bowl of water, filled with iron filings and a magnetic needle. The plan was to cause an electrical spark between the bar and the filings. According to his assistant, what happened to Richmann was much more dramatic. As he watched, he saw 'a Globe of blue and whitish Fire, about four inches Diameter, dart from the Bar against M. Richmann's Forehead, who fell backwards without the least Outcry. This was succeeded by an Explosion like that of a small Cannon'.

Richmann was killed instantly (though the lightning left only a small red mark on his forehead); the assistant had his clothes singed and torn by pieces of burning wire, and the door to the room was ripped off its hinges.

Franklin had other, less perilous, insights. He was puzzled by the fact that mail ships leaving Falmouth in Cornwall took two weeks longer to reach New York than merchant ships leaving from London. To solve the mystery, he took the direct approach and invited his cousin Timothy, a Nantucket whaler captain, to supper. Learning about the fierce ocean current that the whalers and the merchants avoided, but that the mail boats regularly sailed into, Franklin commissioned a group of experienced sailors to map the current and gave it a name: the Gulf Stream. This was typical of Franklin: if he didn't understand something, he studied it carefully and asked for his friends for their advice – an approach Epicurus would have applauded. He wasn't always right – he called the Gulf Stream a river, which it isn't – but his instincts were sound. In 1756 his scientific achievements received the highest possible accolade when he became one of the very few Americans to be elected to the Royal Society in London.

When he wasn't inventing things, making money or pushing back the frontiers of scientific knowledge, Franklin worked as a diplomat, first in London and then Paris, skilfully negotiating America's case and ultimately getting the newly independent United States recognised by the world's two superpowers, France and Great Britain. He is the only one of the Founding Fathers to have signed all three of the key documents: the Declaration of Independence, the US Constitution and the Treaty of Paris that ended the Revolutionary War. His success as both diplomat and businessman was due to the fact that people enjoyed doing business with him. He was charming, witty and a natural deal-maker, always alert to the possibilities of compromise. Crucially, he could laugh at himself, which is one of the reasons his un-finished autobiography is so likeable. Describing how, at the age of twenty, he started on 'the bold and arduous project of arriving at moral perfection', he set about it with scientific rigour, drawing up a list of the thirteen virtues he wanted to acquire (with temperance at the top of the list), quickly deciding he can't manage all at once and so deciding to take on one a week. The account of his struggles – particularly his failures (which, with a dry printer's wit, he calls 'errata') – is both very funny and very inspiring: *The Seven Habits of Highly Effective People* with jokes.

Here's a good story from the book. Franklin had been asked to publish a 'scurrilous and defamatory' article in his newspaper, *The Pennsylvania Gazette,* but he strongly disagreed with both the tone and the content:

> *To determine whether I should publish it or not, I went home in the evening, purchased a twopenny loaf at the baker's, and with the water from the pump made my supper; I then wrapped myself up in my great-coat, and laid down on the floor and slept till morning, when, on another loaf and a mug of water, I made my breakfast. From this regimen I feel no inconvenience whatever. Finding I can live in this manner, I have formed a determination never to prostitute my press to the purposes of corruption and abuse of this kind.*

It was typical of the man: at once morally admirable, rigorously original and faintly absurd. And, in realising that he could survive perfectly well living on bread and water and sleeping on the floor, he was a true Epicurean.

But there was to be no 'hidden life' for Franklin. In his seventies, as US ambassador to France, though he dressed like a simple backwoodsman in a fur hat and a plain brown suit, there was no escaping the fact he was one of the world's most famous men. As he wrote to his daughter:

*My picture is everywhere, on the lids of snuff boxes, on rings, busts. The numbers sold are incredible. My portrait is a best seller, you have prints, and copies of prints and copies of copies spread everywhere. Your father's face is now as well known as the man in the moon.*

He was also – despite being old, bald and fat – very popular with the ladies. Although, as a younger man, he did admit to at least one illegitimate child (his son William), he probably wasn't as much of an old goat as some have painted him. He certainly liked women – and had an uncanny ability to write as though he were one (as his many female pseudonyms show) – though most of his amorous liaisons seem to have been intimate but not sexual friendships, usually with him in the role of mentor. Which isn't to say he didn't get up to mischief. At one of the endless parties the French threw for him, a young woman patted his portly belly and remarked, 'Dr Franklin, if this were on a woman, we'd know what to think.' To which he replied, 'Half an hour ago, mademoiselle, it was on a woman and now what do you think?' In this vein, when asked by a young male friend for advice in choosing a mistress, Franklin wrote back extolling the virtues of older women. He listed eight good reasons, including:

*5. Because... The Face first grows lank and wrinkled; then the Neck; then the Breast and Arms; the lower Parts continuing to the last as plump as ever: So that covering all above with a Basket, and regarding only what is below the Girdle, it is impossible of two Women to know an old from a young one. And as in the dark all Cats are grey, the Pleasure of corporal Enjoyment with an old Woman is at least equal, and frequently superior, every Knack being by Practice capable of Improvement.*

His final reason was even more to the point: 'They are so *grateful!*' As always with Franklin, it's difficult to tell just how serious he was being, but the letter, first discovered in 1881, has done him no harm. In 2003 *Time* magazine published an article on him entitled 'Why he was a babe magnet'. Franklin's more self-deprecating name for himself was 'Dr Fatsides'.

Benjamin Franklin – scientist, diplomat, philosopher, inventor, businessman, civic leader, patriot, humorist, revolutionary and ladies' man – died in 1790, aged eighty-four. Sixty years earlier he'd written his own immortal epitaph:

*The Body of B. Franklin Printer; Like the Cover of an old Book, Its Contents torn out, And stript of its Lettering and Gilding, Lies here, Food for Worms. But the Work shall not be wholly lost: For it will, as he believ'd, appear once more, In a new & more perfect Edition, Corrected and Amended By the Author.*

Half the population of Philadelphia – 20,000 people – attended his funeral, and his pallbearers included representatives of all the main religious denominations. (Ever the pragmatist, Franklin had been careful to contribute to each of their building funds, including one for a new synagogue.) Few men can honestly say they have left the world a better place. Through the warmth and courage of his character and the deep originality of his mind,

Citizen Ben Franklin, the first self-taught American genius, was certainly one of them.

~

The career of the English doctor **Edward Jenner** (1749–1823) can't possibly match Franklin's for excitement. He spent most of his life working quietly in his home village of Berkeley in Gloucestershire, but he too changed the world beyond all recognition. The two men shared the same sunny outlook and the same voracious enthusiasm for learning and experiment. In Jenner's case, this led to a discovery that has probably saved more human lives than any other.

The eighth of nine children, he lost both his parents before he was six but his elder siblings looked after him well. His sister Deborah took him in to her family home, and his brother Stephen planned out his education, so that by the age of thirteen he was apprenticed to a surgeon in nearby Chipping Sodbury. Edward was a happy, self-absorbed child, obsessed with fossil-hunting and natural history. By the time he was nine he had a large collection of dormouse nests and would always carry a large pocketbook to record his observations. He could never walk past a butcher's shop without peering at the various organs on display in case they revealed something anatomically interesting. He maintained his interest in such things throughout his life, long after he became famous. As an old man, he was delighted to be the first to find and identify the fossilised bones of an aquatic dinosaur (the plesiosaur) near his home. To him, fossils were no dusty old bits of rock; they were 'monuments to departed worlds'.

Edward Jenner would have liked Epicurus' belief that happiness comes from living an unobtrusive life. 'As for fame, what is it?' he wrote to a friend. 'A gilded butt for ever pierced with the arrows of malignancy.' But, try as he might, anonymity was not to be his destiny. Aged twenty-one he went up to London to study anatomy, physiology and midwifery under the eminent surgeon John Hunter (1728–93). Hunter was the most disting-uished anatomist of his day, and it was he who encouraged Jenner to experiment rather than speculate about his scientific ideas. His motto was: 'Don't think, try!' On his two acres of land at Earl's Court, Hunter kept ostriches, leopards, buffaloes, jackals and snakes, all for his students to carve up and investigate. If need be, he supplemented his supply by bringing in the carcasses of exotic beasts from the Royal Zoo at the Tower of London.

In 1771, when Joseph Banks returned from James Cook's first voyage, Hunter recommended Jenner to catalogue his botanical collection. Banks agreed, and was so impressed with Jenner's work that he invited him to join Cook's second voyage in 1772. After some hard thought, Jenner decided against it and went back home to set up his own general practice in Gloucestershire. He had also turned down John Hunter's offer of a partnership, but the two men kept in close touch, with Hunter directing Jenner's research into natural history by letter. After Jenner suffered a romantic setback, Hunter wrote to him saying:

> *Let her go, never mind her. I will employ you with hedge-hogs, for I do not know how far I may trust mine. I want you to get a hedge-hog in the beginning of winter and weigh him; put him in your garden, and let him have some leaves, hay or straw, to cover himself, which he will do; then weigh him in the Spring and see what he has lost.*

Jenner was fascinated by hibernation and sceptical of

contemporary theories that birds (like bats) hibernated in winter. He dissected them and found seeds that came from other countries. He also noted that returning swallows were not, in fact, 'dirty' – going against the prevailing wisdom that they spent the winter asleep in the mud at the bottom of ponds.

His work on bird migration wasn't published until the very end of his life, but it was an earlier piece of birdlife research that first made his name. In 1787, his 'Observations on the Cuckoo' revealed that cuckoo chicks have hollows in their backs, allowing them to scoop up the other baby birds in the nest and tip them over the side. This unique feature is only present for the first twelve days of the cuckoo's life. Until Jenner's publication, it had been assumed that it was the foster birds that got rid of their own chicks. His theory wasn't universally accepted until photography confirmed he was right in the twentieth century, but it was good enough to get him elected to the Royal Society in 1789.

Close observation was Jenner's forte and it led to another breakthrough: he was one of the first doctors to make a connection between arteriosclerosis of the coronary arteries and angina. In 1786, he noted that, in one of his patients who had suffered from angina, the coronary arteries were 'blocked' with a 'white fleshy cartilaginous matter' that made a grating sound when he cut through them. 'The heart, I believe,' he wrote, 'in every subject that has died of the *angina pectoris*, has been found extremely loaded with fat.'

Jenner thoroughly enjoyed life in Gloucestershire. He was a popular country-house guest, highly regarded as a witty raconteur, poet and violinist. He was also a natty dresser. According to his friend Edward Gardner, he was usually to be seen in 'a blue coat, and yellow buttons, buckskin, well polished jockey boots with silver spurs, and he carried a smart whip with a silver handle'. Like Ben Franklin and Epicurus, he loved like-minded company, and founded two clubs: the Convivio-medical Society and the Medico-convivial Society. They met in separate inns and had, as their names imply, similar interests but opposite priorities. Jenner was also a keen balloonist, a hobby that terrified the local farmers but was to lead him to his future wife, Catherine. His unmanned, varnished-silk balloon landed in the grounds of her father's estate.

Edward and Catherine were married in 1788 and had four children. The eldest, Edward, died of tuberculosis aged twenty-one. Jenner was devastated, but, ever the scientist, used the blood from his son's frequent bleedings to enrich his manure and see if it had any effect on the growth of plants.

He was forty-seven when he made the discovery that would make him famous. By the late eighteenth century, 60 per cent of the population of Europe was infected with smallpox. A third of those who contracted the disease died and survivors were left horribly disfigured. Elsewhere in the world, the toll was even worse: an estimated 95 per cent of the indigenous peoples in the Americas perished from the disease after the Conquistadors brought it with them in the fifteenth century. When Jenner was a child, the only hope of staving it off was a process called variolation (*variola* was the scientific name for smallpox, from the Latin *varius*, 'spotty') where dried smallpox scabs were rubbed into a cut on the hand in the hope that the body would develop resistance to the full-blown disease. It was reasonably effective, but the side effects were unpleasant and the risk of contracting smallpox remained unacceptably high.

Jenner had suffered the discomfort of variolation as a child – it also involved being starved and purged – and though he introduced it to his village practice as a standard procedure, he began experimenting to see if a safer alternative could be found. Among his patients, he noticed that milkmaids rarely caught smallpox but regularly needed treating for cowpox, a related but much less virulent infection contracted from milking cows. He wondered if country lore that cowpox protected you from small-pox might have some basis in truth.

On 14 May 1796 he took some discharge from cowpox pustules on the hand of a milkmaid called Sarah Nelmes and inserted it into an incision in the arm of eight-year-old James Phipps, the son of his gardener. Other than a slight fever, Phipps was fine. Six weeks later, Jenner inoculated him with pus from a smallpox sufferer. Again, no reaction. This wasn't the first time it had been tried – a Dorset farmer called Benjamin Jesty had deliberately infected his wife and children with cowpox during a local smallpox epidemic twenty years earlier – but it was the first time it had been done scientifically. Two years later, having performed the procedure, which he named 'vaccine inoculation' or 'vaccination' for short (from the Latin *vacca*, 'cow') on more than twenty patients, Jenner published the paper that would change everything: *Inquiry into the Causes and Effects of the Variolae Vaccinae… known by the name of the Cow-pox* (1798).

The conclusion that Jenner reached was that the cowpox vaccine was safer than variolation and provided indefinite protection against smallpox. It could also be inoculated person to person. News of the *Inquiry* spread all over the world and within two years it had been translated into Latin, German, French, Italian, Dutch and Spanish. Jenner's life changed overnight. 'I have decided,' he declared, 'no matter what trials and tribulations lie before me, to dedicate the whole of my life to ridding the world of smallpox.' This modest country doctor became 'the Vaccine Clerk to the World', sending samples of his vaccine to everyone who needed it. In his own garden at Berkeley, he built a small hut, which he called the 'Temple of Vaccinia', where he vaccinated the poor for free. He was feted by London society, presented to George III and Queen Charlotte, met the Tsar of Russia and the King of Prussia, received the freedom of the cities of London, Dublin, Edinburgh and Glasgow and was awarded honorary degrees from Oxford and Cambridge.

Messages of admiration flooded in from all over the world. Thomas Jefferson wrote offering 'to render you my portion of the tribute of gratitude due to you from the whole human family. Medicine has never before produced any single improvement of such utility.' Native Americans sent him a wampum belt and taught their children his name, which they commended to the Great Spirit. The British MP, William Wilberforce, commented that there was 'no man who is so much inquired after, by Foreigners when they arrive in this country'. Jenner even corresponded with Napoleon, securing the release of two English prisoners, one of them a relative. Napoleon had already issued instructions for the mass vaccination of the French people. 'Ah Jenner,' he exclaimed, 'I can refuse him nothing.'

Not everyone was convinced: the variolators saw the vaccine as a serious threat to business and other doctors questioned whether Jenner's sampling and recording methods were rigorous enough. Some patients were wary, too – scared that they might sprout horns or udders if excretions derived from cows were injected into them. But both the army and navy promptly adopted vaccination as standard procedure and many of Britain's most eminent physicians came out in Jenner's support. Nevertheless, the medical authorities dragged their feet: it took until 1840 for the government to set up a national programme of free vaccination.

By then, Jenner had been dead for seventeen years. In 1815 his wife, like his eldest son, fell victim to tuberculosis and Jenner himself, increasingly infirm and tired of the public attention, returned to his haven at Berkeley. He remained there until his own death eight years later. A year before he died, he was appointed Physician Extraordinary to George IV.

In his last years, Jenner occasionally treated patients, but spent of most his time out among nature, his original inspiration, finishing his investigations into the migration of birds and importing and propagating exotic fruits. He also made arrangements to help James Phipps, the cowpox guinea pig, who had also fallen ill with tuberculosis. Poor Phipps had been variolated at least twenty times after Jenner's original experiment by other doctors keen to test the results for themselves. As a mark of gratitude, Jenner designed and built Phipps a small cottage and personally supervised the laying-out of the garden and vegetable patch that went with it. Of the other players in the cowpox drama, nothing more was heard of the milkmaid, Sarah Nelmes, but the hide of her cow Blossom still hangs in St George's Hospital, Tooting. The cow's horns – rather like bits of the True Cross – have multiplied since her death: at least six 'authentic' pairs have been recorded.

It's hard to overstate Jenner's legacy. He founded the discipline we now call immunology. The modern equivalent of his discovery would be if a cure for cancer were announced tomorrow. Smallpox, the speckled devil, 'the most dreadful scourge of the human species' for millennia, was declared finally eradicated by the World Health Organization in 1980, just as Jenner had predicted it would be back in 1801.

*The joy I felt as the prospect before me of being the instrument destined to take away from the world one of its greatest calamities was so excessive that I found myself in a kind of reverie.*

What is truly admirable is Jenner's attitude. He knew he was right; he never gave up; he didn't try to profit from his discovery. He just took quiet pleasure in being the right man in the right place at the right time.

～

There was nothing quiet about **Mary Seacole** (1805–81), although she, too, was an exceptional healer. The Jamaican-born heroine of the Crimean War, forgotten for almost a hundred years, has recently been re-discovered and restored to her rightful place as one of great characters of the nineteenth century.

The daughter of a Scottish soldier and a Jamaican nurse, Mary Grant grew up in a boarding house for sick and disabled members of the armed forces, run by her mother in Kingston, Jamaica. As a teenager, she made her way to England on her own, paying her way with a suitcase full of exotic West Indian pickles. When she returned home to take over the running of the boarding house, she was able to combine her knowledge of traditional Caribbean healing with the latest western medical ideas she had picked up in London. In 1836 she married Edwin Horatio Hamilton Seacole, an English merchant resident in the house, who was rumoured to be the illegitimate son of Horatio Nelson and Lady Hamilton. But her happiness was tragically short-lived. In 1843 a fire wrecked the boarding house and, the following year Mary's husband and mother both died. Grief-stricken and penniless, Mary left Jamaica for a second time to join her brother in Panama, where they jointly ran a hotel. It was there that she first got to practise her medical skills in earnest, nursing the victims of outbreaks of cholera and yellow fever – with remarkable results. Her method was based on careful observation of the symptoms of each individual patient: '...few constitutions permitted the use of exactly similar remedies, and...the course of treatment which saved one man, would, if persisted in, have very likely killed his brother.' Although some of her medications, like sugar of lead, probably did more harm than good, her attentiveness and general empathy with the suffering of those in her care offered a holistic approach to healing that was ahead of its time.

Encouraged by her success, she applied to the British War Office to serve as a nurse in the Crimea. Never one to under-dramatise her life, Mary wrote that she wanted to experience 'the pomp, pride and circumstance of glorious war'. Needless to say, a loud and rumbustious fifty-year-old woman of mixed race and brightly coloured attire was not what either Florence Nightingale or the War Office were looking for. Though laden with letters of recommendation, each of her several applications were rejected.

But Mary was undeterred. She had grown up surrounded by British soldiers and was convinced that her 'sons', as she called them, would need her special form of bedside care. So she borrowed some money, bought a one-way ticket and printed some business cards:

### BRITISH HOTEL
### MRS. MARY SEACOLE
(Late of Kingston, Jamaica),
Respectfully announces to her former kind friends, and to the
Officers of the Army and Navy generally,
That she has taken her passage in the screw-steamer *Hollander*,
to start from London on the 25th of January, intending on her
arrival at Balaclava to establish a mess table and comfortable
quarters for sick and convalescent officers.

It was an astounding declaration, but she was as good as her word. In Balaclava, she bumped into an old business colleague of her husband's, Thomas Day, and they set up a partnership. Using local labourers and any materials they could salvage – packing cases, driftwood, scrap metal – they built a small hotel. It opened in March 1855, on the main supply route to Sevastopol, two miles from the front line.

The British Hotel became a Crimean institution. The restaurant alone was legendary – Mary's rice puddings and sponge cakes reminded the troops of home – but the hotel also served as a bar, a hospital and a general store that stocked anything from 'a needle to an anchor'. From there each day Mary would ride to the trenches surrounding Sevastopol, sometimes under fire, with two mules – one carrying medicine, the other food and wine – to nurse and feed the wounded. Known to all as 'Mother Seacole', she was a warm, reassuring presence amid the slaughter, dressed in startling combinations of yellow, blue and red. She was on hand to care for the British after the ill-fated assault on the Redan outside Sevastopol in June 1855, in which a quarter of the men were killed or wounded. Two months later, after the battle at the

Tchernaya River, she tended wounded Russians as well as French and Italians but was ready the next day to throw 'a capital lunch on the ground' at a British regimental cricket match. In September, when Sevastopol finally fell to the allies, after a horrific year-long siege in which 100,000 Russians died, Mary Seacole was the first woman to enter the burning city.

In 1856, the war over, Mary set off for England, penniless for the third time, ill, alone and pursued by creditors. This would have been an unthinkable disaster for most women of her age, but she was unbowed: 'I do not think I have ever known what it is to despair, or even to despond,' she wrote later. She took to wearing medals to remind people of her outstanding service to the military cause (although there is no record she was ever awarded any) and within a few months had mobilised her friends in the upper echelons of the army and the popular press to set up the Seacole Fund to save her from bankruptcy. It did that and more. In July 1857 the fund staged a four-day festival featuring over 1,000 performers including eleven military bands. It was a kind of SeacoleAid, attended by a crowd of 40,000 people.

A month earlier, Mary had published her autobiography, the *Wonderful Adventures of Mrs Seacole in Many Lands*. It was bound in bright yellow boards, with scarlet lettering and a portrait of Mary on the front in military garb, wearing a Creole kerchief and an extravagantly feathered hat. If that didn't pull in the Victorian reader, the opening paragraph was a real lapel-grasper:

*All my life long I have followed the impulse which led me to be up and doing, and so far from resting idle anywhere, I have never wanted inclination to rove, nor will powerful enough to find a way to carry out my wishes.*

With its vivid and moving account of the war, it became an immediate best-seller and cemented Mary's celebrity status.

The last twenty-five years of Mary's life were (by her somewhat frenzied standards) restrained and comfortable, and she died at her house in Paddington in 1881, aged seventy-six. Both *The Times* and the *Manchester Guardian* ran glowing obituaries. Her subsequent disappearance from the public record is usually blamed on the pre-eminence of Florence Nightingale, who, as we all know, invented modern nursing at her Crimean hospital in Scutari. This is unfair on both women. Mary Seacole was a doer, a force of nature. She restored people's souls as well as their bodies. It's appropriate that she has become a role model for the medical profession only now, after a century of more mechanistic medicine. But she invented no system, left no legacy. And she ran hotels, not hospitals – as Florence Nightingale was keen to point out. In 1870 the Lady with the Lamp wrote a rather vinegary letter to her brother-in-law complaining about Mary's 'bad character' and summing up her contribution to the war effort. 'She was very kind to the men &, what is more, to the Officers – & did some good – & made many drunk.'

Florence Nightingale's disdain raises another issue: Mary's colour. Was she the victim of prejudice? She certainly thought so. Reflecting on her rejection by the War Office, she wrote: 'Did they shrink from accepting my aid because it flowed from a somewhat duskier skin than theirs?' In the 1970s, this became a rallying cry for disgruntled black nurses in the NHS, marking the beginning of a process of rehabilitation for Mary Seacole which ended in her being voted the greatest Black Briton of all time and becoming a settled fixture on the National Curriculum.

Ironically, Mary didn't consider herself 'black' at all. She came from Jamaica where the subtleties of skin colouring mattered intensely. She called herself a Creole 'with good Scotch blood coursing in my veins'. Her father was white and her mother probably mixed race. In Jamaica this meant she was a Free Coloured, less constrained and more socially acceptable than the black former slaves, but still definitely not white. As she wrote in her memoir: 'I am only a little brown – a few shades duskier than the brunettes whom you all admire so much.' And she was fiercely proud of being British. One of the things that makes her autobiography so compelling is the first-hand account of nineteenth-century racism and her sense of disappointment that skin colour should matter at all. There is one powerful exchange from her time in Panama where a 'sallow-looking' American toasts her for all she has done to stem disease in the colony adding: 'If we could bleach her by any means we would – and thus make her as acceptable in any company as she deserves to be.' Mary's response is magnificent:

> *Providence evidently made me to be useful, and I can't help it. But, I must say, that I don't altogether appreciate your friend's kind wishes with respect to my complexion. If it had been as dark as any nigger's, I should have been just as happy and as useful, and as much respected by those whose respect I value; and as to his offer of blessing me, I should, even if it were practicable, decline it without any thanks. As to the society which the process might gain me admission into, all I can say is, that, judging from the specimens I have met with here and elsewhere, I don't think that I shall lose much by being excluded from it. So, gentlemen, I drink to you and the general reform-ation of American manners.*

The *Wonderful Adventures* deserves its new-found status as a modern classic. It was written for money and can be monstrously self-promoting in places, but at its best – in the tender accounts of the young men who died in her arms, or by abruptly breaking off from describing battlefield carnage to give a recipe for a refreshing punch – it is as lively and original as the lady herself.

Despite her all troubles, Mary lived and died a happy woman. She may never have heard of Epicurus but she instinctively embodied his central proposition that true pleasure comes from conquering pain and fear. And, in the other sense of the word, what could be more Epicurean than a bar and restaurant on a battlefield? She left no grand edifice, but she left an unforgettable voice.

~

Everything we know about **Mary Frith**, better known as Moll Cutpurse (about 1584–1659) suggests that her voice was equally unforgettable. For one thing, she had to make herself heard above the roar of the bear-pit. Standing among the office blocks and art galleries of London's Bankside today, it's hard to imagine that, 400 years ago, in a small street still called Bear Gardens, ferocious battles were fought in a circular arena that held over 3,000 people. Here could be seen the most formidable fighting bears of the era – ursine celebrities like Ned Whiting, Sackerson or Blind Harry Hunks – taking on a succession of dogs, swatting them from wherever their jaws had fastened hold, battling it out until either they or the dogs collapsed from exhaustion. As well as being a noisy, gruesome spectacle, bear-baiting was big business. A lot of money could be made betting on the outcome.

It was a brutal, often dangerous, pastime. The animals were tethered to a stake in the centre of the arena, held by a 15-foot chain or rope. The breeders stood in a circle, just out of range, holding their dogs by the ears. Once they were let loose, the contest would rage for as long as an hour. It wasn't unusual for wounded animals to break free and chase their owners round the pit. Injuries were common; health and safety rules rudimentary. This was a man's sport: the bear-pit was no place for a woman.

But Mary Frith wasn't going to let that put her off. She dressed, drank, smoked and swore like a man and the bear-pit was her passion. She bred mastiffs – the muscular, squat-faced, short-necked, strong-jawed ancestors of today's bulldogs. In her own account of her life, published in 1662, three years after her death, we learn that her dogs were pampered like the children she never had (or wanted), each of them sleeping in their own bed, complete with sheets and blankets, and fed on a special food she boiled up herself.

Mary had grown up just over the river, the daughter of a cobbler in Aldersgate Street, but Southwark was her spiritual home. The south bank of the Thames in the early seventeenth century was London's pleasure-centre, though very much not what Epicurus had in mind. Twopence got you into the bear-garden; sixpence, an evening at the theatre or an hour with a whore. Beer was a penny a pint; tobacco, threepence a pipe-load; a decent tavern meal about the same. Given that the average wage was about 7 shillings a week, it's not surprising that theft and gambling were rife. The entertainments brought in huge numbers of punters: an estimated 10 per cent of the entire population of London visited the theatre or the bear-garden every day. In the narrow maze of streets, gangs of professional criminals worked their routines assiduously.

Mary Frith started out as a pickpocket. We first hear of her as a teenager in 1600, when she and two female accomplices were accused of stealing '2s and 11d in cash, from an unknown man at Clerkenwell'. Other arrests followed and, despite her protestations in her autobiography that she 'never Actually or Instrumentally cut any Mans Purse', she certainly worked as a part of gang who did. But Mary had grander ambitions than a life of petty crime. By 1608 she was performing in the streets and taverns of Southwark. Dressed like a man, in a doublet and leather jerkin, a sword hanging by her side and a pipe clamped between her teeth, she would strum her lute, sing rude songs, dance jigs and tell stories. Perhaps the cross-dressing began as part of her pick-pocketing routine – it would certainly have made it easier it to blend into a crowd – but it soon became her calling card.

A woman dressing as a man was far more shocking then than now. It was done in the theatre, of course – all the actors were men and boys in any case – but to do it openly on the streets was more than just an affront to the natural order of things. It was breaking the law. 'Moll Cutpurse', Mary's alter ego, became an overnight sensation. She was more like a contemporary conceptual artist than the stage performers she hung round with – not only did she dress and perform as a man, she lived like one too. From the tavern to the bear-pit, her art was her life. By 1610, she had inspired one of the first female celebrity biographies, *The Madde Prancks of Merry Moll of the Bankside with Her Walks in Man's Apparel and to What Purpose*, by the playwright John Day. In 1611 two of the most successful writers of the age, Thomas Dekker and Thomas Middleton, asked her to close a performance of the play they had written about her, *The Roaring Girl*. This was the big time – an audience of 2,000 people watching Moll Cutpurse playing herself.

This stunt proved too much for the authorities. Mary was arrested for immoral behaviour and thrown into the correction house at Bridewell where she was subjected to the punishment usually reserved for prostitutes. She was soundly whipped and then forced to beat the stalks of hemp plants to make fibres for rope. But if this was intended to make her see the error of her ways, it failed abysmally. After three months, she re-emerged and took up where she left off. On Christmas Eve, 1611, she was arrested again for exactly the same offence, 'to the disgrace of all womanhood'.

This time she was hauled up in front of the Bishop of London, charged with prostitution as well as cross-dressing. The Bishop pressed her to confess that she was 'sexually incontinent', but Mary would have none of it. She cheerfully admitted to being a foul-mouthed, drunken thief, a gambler and a bear-baiter, but she strongly objected to the accusation that she had sold her body. Though she looked like a man, she told the assembled clerics, a visit to her lodgings would show she was every bit a woman. This saucy response outraged the judge. She was sentenced to public penance (dressed in a very unmanly white shift) at the cross outside old St Paul's. Mary turned it into a command performance, drinking herself insensible on six pints of sherry first and then weeping so piteously that the authorities released her to preserve the peace.

Mary had a very modern instinct for making money from fame. By the time she was thirty, she was a major player in the London underworld. Her days as a thief and her hours spent in the bear-gardens and taverns had built up an unrivalled network of contacts on both sides of the law. As far as her manor was concerned, she always knew who was doing what, and where. This made her the perfect broker for stolen goods. If a purse or a watch went missing, a visit to Moll Cutpurse would usually see it restored on the same day, provided a decent cash reward was produced. It was a protection racket, tolerated by the authorities because it kept the mean streets of Southwark under control, and welcomed by the theatres and sporting rings because it allowed them to turn a profit unmolested.

In 1614 Mary married Lewknor Markham, scion of a well-off, upper-class family from Nottinghamshire. Mary's new father-in-law, Gervase Markham (1568–1637), was an astonishingly industrious author, churning out poems and treatises on everything from forestry, agriculture and military training to veterinary medicine, archery and wildfowling. The booksellers were swamped with his oeuvre. In 1617 he had five different books on horses all in print at the same time. This exasperated the Stationers' Company, who forced him to sign an unprecedented agreement in which he promised 'never to write any more book or books to be printed of the deseases or Cures of any Cattle, as Horse, Oxe, Cowe, Sheepe, Swine, Goates etc.' His best-known work is *The English Hus-wife* (1615), a kind of early Mrs Beeton, full of recipes and handy hints on running a successful household. Quite what drove his son to marry a cross-dressing, bear-baiting gangster is a mystery.

In any event, it seems to have been a marriage of convenience rather than passion, as there is no evidence of them ever having lived together. From Mary's point of view, having a husband brought respectability, which was good for business. She invariably referred to herself as Mrs Mary Markham from then on, although she failed to mention her husband at all in her autobiography. In fact, other than the marriage, there is no mention of Lewknor Markham in any historical records. The couple married at St Mary Overbury, now Southwark Cathedral, at that time the actors' church, so it's possible he was involved with the theatre. Why did he marry Mary? Perhaps he was gay? That wouldn't have been unusual in the Southwark of the day. Or, given that the subtitle to *The English Hus-wife* was '*Containing the Inward and Outward Virtues Which Ought to Be in a Complete Woman*', it might have just been two fingers up to his annoyingly successful father. But the most likely reason is money, Lewknor taking a cut from Mary's business in return for use of the Markham name. That would have been worth hard cash to her.

Mary's sex life is another mystery. There's no record of her having had sexual relationships with anyone, male or female. However scary Moll Cutpurse may have been in public, the private Mary Frith sounds rather nice, and her house in Fleet Street, full of dogs and parrots, surprisingly feminine. It was always immaculate – kept spotless by no fewer than three maids – and the walls were covered with looking glasses, 'so that I could see my sweet self all over in any part of my rooms'. Self-esteem was clearly not the problem. On rare occasions she did admit to finding a man attractive – one such was Ralph Briscoe, the clerk at Newgate Prison, who was 'right for her tooth' and whose life she saved by pulling him out of the ring when a bull had him by the breeches. But sex just seems to have been too much bother, except as a source for humour. Coming across a worse-for-wear neighbour late one night, she called out to him cheekily: 'Mr. Drake, when shall you and I make Ducklings?'

To which he responded 'that I looked as if some Toad had ridden me and poisoned me into that shape', that he was altogether for 'a dainty Duck, that I was not like that Feather, and that my Eggs were addle. I contented my self with the repulse and walked quietly homeward.'

Good humour, self-deprecation, vulnerability are all there. Perhaps she was happier alone with her dogs and parrots, who loved her unconditionally.

The lusts of others were a different matter. Hovering between the criminal underworld and polite society, Mary was perfectly placed to offer more intimate services than the sale of stolen property. And she had spotted a gap in the market: wealthy women looking for male companions. With the single-mindedness she brought to all her business ventures, she 'chose the sprucest Fellows the Town afforded' and turned her house into an escort agency. One of her most audacious coups was to get the male lovers of a woman who had been (with Mary's help) serially unfaithful to her husband to contribute to the maintenance of her children after she'd died of the clap.

Busy as she was with fencing and pimping, Mary still found time to play Moll for the occasional public performance. The vintner and showman William Banks bet her £20 that she wouldn't ride from Charing Cross to Shoreditch dressed as man. Of course, she did so in style, flaunting a banner, blowing a trumpet and causing a riot in the process. Part of the excitement was due to the fact that the horse she was riding was Banks's 'Morocco', the most famous performing animal in London. Shod in silver, it could dance, play dice, count money and generally astonish an audience with its intelligence and dexterity. Its most famous trick was climbing the hundreds of narrow steps to the top of the old St Paul's and dancing on the roof, watched by thousands below. In the annals of popular entertainment, Moll Cutpurse riding Banks's horse would have been the Jacobean equivalent of the Beatles reforming and playing on the same stage as the Rolling Stones.

Even at four centuries distance, it is this irrepressible side to Mary's character that seems as fresh as ever. If the idea of 'bawdy' has fallen victim to endless over-the-top costume dramas, full of ale-swigging wenches in low-cut dresses, it's worth remembering the word originally meant 'joyous'. The joy that Mary brought to others with her unconventional life was borne out by the people who knew her. 'She has the spirit of four great parishes,' wrote Middleton and Dekker, 'and a voice that will drown all the city.' She was a show-off – even sometimes a bully – but the dens and alleyways of south London were a brighter place for her presence. One can imagine her getting on well with Mary Seacole. Both rose from poverty and lived their lives as independent women, on their own terms, in a man's world.

After the Civil War, the Puritans banned bear-baiting. Though Mary outlived Cromwell, she didn't quite live long enough to see the monarchy restored and her beloved bear-garden re-opened but, in any case, the Southwark of old was never quite the same again. Mary Markham died wealthy enough to be buried inside St Bridget's Church in Fleet Street. Her final request was to be laid face down in her coffin because 'as I have in my Life been preposterous, so I may be in my Death' – but whether it was carried out, we'll never know.

~

One person who would have appreciated Mary's last wish was the great twentieth-century physicist **Richard Feynman** (1918–88). He was also an eccentric prankster with a huge appetite for the preposterous. Tall, handsome and funny, his own last words were in the same spirit: 'I'd hate to die twice. It's so boring.' For Feynman, to be bored, in life, work or death, was the ultimate sin.

He was born into a tight-knit New York Jewish family and didn't talk until he was well past three years old. Not long afterwards, his father, somewhat optimistically, bought him the entire *Encyclopedia Britannica*. But the young Feynman devoured it: it was his constant companion throughout his childhood and by his early teens he had read it cover to cover. His father, Melville, a Byelorussian car-polish salesman, stretched him in other ways, too. He taught him to predict mathematical patterns using building blocks and took him on long walks where he showed him how to pay close attention to nature. It was his father, Feynman always said, who taught him the difference between 'knowing the *name* of something and knowing something'. Years later he would write:

> *You can know the name of a bird in all the languages of the world, but when you're finished, you'll know absolutely nothing whatever about the bird. So let's look at the bird and see what it's doing – that's what counts.*

Melville also had a wonderful knack of turning abstract scientific ideas into stories, something his son would inherit and make his trademark:

> *For example, when I was playing with my electric trains, he told me that there is a great wheel being turned by water which is connected by filaments of copper, which spread out and spread out and spread out in all directions; and then there are little wheels, and all those little wheels turn when the big wheel turns. The relation between them is only that there is copper*

*and iron, nothing else – no moving parts. You turn one wheel
here, and all the little wheels all over the place turn, and your
train is one of them. It was a wonderful world my father told
me about.*

As a result, science and fun were indistinguishable for the young
Feynman. He accumulated tubes, springs, batteries, anything
mechanical he could get his hands on, and performed experiments.
He paid his younger sister Joan (who also became a physicist) four
cents a week to act as his lab assistant. Part of her role was to agree
to be electrocuted (mildly) in front of Dick's friends. He also
created a rudimentary burglar alarm for the house and an electric
motor that would rock his sister's cot. He was known in the
neighbourhood as 'the boy who could fix radios by thinking'.

He hated school, of course – except for the Maths Team,
where he reigned supreme. In the school yearbook, he was given
the soubriquet 'Mad Genius', which he did his best to live up to.
Studying for his bachelor's degree at the Massachusetts Insitute
of Technology, his maths and physics results were off the scale,
and later, in the entrance exam for Princeton, he achieved a
perfect score in both subjects – a feat never achieved before or
since. Feynman's happiest times at university were spent playing
in his room, trying to figure out how ants communicated or the
physics required to explain how a jelly set. Nevertheless, his
doctoral thesis caused a sensation. In it, he created an entirely
fresh approach to quantum mechanics – unlike anything anyone
had done before – and applied it with spectacular success to
describe the interactions of electrons and photons. Rather as
Oliver Heaviside (q.v.) had done with Maxwell's equations for
electromagnetism, the twenty-three-year-old Feynman had come

up with a simpler, more elegant solution than anyone had thought possible. He later claimed that he had a synaesthetic gift: he could see the underlying patterns in a sequence of equations marked out in different colours.

This unconventional brilliance earned him a junior role in the Manhattan Project, helping to develop the atomic bomb at Los Alamos in New Mexico. Glamorous though this sounded, he soon got bored: 'There wasn't anything to *do* there,' he complained. To while away the time, he taught himself to pick the combination locks on the security complex's top secret filing cabinets, or disappeared out into the desert to chant and drum in Native American style, gaining himself the nickname 'Injun Joe'. Despite his initial euphoria at the success of the tests (typically, he was the only one to see the bomb explode without protective glasses, reasoning – correctly – that the a car windscreen was sufficient to screen out the harmful alpha radiation) he later regretted his involvement, likening it to tickling the tail of a sleeping dragon.

In 1948 he won the Nobel Prize for Physics. He was only thirty. As with his graduate thesis, the prize was awarded for improving and clarifying the work of others. Quantum Electrodynamics (QED) was the discipline that explained the behaviour of light, magnetism and electricity, but it was irritatingly unreliable. With two other physicists, Feynman fixed the flaws in the theory but his most important contribution was to describe the motions of subatomic particles using a sequence of small, elegant diagrams. He always downplayed the work he did at this period as so much 'mathematical hocus-pocus', but he liked his 'Feynman diagrams' enough to paint them all over his van. They are still the best way of describing the quantum world.

The major portion of Feynman's professional life was spent at the California Institute of Technology. It is sometimes said of him that, although he was unquestionably one of the great physicists of any century, he didn't make a major theoretical breakthrough or give his name to an important new discovery. That may be less to do with him than the nature of physics in the period – few of his contemporaries could claim to have done so either. It also obscures what is Feynman's greatest achievement: he was the best and most charismatic teacher of his generation. He loved teaching and believed that, if a theory couldn't be explained to a non-scientist, there was something wrong with the theory. In the introduction to his best-selling collection of lectures he tells his audience:

> *What I am going to tell you about is what we teach our physics students in the third or fourth year of graduate school... It is my task to convince you not to turn away because you don't understand it. You see my physics students don't understand it. That is because I don't understand it. Nobody does.*

But this, as he explains, is neither demoralising nor defeatist:

> *We can imagine that this complicated array of moving things which constitutes 'the world' is something like a great chess game being played by the gods, and we are observers of the game. We do not know what the rules of the game are; all we are allowed to do is to* watch *the playing. Of course, if we watch long enough, we may eventually catch on to a few of the rules.* The rules of the game *are what we mean by* fundamental physics.

Feynman always described his physics as 'fiddling about' or 'a game'. For him, it was play rather than work: just a matter of looking closely, and wondering:

*When someone says, 'Science teaches such and such,' he is using the word incorrectly. Science doesn't teach anything; experience teaches it. If they say to you, 'Science has shown such and such,' you might ask, 'How does science show it? How did the scientists find out? How? What? Where?'*

He spent most of the second half of his life trying to supply intelligible answers to these questions. Perhaps the perfect Feynman moment came in the enquiry into the *Challenger* space-shuttle disaster in 1986. The commission had become mired in evasions and technical obscurantism and was finding it impossible to pinpoint the cause of the accident. One suspect was the rubber O-rings used as seals between the sections of the solid fuel rockets. The failure of these immense but fragile rings – only a quarter of an inch in diameter but 37 feet in circumference – would certainly have caused the disaster, but nobody could (or would) say for certain whether they had or not, or why. Feynman was convinced the O-rings were to blame. Live on camera, in front of the commission and all the witnesses, he cut through the whole tangle of evidence by taking a small section of O-ring and dipping it into a glass of iced water. It was immediately obvious to everyone that the rubber instantly lost its elasticity at cold temperatures, which would have caused the seals to fail and the rocket to break up. On that fateful morning, the temperature had been 24° lower than the engineers recommended. Case closed. It was science at its simplest and most powerful: Epicurus would have been proud.

The rest of Feynman's life can sometimes look like a parody of the groovy 1960s professor. He taught himself to play bongos in the Brazilian manner, held exhibitions of his own paintings,

experimented with drugs, learned how to decipher Mayan hiero-
glyphs and studied comparative religions. He had a 'second
office' in a topless bar in Pasadena, where he would scribble
equations and new Feynman diagrams on the back of his beer
mat. But these were more than the affectations of a geek:

> *The fact that I beat a drum has nothing to do with the fact that
> I do theoretical physics. Theoretical physics is a human en-
> deavor, one of the higher developments of human beings – and
> this perpetual desire to prove that people who do it are human
> by showing that they do other things that a few other humans
> do (like playing bongo drums) is insulting to me.*

He didn't play the bongos because he was a physicist; he played
bongos because he was Richard Feynman, a man with a lifelong
aversion to boredom. As he once wrote: 'You cannot develop a
personality with physics alone, the rest of life must be worked in.'
In his final years, dying of cancer, he became fascinated by the
central Asian republic of Tuva, researching its history and culture
– particularly the throat-singing, which he loved – and planning a
visit. The story of his cat-and-mouse, decade-long game with
Russian bureaucracy became his last book, *Tuva or Bust!* It's as
funny, quirky and life affirming as you'd expect. His visa finally
arrived the day after he died.

~

Richard Feynman's absorption in his subject, and his defiant
determination to have fun right to the end, sums up the attitude
that animates each of these six lives. Each learned to be happy in
their own skin and to do so by being positive. Of those who went
to school at all, none of them were particularly attentive pupils:

they taught themselves by observing the world and people around them. The philosopher Wittgenstein once remarked that although he wasn't sure why we were here, he was 'pretty sure that it is not in order to enjoy ourselves'. Epicurus would have had words with him about that. Enjoyment for each of the six came from doing what they loved to do. And that spirit is infectious. Who wouldn't want to sit down to 'a capital lunch' with Mary Seacole, go for a county walk with Edward Jenner, eavesdrop on Ben Franklin at a party, or spend an evening in a bar where Moll Cutpurse was singing, accompanied by Richard Feynman on bongos? This is the real meaning of genius: to expand our sense of what's human, to cheer us up. Nietzsche – not himself, perhaps, at the top of anyone's cheerful list, but a great admirer of Epicurus – certainly thought so: 'There is one thing one has to have: either a soul that is cheerful by nature, or a soul made cheerful by work, love, art, and knowledge.'

# CHAPTER THREE

# Driven

*If we did all the things we are capable of doing,*
*we would literally astonish ourselves.*

THOMAS EDISON

What drives you? What gets you up in the morning? Is it the same thing that compels a person to sail round the world in a coracle or spend forty years trying to grow a black tulip? The word 'motivation' is (rather surprisingly) little more than a hundred years old, but the thing itself (whatever it may be) is as ancient as our species. Consciously or unconsciously, and for reasons no one really understands, the 'reward centres' of our brains are chemically stimulated by activities like making money or exacting revenge, as well as by more abstract pleasures such as witnessing beauty or solving puzzles. As habit-forming as eating, drinking or exercise, they can drive people to the most astonishing places. Here are six people who never even paused to look up from the road.

∼

If there is a more driven person in human history than **Genghis Khan** (about 1162–1227) we should pray we don't bump into him on a dark night.

The Mongol Empire stretched all the way from the Pacific coast of China to Hungary and covered almost a quarter of the land mass of the planet. It was the largest empire the world has ever seen: four times bigger than Alexander's and twice the size of Rome's, and Genghis Khan created it from nothing in just twenty years. Under his leadership, the Mongols were the most successful military force of all time. From a population base of well under a million people they were responsible for the deaths of over 50 million human beings, roughly a third of the inhabitants of the lands they conquered.

What bound the Mongols together wasn't a lust for blood, but a new-found sense of nationhood. Until the time of Genghis Khan there was no 'Mongolia'. Asia north of the Gobi desert was home to half a dozen loose confederations of nomadic tribes of which the Mongols were only one. Competing for sparse grazing land for their herds of sheep and horses, they were often unfriendly towards each other. Raiding, feuding and revenge killings were common.

'Genghis Khan' was his title, not his name. As a boy, he was called Temüjin ('iron one'). He was of noble birth: his father, Yesügei, was a *khan* or clan chieftain. When Temüjin was nine, a group of treacherous Tatar bandits poisoned his father while sharing a meal.

Temüjin claimed the chieftainship but the clan laughed at him as he was too young to take on his father's role: he and his family were cast into the wilderness. For three years he scraped a subsistence living for them, hunting small game and gathering wild fruits. At the age of twelve he killed one of his half-brothers for stealing food, cementing his role as leader of the family.

Married at a very young age, and before long his wife Börte

was abducted by the savage Merkit tribe. To get her back, Temüjin made an alliance with his father's old blood brother, Toghrul, khan of the powerful Kerait. She gave birth to a son when she came home: she had been away for eight months, and raped, so the paternity of the child was in doubt. Nevertheless Temüjin accepted him, and he was given the name Jochi, 'The Guest'. Encouraged by their victory over the Merkit, Temüjin and Toghrul began to build a new tribal confederation.

Temüjin's great contribution was to draw up new set of laws, called the *yassa*. Based on what he had experienced, the laws were designed to eliminate the anti-social opportunism – casual theft, violent bickering, tit-for-tat kidnapping and murder – that made life on the steppe so difficult and dangerous. (Even his own father had carried off his mother from a neighbouring tribe.)

Under the *yassa,* food was to be shared. Everyone was free to follow any religion they wished. All men (other than religious leaders and doctors) were obliged to join the army, but recruits were rewarded for their skill not for their family affiliations. Kidnapping women and stealing livestock were forbidden. The pillaging of enemy corpses and property was not allowed until ordered by field commanders. When it was permitted, individual soldiers were allowed to keep the spoils. The children of conquered peoples were to be adopted by Mongol families and treated as equals not as slaves. Captured troops were to be re-trained as Mongol soldiers and given the same rights.

A combination of warrior code, state constitution and Geneva Convention, the *yassa* was ruthlessly enforced: disobedience brought immediate execution. Although in some ways it was really just a clear codification of existing tribal customs, its tough justice took hold at once, producing professional discipline among the existing troops, gratitude from the new recruits (and their families) – and loyalty from everyone. The ranks of the Mongol army swelled and, with each new conquest, Temüjin's power base increased.

If this gives the impression that Temüjin was some sort of Mongol version of the Dalai Lama, then it would be inaccurate. He was fair but he was implacable. When, to establish his supremacy, Temüjin eventually had to impose his will on his original allies, the Kerait, he first offered them the chance to surrender and when they refused he crushed them in a series of great battles. The Kerait were by then led by Jamuga, son of Toghrul (and Temüjin's own blood brother and boyhood friend). When the vanquished Jamuga asked if could meet his end without his blood being spilled, Temüjin graciously had him wrapped in two felt blankets and then beaten and asphyxiated to death.

By 1206 Temüjin had achieved the unthinkable, linking all Mongol tribes for the first time into a single league. At the age of forty-two, having outmanoeuvred or defeated his rivals, he was declared Genghis (or more accurately *Chinggis*) Khan. Many suggestions have been put forward for the precise meaning of this name – Lord of the Oceans, Universal Leader, Precious Warrior, Spirit of Light, True Khan – but the general idea is unmistakeable: he was the *khan* of *khans*. No other Mongol leader ever bore this title.

You cannot operate an effective legal system without writing, so Genghis Khan borrowed the alphabet of a nearby people, the Uighur, to create standardised written Mongolian. (Uighur derives from Aramaic, the language spoken by Jesus, though Aramaic, ironically, never developed a written script of its own.) He also instituted a rapid communication system known as the *yam*. This operated like an Asian Pony Express, consisting of a chain of manned refuelling stages at 140-mile intervals all over the empire. To run a *yam* station was a well-rewarded, high-status job. A messenger would arrive, hand his package on to a fresh horseman and then rest and recuperate. In this way, a message could travel over 200 miles in a single day, outstripping the fastest army. The service was safe and secure: for merchants wanting to move goods or information it was also free. The *yam* was to turn the Silk Road into the medieval world's most important highway.

None of this would have been possible without the superiority of Mongolian troops. Highly skilled, mobile and disciplined, Mongolian mounted archers were self-contained fighting units. Protected by light helmets and breastplates made of leather or iron plates, they carried two powerful small composite bows made from horn, wood and sinew, each as powerful as an English longbow but much quicker to use and re-load. Their quivers contained a selection of arrows for different jobs: armour-piercers, blunt 'stun' arrows, even arrows that whistled, which were used for sending messages. They also carried a small axe or mace. Each man had a saddlebag with his own food rations, rope and sharpening stone, and a string of five or six spare horses. This meant there was no baggage train or camp followers to slow things down. A Mongol army could travel well over a hundred miles a day – they ate on the move and even stood up in the saddle to evacuate themselves while galloping along.

Genghis was a superb military planner. Each campaign was mapped out in advance and extensive use was made of spies and field intelligence. The troop structure was based on the decimal system: squads (10 men), companies (100), regiments (1,000) and divisions (10,000). Commanders controlled regiments and were given a high degree of independence.

*Driven*

A Mongol attack was devastating and virtually impossible for a traditional army to withstand. Appearing at terrifying velocity, the cavalry suddenly split into three or more columns and mounted a multi-pronged assault. The tactics required remarkable horsemanship and the troops were rigorously trained. This was done through hunting exercises. A posse of horsemen would set out into the steppe until game was sighted, surround the animals at speed and at a distance, and then gradually close the circle making sure nothing escaped.

The Mongols usually tried to ambush an army and destroy it in the field rather than besiege a major city, but when the time came they were both ruthless and highly original. Innovative siege warfare was another of Genghis Khan's great skills. First, small undefended local towns would be taken and the refugees driven towards the city, putting pressure on living space and food resources. Next, rivers were diverted to cut off the water supply. If necessary, siege-engines were then deployed, built on site from local materials by prisoners of war. Mongol catapults were particularly effective, sometimes firing the bodies of plague victims over the city walls: one of earliest examples of germ warfare. Once a city was taken its leaders were captured and executed to remove the focus for any future rebellion.

Brutal though this sounds, even Mongol siege techniques bore witness to the sense of fairness that Genghis Khan had enshrined in the *yassa*. Arriving in front of a doomed city, the Mongol commander would issue the order to surrender from a white tent: if the city complied, all would be spared. On the second day, he would use a red tent: if the city surrendered, the men would all be killed, but the rest would be spared. On the third day, he would use a black tent. After that, no quarter was given.

Genghis Khan's achievements can hardly be overstated. By the time he died (still fighting, in north-western China in 1227) he had transformed a haphazard patchwork of squabbling goatherds into an empire of unparalleled military strength, with a language, a constitution and an international postal service. In Mongolia today, he is still considered a national hero.

Though he was said to have more than 500 concubines (and untold numbers of bastards), Genghis Khan stayed loyal all his life to his original wife Börte and their four legitimate sons. He had appointed his third son, Ogedei, as his successor and for fifteen years things went well. Under Ogedei's leadership the Mongols put down a rebellion in Korea and demolished the Russians, Ukrainians, Poles and Hungarians. By 1241 the Golden Horde had reached the gates of Vienna. It felt like the end of civilisation. Then, in what seemed to be a miracle, the Mongols mysteriously melted away. They went home to Mongolia: a *quiriltai* had been called to choose a successor to Ogedei, who had died in a binge-drinking spree after a hunting expedition. From then on the Mongols became increasingly directionless and needlessly destructive. At the sack of Baghdad in 1258, centuries of priceless Muslim scholarship were burnt and thrown in the Tigris. The Mongol Empire eventually disappeared and left little trace on the cultures it had conquered, but this only bears testimony to the strength of Genghis Khan's leadership; he was irreplaceable.

As was the custom among Mongols, he was buried in an unmarked grave. His four legitimate sons were so paranoid about keeping its location secret (to avoid it being despoiled) that their men slaughtered every single person the funeral cortege came across – Marco Polo later claimed this exceeded 20,000 people. Leaving nothing to chance, they then got soldiers to execute the slaves who had excavated the tomb, and then had those soldiers executed in turn. To find it again themselves, they sacrificed a suckling camel in front of its mother and buried it in their father's tomb. Camels have long memories so, once a year, they released the mother camel, which unerringly returned to the precise position it had last seen its offspring. The only flaw in the plan was that when the old mother camel finally died all knowledge of the location was lost. Despite many false claims Genghis Khan's grave has never been found.

As for his permanent legacy, it stretches far beyond the boundaries of Mongolia. Recent genetic studies have found that 8 per cent of the current male population of central Asia are direct descendants of Genghis Khan.

~

Among the direct descendants of the American naval officer and polar explorer, Rear-Admiral **Robert E. Peary** (1856–1920) are Peary S. Fowler, a female county circuit judge in Florida, and several Inuit.

Robert Peary believed it was his pre-ordained destiny to be the first man to reach the North Pole. He talked about the Arctic as though it were his own private property, treating other expeditions as infringements and becoming visibly upset when it was pointed out that he was re-tracing the routes of previous explorers. With astonishing will-power, superhuman powers of endurance and a fanatical ability to ignore pain, he made eight separate attempts on the Pole in ten years, losing all but two of his toes to frostbite.

Peary decided from an early age that he wanted to be famous. In his twenties, when he was just beginning his career in the navy, he wrote to his mother: 'Remember, mother, I must have fame, and I cannot reconcile myself to years of commonplace drudgery.' Robert's father died suddenly when he was three and his mother Mary's way of coping with the tragedy was to devote her life to her son: protecting him from the world at every turn, not letting him play with other boys, telling him he was too delicate, making him wear a sun bonnet. It was a deep but suffocating bond: his mother went with him everywhere, even on his honeymoon. Robert Peary married Josephine Diebetsch in 1888. At the time, he had only made one short, failed expedition to Greenland, but that was soon to change. In twenty-three years of marriage, they would spend only three of them together. Nonetheless, Jo would be Peary's rock: remaining his principle encourager, confidante and public mouthpiece until his death.

In 1891 she went with him on a reconnaissance mission to Greenland, becoming the world's first non-native female Arctic explorer. She wrote a surprisingly cheerful journal and the following year gave birth to their first child, Robert Jr. The family lived among the Inuit and Jo thought her hosts the 'queerest, dirtiest-looking individuals' she had ever seen, reminding her 'more of monkeys than human beings'. She was tough, unsentimental and above all, on her husband's side. Those who crossed the Pearys or let them down were cut off immediately. One young geologist, John Verhoeff, who had put his life savings into the venture, was so traumatised by the way the Pearys treated him that he effectively committed suicide. Disappearing into the snow, alone and against specific instructions, he shouted back to no one in particular: 'I hate them! Her and him both!' and shortly afterwards fell down a crevasse.

Peary, meanwhile, set off north. He had a hunch that

Greenland was an island and, after an incredible journey, sledging 1,000 miles in three months, he and his men finally reached open water, naming it Independence Bay. They believed they had found the northernmost point of Greenland and were looking at the Arctic Ocean. In fact, it was what today is called Independence Fjord, an immense inlet on the north-east coast, some 160 kilometres long by 25 wide. They were still 200 kilometres short of where they thought they were. It was an impressive feat all the same. That part of Greenland is still called Peary Land, and Peary had gone much of the way with a broken leg, which was saved with an improvised splint by the expedition's doctor, Frederick Cook.

Returning a hero to America in 1892, Peary threw himself into a fund-raising tour for an assault on the North Pole. He travelled the length of the country, delivering 165 lectures in 103 days – earning up to $2,000 a night (about $5,0000 today). He looked every inch the bluff polar explorer: almost six feet tall with deep blue eyes, a mane of red hair and a large handlebar moustache. He delivered his lectures in polar furs, on a stage dressed with an elaborate reconstruction of an Inuit camp, accompanied by five huskies trained to howl in unison at the end of his speech.

His public image concealed a touchy and insecure human being. He suffered all his life from a stutter. Opaque and emotionally distant with everyone, the least hint of disloyalty sent him into a furious rage. Though he was capable of being charming when he wanted something – and was always decisive out on the ice – in private he was a brooder, seeing conspiracies on every side. The wrong side of Robert Peary was a cold, dark place to be, and sooner or later everyone found themselves there – even his wife.

In 1898, leaving Jo behind to bring up their two children and manage their precarious finances, Peary returned to live among the Inuit for three years. Photographs of him standing imperiously in his sealskins help explain why he was almost a godlike figure to them. Exercising his *droit de seigneur*, Peary now chose an Inuit mistress. 'The presence of women,' he wrote, 'is an absolute necessity to keep men happy.' Aleqasina was a fourteen-year-old girl who had originally come to the house as a cleaner. She was to bear him two sons, Anaakkaq (born 1900) and Kaalipaluk (born 1906). While she was pregnant with the first of these, Jo Peary turned up unexpectedly. She had had no news of her ice-bound husband for several months and was profoundly shocked by what she found. 'Had I known how things were I should not have come', she wrote afterwards. Somehow Jo reconciled herself to this unconventional ménage, returning twice more in 1902 and 1903, but her journal shows that she was often very low. In 1906 she wrote in her diary, 'The Pole will never thank me for the anxiety and suffering I have endured.'

Peary's relationship with Aleqasina was similar to his relationship with the Inuit as a whole. His attraction was genuine enough, but he never took the trouble to learn the language properly, still less to understand their culture. He considered them brave and resourceful, he admired them as 'anarchistic philosophers', but he was no more able to make an emotional connection with them than anyone else. He preferred striding around as 'Pearyaksoah', the great white God, dispensing largesse and barking orders. 'They value life only as does a fox, or a bear; purely by instinct,' he wrote. Their sole contribution would be to help him discover the Pole.

In fact, they did much more than merely help him. The 'Peary System' for polar exploration, which he trumpeted as his great technical breakthrough, was nothing more than the application of Inuit survival techniques. Without their local knowledge and the huge numbers of their dogs (most of which died en route), his expeditions would never have happened at all. It is possible that the years he spent snuggled up with Aleqaina, waiting for a set of prosthetic toes to arrive, obsessively planning his next assault on the Pole, were the happiest in his life. But Peary was only really happy behind a sledge.

After he left the Arctic for good in 1909, he never attempted to contact Aleqasina or his two Inuit sons and nor – despite the wealth his fame had brought him – did he ever make any financial provision for them or the people who had served him so faithfully. Though in awe of him and proud of their role in his mighty project, the Inuit of northwest Greenland still remember Peary today as their 'Great Tormentor'.

In 1897, in an act of spectacular vandalism, Peary stole the four sacred meteorites they had used for millennia as a source of metal flakes for knives and arrowheads, took them back to New York and sold them to the American Museum of Natural History for $40,000 (worth over $1 million today). None of the money found its way back to Greenland. Peary also brought six Inuit back with him, so he could show them off as part of his lecture series. Four of them died almost immediately of pneumonia. Peary cynically faked their burial and sold their physical remains to the museum. The youngest surviving Inuit was an eight-year-old boy called Minik. He was adopted by the family of the museum's superintendent, William Wallace, and named 'Minik Peary Wallace'. Shortly afterwards Wallace resigned. It wasn't until nine years later, as a teenager, that Minik visited the American Museum of Natural History for himself. There he was horrified to be confronted with the sight of his father's bleached bones in a glass case in the ethnographic department. Minik begged to have the remains returned to him for a ritual burial but the museum refused. Peary reluctantly agreed to pay for Minik to return home, from where Minik fought a running battle with the museum for the rest of his life. He died in 1918, aged twenty-nine, two years before Peary himself. The skeletons weren't released and reburied in Greenland until 1993.

Though Peary made several attempts on the North Pole in the early part of the twentieth century, all of them ended in failure, and some in disaster. But his reputation in America continued to grow. He befriended Theodore Roosevelt, who adored adventure of all kinds and through whom he acquired a number of wealthy patrons to cover his exponentially mounting expenses. (The average cost of each expedition was over $400,000, or $10 million in today's terms.)

In 1909, now well into his fifties, Peary was ready to make his final assault on the North Pole. A team of twenty-four men with nineteen sledges and 133 dogs set out, but of these only Peary and five companions went the whole way. One was Matthew Henson, the world's first black polar explorer. This talented, self-taught man was the son of a poor farmer. His parents died when he was small, and at the age of twelve he walked the 30 miles from Washington DC to Baltimore and went to sea as a cabin boy. He was a skilled navigator, carpenter and mechanic. He had ac-companied Peary on all his major expeditions since they had met twenty-five years earlier. Like Peary, Henson had married an Inuit woman and fathered a son. Peary owed much of his success to Henson's logistical genius and his fluency in the local language. The rest of the party consisted of four Inuit who drove the sleds.

They had to sledge across melting ice riven by treacherous water channels, led by a fifty-four-year-old man with no toes. Henson had an almost infallible sense of direction, but no one except Peary knew how to take the sequence of latitude readings that would indicate their arrival at the pole. Peary never took them. Since there were no independent witnesses, there was no evidence other than Peary's word that they had reached their destination. Given that this was the moment he had spent two decades working towards, it's very odd that Peary's diary was left empty on the day of their alleged arrival (he later inserted a loose leaf page recording the appropriate sentiments). More damning still, to cover the distances that he claimed they had, they would have had to travel over 70 miles a day. No polar explorer has matched this before or since. When the British adventurer Sir Wally Herbert retraced the voyage in 1969, he estimated that Peary's 'Pole' was at least 50 miles short of the real one.

Peary's behaviour on regaining the expedition's ship was far from triumphant. He had hardly spoken to Henson on the journey back, and Henson was tight-lipped: 'We had a little argument at the Pole, but that's all I'll ever say.' (Years later Henson intimated that the argument resulted from Peary's resentment at having to share *his* moment with someone else.) The ship's crew were eager to know if they'd reached the pole but, even when asked directly, all Peary would say was: 'I have not been altogether unsuccessful.'

When the expedition returned to New York, they found there was a rival claim. Dr Frederick Cook, the man who had saved Peary's leg eighteen years before, had emerged from the ice saying he had reached the Pole a whole year earlier. This stung Peary into action. All sheepishness forgotten, he set about destroying Cook's claim (which was even less credible than his own). Peary pulled in every favour he had ever been owed. The resultant publicity savaged Cook's moral character and previous polar experience with such ferocity that his reputation never recovered. The press didn't give Peary the unequivocal acclamation he had hoped for, and questions continued to be asked in private, but as far as the world was concerned, it was Robert Peary who had conquered the North Pole. 'I have got the North Pole out of my system after twenty-three years of effort,' he proclaimed.

Twenty-two gold medals from the world's leading geographical societies followed, along with three honorary doctorates and the French Cross of the Grand Officer of the Legion of Honour. He was received by royalty all over Europe and promoted to the rank of rear-admiral at home. His ghost-written memoirs became best-sellers, enthralling a whole generation of armchair explorers. Peary had got all the fame he ever wanted. He withdrew from public life to Eagle Island, his retreat off the coast of Maine, to enjoy his retirement.

But he did not enjoy it in the least. His health collapsed and he suffered severe bouts of depression. His wife blamed his decline on the doubters who had subjected him to such a grilling on his return, saying that it 'did more toward the breaking down of his iron constitution than anything experienced in his explorations'. After all he had done, Peary must have had a terrible sense of anti-climax and boredom – and (one can only hope) regret for the way he had treated his innocent Inuit. And perhaps, in the dark watches of the night, he turned over in his mind the guilty knowledge that he had never reached his goal, and that all the fame he'd craved and won was based upon a lie.

Peary desperately wanted the approval of the world because he had never had the approval of a father. His mother had smothered him with love and he loved her in return – his gushing letters to her are full of tenderness – but he needed to be free of her. Psychotherapists call this 'spousification', where the child develops guilt and anxiety because the parent is acting like a lover: Peary's mother joining him on honeymoon is a classic example. The North Pole was a long way to go to get away from her, but it was where Robert Peary felt safe and free and where he could try to prove himself a hero to the father he never knew. He died of pernicious anaemia aged only sixty-three.

The first definitely verifiable successful land assault on the North Pole did not take place until 1968. The name we should remember is not Robert Peary but Ralph Plaisted, a high school dropout and former insurance salesman from Bruno, Minnesota.

~

The Victorian explorer **Mary Kingsley** (1862–1900) also had difficulties with her parents, but her escape from what Peary referred to as 'commonplace drudgery' could not have produced a greater contrast.

Mary's father was Sir George Kingsley, a physician and amateur scientist. Her mother was one of his kitchen staff whom he made pregnant by accident. They married just four days before Mary was born. Although Mary had avoided the stigma of illegitimacy, her childhood hardly differed from that of a servant. Her mother was an invalid and Sir George was rarely there: he worked for wealthy patrons who felt they needed a doctor in attendance as they toured the world. Leaving the house within weeks of Mary's birth, he was sometimes away for years at a time, writing sporadic and alarming letters home, giving his address as 'Abroad'. When Mary was fourteen, he casually wrote to say that a last-minute change of plan had narrowly avoided his accompanying Custer to certain death at the Battle of the Little Big Horn.

The conditions in which Mary found herself meant no school and hardly any social life: the only people she met were domestics. As a result she had a strong cockney accent and the vocabulary of a builder. Her earliest memory was of her father on one of his whistle-stop visits, carrying her downstairs to her mother and bellowing, 'Where does this child get her language?' When she was old enough Mary ran the household, nursing her mother and bringing up her brother Charley. She was fiercely intelligent, teaching herself to read and working her way through all the literature in the house, mastering Latin, German, physics and chemistry and losing herself in the lives of renowned explorers. As she later wrote: 'I had a great amusing world of my own other people did not know or care about – the books in my father's library.' Soon she was acting as her father's assistant, cataloguing the scientific and anthropological specimens he sent back from his travels. Though physically rooted in north London, Mary's imagination was travelling the world.

While her contemporaries went to dances and got engaged, she stayed home and studied. By 1887 her mother needed constant nursing. Mary consoled herself by learning Arabic and Syrian. Then in one six-week period in 1892 her whole life changed. Her father died suddenly of rheumatic fever and her mother followed soon afterwards. Mary, at thirty years of age, found herself without any obligations for the very first time.

What she decided to do with that freedom was to go to West Africa – the most dangerous and mysterious place on earth –

entirely on her own. She planned to fund her travels by trading in ivory and tobacco, eating the local food and staying in the houses of native people. For a young Englishwoman of limited means, this was brave bordering on reckless, but Mary was determined. She sent letters of introduction to traders, government officials and missionaries and solicited advice from everyone she could find. One old Africa hand gave it to her straight: 'When you have made up your mind to go to West Africa the very best thing you can do is to get it unmade again and go to Scotland instead.'

Mary refused to be put off. The reason for her journey was 'the pursuit of fish and fetish'. The fishes were for Dr Günther of the British Museum and the fetishes were to enable her to complete her father's study of primitive religion. Her extensive reading had prepared her well for what awaited her. One story that made a particular impression was that of the Dutch explorer, Alexandrine Tinné (1835–69), who had set out twenty-five years earlier to become the first European woman to cross the Sahara – but she got drawn into a vicious tribal altercation among the Tuareg and ended up with her hands chopped off and left to die by her guides. This persuaded Mary she needed to travel light and to be properly equipped. She landed in Africa in August 1893 with one suitcase, a holdall, a large bowie-knife and a revolver.

As for attire, she made no concession to the climate: she had always worn black silk and saw no reason to change. In her voluminous, high-collared, cinch-waisted dresses and little black hat, she looked as though she was about to take a hansom to the West End rather than a dug-out up the Ogooué River. This worked to her advantage: wherever she went she was instantly recognisable. Businesslike, humorous and unflappable in the face of danger, she would march into remote jungle villages with a cheery 'It's only me!' In a canoe on the Congo River a crocodile reared up over the boat's stern. She whacked him on the snout with a paddle and sent him packing. Confronted by a leopard about to pounce, she coolly lobbed a large earthenware pot, which 'burst on the leopard's head like a shell'. Her friend Rudyard Kipling shook his head in wonderment. 'Being human,' he said, ' she must have been afraid of something, but one never found out what it was.'

Her two long journeys in 1893 and 1894 explored what are now Nigeria, Sierra Leone and Gabon. She became the first woman to climb the active volcano Mount Cameroon (4,095 m or 13,435 ft). To her deep disgust, the summit was wreathed in thick cloud, robbing her of her main object in going up it, which was 'to get a good view'. Of more than a hundred fauna samples she collected for the British Museum, there were eighteen species of reptile and sixty-five species of fish, seven of which were new to science and three of which have since been named after her. She was also one of the first Europeans to see the mythical gorilla with her own eyes. 'Never have I seen anything to equal gorillas going through the bush; it is a graceful, powerful, superbly perfect hand-trapeze performance.' On the other hand, she had never seen anything so ugly. She admitted to a 'feeling of horrible disgust that an old gorilla gives on account of its hideousness of appearance'.

She turned her adventures into two books, *Travels in West Africa* (1897) and *West African Studies* (1899). Models of great travel writing, they are witty, full of robust opinions and vividly observed. If you want to know what a python tastes like, re-live a locust attack or learn how to survive a tornado, Mary Kingsley is your woman. She makes Peary's work read like a railway timetable. Particularly appealing is her tone of voice – what one reviewer called her 'light, chaffy style' – forthright, unpretentious and delivered with jolly-hockey-sticks enthusiasm. Here she is on African insects:

*Undoubtedly one of the worst things you can do in West Africa is take any notice of an insect. If you see a thing that looks like a cross between a flying lobster and the figure of Abraxis on a Gnostic gem do not pay it the least attention – just keep quiet and hope it will go away – for that is your best chance; you have none in a stand up fight with a good thorough-going African insect.*

The books were best-sellers and are still in print. Apart from her gifts as a storyteller, they present a remarkably rounded view of African life. Mary's close study of the Fang people of Gabon had led her to respect a way of life she found preferable, in many ways, to the 'second-hand rubbishy white culture' of the colonial administrators and missionaries. She had learnt, she said, to 'think in black', enabling her to look on the bright side of cultural practices such as polygamy, even cannibalism. Once, when staying in a Fang hut, a 'violent smell' alerted her to a bag suspended from the roof. Emptying the contents into her hat, she found 'a human hand, three big toes, four eyes, two ears and other portions of the human frame'. She showed no squeamishness: 'I subsequently learnt that the Fang will eat their fellow friendly tribesfolk, yet they like to keep a little something belonging to them as a memento.'

She saw a future for Africa that was based on developing trade, not colonial control: 'Officialdom says it won't have anything but its old toys: missionaries, stockbrokers, good intentions, ignorance and Maxim guns. We shall see.' Her refusal to accept that Africans were less intelligent or less well behaved was far ahead of its time. 'You see more drunkenness in the Vauxhall Road on a Saturday night,' she pointed out, 'than in the whole of West Africa in a week.' As she wrote to her friend Alice Stopford Green in 1897, 'These white men who make a theory first and then go hunting travellers' tales to support the same may say what they please of the pleasure of the process. Give me the pleasure of getting a mass of facts and watching them.'

Adding to her 'mass of facts' about West Africa was to take up the rest of her short life. Africa had become her *raison d'être*. Surveying the damp English winter of November 1895 only confirmed her desire to get back there as soon as she could. She missed life in the forest with a passionate intensity: 'If you do fall under its spell, it takes all the colour out of other kinds of living.' She tried to make up for it by turning up the heating in her brother's Kensington flat to tropical levels and by going shopping with a monkey perched on her shoulder. Her more regular public appearances were at her lectures, which she gave, accompanied by magic lantern slides, to a huge array of admirers – geographical societies, gatherings of academics, students, nurses, boys' clubs in city slums – and she was the first woman ever to address the chambers of commerce at both Liverpool and Manchester. Attendances of over 2,000 were not uncommon. Tall, angular and very thin, with her matronly black outfits and her hair pulled severely back and pinned under her cap, she looked much older than a woman of thirty-five. The combination of her old-fashioned, no-nonsense appearance and her wonderfully crafted funny stories allowed Mary to be thoughtful, controversial and entertaining all at once, and audiences loved it. So did she, playing up to her slightly antiquated image: 'I expect I remind you of a maiden aunt – long since deceased,' she began one talk.

When the *Daily Telegraph* reported her return from Africa under the title 'The New Woman', she reacted angrily. She was no feminist: she disparaged agitators for equal rights as 'androgynes' or 'men-women'. 'As for encasing the more earthward extremities of my anatomy in trousers,' she wrote in *Travels in West Africa*, 'I would rather have perished on a scaffold.' Despite this ardent assertion of her womanhood, she never came close to marrying, and her one serious crush (on Matthew Nathan, the acting governor of Sierra Leone) went unrequited. Perhaps her 'maiden aunt' persona put him off. In Rudyard Kipling's autobiography, *Something of Myself* (1937), he tells a revealing story. He first met Mary at one of his own aunt's tea parties and was so entranced by her that he offered to walk her home. When the conversation strayed to cannibalism, he invited her up to his rooms 'to talk it out there'. Mary at first accepted the invitation, 'as a man would', and then suddenly remembered herself: 'Oh, I forgot I was a woman. 'Fraid I mustn't.' Is there a faint hint of flirtation here? Kipling doesn't say. It's more likely that her time in Africa had blunted her English social radar. She once wrote to a friend that she did not go to Africa as a 'tonic'. Rather, after the trauma of her parents' deaths, she thought 'having been for so many years so close to death and danger in the most dreadful form they can come to one, namely the fight for the life of one we love, that a mere English social life was, and ever will remain, an impossibility to me, so I went off to carry on the old fight, where it is at its thickest, in the Terrible Bight of Benin.' Like Peary and his Arctic, Mary had found her soul mate in a place rather than a person.

In 1899 she set out for Africa for the last time. Her objective was to collect samples of freshwater fish for the British Museum from the Orange River in South Africa, and then make her way 'home' to West Africa. However, by the time she arrived, the Anglo-Boer War had broken out. Mary volunteered as a nurse and was sent to tend injured Boer prisoners of war in Simon's Town camp near Cape Town. The conditions were dreadful and disease was rife. Mary drank wine in place of water to reduce the risk of infection but it was to no avail; within a few months she succumbed to typhoid. She died alone, asking her nurses to leave the room as she was dying. Only thirty-seven years old, she was buried at sea, as she had requested; but with full military honours, which she had not. It was not quite the end of the story. The coffin was insufficiently weighted and bobbed off over the waves. A lifeboat had to be launched in pursuit and the casket dispatched to the deep by attaching anchors to it. Mary Kingsley had never been easy to pin down.

~

If Genghis Khan sought power, Peary fame and Mary Kingsley freedom, what drove the Prussian polymath, **Alexander von Humboldt** (1769–1859) was knowledge. Explorer, geographer, cartographer, geologist, mineralogist, botanist, sociologist and volcanologist, he is a giant of nineteenth-century science, linking the heroic voyages of Captain Cook and the conceptual revolution of Charles Darwin. He died just six months before the publication of *On the Origin of Species* in 1859, but without him, it might never have been written. When Darwin boarded the *Beagle* in 1826 he had Humboldt's *Personal Narrative* tucked into his knapsack, a book he was still reading and re-reading (and still taking notes from) right up until his death in 1882. 'He was the greatest travelling scientist who ever lived,' Darwin wrote in his diary. 'I have always admired him; now I worship him.' He wasn't the only one. Goethe claimed that he had learned more in an hour's conversation with Humboldt than in eight days of studying books. Thomas Jefferson counted him a close friend and sought his advice on what vines to plant at his country estate in Virginia. By his early thirties, Humboldt was said to be the second-most-famous man in the world after Napoleon. When the two met briefly in 1804, the yet-to-be-crowned Emperor greeted him patronisingly: 'You collect plants, Monsieur?' When Humboldt modestly agreed that he did, Napoleon turned smartly on his heel with a curt 'So does my wife!' He later tried to deport him as a spy.

Humboldt did a very great deal more than 'collect plants'. His name is in every botany and biology textbook – as well as every atlas – in the world. He has a penguin named after him, and a squid, a dolphin, a skunk, a lily, an orchid, and countless other plant and animal species. The Humboldt Broncos are an ice-hockey team from Humboldt, Saskatchewan, one of a swathe of North American places named for him including Humboldt Bay, the Humboldt Sink, the Humboldt River, Humboldt Lake, Humboldt Salt Marsh and Humboldt mountains. More important still, the greatest marine ecosystem on earth, the vast upwelling from the Antarctic Ocean that runs along the coasts of Chile and Peru and keeps them cool and dry is called the Humboldt Current. Few human beings have inscribed themselves on the planet on such a scale.

Scale is a word that suits him. He invented what we now call earth science. He turned geography into an academic discipline and re-wrote the history of the planet. He was the first real ecologist. The idea that the earth is a single interconnected entity had its first and most eloquent champion in Humboldt. He collected data from every possible source: animals, plants, fossils, rocks, the movements of stars and weather patterns. He sought to combine all this information into one dynamic system, which he called 'harmony in nature'.

Humboldt's early life has some similarities to Peary's. His father, a major in the Prussian army and one of Frederick the Great's closest advisors, died when he was ten. His mother loomed large in his life as Peary's had done, but far from smothering him with love Maria von Humboldt drafted in a corps of private tutors to educate Alexander and his older brother, Wilhelm, to an appropriate standard. Alexander did not meet it. He was an inattentive student, preferring to spend time poring over his collections of plants, insects and rocks, earning him the nickname 'the little apothecary'. He also had a gift for languages and could draw beautifully, particularly landscapes, but Maria was unimpressed. She wanted him to be a politician. Carted off to a succession of universities, he failed to graduate from any of them. Toiling away at finance and economics to please his mother, he quietly developed his languages and studied geology, botany and history on the side.

At Göttingen University he made friends with Georg Forster, son of Johann Reinhold Forster, the naturalist on James Cook's second voyage to the South Pacific. Talking with Georg, Humboldt suddenly realised what he wanted to do: scientific exploration was to be his destiny. Sensing that geology was the quickest way to get there, he entered the Freiberg School of Mines, a new and progressive establishment with a growing international reputation. Humboldt was the star student of his year, staggering everyone with his ability to memorise immense amounts of technical information and with his capacity for hard work. Once again, he didn't graduate, but he didn't need to: the Prussian government offered him a job as an assessor of mines. Posted to rural Bavaria, he spent five years reorganising a series of semi-redundant gold and copper mines, re-equipping them, hiring new staff and introducing the latest mining technology. He invented a safety lamp, and, using his own money, founded a technical school for young miners. The government was so taken with him they sent him on several diplomatic missions to France. Louis Philippe, King of the French always looked forward to his visits. Then in 1796 Alexander von Humboldt's mother died.

Like Mary Kingsley at a similar age, Humboldt all at once found himself free of family obligations. What's more, he had been left a sizeable inheritance. He began to plan, but a chance meeting with a diplomat led to an introduction to Charles IV of Spain. The Spanish empire was sitting on a vast hoard of mineral wealth in South America and Humboldt made a favourable impression on the king, talking him through the latest developments in mining. The result was an invitation to visit the Spanish colonies in South America, at that time completely closed to the rest of the world. This was the break that Humboldt had waited for and he immediately went out and spent a fortune on scientific and astronomical instruments. He set sail from Marseilles with the French botanist Aimé Bonpland in 1799. Together they spent five years in Central and South America, covering 6,000 miles on horseback, in canoes and on foot. It was a journey that would change our understanding of the world.

The revolutionary general and liberator of South America, Simón Bolívar (1783–1830), called Humboldt 'the true discoverer' of the continent. Before him no one had guessed that the Amazon rain forest was the planet's richest and most diverse habitat. With Bonpland he collected over 60,000 samples and discovered over 3,500 new species: no single trip has ever yielded as many. Humboldt's vision went far beyond the work of his contemporaries, who were busily filling in branches on the sprouting tree of species devised by Linnaeus. He was intent on uncovering the hidden connections between apparently unconnected phenomena. He wasn't just interested in what a plant looked like. He wanted to know why it lived where it lived, the type of rocks that produced the soil it grew in, the prevailing climatic conditions, the other species that grew near it – as well as the species that fed on it, near it, or under it and how the whole ecological cycle it was part of worked. That was why he had to travel. It was not enough to give his samples a label and a Latin name: he had to understand the context. One of the pleasures of reading Humboldt is that he never lost his childlike sense of awe: 'The stars as they sparkle in the firmament fill us with delight and ecstasy,' he wrote, 'and yet they all move in orbit marked out with mathematical precision.'

Humboldt was incapable of noticing anything without then asking 'why?' When he observed the 'brilliant fireworks' of the Leonid meteor shower in northern Venezuela, he went on to calculate when they would next return. Confronted with volcanoes, he perceived that they were lined up along subterranean fissures in the earth's crust and was able to demonstrate the course of those faults. He proved that many mountain ranges were volcanic in origin, destroying the then fashionable theory of Neptunism, which suggested that all rocks were originally oceanic sediments. He was the first to show that the Earth's magnetic field weakens as you travel from the poles towards the equator. He covered so much ground he was able to plot lines linking places with same temperature to map the planet's climate, for which he coined the word 'isotherm'. His discovery of the guano deposits on the Peruvian coast revolutionised agriculture in Europe and America, providing entrepreneurs with a lucrative and potent source of fertiliser.

His scientific curiosity extended to human culture, too. In South America he saw that the continent's startling range of plant and animals species was mirrored by its ethnic diversity: 'A traveler, however great his talent for languages, can never hope to learn enough to make himself understood along the navigable rivers.' On the Orinoco he found a parrot that was the last remaining speaker of a language belonging to a tribe exterminated by its neighbours, and dutifully recorded the bird's forty-word vocabulary. Aztec and Inca ruins led him to suggest, heretically for his time, that their cultures had once rivalled the ancient civilisations of Europe and the Middle East – and he was the first to speculate that the native peoples of South America had originally come from Asia, a hypothesis now confirmed by genetics. Wherever Humboldt looked, new possibilities emerged.

He was a remarkably hands-on scientist. While still a mining inspector back in Bavaria, his fascination with Luigi Galvani's theories of animal magnetism had led him to conduct over 4,000 experiments, many on himself, in which he attached electrodes to his skin and recorded the sometimes excruciating pain they caused. In South America he and Bonpland climbed to 19,260 feet (5,870 metres) on Chimborazo, the Ecuadorian volcano then thought to be the world's highest mountain. Although they didn't quite make the summit, no one had ever climbed so high before. Humboldt, his nose streaming blood, became the first person to note down the effects (and correctly guess the cause) of altitude sickness. In the jungle he reported being unable to breathe because of the dense clouds of mosquitoes. Seeing how the Orinoco Indians prepared curare, a poison from plants, he tested it on himself then on captured monkeys, giving them gradated doses and even resorting to mouth-to-mouth resuscitation to keep them alive. To penetrate the mystery of electric eels, he 'imprudently' placed both his bare feet on one ('the pain and the numbness are so violent it is impossible to describe the nature of the feeling they excite') and then asked the Indians how to collect specimens safely. They showed him how by driving a herd of thirty wild horses into an eel-infested lake. As the water crackled with electric charge, the terrified horses lunged frantically about with bulging eyes; several succumbed to the shocks and drowned, but gradually the eels ran out of battery. Once the horses were either calm (or dead), Humboldt could pick up the exhausted eels (using dry lengths of wood to act as an insulator) and begin his dissections, meticulously noting down all the various shocks he received in the process.

Humboldt arrived back in Paris to find himself famous. It wasn't altogether a surprise: he had shrewd marketing instincts. He had sent back many of his most exciting samples well in advance. He had also written letters to friends that began 'By the time you receive this I will probably be dead . . .' – all of which helped to create a sense of anticipation.

As Bonpland embarked on cataloguing the contents of the teetering stacks of sample cases, Humboldt set out to turn his notes and sketches into a book. His initial estimate of two years' work proved hopelessly optimistic. The thirty volumes of *Personal Narrative: A Voyage to the Equinoctial Regions of a New*

*Continent 1799–1804* took him almost thirty years (and almost all of his money) to complete. It is one of the great milestones of scientific literature and one of the very few that reads with the mounting excitement of an adventure story.

One of the reasons the book took so long to finish is that Humboldt had so much else to do. Over the next three decades, he climbed Vesuvius three times, went under the Thames in the diving bell used by Isambard Kingdom Brunel during the construction of the Thames Tunnel, and led a six-month expedition across Russia to the Chinese border. This didn't quite match the South American journey for new discoveries or excitement but it did lead to the establishment of a network of meteorological stations that stretched first across Russia and then around the world. The data they collected transformed our understanding of the weather and the operation of the earth's magnetic field. The 1911 edition of *Encyclopaedia Britannica* described it as 'the first truly international scientific collaboration'.

Little is known of Humboldt the private man. The mask of the suave diplomat rarely slipped, although his close friend and fellow scientist François Arago hinted at a more unbuttoned Humboldt behind closed doors: 'He has the most malicious tongue of any man I know and the best heart.' He never married. His close friendships with men have led many to suppose he was gay, but he destroyed all his personal papers so the evidence either way is thin. First-hand testimonies of his participation in the lively subculture of nineteenth-century Berlin mostly consist of dark mutterings about him consorting with 'obscene, dissolute youths' and tend to come from the more conservative and religious-minded of his younger colleagues. There is also the mystery of why he bequeathed his whole estate to an elderly male valet, but again that hardly offers conclusive proof of anything, especially as he had no immediate heirs. We'll never know for sure. It may have been that, like Mary Kingsley, he suppressed whatever sexual urges he had in order to concentrate on his work. This was a man, after all, who survived for eight decades on no more than four hours' sleep a night.

Humboldt ended his life in triumph. As he approached seventy, long after most of us have retired, he conceived his crowning achievement: 'I have the crazy idea to represent in one work the entire material universe.' The five volumes of *Kosmos* pulled together his experience of over half a century at the front line of scientific research. The product of what he called his 'improbable years', it was a magnificent achievement, rapturously received across Europe and in America. Humboldt lived to see all but the last volume published and died quietly in his sleep just a few months short of his ninetieth birthday.

After his death, Humboldt's reputation plummeted rapidly. His works were hardly read at all in the first half of the twentieth century and far more people today recognise the names of Linnaeus and Darwin. Given the pre-eminence he had enjoyed during his lifetime, this is hard to understand. It may be that Humboldt's work, for all its density and richness of detail, lacks what his greatest disciple, Charles Darwin, could offer; a simple, organising theory that binds it all together. Fascinating as *Kosmos* is to read, most of the science in it has been superseded by more recent research. Nevertheless, if the last 150 years of biology have been a series of footnotes to Darwin's theory of natural selection, Humboldt's time is now. Faced with the possibility of catastrophic global warming, we can see just how prescient he had been about the Earth as a single system. Darwin might have helped us join the dots in the tree of life, but to comprehend the climatic and geological forces that create and sustain it, Humboldt is still the man.

His work is imbued with the spirit of liberty and freedom that had animated the revolutions in America and France. His experiences in South America left him with a strong distaste for colonialism, for much the same reasons as Mary Kingsley: it demeaned both parties. And *Kosmos* makes his views on race plain: 'While we maintain the unity of the human species, we at the same time repel the depressing assumption of superior and inferior races of men . . . All are in like degree designed for freedom.'

Darwin enthusiastically endorsed this sentiment, but one of the unforeseen consequences of his evolutionary theory was it that it encouraged the idea that human beings were 'improvable'. In the last paragraph of *The Descent of Man* (1871) Darwin writes: 'Man may be excused for feeling some pride at having risen, though not through his own exertions, to the very summit of the organic scale.' The crucial phrase here is *'not through his own exertions'*. Man has been 'improved' by the operations of natural selection, not by the imposition of his own will. Darwin's point is that, for all man's noble qualities and achievements, he still bears the 'the indelible stamp of his lowly origin'.

~

At some point, this distinction became confused in the otherwise brilliantly original mind of his cousin and occasional collaborator, the statistician **Francis Galton** (1822–1911). Galton will forever be associated with the theory of eugenics (from the Greek for 'well born'), which proposed that selective breeding could be used to create a race of fitter, stronger and more intelligent humans. 'What nature does blindly, slowly, and ruthlessly, man may do providently, quickly, and kindly,' he wrote. The idea of breeding out the bad traits in humanity isn't intrinsically immoral; it's just based on bad science. There is no evidence that intelligence, still less virtue, is inherited. But Galton believed it and persuaded many others it was true. H. G. Wells, Sylvia Pankhurst, George Bernard Shaw and John Maynard Keynes were all eugenicists. Their motivations were honourable – they genuinely thought that 'breeding out badness' would deliver a better world. But the potential applications of Galton's ideas – most notably in Nazi Germany – have made eugenics a word that produces a shudder of disgust.

Galton's intellectual pedigree was impeccable. He shared a grandfather, Erasmus Darwin, with his cousin Charles, and the families were closely interknit (two of Francis's brothers were called Erasmus and Darwin). The Darwins were doctors and scientists; the Galtons were free-thinking Quaker bankers. Both families had produced members of the Royal Society and both helped found the Lunar Society, the influential think-tank of industrialists, scientists and philosophers that included James Watt, Joseph Priestley and Josiah Wedgwood. Young Francis was an infant prodigy. He learned to read at two and a half and got extra coaching from his older sister Adele, who had a congenital spinal defect that confined her to the house. She proved to be a talented teacher, though her baby brother took most of the credit:

> *I am four years old and can read any English book. I can say all the Latin Substantives and Adjectives and active verbs besides 52 lines of Latin poetry. I can cast up any sum in addition and multiply by 2, 3, 4, 5, 6, 7, 8, 10. I can also say the pence table. I read French a little and I know the Clock.*

This conceitedness, amusingly forgivable in a precocious child, never left Galton. He was clever but socially inept. At the age of five he was sent to a small school in Birmingham. He hated it. 'No one had heard of, let alone read, *The Iliad*,' he complained. The narrowness of the curriculum oppressed him and turned him into a disruptive influence. This carried over into his studies at medical school. Always suspicious of received wisdom, he decided to try all the drugs on himself, working his way through them alphabetically. He got as far as croton oil, a powerful purgative. Thinking that two drops wouldn't have much effect, he took some, but it produced such alarmingly unpleasant effects that he abandoned both the experiment and medicine altogether. He switched to mathematics, enrolling at Trinity College, Cambridge, in 1840.

Galton loved the social life at Cambridge and, much like his cousin Charles, made no great impression there academically. At the end of his fourth year, he suffered a nervous breakdown. He later claimed he had a 'sprained brain' from working too hard, but he left with a 'pass', the lowest level of degree awarded. Shortly after this, he was dealt a further blow by the death of his father. But, like Humboldt and Mary Kingsley, once the initial grief passed, he realised he was free. What's more, he discovered he was extremely rich. And, like Humboldt and Mary Kingsley, he decided to travel.

He made his first foray to Egypt and the Sudan, crossing the Nubian Desert by camel and learning Arabic. While sailing down the Nile at night, a shore party set off to shoot a hippo but, mistaking their target in the dark, bagged a cow that had come down to the water's edge to drink. They had to leave in a hurry. Nor did Dalton make it to his intended destination – the Holy

Land. In Damascus his faithful servant Ali died of violent dysentery. Again, Dalton had to make tracks, pursued by a horde of Ali's 'grieving relatives' with threats of legal action (or worse). He arrived back in London with two monkeys, a bad case of gonorrhoea contracted from a prostitute and a strong desire to improve his marksmanship. The monkeys perished when a friend's landlady left them in a cold scullery overnight but the venereal disease was treated successfully, and Galton spent a good deal of the next three years teaching himself to shoot on various Scottish estates. By 1850 he was ready to risk the tropics again. He bought a *papier maché* crown in Drury Lane, announced his intention to place it on the head of 'the greatest or most distant potentate I should meet with' and set off to un-mapped South West Africa. His thousand-mile accident-prone journey produced two very successful books. The first, *Tropical South Africa* (1852) won him the Royal Geographical Society's Gold medal and a Fellowship of the Royal Society. The second, *The Art of Travel* (1855), a practical handbook, quickly became an essential part of any gentleman's travelling kit, stuffed with useful tips on making your own pemmican, catching fish without a line, and managing 'savages'. He advised: 'A frank, joking but deter-mined manner, joined with an air of showing more confidence in the good faith of the natives than you really feel is the best.'

In South West Africa, Galton developed the fixation for statistics that would become his lifelong trademark. Adopting the motto 'Whenever you can, count', he fastidiously measured everything he came across: horses, cats, plants, human head shapes, portraits, reaction times. He surveyed the heights of mountains by climbing them and boiling kettles at regular intervals to ascertain their altitude, and he devised a method for measuring the size of African women's breasts and buttocks by using a sextant. When he finally reached his goal, placing his paper crown on the head of the immensely fat King Nangoro, chief of the Ovambo in northern Namibia, he passed up the chance to verify his instrumental readings at first hand. The chief offered him, by way of thanks, 'temporary marriage' to his daughter. When the girl arrived in his tent, naked, smeared with red ochre and butter, Galton ejected her 'with scant ceremony'. He had no intention of letting her spoil his white linen suit.

His compulsion for measurement continued on his return to England. He kept a home-made pin-and-paper device in his pocket allowing him to record data unobtrusively. A trip around the country notating the frequency of attractive women led to his publication of a 'beauty map' of the Britain, stating that London, proportionally speaking, had the most beauties and Aberdeen the highest concentration of the 'repellent'. At one rather dreary meeting at the Royal Geographical Society he created a 'boredom' chart, logging the total number of fidgets per minute. He mapped optimists and pessimists, people with blond hair and blue eyes, and scoured international court cases to come up with his 'honesty' index. Britain (naturally) came top, while Greece was 'the centre of gravity for lying'. He 'proved' that prayer was ineffective by noting the average ages of the British royal family (for whom, in those days, every congregation in the country dutifully prayed each Sunday) and demonstrating that they lived no longer than anyone else. He even developed a mathematical formula for a perfect cup of tea, designing and building his own thermometer to test it. (The water, according to Galton, should be 82–87 °C and sit on the leaves for precisely eight minutes – the result will be 'full bodied, full tasted, and in no way bitter or flat'.)

In over 300 books and articles, Galton alternated between serious scientist and mad boffin. For every 'Gumption-Reviver Machine' (a mobile dripping tap positioned above the head to keep students alert) there were genuine scientific insights. His pioneering work in meteorology produced the first working weather map. His 'anthropometric laboratory', based in the South Kensington Museum in London, collated the measurements of almost 10,000 human bodies revealing for the first time that fingerprints were unique and invariable throughout a person's life. Galton's 200-page book *Finger Prints* (1890) led to the adoption of fingerprint identification by the Metropolitan Police.

Galton had always had a knack of seeing patterns in pages of dull numerical data that eluded other people. His cousin's publication of *On the Origin of Species* had a galvanising effect on him. He became fascinated by the idea of measuring the apparently random variations produced by natural selection. By plotting the height of parents against that of their offspring he noticed that exceptionally tall parents tended to have children that were less tall than they were. In fact, by drawing a line on his graph he was able to show that their offspring were only two-thirds as exceptional. Galton had uncovered a mathematical law: 'regression towards the mean', the tendency for a series of measurements over time to move closer to the average point. This was a major breakthrough, especially for a mathematician of unexceptional ability, and it was to transform statistics into a proper science. There was 'scarcely anything so apt to impress the imagination as the wonderful form of cosmic order expressed by the Law', wrote Galton with characteristic immodesty. 'It would have been personified by the Greeks, and deified, if they had known of it.' Outstanding though it undoubtedly was, Galton came unstuck when he tried to apply the law to far more complex human qualities such as intelligence.

In *Hereditary Genius* (1864) he became the first person to frame the 'nature versus nurture' debate, and the opening sentence makes plain which side he is on: 'I propose to show in this book that a man's natural abilities are derived by inheritance.' What follows is an attempt to prove that 'greatness' runs in families. It is full of powerful ideas and the statistical evidence is impressively marshalled – Darwin said that he did not 'think that ever in all my life I read anything more interesting or original' – but it is also wilfully selective. Geniuses like Leonardo da Vinci or Michael Faraday, whose families showed no obvious aptitude for art or science, are omitted. The argument is based on a false premise; Galton's own experiments had shown that the expression of intelligence can be markedly different even between identical twins, and there is, in fact, no single 'intelligence' gene. Worse, the work is disfigured by a casual racism that today is deeply uncomfortable to read. In the chapter 'The Comparative Worth of Different Races', Galton places human intelligence in a hierarchy with the ancient Greeks at the top, two classes above the average Anglo-Saxon, who is in turn two classes above black Africans, with Australian Aboriginals at the bottom. 'The number among the negroes of those whom we should call half-witted men', Galton blithely opined, 'is very large'.

Galton was knighted in 1909 and died two years later, just a few months before he turned ninety, like Humboldt. Eccentric to the last, he experimented with controlling his bronchial problems by smoking hashish. To the very end, he was sure he knew best. Odd as he undoubtedly was – inventing ridiculous gadgets like underwater spectacles so he could read in the bath –he was also one of the most respected and influential members of the Victorian scientific establishment and feted as one of the great men of his day. The final irony is that, for all his eugenicist talk of creating a 'better' world by sterilising 'those who are seriously afflicted by lunacy, feeble-mindedness, habitual criminality, and pauperism', it was Galton himself who died childless.

~

**William Morris** (1834–96) was a decade younger than Galton. Given their respective political views it's unlikely they ever met, although perfectly possible that Galton's elegant South Kensington home was furnished using Morris's designs. Morris is still best known as a designer, the Terence Conran of the nineteenth century: his work has spawned a thousand tea cosies, spectacle cases and napkins. This has tended to obscure his other achievements as a poet, painter, engraver, weaver, dyer, printer, retailer and revolutionary. Morris elevated 'busyness' to a kind of art form, so much so that, when he died in 1896, his doctor attributed his demise to 'his simply being William Morris, and having done more work than most ten men'.

For Morris 'useful' work (which he distinguished from 'useless' toil) was no different from play: an enjoyable occupation that engaged both the mind and the senses. Confucius had said much the same thing 2,500 years earlier: 'Choose a job you love and you'll never have to work again.' In a century when industrialisation was rapidly reducing human beings to automata, Morris's ideas were a powerful call for change. Few have people have lived their work as thoroughly.

Morris's father was a city broker who died young, but whose shares in a Devon copper mine ensured the family enjoyed a comfortable life. As a result, Morris could afford to be generous to his friends, entertaining them royally and bankrolling their artistic joint ventures. It also left him with a devil-may-care disrespect for class distinctions that gives his prose a blunt honesty we don't usually associate with the High Victorians. In a letter to a friend he writes: 'I am a boor and the son of a boor . . . How often it consoles me to think of barbarism once more flooding the world and real feelings and passions, however, rudi-mentary, taking the place of our hypocrisies.'

His early childhood was idyllic. Growing up near Epping Forest his father had bought him a pony and toy suit of armour, and he would ride into the forest as a miniature knight, carrying out quests and making up tales of chivalry while sketching the birds and wild flowers that would become central to his designs. He loathed formal education. At Marlborough, he recalled, 'I had a hardish time of it, as chaps who have brains and feelings generally do at school.' His nickname was Crab, and he was famous for his stormy temperament, rushing after those who teased him 'with his head down and his arms whirling wildly'.

This restless, impulsive quality persisted throughout his life and made him both lovable and exasperating. Before going up to Oxford, he toyed with the idea of becoming a High Church Anglican clergyman, but the work of John Ruskin converted him to architecture instead. Next, he became a passionate advocate of medieval art and communal living. After he graduated, he was apprenticed to G. E. Street, the Gothic revival architect, whom he later came to despise as a 'vandal'. Inspired by his best friend, the Pre-Raphaelite artist Edward Burne-Jones, Morris decided that his real calling was painting. Then poetry took him over and he wrote *The Earthly Paradise* (1869), a kind of re-invention of the

*Canterbury Tales*, in which a group of medieval Norwegian wanderers set out in search of a land of eternal life. This mythic verse epic became an immediate best-seller, establishing him as one of the most popular poets in the country. From then on, most people knew him as the 'author of *The Earthly Paradise*', and the poem was still popular enough, more than twenty years later, for Morris to be offered the Poet Laureateship when Tennyson died in 1892. As well as poetry, novels, fantasies and essays flowed out of him – his *Collected Works* come to twenty-four large volumes. After poetry, his next preoccupation was dyeing, a complex technical process that he taught himself. Having mastered that he learnt weaving, then tapestry, then printing. On top of all this, he found time to become a political activist: first a liberal, then a socialist and the spiritual godfather of the British Labour Party. His friend Burne-Jones encapsulated the roller-coaster ride of Morris's life: 'All things he does splendidly . . . every minute will be alive.'

Morris never felt more alive than when he was making something. He summed up his philosophy in saying: 'If a chap can't compose an epic poem while he is weaving a tapestry, he had better shut up.' His infectious enthusiasm rubbed off on all those around him. Whether at home, or in the factories and shops he built, Morris had a genius for getting everyone to join in. Much of this was due to his bonhomie and unconventional sense of fun. At Oxford, he was noted for his purple trousers and once ate dinner in a suit of chain mail he'd had made by a local blacksmith. His unruly mop of hair led his friends to nickname him 'Topsy' (as in the phrase 'growed like Topsy') after the ragamuffin slave girl in the popular contemporary novel *Uncle Tom's Cabin* (1852).

William Morris was a short, portly, barrel-chested, bright-eyed, tousled ball of energy: absent-minded, charming, continually breaking chairs by means of what Ned Burne-Jones called 'a muscular movement peculiar to himself' and capable of terrifying fits of foul-mouthed temper. When in a rage, he could crush forks with his teeth and smash holes in plaster walls with his head: one Christmas Day he threw an under-cooked plum pudding through a window. In return, his friends would wind him up terribly, re-sewing the buttons on his waistcoat to make him seem even fatter, or refusing to answer his questions at dinner. Mostly it was with Morris's cheery compliance. He liked being the centre of attention, even when it cast him in an absurd light.

He was a man of large appetites: he 'lusted for pig's flesh' and always kept the dinner table groaning with good wine. 'Why do people say it is so prosaic to be inspired by wine,' he protested. 'Has it not been made by the sunlight and the sap?' He liked the grand gesture: on becoming a socialist he sat on his top hat to mark his resignation from the board of the family's copper mine. With his shaggy beard, blue work-shirt and rolling gait, he was often mistaken for a seaman, though he sometimes seems more like a Viking that has stepped out of one of his beloved Norse sagas.

Perhaps because of his lovable, faintly batty streak, Morris's contributions to public life are often overlooked. He has been called the father of Modernism in architecture, the most important English socialist thinker and the first environmentalist. The Society for the Protection of Ancient Buildings and the Art Workers Guild, both of which he helped found, continue to thrive. Even in literature, where his reputation has suffered its steepest decline, C. S. Lewis and J. R. R. Tolkien both cited his prose romances like *The Wood beyond the World* as inspirational for their own work.

Considering why Morris's poems were no longer read, G. K.

Chesterton once remarked: 'If his poems were too like wallpapers, it was because he really could make wallpapers.' Morris's design has become a by-word for English bourgeois good taste. It appears everywhere – often in contexts that Morris could not possibly have foreseen, still less approved of. Morris's ideal house was a big barn, 'where one ate in one corner, cooked in another corner, slept in a third corner and in the fourth, received one's friends.' His own actual houses were, quite literally, hand-made works of art. The core idea of his thought is that art begins at home, in the making and furnishing of a house. True art, for Morris, is indistinguishable from craftsmanship: it isn't about abstract 'self-expression' but practical collective labour that gives pleasure in the doing and creates beauty that everyone can share. He was extraordinarily influential in his life-time: the social progressives who applauded Galton's eugenics – George Bernard Shaw, the Webbs, the Pankhursts, J. M. Keynes – had homes that were veritable shrines to Morris & Co.

Morris was well aware of the contradiction of being a socialist visionary, on the one hand, and a businessman who supplied decor to the rich and famous on the other. But he was far too busy to wallow in guilt. He pointed out that he paid his staff over the odds and taught them to make beautiful things that would last a lifetime. What would be the point, he asked, of him giving his money away? The poor would be just as poor. 'The world would be pleased to talk to me for three days until something new caught its fancy. Even if Rothschild gave away his millions tomorrow, the same problems would confront us the day after.'

In some ways, the brand of socialism that Morris championed has fared no better than Galton's eugenics, but he was never a hard-line party man – Engels and the other London-based communists were deeply suspicious of him. Neither he nor they could have foreseen the Gulags, any more than Galton could have predicted the Nazis. What Morris did see coming, though, with great clarity and dismay, was the consumer society. Even as a teenager he refused to go into the Great Exhibition of 1851 with the rest of his family, suspecting it would be brimful of industrial ugliness and wasteful luxury goods. 'I have never been in any rich man's house which would not have looked the better for having a bonfire made outside of it of nine-tenths of all that it held,' he wrote. Far ahead of his time, Morris saw that consumerism would come to oppress those who did the consuming: he foresaw a nation drowning in cheap tat and clutter, its people ruled by their own possessions. 'Luxury,' he said, 'cannot exist without slavery of some kind or other.'

He also saw how capitalism would get round the growing clamour for freedom and equality. In 1869, long before the Labour Party was founded, he predicted that the Establishment would survive by adopting 'quasi-socialist machinery' with 'the workers better treated, better organised, helping to govern themselves, but with no more pretence to equality with the rich, nor nay more hope for it than they have now'. They were prophetic words. Though the overall standard of living has improved in the 140 years since Morris was writing, inequality in British society has actually widened. The top 20 per cent in Britain today now earn seven times as much as the bottom 20 per cent.

As the novelist Henry James said of Morris, he is 'wonderfully to the point and remarkable for clear, good sense'. He wasn't a sophisticated political theorist; he was a problem-solver, a doer, and he was the first major figure to utter the heresy that unless art is accessible to everyone it is worthless.

His personal life, friendships and merriment aside, was painful. His wife, Jane, had two long affairs, one with his friend, the poet and painter Dante Gabriel Rossetti (who rather cruelly called his pet wombat Topsy) and the other with the louche poet Wilfrid Scawen Blunt. Her infidelities wounded Morris deeply, although his own emotional inadequacies were partly to blame. His view of romantic love never developed beyond adolescent idealisation and fell far short of the emotional intimacy that Jane needed. She was a depressive and Morris escaped her moods by burying himself in his work. Nevertheless, they remained together and he managed the situation over forty years with tact and kindness. By way of compensation for his failings as a husband, he was endlessly attentive to his children – particularly his daughter Jenny who lived life as a semi-invalid because of her epilepsy. They, in turn, adored him.

In the last two years of his life his great passion was the production of a hand-printed edition of Chaucer's *Canterbury Tales,* in type he designed himself, with eighty-seven illustrations by Burne-Jones. A masterpiece of book design, it is the embodiment of his theory that work should be collaborative and the results both beautiful and useful. Burne-Jones called it 'a pocket cathedral'.

In 1895 trouble with Morris's lungs proved to be tubercular and he started to weaken. But, visiting a badly restored Norman church in Sussex, he still had the energy to unleash paroxysms of fury at the absent architects: 'Beasts! Pigs! Damn their souls!' On hearing that John Ruskin had described him as 'the ablest man of his time', he summoned his old jollity to order up a bottle of Imperial Tokay (one of his favourite wines) from the cellar. But he knew the end was near. 'I cannot believe I will be annihilated!' he fumed. His final words were defiant: 'I want to get mumbo jumbo out of the world,' but his death was peaceful. Several of his friends noted how beautiful he looked lying there in repose – and, being motionless, how unlike himself.

~

Morris's contemporary, the tireless naturalist T. H. Huxley, had died the previous year. He wrote that 'the great end of life is not knowledge but action'. Genghis Khan conquered most of the known world; Peary and Mary Kingsley charted unknown lands; Humboldt took on the cosmos; Galton and Morris designed the future. For all of them, 'doing' was the only setting on their dial. Yet none had happy marriages and only Morris passed muster as a loving parent. They probably hardly noticed: the job in hand was what mattered and absorption in the task was reward enough in itself. All would have agreed for sure with that other nineteenth-century over-achiever, Benjamin Jowett, Master of Balliol, Oxford: 'Never retreat. Never explain. Get it done and let them howl.'

# CHAPTER FOUR

# Let's Do It

*Personally I know nothing about sex because I have always been married.*

ZSA ZSA GABOR

Sex is the most natural but least straightforward of all human urges. It fascinates and repels us, and it's the ultimate leveller. Rich or poor, prince or plumber, saint or private equity fund manager, we all got here because somebody, somewhere, had sex with someone else. Yet human sexual activity takes up less of our time than eating, sleeping, watching television or even choosing what clothes we wear in the morning. Of the twenty-five years the average couple spends in bed, only two months are spent making love. And, despite what you read in the papers, we don't think about it all the time, either. The cliché about men's minds straying to sex every seven seconds is pure invention. The Kinsey Institute found that almost half the men they survey only think about sex once or twice a week.

~

This was not the case with **Giacomo Casanova** (1725–98). His twelve volumes of memoirs, *The Story of My Life*, are a 3,600- page catalogue of debauchery and sexual conquest. They are in French, which Casanova thought more sophisticated than his native Italian, and were not published in full until 1960. They record each significant moment in Casanova's life up until the summer of 1774 (when he was forty-nine), at which point the narrative stops in mid-sentence. The author was then in his sixties, a washed-up, impotent, pox-raddled librarian in an obscure Bohemian castle. Bored out of his mind, he began to write as 'the only remedy to keep from going mad or dying of grief'.

Giacomo Casanova was born in Venice. His father, Gaetano, was an actor. Even in the most licentious city in Europe, infamous for gambling, prostitution and its wild abandoned carnival, acting was a low calling, scarcely better than burglary. When Gaetano Casanova married Zanetta Farussi, her father, a humble shoe-maker, died of shame (or so they said) within a month of the wedding. His son wasn't proud of him either. His memoirs begin with a tortuous attempt to make up for it by proving that his father was the descendant of a Spanish nobleman, tracing the family tree back three centuries, only to conclude that his *real* father wasn't Gaetano at all, but an aristocratic theatre-owner called Michele Grimani. Casanova's mother, 'beautiful as the sun-light', was a flirt of epic proportions: alternative paternities have been suggested for all six of her children. Casanova's lifelong anxiety over his legitimacy would drive him to create an ideal self – the suave, witty, patrician libertine of legend – but that's not how it began.

As a boy, Giacomo had 'an air of madness' about him. His mouth hung open slackly and he had a perpetual nosebleed:

*My illness made me a gloomy child, and not the least bit amusing. Everyone felt sorry for me and left me in peace; they thought my time on earth would be brief. My father and mother never spoke to me at all.*

Luckily for Giacomo, he had Marzia, an Italian grandmother straight from central casting. She bossed, bullied and fussed over him, took him to see a witch to try to sort out his nose, and then, with the help of the Abbé Grimani (the brother of his true father), arranged for him, aged nine, to be privately educated in Padua. He spent some miserable months starving in a rat- and flea-infested boarding house but Marzia came to the rescue, travelling to Padua herself, tearing a strip off his sadistic Croatian landlady and transferring him to the family home of his young tutor, the Abbé Gozzi. Giacomo proved himself an excellent student and was soon out-pointing his teacher in theological discussions. Extra-curricular activities were also on offer. The priest's teenage sister, Bettina, seduced him, inflaming his ardour one morning by washing his thighs, using the flimsy excuse that she wanted him to try on a new pair of white stockings. As Casanova recalled, she 'struck the first sparks of a passion that was to become the dominant one in my heart'. The eleven-year-old Giacomo quickly lost control ('the sweet pleasure her curiosity caused in me did not cease until it could increase no more') and then tormented himself, wondering if, after this terrible crime, he should offer to marry her. But Bettina had already turned her attention elsewhere, to older boys – teaching Giacomo another, less enjoyable lesson: after love comes melancholy.

For the next four decades, Casanova devoted himself to the pursuit of pleasure and a lavish lifestyle. His working life, by contrast, was chaotic. He graduated from Padua University as a lawyer but felt an 'unconquerable aversion' to the legal profession. Instead, he took holy orders. This started well. He landed a job working for a powerful cardinal in Rome, where he met the Pope and persuaded him to allow him access to 'forbidden books' and grant him special dispensation to eat meat on 'fish only' days (on the grounds that fish 'inflamed' his eyes). After being caught in a three-in-a-bed romp with two sisters and then arrested for gambling debts, he left the church in a hurry, though a distinctly ecclesiastical flavour lingers on in the records of his romantic encounters (he 'approaches the altar frieze', 'performs the gentle sacrifice' and on one occasion 'reaches the porch of the temple, without gaining free entrance to the sanctuary'). Casanova's next temping job was as an officer in the Venetian army. Initially attracted by the smart uniforms, he almost immediately got bored with the repetitiveness of military life, so he had a stab at being a theatre violinist, followed by trying his hand as secretary to a Venetian senator. And so it went on. Casanova's charm and intelligence would get him work, after which he would be distracted by women, rack up huge gambling debts and be forced to flee from his creditors. His story reads like half a dozen airport thrillers with the pages shuffled and put back together in the wrong order. He was a diplomat, mathematician, spy, alchemist, Freemason, card sharp, magician, entrepreneur, faith healer, actor, playwright, duellist, lawyer, physician and, finally, librarian. Fluent in Italian, French, Latin and Greek, with a smattering of German, English and Russian, he travelled some 40,000 miles and negotiated his way in twenty-seven different currencies. Work, for Casanova, was only ever about status: he would do anything for anyone, in any country, as long as it allowed him freedom and the semblance of wealth and influence. Throughout his life, most of his 'income' came from gifts. When he needed serious money, he gambled:

*Why did I gamble when I felt the losses so keenly? What made me gamble was avarice. I loved to spend, and my heart bled when I could not do it with money won at cards.*

And he was good. Over the period covered by his memoirs, his winnings came to over £11 million in modern terms, with his losses running at less than a million. The low boredom threshold he exhibited when trying to hold down a job never affected him at the card table. One marathon session of piquet lasted for forty-two hours without a break.

But gambling, however addictive he found it, was always a means to an end – and the end, with Casanova, was always a woman. 'Love is three-quarters curiosity,' he wrote – and his was insatiable: any woman, under any circumstance, was fair game. Tall and skinny with a beaked nose, bulbous eyes and heavy eyebrows, he was not classically handsome, but it was his unshakeable conviction that he – or indeed any man – could seduce any woman if she felt herself the sole object of his undivided attention. 'I don't conquer, I submit,' he explained. Women trusted him and he was an appreciative and considerate lover. He liked to give them pleasure and even practised safe sex, using a variety of condoms made from sheeps' intestines and linen or – if all else failed – half a lemon inserted as a kind of improvised Dutch cap. His list of conquests is surprisingly modest given his reputation: he slept with perhaps no more than 140 women (a total trounced by Byron, when he lived in Venice, in just two years). On the other hand, it was enough to give him gonorrhoea at least eleven times, and when he died in 1798 it was from a bladder complaint probably caused by repeated venereal infections.

The detail and humour of Casanova's memoirs make for a compelling read. He relates that he lost his virginity to two sisters and that their lovemaking was punctuated by an impromptu dinner of bread and cheese. Falling for a castrato singer called Bellino, and convinced she is a woman in disguise, he groped her crotch, only to find an unmistakable bulge. Indefatigable as ever, he reasoned this must be a 'monstrous clitoris', and his persistence paid off. 'Bellino' was indeed a woman called Teresa, who wore a false phallus to get round the papal ban on women singing in church choirs. Needless to say, she became his mistress. In Venice, he enjoyed a *ménage-à-trois* with the French ambassador and a nun. He nearly seduced a beautiful young woman who turned out to be his own daughter by a former lover. A few years later, they met again and this time he deliberately seduced her and slept with her and her mother simultaneously. Untroubled by shame, he also bedded his niece, encouraged a twelve-year-old novice nun to fellate him through a grille, and seduced all five daughters from one family in exchange for rescuing their parents from ruin. But he didn't get it all his own way. In London a courtesan called Marianne Charpillon refused to go to bed with him and then stole all his money. He was so upset by this that he decided to kill himself by jumping into the Thames, and only stopped when a friend persuaded him to go a pub and get drunk instead. To get revenge, he trained a parrot to recite: 'Miss Charpillon is more of a whore than her mother.' This so enraged Miss Charpillon that she took legal advice on whether or not she could sue a parrot for libel.

Casanova had better luck with the Marquise D'Urfé, one of the richest women in Paris, who was impressed by his deep knowledge of the Cabbala. He convinced her that he could help her be reincarnated and that part of the necessary ritual involved his having sex with her. The Marquise was so physically repulsive he had to fake two of his three orgasms. This wasn't his usual problem – he was afflicted by premature ejaculation through most of his life – although he claimed he could make love at least six times a night with the help of a special concoction of chocolate and egg-white. He also fixed the oyster's reputation as an aphrodisiac, sometimes eating fifty for breakfast, declaring that the best sauce for an oyster was his lover's saliva. A special treat was eating live bivalves off a girlfriend's breasts.

In 1755 Casanova's sexual intrigues, combined with his dabbling in banned Masonic rites and magic, earned him a five-year sentence in Venice's Piombi prison. He stuck it out for nine months before escaping by breaking through the roof of his cell and walking out of the main gates when they were opened the next morning. Forced to seek exile in France, he came up with his greatest and most lucrative financial scam – inventing the French national lottery. Now in his mid-thirties, he enjoyed a brief spate of wealth and fame, styling himself the Chevalier de Seingalt (an entirely bogus title). He met – and was disappointed by – Voltaire, arguing with him over religion; he discussed powered flight with Benjamin Franklin and taxation policy with Frederick the Great; and made friends with Lorenzo Da Ponte, Mozart's favourite librettist. (It seems likely that Da Ponte's masterpiece, *Don Giovanni*, was based at least in some part on Casanova, who may even have contributed to the writing himself.)

Casanova's own literary ambitions never quite came together until the very end of his life. He wrote forty-two books, including a history of Venetian government, a history of Poland and a much-admired translation of Homer's *Iliad* into modern Italian.

He even produced a five-volume science-fiction novel, *Isocameron*, which predicted the motor car, the aeroplane, television and many other inventions. His plays were performed across Europe but he was never in one place long enough to capitalise on his reputation. Fame, money and love all had a way of deserting him. He never came close to getting married, although he did, in his late twenties, fall heavily for a young Frenchwoman called Henriette:

> *They who believe that a woman is incapable of making a man equally happy all the twenty-four hours of the day have never known an Henriette. The joy which flooded my soul was far greater when I conversed with her during the day than when I held her in my arms at night.*

Henriette was smart and cultured as well as beautiful, and she seemed to sense Casanova was in the grip of a pathology he couldn't control. She turned the tables on him, and stole away in the night, having scratched a message on his bedroom window with her diamond ring. It said, 'You will forget Henriette, too.' She also slipped 500 gold louis into his jacket pocket (worth about £30,000 today): the perfect 'thanks, but no thanks' gesture. She had his number: clever, charming and expensive to run. Casanova was bereft and cheered himself up the only way he knew how: more travel, more women and more gambling. It would be easy to argue that he squandered his talents and that, but for his addiction to sex, he might have ended up, in some way, as one of the great men of his day. Surveying the wreckage at the end of his life, he fantasised about the different course he might have taken:

*If I had married a woman intelligent enough to guide me, to rule me without my feeling that I was ruled, I should have taken good care of my money, I should have had children, and I should not be, as now I am, alone in the world and possessing nothing.*

Anyone familiar with his effervescent memoirs will see this as self-pitying, self-indulgent humbug: Casanova got the life he wanted and the fate he deserved. As he sat in the castle at Dux, hunched over his manuscript in a draughty library, scribbling away for thirteen hours a day, he had come full circle. The nine-year-old boy who had watched his father die and kissed his beautiful mother goodbye was alone again once more.

*The chief business of my life has always been to indulge my senses; I never knew anything of greater importance. I felt myself born for the fair sex, and I have been loved by it as often and as much as I could.*

Sex may not have made him happy, but it made him laugh and it made him famous, more famous than almost anyone else of his era.

~

In 1765 Casanova was granted an audience with **Catherine the Great** (1729–96). Both were in their prime: he was forty, she thirty-six. Here were two of the most famous sexual appetites of all time engaged in an animated discussion. What did they talk about? Bringing the Russian calendar into line with the rest of Europe is what. They clearly got on. He said of her that she 'thoroughly understood the art of making herself loved. She was not beautiful, but yet she was sure of pleasing by her geniality and her wit.' She said of him that he was 'not precisely handsome' but agreed to see him again and was obviously charmed. Their encounter ended with Casanova's failure to persuade her either to reform the calendar or introduce his lottery scheme. He praised her tact and judgment but ended with an arch (and somewhat ironic) aside to the reader, saying that, for all her greatness, 'the moralist will always consider her, and rightly, as one of the most notable of dissolute women'.

Catherine the Great, Empress of Russia, wasn't Russian, wasn't called Catherine and hated being referred to as 'the Great'. She was a Prussian aristocrat, born Sophie Frederica Auguste, Princess von Anhalt-Zerbst.

Almost three centuries after her death her name is still synonymous with wanton lust. Her notoriety is based on having had 'legions' of lovers, combined with the entirely apocryphal story that she died while attempting to mate with a horse. In fact, her death was one of the least remarkable things to happen to her: she collapsed from a stroke while on the lavatory and died some hours afterwards in bed. What she left behind her was a powerful, modernised Russian empire that made other European states nervous. Most of the rumours concerning her death were probably spread by her enemies, of which the post-Revolutionary French were the most prominent. Tales of sexual excess were the standard way of disparaging a powerful woman: the rumours about Queen Marie Antoinette's sex life were even worse.

To get to the truth about Catherine we need to start with her very odd and unsatisfactory marriage to her cousin, the Grand Duke Peter of Holstein-Gottorp (1728–62), heir to the Russian throne. Badly disfigured by smallpox, and physically quite weak, Peter preferred playing soldiers to managing affairs of state. His absorption in these games was total and he would change uniform up to twenty times a day while having mock battles with his valets, guards and a selection of companion dwarfs. Catherine was expected to join in and often had to stand on guard as a sentry in the doorway between their two rooms when she was his fiancée. Peter had several other lovers, one of whom Catherine described as being as 'discrete as a cannonball'. After their wedding in 1745 they moved into the Oranienbaum Palace on the Gulf of Finland, near St Petersburg. Catherine realised the marriage was doomed from the start, writing in her journal that he was 'unlovable' and telling herself 'if you love him you will be the most wretched creature on earth'. Fortunately, the marriage wasn't consummated for several years and, by the time it was, Catherine had already started on her own sequence of dashing lovers, beginning with a handsome chamberlain called Sergei Saltyov and a suave Polish nobleman, Stanislaw Poniatowski, whom she visited disguised as a man (Catherine later made him king of Poland). She insisted that her first son, Paul, was the result of her affair with Saltyov, though he was both physically and emotionally very like the Grand Duke Peter, a weak-willed bully who shared the older man's love of dressing up. In an effort to stop him becoming an effeminate laughing-stock like her husband, Catherine arranged for a young widow to instruct him in the art of love when he was fourteen.

In 1762, on the death of his mother, Grand Duke Peter became Emperor Peter III. He was a German, born in Kiel, and he hated Russians. At his mother's funeral he disgraced himself by deliberately walking slowly so that the cortège drew ahead and then sprinting after it so that the elderly courtiers were left gasping for breath. Six months later, a group of Russian nobleman deposed him in a *coup d'état*, provoked by both his incompetence and his support for Prussia's land claims in Poland. The feeble-minded Peter seemed quite happy to retire to his country palace with his mistress and, despite her own lack of Russian blood, Catherine was proclaimed Catherine II, Empress of All the Russias. She'd been careful not to implicate herself directly in the coup but she ordered that the victorious army be given free drinks in St Petersburg, paying the bill herself. It came to over 100,000 roubles (around £20 million today). Three days later, a young officer called Alexei Orlov assassinated Grand Duke Peter.

Orlov was the third of four brothers, the second of whom, Grigory, had been Catherine's paramour since 1759 and was one of the leaders of the military coup. Historians generally exonerate Catherine from her husband's murder, but she rewarded all four Orlovs by creating them counts, and Grigory got a palace in St Petersburg as well. He had obvious attractions as a lover. He was a powerfully built guardsman who had been wounded several times on the battlefield and enjoyed bear-hunting, cock-fighting and boxing. Catherine almost married him but, though they stayed friends, she decided he wasn't up to the politics and she'd have more freedom as the Dowager Empress. In the meantime, she continued to enjoy the services of younger, physically im-pressive men. Perhaps the most important of these was General Grigori Potemkin, who remained a confidant and ally even after their love affair was over. They wrote to each other several times a day even when they were in the same building – she called him her 'lion of the jungle', 'golden tiger', 'wolf' and her 'Cossack'. He called her 'Sovereign Lady', and occasionally 'Little Mother' (*Matrushka*). After their affair, it was rumoured that he acted as her bedroom advisor, choosing young men she would find suitably attractive and interesting. Catherine was sexually active until the end of her life: one of her last lovers was Prince Platon Zubov. He was only twenty-two, more than forty years her junior. She was devoted to him, referring to him as her 'baby', and telling everyone he was 'the greatest genius Russia has ever known'. Under her patronage, he amassed great wealth and eventually succeeded Potemkin as governor general of New Russia, the newly conquered lands in what is now southern Ukraine.

What Zubov, Potemkin and many of Catherine's other partners shared was their capacity to engage her intellectually. She liked her boys beefy, but wit was much more important. Arriving in St Petersburg as a teenager, she had been horrified by the ignorance and lack of education she found in royal circles: almost half the courtiers were illiterate. In 1774 she was thrilled when the French philosopher Denis Diderot visited the city, feeding her mind with long discussions about science, art and politics. He was equally delighted, describing her as having 'the soul of Caesar with all the seductions of Cleopatra'.

Catherine's active sex life was just one facet of her passionate and energetic personality. She could stay awake for twenty-four hours, working late into the night on state papers; she could ride a horse as well as most men; and she was both highly intelligent and creative, writing plays and corresponding with the great philosophers of the Age of Enlightenment such as Voltaire and D'Alembert, and incorporating their ideas into her *Nakaz*, or 'Instruction' of 1767. Designed as a template for an enlightened monarchy, it anticipated many of the themes of the American republican constitution by twenty years. All men were equal before the law and the death penalty and torture were discouraged.

The same progressive attitude and openness to new ideas

informed her personal life. As a strong, intelligent woman she was far ahead of her time in the ultra-conservative backwater of Russian politics. In that chauvinistic world, a mere woman could not succeed on merit alone. Her enemies would destroy her reputation in any way they could, even if it meant claiming that she was so debauched that no man could fully satisfy her inhuman appetites.

~

If Catherine the Great sought out sex because she enjoyed it, **Cora Pearl** (1835–86) turned her sexual expertise into a business. One of the great Parisian courtesans of the 1860s (known collectively as *les Grandes Horizontales*), she called her succession of male friends 'a golden chain'. They weren't merely wealthy, they were prominent members of high society: Prince Wilhelm, heir to the Dutch throne; Prince Achille Murat, grandson of the King of Naples; the Duke of Rivoli; the Duke of Morny, half-brother of the Emperor Napoleon III; and the Emperor's cousin 'Plon-Plon', better known as Prince Napoleon. Showered with gifts from these wealthy lovers, Cora was able to buy two houses in Paris, keep sixty horses and amass a collection of jewellery worth more than a million francs.

This darling of the French nobility was actually English, formerly Eliza Crouch of Plymouth. Daughter of the cellist and conductor Frederick Nicholls Crouch and Lydia Pearson, singer, her father deserted the family when Eliza was ten and emigrated to the United States, where he reputedly fathered another twenty offspring. Eliza never saw him again. Lydia remarried and moved to Guernsey and Eliza was sent to a convent school in Boulogne, afterwards returning to London to live with her grandmother. She was just nineteen when a man in the street accosted her, gave her gin and took advantage of her. Too ashamed to go home, and completely distrustful of men, she began to earn her living as a prostitute. She befriended Robert Bignel, owner of the Argyle Dancing Rooms where she plied her trade. He took her to France on holiday as his mistress, but she refused to return to England, throwing her passport on the fire so that he had no choice but to leave her behind. Adopting the name Cora Pearl (because she liked the sound of it), she set about acquiring a circle of wealthy admirers. There was no better place for that than Paris during the Second Empire. The city was the centre of the civilised world, a non-stop succession of balls and parties where, as Alexandre Dumas *fils* described it, 'Women were luxuries for public consumption like hounds, horses and carriages.'

Cora, the Devon girl who spoke 'Cockney French', quickly turned herself into the most desirable woman in Paris. She wasn't classically beautiful; one critic writing in the *London Truth* said she had 'a round face, carroty hair, an unamiable temper, and a laugh which if bereft of jollity stretched her coarse mouth from ear to ear. That mouth was visibly formed to eat and drink, to talk slang and to swear.' But Cora's red hair quickly became legendary, earning her the nickname '*La Lune Rousse*' (the Red Moon).\* Plus she had an unblemished complexion and a body that was a 'marvel of nature': her breasts were accounted so perfect that plaster casts were taken of them to make bronze sculptures. She also gained a reputation for being life-changingly

---

\* Literally, *The Red* (or *Auburn*) *Moon*, from her round face and red hair, but it's cleverer than that. In French *La Lune Rousse* also means 'The April Moon', one that coincides with the frosts that can destroy the shoots of young plants.

adventurous in bed; one of her (anonymous) admirers described her 'as a specimen of another race, a bizarre and astonishing phenomenon'. It was rare to find a courtesan who loved sex as much as Cora did, and this added greatly to her mystique. If the appeal of undreamt-of sensuality wasn't enough to ensnare a potential lover, Cora was also a consummate hostess.

Her parties were like no others in the city, a combination of lascivious cabaret and fine cuisine. As many as fifteen lucky gentlemen at a time would be invited to see her immersed in a bath of champagne, dancing naked on a bed of orchids or served up for dinner on a silver platter, wearing nothing but a few sprigs of parsley. She wore shimmering body paint, covering herself in silver, stars and pearls. She dyed her hair red, black and blonde, and transformed her eyes with brilliantly coloured eye-shadow and mascara. Once, she even dyed her dog blue to match an outfit (it died shortly afterwards). She was bright, witty, outrageous and reassuringly expensive. At her peak during the 1860s, she was burning through an income of 50,000 francs a month (equivalent to about £90,000 today), all of it provided by her 'protectors', most of them members of the French royal family. When the Emperor's half-brother, the Duke of Morny died, she took up with his cousin 'Plon-Plon', Prince Joseph Charles Bonaparte (1822–91), Napoleon's nephew. In return for her exclusive attention, he gave her a mansion and the money to buy a large collection of racehorses, which she ran with English jockeys. As her reputation grew, women copied her style. At a dinner one night, she boasted that whatever she wore in public would be in the shops the next day. To prove her point, she took one of the gentlemen's hats, crushed the brim, stuck an ostrich feather in the peak and walked down the Bois de Boulogne. Sure enough, the next day, a copy of the ludicrous headgear was for sale in a fashionable boutique. Cora usually preferred something classier, and she helped establish the reputation of the English couturier Charles Worth whose wincingly expensive dresses she bought by the armful. Through her patronage, he became one of Paris's most celebrated designers and was the first one ever to sew a named label into an item of clothing.

In 1870 the outbreak of the Franco-Prussian war brought all partying to an abrupt halt. The defeat of Napoleon III sent him and most of his family into exile, depriving Cora of her protectors. She went to London but her reputation got there first: she was snubbed by polite society and refused a room at the Grosvenor House Hotel. She returned to a very different Paris. To starve the city into submission, Prussian troops blockaded it for four months. Conditions deteriorated rapidly and the citizens were forced to eat rats, dogs and horses. Even the animals at the city's zoo weren't spared: restaurant menus survive that feature dishes made from elephants, camels, wolves and bears. On 25 January 1871, Bismarck ordered the bombardment of Paris with heavy artillery and, three days later, it surrendered. Since the siege began, over 47,000 civilians had been killed or seriously wounded. By the end of May 1871 another 30,000 had fallen in the street battles of the Paris Commune. The pleasure-seeking days of the Second Empire seemed a very distant memory.

Cora responded to this change in her fortunes in a surprisingly practical way, turning her large house into an impromptu hospital, tearing up bed linen to make bandages and making sure her patients were given the best possible care. This made a serious dent in her finances but by early 1872 she had found a new admirer. Handsome, wealthy and deeply unstable,

Alexandre Duval was the son of a successful restaurateur. He fell in love with Cora, squandering the several million francs of his inheritance on her to prove his devotion. When bankrupt, and thus of limited value to Cora, he continued to stalk her, alternating between jealous rages and proposals of marriage. It all came to a head one afternoon when Duval arrived at Cora's apartments on the rue Chaillot and begged to be allowed to stay. She ignored him and tucked herself up in bed. In the meantime, he shot himself in the chest on her doorstep.

Somehow he survived, but the story circulated that Cora had left him bleeding in the street and wouldn't call for help. She countered that she had no idea he'd used the gun on himself, protesting that he was always prone to over-exaggeration and melodramatic gesture, but the damage to her reputation was done. She was portrayed as cruel and heartless and overnight she found herself *persona non grata* in Parisian society. She laid low in Monte Carlo where she stayed with a friend until the scandal died down, but it quickly became clear that her career as a courtesan was over. Without a protector or an income, pursued by her creditors, she was forced to sell her houses and possessions and for the last ten years of her life lived as an itinerant gambler, drifting round the racetracks and casinos of Europe, rather like Casanova.

Unlike him, she didn't have much luck and by the time the French journalist Henri Rochford bumped into her in the early 1880s she was an 'ugly old wreck' who accosted him for racing tips. The woman whose beauty and wit had once brought in over a million pounds a year was reduced to playing roulette at the Monte Carlo casino – on the cheap tables where only 5-franc bets were allowed. One night, her former lover Alexandre Duval (now recovered and married to someone sensible chosen by his mother) was spotted at the next table, where the minimum bet was 100 francs. He did not even acknowledge her.

Just before her death from cancer in 1886, she published her memoirs in an attempt to make some money. They attracted disappointed reviews, largely because she refused to the dish the dirt on her former lovers. The *New York Times* was typical: 'One has only to read her book to see she has no wit at all. The volume makes no appeal to unhealthy curiosity. It is dull. The woman is not even malicious.' In fact, her memoirs, while not remotely in the league of those written by Casanova or Catherine the Great, have a warmth and honesty that is genuinely moving. The French novelist Zola portrayed her sympathetically in his novel, *Nana* (1880).

Cora Pearl was only fifty-one when she died. She went peacefully and without bitterness.

> *I have had a happy life; I have squandered money enormously. I am far from posing as a victim; it would be ungrateful of me to do so. I ought to have saved, but saving is not easy in such a whirl of excitement as that in which I have lived. Between what one ought to do and what one does there is always a difference.*

~

Cora would have got on well with the novelist and social commentator **H. G. Wells** (1866–1946). Wells liked to call himself 'the Don Juan of the intelligentsia': even at the age of seventy-four, having lost all his teeth, he was proud that he could still enjoy the company of prostitutes. He once said that 'to make love periodically, with some grace and pride and freshness, seems to be, for most of us, a necessary condition to efficient working'. If Cora turned sex into work, Wells turned to sex in order to work.

Wells inherited infidelity from his father, Joe, a nonchalant lady's man who supplemented the modest income he made in his china shop as a fast bowler for Kent: he had once taken four wickets in four balls against Sussex. His sporting career was permanently interrupted when he fell off a ladder and broke his thigh. The accident happened while he was helping a girlfriend climb over a wall one Sunday morning while his wife was at church. The service ended sooner than expected and Joe – pretending to prune a vine – was caught red-handed. Some years earlier, his son Bertie (never Herbert) had also broken his leg, aged seven. He always said this was the beginning of his love of books: his father brought him piles of them to read in bed while he recovered. When he was thirteen Wells wrote his first story, a comic-strip called 'The Desert Daisy', but his literary ambitions were put on hold after his father's accident. Never particularly well off, the loss of Joe's cricketing income meant Bertie could no longer be sent to school at the Bromley Academy. To bring in money he was apprenticed at a draper's shop, but was sacked for being too common, an experience he was to chronicle in his novel *Kipps* (1905) about a draper who comes into money and tries to mingle with the upper classes. Wells himself was more interested in mingling with women – lots of them.

During his two years as a draper, Wells showed extraordinary powers of self-discipline. He devoted every scrap of spare time to educating himself and was proud to say that during these years he never read a work of fiction or played a single game. His hard work paid off and he secured a scholarship to the Normal School of Science in London studying biology under the great T. H.

Huxley. Dirt poor, shabbily dressed and permanently hungry, Wells graduated with a degree in zoology, discovering the joys of English literature and socialism en route. He worked as teacher, first at a boarding school in Wales and then in Kilburn, where his star pupil was A. A. Milne, author of *Winnie-the-Pooh*. While lodging with relatives, he fell in love with, and married, his cousin, Isabel Mary Wells. He was twenty-five and she was twenty-two. Until then, his only sexual experience had been with a prostitute several years earlier.

The newly-weds moved to Wandsworth, where Wells continued to teach, earning extra money by writing educational journalism and producing his *Textbook of Biology*, which stayed in print for thirty years. On the side, he was also making up for lost time in the sack. By 1894 the marriage was over. Wells moved in with, and then married, one of his students, Amy Catherine Robbins, whom he called Jane. Although Wells wasn't your typical Lothario – he was short and scrawny, with a limp moustache and a squeaky voice – he bubbled with ideas, self-confidence and loved to talk, fixing people with his piercing blue eyes. He discovered that women found him irresistible.

His political awakening, his immersion in Darwinism and his struggle to pull himself out of poverty led him to believe that love meant freedom from restraint and the judgement of others and this could only be achieved if he had more than one sexual relationship. In Jane he found a woman who seemed happy to go along with this radical logic, allowing him to keep an apartment in town for assignations and hang photographs of his lovers in the family home. She was even prepared to deal with the human fall-out of Wells's endless bacchanals, taking one of his spurned lovers, the Austrian journalist Hedwig Gatternigg, to hospital after she had slashed her wrists outside his flat, distraught at the idea that he didn't truly love her.

Wells's health had troubled him since his time at the boarding school in North Wales. He had been aggressively fouled while playing football and, falling badly, had acquired a crushed kidney and haemorrhaged lung. The lung problems developed into a condition that his doctors suspected was tubercular and he wasn't given long to live. This added urgency to his sexual conquests, but also gave him time while convalescing to begin writing the scientific romances for which he is still best known. In a tremendous four-year burst of creativity he produced *The Time Machine* (1895), *The Island of Doctor Moreau* (1896), *The Invisible Man* (1897) and *The War of the Worlds* (1898). He founded modern science fiction at a stroke, marrying thrilling, apocalyptic stories with the latest scientific and political ideas. He would later come to disparage their popularity, but they propelled him to the front rank of English novelists and gave the couple much needed financial security. Moving to the healthier air of Sandgate on the Kent coast, he discovered a thriving community of fellow writers, with whom he soon became good friends, including Joseph Conrad, Ford Madox Ford and George Bernard Shaw. He gradually got fitter and began a lifelong passion for cycling: 'Every time I see an adult on a bicycle, I no longer despair for the future of the human race,' he wrote. By 1909 he felt well enough to re-enter the intellectual foment of London and he and Jane and their two boys, Gip and Frank, moved to 17 Church Row in Hampstead.

The Wells's 'open marriage' scandalised literary London, but it worked for them. He called her 'Bits' and 'P.C.B.' (Phylum: Companion of the Bath). She called him 'Bins' (short for '*husbinder*') or 'Mr Binder' or sometimes 'Pobble'. They communicated in 'Picshuas' – little scrawled cartoons that caricatured incidents in their marriage and which, Wells said, 'softened our relations to the pitch of making them tolerable'.

This childlike domestic contentment gave Wells a secure base from which to sally forth on his carnal adventures, to explore the 'sexual imaginativeness' that Jane could not provide. His lovers included the birth-control campaigner Margaret Sanger and the novelists Dorothy Richardson and Elizabeth von Arnim. Richardson was a school friend of Jane's and her underrated novel *Pilgrimage* (1915) invented the 'stream-of-consciousness' technique that Virginia Woolf later made famous. It also contained a vivid portrait of life in the Wells household. An affair with Bertie, it appeared (rather as with Casanova) could be great fun and a tonic for the ego. Here he is writing to Margaret Sanger:

> *My plans in New York are ruled entirely by the wish to be with you as much as possible – & as much as possible without other people about. I don't mind paying thousands of dollars if I can get that.*

He added that she was, at all costs, to dress up in the 'costume of a tropical island . . . Everything else is secondary to this.'

In 1907 Wells addressed the Cambridge University Fabian Society, which had been founded the previous year by a sparkling young undergraduate called Amber Reeves. After the talk, Wells bundled her onto a train and took her to Paris for the weekend. She was, he wrote:

> *a girl of brilliant and precocious promise . . . a sharp, bright, Levantine face under a shock of very fine abundant black hair,*

*a slender nimble body very much alive, and a quick greedy mind.*

Two years later, she was pregnant with Bertie's child. This dismayed her mother and father (they were friends of Wells), and the couple ran away to Le Touquet and tried to make a go of it. It lasted three months. Amber was lonely and depressed and Wells put her on a ferry back to England. There, she found comfort in the arms of a mutual friend, a young lawyer called George Rivers Blanco White, who gallantly married her before the child was born. Amber's daughter, Anna-Jane, was eighteen before she found out that H. G. Wells was her real father.

In 1912 the precocious feminist journalist Rebecca West wrote a critical review of Wells's novel *Marriage,* calling him an 'old maid'. As we know, Wells liked spirited young women so he (forty-six) invited her (twenty) to tea. She gave birth to his son Anthony in 1914, and the boy was told that Wells was his 'uncle'. Anthony's second name was 'Panther', the nickname Wells had used for Amber. (Amber had called him 'Jaguar'.) Messy as all this sounds, it actually worked out quite well for everyone. In 1939 Amber wrote to Wells to say that neither she nor her daughter had ever, for a moment, felt 'they were not worth the price'.

Wells visited Russia twice, in 1914 and 1920, and he met and impressed the writer Maxim Gorky there. Not everyone was so generous. After a brief meeting, Lenin called him 'a dreadful bourgeois and a little philistine!' For his part, Wells disliked the cult of personality that surrounded Karl Marx, whose face loomed from every wall and notice board:

*About two-thirds of the face of Marx is beard, a vast solemn woolly uneventful beard that must have made all normal exercise impossible. It is not the sort of beard that happens to a man, it is a beard cultivated, cherished, and thrust patri-archally upon the world. It is exactly like Das Kapital in its inane abundance, and the human part of the face looks over it owlishly as if it looked to see how the growth impressed man-kind. I found the omnipresent images of that beard more and more irritating. A gnawing desire grew upon me to see Karl Marx shaved.*

The highlight of the second trip for Wells was, true to form, the addition of a new lover. She was his interpreter, Baroness Moura Budberg (1892–1974). The Baroness had been married twice, firstly to the Tsarist diplomat Count Johann Benckendorff and then, after he was shot by the revolutionary authorities in 1919, to Baron Nikolai von Budberg-Bönningshausen. She had also been the mistress (at different times) of Maxim Gorky (who had recommended her to Wells) and the British spy Sir R. H. Bruce Lockhart, author of the bestselling *Memoirs of a Secret Agent* (1932). Moura was known as 'Mata Hari of Russia'. Her MI5 file recorded 'that she can drink an amazing quantity, mostly gin'. It was she who, as early as 1951, was to tip off MI6 that Sir Anthony Blunt was a communist, her other claim to distinction being that she was the great-aunt of Nick Clegg, leader of the Liberal Democrats. She was twenty-four years younger than H. G. Wells, but it was no casual fling. After the death of his wife Jane in 1927, Moura became Wells's closest female friend and he would later confide: 'She was the only woman I really loved.' Moura was equally smitten. When quizzed by Somerset Maugham on what she saw in 'the paunchy, played-out writer', Moura replied: 'He smells of honey.'

If Wells showed no signs of slowing down in his personal life, this was matched by his phenomenal productivity as a writer. In a career spanning fifty years, he published over 130 books. Instead of mellowing, his political and social philosophy got more extreme as he got older and his later books alternate between a kind of Utopian authoritarianism (he was keen supporter of eugenics) and muscular 'we're all doomed' pessimism. His finest work of non-fiction, *The Outline of History* (1920) became an international best-seller, describing the modern world as 'a race between education and catastrophe'. Wells was a passionate advocate of world government and he knew his subject, interviewing both Theodore and Franklin D. Roosevelt *and* Lenin and Stalin. He rejected both communism and fascism from the start and, if few people now take his political philosophy seriously, the Nazis, at least, felt otherwise. Top of the blacklist of intellectuals to be liquidated after their planned invasion of Britain was the name H. G. Wells.

For all Wells's talk of the Great Sexual Liberation and his socialist dislike for the bourgeois institution of wedlock, Wells was happily married for much of his life. The final volume of his *Experiment in Autobiography* was published in 1984, after the last of his lovers had died. In it, he admits that he often wanted to leave Jane and the drudgery of family life for one of his younger, eager-minded lovers, but knew that she was a steadfast presence, a true friend that he couldn't do without. This was not the case with the other women he had known: 'The women I have kissed, solicited, embraced and lived with, have never entered intimately, and deeply into my emotional life.' Sex with his mistresses occupied 'much the same place in my life that fly-fishing or golfing has in the life of many busy men'. This is hardly a mission statement for a new world-order of sexual liberation; it sounds more like a man having his cake and eating it. Jane forgave Wells and put up with his philandering because it posed no real threat. The 'World-Man', the 'hero of the future', always came home for the sympathy, support and encouragement that only she could give him. As he himself once confessed:

> *I can't bank on religion. God has no thighs and no life. When one calls to him in the silence of the night he doesn't turn over and say, 'What is the trouble, Dear?'*

~

The story of the loyal wife making sacrifices to support the career and unruly appetites of a gifted husband is a familiar one. But what happens when the boot is on the other foot? What if Jane had written about the marriage instead of Bertie? Reading the work of **Colette** (1873–1954) is practically a rite of passage for adolescent girls in France. In more than fifty novels, she lays bare the ambiguities of female love with such acuity and startling originality that they make H. G. Wells's social novels look like so much high-minded puffery. If a chap wants to understand women's sexuality, Colette is the perfect place to start. She laid out her stall early on. While still a schoolgirl, she decided she would be known by her surname, as the boys were. None of her friends in Burgundy ever used her Christian names – Sidonie-Gabrielle – and she continued the habit when, aged twenty, she married Henri Gauthier-Villars. Fifteen years her senior and an art critic who dabbled in fiction, he saw at once that she was the better writer, encouraging her to produce a series of novels based on her character 'Claudine', and locking her in her room until she had produced the requisite number of pages. First published under his pen-name 'Willy', they were runaway best-sellers, titillating French society with their implied lesbian relationships among schoolgirls.

'Willy' had an adventurous sex life himself, openly bringing a succession of young lovers back home and giving Colette at least one dose of gonorrhoea. She left him in 1906, earning her living as an actress, where she formed a close lesbian relationship with the aristocratic Mathilde de Morny, Marquise de Belboeuf, better known as 'Missy'. Colette and Missy were a scandal. At perform-ances of *Rêve d'Egypte* in 1907, there were riots when they bared their breasts and exchanged a kiss on stage. Fleeing Paris, Missy bought Colette a house in Brittany where she could write after her divorce from Willy. (Willy, unfortunately, had kept the copyright to Colette's early successes, and she needed an independent income.) Colette started writing a column for the daily newspaper *Le Matin*. Aged thirty-seven, she fell in love with twenty-four-year-old Auguste Heriot but abandoned him in 1912 to marry the editor of *Le Matin*, the wealthy Baron Henry de Jouvenel. He was to prove just as unfaithful as her first husband. In 1913 they had a daughter, Bel-Gazou, whom Colette referred to as 'a rat'. Motherhood was not going to interrupt her career. 'My strain of virility,' she wrote,' saved me from the danger which threatens the writer, elevated to a happy and tender parent, of becoming a mediocre author.' Bel-Gazou was left in the care of a nanny: it wasn't unusual for Colette to pass six months without seeing her. At eight the child was sent to boarding school, and a friend of Colette's revealed that 'all weaknesses are forbidden her, above all asking for love . . .'

Henri de Jouvenel had a teenage son, Bertrand, who was sixteen in 1919 when Colette seduced him. To be fair to forty-nine-year-old Colette, she had initially hired two prostitutes to take his virginity, but he was unable to perform. Colette persevered and succeeded where the professionals had failed. Bertrand later described his stepmother as 'demanding, voracious, expert and rewarding'. Colette, by her own account, remained in love with Bertrand's father, but he was preoccupied with work and other mistresses. Eventually they divorced but she carried on living with her stepson lover, an affair that lasted until he was twenty-three. Colette had a savage perm and a face-lift in an effort to ward off old age – quite an experimental operation in the 1920s. She told a friend that the secret of life was to 'content yourself with a passing temptation, and satisfy it. What more can one be sure of than that which one hold's in one's arms at that very moment?'

In 1935 she got married for the last time, to forty-five-year-old Maurice Goudeket. He soon ran out of money and before long he was selling second-hand washing machines and devices to unblock lavatories. Colette supported him with her royalties, and although he, too, took other lovers, he was jealous of any other men who paid her any attention right up until her death in 1954 at the age of eighty-one. His infidelities had never troubled Colette. She knew who was running the relationship. She understood that nothing sexual was ever straightforward, explaining to a friend that Maurice stayed with her because of her 'male virility, which shocks him. When he sleeps with another woman he chooses one who is feminine, but he couldn't actually live with a woman like that.'

~

For **Marie Bonaparte** (1882–1962) it was the *lack* of male virility that posed a problem – not hers, but her husband's. Marie was the great-grand-niece of Napoleon, and the last of the Bonaparte line. Her marriage to Prince George of Greece connected her to the royal families of Denmark, Russia and Great Britain (she was Prince Philip's aunt). Prince George was tall, fair and handsome, but he never even kissed Marie while they were engaged, something she put down to his chastity and good breeding. On her wedding night George could not perform and scurried off to his uncle Waldemar's bedroom for a pep talk. Returning with instructions on how to consummate the marriage he confessed, 'I hate it as much as you do, but we must do it if we want to have children.' When they left for their honeymoon, Uncle Waldemar helpfully came with them, and George cried when he left three days later. He was soon back, though, and as it was clear she wasn't going to be able to shake him off Marie resolved to enjoy Uncle Waldemar's company. He would kiss her passionately while George looked on. Marie sometimes joked that she had two husbands, but that she thought of George more as a brother than a husband. When Marie was a teenager, she had had an affair with her father's secretary, a man called Leandri, who then blackmailed her with the love letters she wrote to him. Undeterred by this unpromising start, Marie took numerous other lovers throughout her life, including the French prime minister Aristide Briand, although none of them were to bring her physical satisfaction.

As a young woman, Marie told her father, Prince Roland, that she wanted to train as a doctor, but he forbade it as an unseemly choice for an aristocratic woman. However, he permitted her to keep a human skeleton in her bedroom, so that she could study anatomy. This gave her nightmares, transforming in her dreams into a Hindu mummy that attacked her. Marie decided that the skeleton was a subconscious symbol for her dead mother, and that she must keep it in her room to force herself to conquer her terrors. Her neuroses multiplied: she had her bedroom curtains removed in case they harboured germs, and would not light a fire in case it sucked all the oxygen from the house.

Forbidden to become a doctor, and fascinated by her inability to enjoy sex, Princess Marie formed the idea that she would become an expert on frigidity. Her father was bedridden for months before his death, and Marie sat with him, quietly reading books on psychology. Freud's works particularly inspired her and in 1924 she went to Vienna to be analysed by the master, prior to becoming a psychoanalyst herself.

Freud had plenty of material to work with. Marie's mother had died when she was a tiny baby and her childhood was lonely. Brought up by servants, she was kept away from other children because her grandmother, Princess Bonaparte, thought that having too many friends was common. Marie developed a range of phobias (including an irrational fear of buttons) and an unhealthy interest in reading anything she could about gruesome crimes, especially articles about Jack the Ripper's victims and anarchists executing people with bombs. Her earliest memory of sexual pleasure was when her nursemaid sat her astride her foot and bounced her vigorously up and down but, as she explained to Freud, such pleasure eluded her as an adult. She wondered if this might have been caused by a repressed memory of her nursemaid having sex with a groom, but Freud suggested she was a lesbian, and that matters had been made worse because her husband was probably a homosexual. Marie became obsessed about her sexuality and even sought out the groom and asked him if it was possible that he had had sex in her presence when she was a small child. He confessed that it was.

In 1926, supposedly now sane, Marie co-founded the Société Psycholanalytique de Paris and started taking on her own patients. She had unusual methods. She crocheted while she listened, analysed her patients in the garden, and sent splendid, chauffeur-driven cars to collect them. Sometimes she would take patients away with her when she went on holiday to Athens or Saint-Tropez. As a child, men in the Bois de Boulogne had frightened Marie by exposing themselves to her. Confronting her fears, she returned to the scene of the trauma on a regular basis. When a man did flash her, she would walk up to him, give him her card, and say, 'Put that away, I'm not interested! But please come and see me tomorrow, I would like to talk to you.' When a senior Parisian academic came to her for analysis, she told him that his daughter's phobia of touching the soap in the bath was related to her wish to massage his testicles. The professor was appalled and fled the room in horror, with Marie chasing him down the corridor, shouting, 'But you cannot behave this way.'

One of Marie Bonaparte's few practical achievements was to recruit 243 women and measure the distance between their clitoris and their vagina, concluding that if they were too far apart it would be impossible to achieve orgasm. Marie's own anatomy convinced her that this was her problem too, and she volunteered to have surgery to move her clitoris closer to her vagina. When it didn't have any effect, she had it done again, but there was still no improvement.

Marie Bonaparte's association with Sigmund Freud developed into a close friendship and when he fled Austria for England she gave him financial assistance. They also collaborated professionally, and she respected his controversial belief that vaginal orgasms were superior and more natural than those involving the clitoris. She confessed to him that she had been tempted to commit incest with her son Peter, and took Freud's advice not to try it. When she visited a rival analyst – with whom she also had an affair – she immediately confessed her 'analytic infidelity' to Freud, and (when he gave his permission) she felt so guilty that she vomited. Marie and Freud shared a love of dogs, and she gave him a Chow as a present. She wrote four books about her own dog Topsy, another source of anxiety in her life: she lived in terror of the dog's eventual death. She and Freud spent a lot of time analysing the nature of inter-species love. Apart from her books about Topsy, she also published a study of female sexuality and a 700-page psychoanalytic interpretation of the works of Edgar Allan Poe, whom Marie was convinced was a necrophiliac.

Marie continued as an analyst until her death in 1962. One of her last public duties was to represent her nephew, King Paul of Greece, at the coronation of Elizabeth II in 1953. She struck up a conversation with the gentleman sitting next to her, offering to analyse him. He agreed and they spent the rest of the ceremony in deep conversation. His name was François Mitterrand, the future President of France. It was to Marie that Freud made one of his most famous pronouncements: 'The great question that has never been answered and which I have not yet been able to answer, despite my thirty years of research into the feminine soul, is "What does a woman want?"' In 1920 the Romanian sculptor Constantin Brancusi produced his own answer. Immortalising Marie Bonaparte in sculpture, he unveiled his portrait of her at the Paris Salon. Entitled *Princess X*, it consisted solely of a giant bronze phallus and testicles.

~

The organ itself was 15.9 inches (40.5 cm) long. This would have been of great interest to the American academic **Alfred Kinsey** (1894–1955) who measured more than 5,000 penises in his lifetime. Their dimensions appeared in his painstaking scientific study *Sexual Behaviour in the Human Male* (1948). Dry and statistical in tone, and based on over 18,000 intimate case histories, the book was distributed by a medical publishing house, which expected around 5,000 sales. Instead, the book shot straight to the top of the best-seller list, selling hundreds of thousands of copies. Buried in the text, for those who could be bothered, was every possible bizarre detail of how Americans had sex, how often, what whom or what, and which bits of their bodies were involved.

Kinsey took his inspiration from the pioneering sexologist Henry Havelock Ellis (1859–1939), whose *Studies in the Psychology of Sex* (1921) helped establish sex as an appropriate subject for academic research. Ellis had coined the word 'homosexual' and made his own (controversial) stab at answering Freud's question by stating that 'women's brains are in a certain sense . . . in their wombs'. But the author himself was spectacularly unqualified in terms of his own experience. He was impotent until he was sixty years old, and it's doubtful if he ever consummated his marriage. His wife Edith used to refer to his penis as 'the Holy Ghost' and wrote a novel about a woman married to a man made impotent after a mining accident. She conducted numerous lesbian relationships during their marriage. When Henry finally got the hang of sex (after the death of his wife, with the help of his younger lover, Françoise Delisle) he became quite addicted to it. Until then he much preferred masturbation. The thing he found most arousing was the sight of a woman urinating, something he put down to having seen his mother caught short in a London park as a child.

Kinsey, too, was something of a late starter in the bedroom, and also like Havelock Ellis, bore the scars of a deeply religious upbringing. He hated his childhood. The son of a carpenter, he grew up in extreme poverty, suffering from rickets, which gave him double curvature of the spine. He was frequently ill as a boy and, as well as suffering all the usual childhood diseases, got rheumatic fever and typhoid. He was bullied at school because his clothes were so heavily darned. Like H. G. Wells, everyone was convinced that Alfred would die young and because of his frequent absences from school through illness he made very few friends. The abject poverty of his youth left him with a lifelong horror of debt and a furious hatred for the potato, which had often been the only food available when he was a boy.

His father, Alfred Senior, was a religious zealot and a bully. Every Sunday, he dragged the family along to three interminable church services and Sunday school as well. On the Lord's Day, no entertainment or activities of any kind were permitted: not even reading the paper. The milkman was forbidden to deliver milk and Mrs Kinsey had to cook all of Sunday's meals the day before. Alfred's aunt was turned out of the family home for playing the piano on the Sabbath. Suspecting his neighbours of lax moral standards, Alfred's father used his son as bait to see if shopkeepers would sell cigarettes to a minor. All references to sex were taboo, no adult was ever seen naked in the house, and Alfred was banned from seeing girls.

Kinsey finally escaped to study biology (against his father's wishes). For the first twenty years of his scientific career there was nothing to suggest that this polite, shy man was going to unleash a sexual revolution. Instead, he forged a reputation as the world's foremost expert on North American gall wasps. After earning a doctorate from Harvard, he travelled across the USA collecting 300,000 wasps from thirty-six states and posting them back to Boston. Many of these hatched before he got back, causing chaos in the postal service. Kinsey took twenty-six individual measurements on every single wasp, enabling him to identify seventy new species unknown to science. He always did everything obsessively – he collected irises and planted more than 250 species in his garden; he plaited home-made rugs twice as thick as anyone else's; even as a Boy Scout he had amassed seven years' worth of merit badges in just two. His talent for extreme detail and meticulous research stood him in good stead when he began to tire of wasps and take an interest in human beings.

Kinsey followed up his study of male sexual behaviour with *Sexual Behaviour in the Human Female* (1953), which was also an immediate best-seller. Having grown up in a family where nudity was anathema and sex never mentioned, Kinsey realised many of his undergraduate students were as ill informed about their sexual needs as he was. He also came to see that repressed sexual urges were psychologically damaging. As in everything else he did, Kinsey's attention to his subject was all consuming. He regularly worked sixteen hours a day, which prompted his wife to remark drily: 'I hardly ever see Alfred at night at any more, now that he's taken up sex.'

Kinsey's crusade to rid the world of sexual ignorance started in his own bedroom. His marriage to Clara McMillen – always known as 'Mac' – in 1921 wasn't consummated for several months. This may have had something to do with his unusually large penis and her short stature, but they hardly gave themselves the best start. For their honeymoon they went on a gruelling climbing expedition and their first attempts at sex were on a mountainside in the middle of a storm. The gradual release of personal documents by the Kinsey Institute means we now know that the Kinseys' marriage and sex life was liberated in a way that H. G. Wells could only dream of. They loved nudism and took their clothes off whenever they decently could. They operated a system of interacting open marriages with colleagues at the Institute for Research in Sex, Gender and Reproduction, which Kinsey had founded in 1947. He had casual affairs with many of his colleagues, male and female. Lots of his staff had affairs with his Clara. During a research trip to Chicago, he was delighted to find an outlet for his homosexual urges, and frequently went cottaging among the gay community there. Kinsey was particularly keen to get the man-on-man taboo out in the open and when one of his assistants confessed that he had no experience of homosexuality, Kinsey said he could personally help him 'tick that box'.

He also experimented with masochism, inserting objects into his urethra while masturbating, enjoying the pleasure and the pain equally. As this organ became less sensitive over the years, he started putting larger and larger things up it. By 1949 he was able to insert pencils into his penis and even a toothbrush, bristles first. He also tried self-piercing, which culminated with him successfully circumcising himself with a penknife in the bath. Kinsey was proud to call himself 'unshockable'. As he was keen to drill into his researchers, the key thing was gathering data: 'We are the recorders and reporters of facts – not the judges of the behaviours we describe.' The results were often controversial; he reported that almost half of American men had

had a homosexual experience, that almost half of married men had committed adultery and that a quarter of married women found their sex life unsatisfactory.

To Kinsey anything was 'biologically normal' provided it was performed by a sizeable number of people – or animals. He would have found the experiences of Casanova or Cora Pearl interesting but unremarkable. He once said that 'the only unnatural sex act is one which you cannot perform'. This was mind-blowing stuff for the 1950s and ushered in attitudinal changes from which our society is still reeling. The modern view of sex – where masturbation isn't evil or harmful, homosexuality is widespread and enjoying sex doesn't mean you are depraved – owes a huge amount to Kinsey's work. By documenting behaviour that many people at the time thought was 'abnormal' and showing how widespread it actually was, he helped create a culture where sex could be seen as just another aspect of ordinary life.

~

Some people didn't wait for Alfred Kinsey to come along to know they needn't be ashamed of their sexual desires, among them the actress **Tallulah Bankhead** (1902–68) who bragged that she had over 500 lovers. When the Kinsey report was published, she'd seen it all before: 'The good doctor's clinical notes were old hat to me,' she remarked.

As a girl Tallulah was short and plump, weighing almost 10 stones and just 5′2″ tall, but by the age of fifteen she had shed enough puppy fat to win a beauty contest in her home town, Montgomery, Alabama. This decided her to head for New York and try her luck as an actress. She went on to appear in over fifty plays and eighteen films, with her final appearance as a character called the 'Black Widow' in a 1967 episode of *Batman*. Early on, she got a reputation for partying, and was a regular user of cocaine and marijuana. She was annoyed by what she saw as *petit bourgeois* fears about drug misuse, but chose humour to confront it: 'Cocaine isn't addictive,' she said, ' I should know: I've been using it for years.' She was equally blasé about sex. She was once asked if it was true that she had been raped as a twelve-year-old on the drive of her father's home. 'Yes, it was awful, truly awful,' she said. 'You see, we had so much gravel.'

Her early career on Broadway was a series of false starts but in 1923 she came to London to appear in a play called *The Dancers* opposite the suave elder statesman of the West End stage, Gerald du Maurier. Her lustrous hair, husky voice and exuberant cartwheels turned her into an overnight star. The writer and actor Emlyn Williams wrote that her voice 'was steeped as deep in sex as the human voice can go without drowning'. Her most devoted fans were her 'Gallery Girls', a group of Cockney teenagers who cheered, stamped their feet and threw flowers onto the stage whenever she said a line. The writer Arnold Bennett was dazzled:

> *Ordinary stars get 'hands'. If Tallulah gets a 'hand' it is not heard. What is heard is a terrific, wild, passionate, hysterical roar and shriek. Only the phrase of the Psalmist can describe it: 'God is gone up with a shout.'*

Winston Churchill was a regular at her shows and before long 'to Tallulah' had become a verb. She told an American reporter: 'Over here they like me to "Tallulah". You know – dance and sing and romp and fluff my hair and play reckless parts.' After a triumphant and extravagant eight years, she returned to the USA to be signed up by Paramount who planned to make her 'the new

Dietrich'. They didn't: they made a string of turkeys. There was something about the nature of film that failed to capture what made her so sexy and delicious in the flesh. She continued to make the occasional movie but, through the 1930s and 1940s, her best work was on Broadway.

Tallulah was bisexual but liked to joke that she couldn't be a lesbian because 'they have no sense of humour', and she once let slip that she could never have an orgasm with anyone she was in love with. The only man she truly loved was an English aristocrat called Napier Sturt Alington, known as 'Naps', who was also bisexual. He married someone else, became a fighter pilot and died in the Battle of Britain. Tallulah married only once, in 1937 to the bit-part actor John Emery. She told friends that she had chosen him because he was 'hung like John Barrymore', but later confided that 'the weapon may be of admirable proportions but the shot is weak'. They never had children and were divorced after four years. When she was thirty, Tallulah had to have a hysterectomy brought on by a bad case of gonorrhoea, an infection she blamed on going to bed with Gary Cooper. Leaving hospital in a very weakened condition, and having lost a lot of weight, she barked at her doctor, 'Don't for one minute think this has taught me a lesson!'

She was the mistress of the one-liner. When a former lover came up to her excitedly babbling that he hadn't seen her for many years, she shot back: 'I thought I told you to wait in the car.' Arranging an assignation, she scribbled a note: 'I'll come and make love to you at five o'clock. If I'm late start without me.' She talked non-stop: one of her friends followed her around for a day, timing her with a stopwatch, and estimated that she spoke 70,000 words – the length of a short novel. As the Hollywood publicist

Howard Ditz wearily remarked, 'A day away from Tallulah is like a month in the country.' Sometimes her mouth got her into serious trouble. Speaking to a fan magazine in 1932, Tallulah confessed that she hadn't had an affair for six months, adding, 'Six months is a long, long while, I WANT A MAN!' This drew a sharp reprimand from Will Hays, Hollywood's censor and moral guardian, for allowing a star to indulge in 'verbal moral turpitude'.

Tallulah took her clothes off in public so often that her friend Estelle Winwood asked, 'Why do you do that, Tallulah? You have such pretty frocks.' She was notorious for not wearing underwear, and delighted in showing off the fact to as many people as possible. When the film crew complained of her regular exposures on the set of *Lifeboat* in 1944, Hitchcock's laconic reply was: 'I don't know whether that's a concern for wardrobe or hairdressing.'

Interviewing Tallulah was never easy. When *Time* magazine tried it in 1948, their reporters came away bemused. She had played the piano, performed some ballet, told jokes, done impersonations, made them lunch, plied them with mint juleps and talked without pause – accompanied by several dogs and her free-flying budgie, Gaylord, whom she had taught to drink champagne. (Luckily, by that time, she had got rid of her pet lion, Winston, and her chimp, King Kong.) As usual, her conversation was peppered with *bon mots*, which included, 'I never think out anything, dahling; I do it instinctively or not at all. I do things I'd loathe in anybody else.' Trying to pinpoint her age, the reporters sought verification from her younger sister Eugenia who sighed: 'Every time Tallulah knocks a year off her age, I have to, too. I'm not sure how long I can keep it up.'

Success, as opposed to notoriety, returned to her life from two unexpected quarters. In 1950 she became the host of a weekly celebrity talk radio slot called 'The Big Show'. It featured Tallulah reciting Dorothy Parker monologues, interviewing other stars and introducing comic turns by the likes of Jimmy Durante and Groucho Marx. Held together by her unpredictable charm, it became an instant hit. Then two years later her autobiography *Tallulah* went straight to the top of the best-seller lists. She had recorded most of it on a tape recorder and it reads like one long, frank, funny, opinionated Tallulah monologue.

This welcome return to the limelight couldn't mask her rapid descent into dependency on drink and sleeping pills. She recruited a bevy of young men as her assistants, calling them her 'caddies'. Although they were usually gay, they often had to sleep in her bed because she was terrified of being alone. At night, one of her boys taped her wrists together at night to stop her taking any more pills. Raddled, frequently irrational, her looks a grim parody of her former beauty, she still had her sense of humour. Not long before she died, a fan approached her and asked if she was Tallulah Bankhead. 'Well, I'm what's left of her, darling,' she replied.

Long after her death, declassified British government papers revealed that Miss Bankhead had been investigated by MI5 in the 1920s over allegations that she had corrupted the morals of pupils at Eton school with indecent and unnatural acts. No conclusive proof was ever found.

~

If there is one thing this chapter does prove conclusively, however, especially in the work of Alfred Kinsey, it is that, between the sheets at least, there is no such thing as normal. Or, as Woody Allen put it, 'Sex between a man and a woman can be a beautiful thing – provided you're between the right man and the right woman.'

# CHAPTER FIVE

# Man Cannot Live by Bread Alone

*Tell me what you eat, and I will tell you who you are.*
JEAN ANTHELME BRILLAT-SAVARIN (1755–1826)

What would Brillat-Savarin have made of Aristotle, who liked camel meat and fried pregnant cicadas, or Friedrich Nietzsche, who gave up alcohol and tobacco and spent a lot of time at the local pastry shop wolfing down cakes and pies?

Trickier still would have been Pliny the Elder, whose larder contained fresh gladiator blood (as a cure for epilepsy), hare's testicles (for relief of pain in the loins) and lynx urine (sore-throat gargle).

Ludicrous though these remedies sound, we should be careful before we write them off. Dietetics is a more complex science than astrophysics – we know less about the effects of the food we eat than we do about the galaxies.

Nothing brings the dead more vividly to life than finding out what they ate. It makes the famous seem more human, and shines a light on the obscure.

~

We know very little about the life of **Helena, Comtesse de**

Noailles (1824–1908), but we know quite a lot about her theories on food and health. Born into the English aristocracy, her marriage to a French nobleman was short-lived and her only child died at birth. Fabulously rich but bored much of the time, Helena migrated between her houses in England, Paris, Montpellier and the French Riviera. In her fortieth year, she saw a striking portrait of a young girl aged about six by the Parisian society painter Ernest Hébert (1817–1908). She asked to buy the picture but was told it had already been sold to Baron James de Rothschild. Undaunted, she decided that if she couldn't own the painting she would acquire its real-life subject instead. She discovered that the child, Maria, had been brought to Paris by her feckless Italian father, Domenico, and that he was willing to allow her to be 'adopted' for two bags of gold, with which he planned to return to Italy and set up his own vineyard. He made only two conditions: that the girl would be brought up as a Catholic and that she would be treated as an equal, not a servant. The Comtesse agreed and Maria's life changed forever.

It was a privileged but peculiar existence. The regulations laid down by the Comtesse dominated Maria's whole childhood and, in due course, the lives of her English husband and their two children as well. They were kept in line by the threat of losing the inheritance promised by their 'grandmother', and dread forebodings passed around the family breakfast table whenever an envelope arrived from France embossed with a capital 'N'.

Loose clothing was one Madame de Noailles's iron rules. So, when Maria was sent to a Catholic boarding school in Sussex she was excused school uniform. She also had to have her own exclusive supply of fresh milk. This was provided by the Comtesse's personal dairy herd, installed in the grounds of a large house she had bought on the nearby Downs. Each winter, the Comtesse left England for fear of catching the flu, and later instructed Maria to do the same with her children in the autumn, the climate being especially unhealthy when the leaves were falling, especially from the oak trees, of which, she said, England had too many.

At mealtimes Helena de Noailles's eccentricities really came to the fore. When Maria and her children came to visit, she would only eat with them if her food was served on plates hidden from view by a two-foot-high silk screen. She never revealed why.

The Comtesse always slept with a loaded pistol beside her bed, even when she stayed in an hotel, where she also demanded that a string of fresh onions be hung on the door to ward off infection. A visitor to her bedchamber noted the silk stockings stuffed with squirrel fur wrapped around her forehead and chin to prevent the formation of wrinkles. To avoid bronchitis, she would eat plate after plate of fresh herring roe. Once Maria and her husband received a gift from the Comtesse of three dozen bottles of Bordeaux and fifty bottles of port. Along with the alcohol came instructions that they should only drink the port at sunset mixed with a little sugar. It was to be diluted with soft rainwater collected from the roof of their house by the servants, under strict supervision by Maria's husband, Philip.

Helena was sprightly and energetic into her mid-eighties, vigilant for the smallest error. Her granddaughter, also named Helena in her honour, recalled the Comtesse shrieking hysterically at the staff because one of the blue silk covers on her bedroom door-handle had fallen off. The glare from the naked brass was, she said, damaging to the eyes. A similar theory led her to replace the lower half of all her windowpanes with red glass, which, she explained, was both healthier and more cheerful. And cows were essential. As well as fresh milk, they produced methane: her herds were always encouraged to graze near the open windows of her houses. She suggested to her grandson Philip that instead of enrolling at medical school he should become a vet, thus contributing much more to the good of humanity. She said she had read in the Royal Agricultural Review that 'children brought up on good milk seldom become drunkards'. If Philip switched to veterinary medicine, she promised, she would give him some money from the sale of land in England, which would otherwise be going to help needy Armenians. He declined.

On one occasion, Maria and her children were summoned to the south of France to mingle with polite society. They were under strict instructions to accept no invitations to afternoon tea at five o'clock. This was the hour when the Comtesse believed most people caught the flu, not by mixing with other people but because there was a dangerous 'miasma' in the air at the end of the day. One of her visitors made the mistake of wearing high heels. After the Comtesse had asked to examine them, she threw them on to the fire. Flat, broad shoes, she always said, were better for the general health and, in 1866, she wrote a letter to the *Medical Times and Gazette* extolling the benefits of going barefoot:

> *Look at the magnificent gait of a barefoot Highland girl and the elastic play of every muscle, and compare her feet with those of girls who have been tortured in boots, too short or too narrow at the toes . . . As for cleanliness, feet freely exposed to the air are not offensive, but the smell of unwashed feet enclosed in dirtier*

*stockings and shoes is very unwholesome, whereas no one ever felt disgusted at the little bare brown feet of Italian peasant children.'*

When Helena de Noailles died, her doctors said she had lasted longer than expected, subsisting largely on a diet of champagne and, of course, fresh milk.

In her will, she endowed an orphanage for the daughters of clergymen, where, even after death, her regulations lived on. Any potential inmates were to have their skulls examined by two independent phrenologists, to ensure that they were 'firm spirited and conscientious'. None of the girls was to be vaccinated – the Comtesse believed vaccinations led to other illnesses – and no girl under ten was to be taught any mathematics except for multiplication tables.

~

There was nothing remotely cranky about **George Fordyce** (1736–1802). He was a respected doctor who fought against quackery, exposing the ineffectiveness of treating epilepsy with a forehead paste made from ground up elk's hooves, and producing important theses on fever, smallpox, diet and metabolism. He also conducted experiments in heated rooms that proved for the first time that the human body could effectively regulate its temperature whatever the environment.

But Fordyce was as famous for his poor bedside manner as he was for his medical expertise. With his patients he was blunt and taciturn: a consultation usually consisted of asking his patients to stick out their tongue and have their pulse taken. 'That will do,' was his usual pronouncement before writing out a prescription.

Born in Aberdeen, he came from a family of high achievers: two of his brothers were doctors, one a Presbyterian minister, one a banker and one a professor. At fourteen he gained his MA from Aberdeen University and spent several years apprenticed to his uncle, a doctor in Rutland. Returning to Scotland, he graduated in medicine at Edinburgh when he was only eighteen. His curt manner may have been exacerbated by the tragic loss of both of his sons in childhood, one of them by drowning in the Thames. He also had two daughters, one of whom married Samuel, brother of Jeremy, Bentham.

Fordyce gave lectures that were renowned for their thoroughness – and their length. For over thirty years, they took place each morning at his premises on the Strand. Gifted with an extraordinary memory, he began speaking, without notes, at seven in the morning continuing until ten. In spite of his reputation for rough manners, Fordyce was elected a fellow of both the Royal College of Physicians and the Royal Society. He knew Dr Johnson, the artist Joshua Reynolds and the actor David Garrick, and was happy to sit quietly in the company of livelier and more famous men, many of whom shared his passion for consuming huge quantities of food.

Fordyce was as regular in his eating habits as in his lecture timetable. For twenty years, he dined every day at four in the afternoon at Dolly's Chop House near St Paul's Cathedral. His theory, laid out in his *A Treatise on Digestion and Food* (1791), was that people should emulate lions in the wild, eating just once a day, rather than over-working the digestive system with frequent meals. His dinner began with a tankard of strong ale, a bottle of port and a quarter-pint of brandy. The meal then gathered pace.

For an appetiser, Dr Fordyce usually took something light –

grilled fowl or a dish of whiting. After this had been washed down with a glass of brandy, he would tuck into two pounds of prime steak accompanied by the remainder of the brandy. For dessert, he had another bottle of port, after which he set off to his home where he would spend much of the night studying. Not surprisingly he was noted for a florid complexion – and for his scruffy appearance: he often appeared for his morning lectures in the clothes he had worn the previous day.

Like many food theorists, Fordyce paid the price for his single-mindedness. For the last weeks of his life, he was bedridden with gout but refused to let any other doctors treat him. One night, while his daughter Maggie was reading to him, he suddenly exclaimed: 'Stop! Go out of the room, I'm going to die!' And so he did.

~

If Fordyce was a typical eighteenth-century trencherman, **Elizabeth, Empress of Austria** (1837–98) comes straight out of a nineteenth-century romantic novel. Married to Emperor Franz Joseph of Austria-Hungary and mother to Crown Prince Rudolf, Elizabeth was a society beauty obsessed with her physique. Throughout her adult life she was determined to maintain her 16-inch waist, which she set off to best advantage with tight corsets that took an hour to lace up. After having three children, her waist expanded to 18 inches but, at 5′8″ tall, she never let her weight go above 7½ stones. If it exceeded that, she ate nothing but oranges until she had lost the extra ounces.

Elizabeth was beautiful and adventurous, famed for her fearlessness on horseback and for her thick dark hair, which fell to the backs of her knees. In public, even when out riding, she carried a fan to conceal herself from sketch artists and photographers who might try to capture a view of her face for the press. Others said she did this to hide her teeth, which were always yellow.

Born to Bavarian royalty at Possenhoffen Castle, Elizabeth was a favourite cousin of 'Mad' King Ludwig II, but her outwardly pampered life was marred by tragedy. She lost her youngest daughter Sophie at the age of two in 1857, and in 1889 her son Crown Prince Rudolf committed suicide in scandalous circumstances. Apart from his body being found with his young lover Mary Vetsera, there were rumours that he had been plotting against his father.

Elizabeth's marriage to the emperor was further strained by the formality of the Hapsburg court, where Franz Joseph was in complete control. When he finished a course at dinner, everyone else had to put down their knife and fork too. He was distrustful of modern inventions like telephones, cars and trains, and said that electric light irritated his eyes. On top of that, his wife's repeated attacks of 'nerves' and her obsession with diet were a constant niggle. For her part, Elizabeth hated everything to do with childbearing, and found sex with the emperor a duty rather than a pleasure. Although she bore him four children, she left them in the care of their grandmother or the servants, and found it difficult to show them affection. She confessed to a friend that only riding helped dispel her frequent bouts of depression.

Known as 'Sisi' to those closest to her, she generally preferred horses to people. She kept portraits of all her horses in her bedroom, describing the ones that had died as 'lost friends' who were 'always more loyal than human beings, and less malicious'. It was said that she 'looked like an angel but rode like a devil' and she hunted all over Europe, often transporting her own mounts by ship and by rail. Fortunately, she had a personal allowance of £5,000 a month to indulge her hobby (worth around £300,000 today). On Corfu she built a holiday villa where she said that she wanted to live 'like a student'. This was about as realistic as Marie-Antoinette's attempts to live like a shepherdess at Versailles: Elizabeth's student digs had 128 rooms and stables for fifty horses.

The empress seemed oblivious of the dangers of riding. She once narrowly escaped death when her horse caught its foot in the planks of a bridge over a steep gorge in the Alps. Later, attempting to vault a wall in Normandy, she was thrown and knocked unconscious, but nothing would slow her down. Riding helped her keep her slim figure – and that tiny waist. Local tailors would be summoned to sew her into her riding costume and, of course, she always watched what she ate. Staying at Combermere Abbey in Shropshire, Elizabeth required the cook to keep a supply of live turtles to make fresh soup and tubs of seawater were shipped to the house from the Welsh coast so that the Empress could have a proper bath.

Elizabeth continued riding until she was in her late forties, after which she channelled her energies into long-distance walks, swimming and gymnastics as well as almost ceaseless travelling, especially after the death of her son. Her fitness regime included daily visits to the gym, so she naturally had gyms built into all of her residences. One visitor described her using the rings to pull herself off the ground dressed in a black floor-length gown trimmed with ostrich feathers. At the edge of the exercise area a rope was stretched across the room, which, she said, was there 'to make sure I don't forget how to jump'.

At state banquets, Elizabeth insisted on having only a cup of consommé, two slices of wheaten bread and some fruit. She also irritated the emperor by skipping dinner entirely sometimes, instead retiring to her room with a glass of milk and a biscuit. When her doctors told her that she was anaemic, she was persuaded to eat red meat for a time, though she soon reduced it to the juice of a rare steak and almost nothing else. One aristocrat described her as 'inhumanly slender'. Her beauty treatments included vigorous massages and being wrapped in wet towels filled with seaweed. She immersed herself in baths of olive oil to smooth her skin and her magnificent hair was washed every three weeks with beer and honey. On her travels she was occasionally seen eating generous portions of cake and drinking hot chocolate, suggesting that she probably suffered from bulimia.

After the death of her son, Elizabeth stayed out of the public eye as much as possible, usually travelling with just one lady-in-waiting. In her diary she wrote: 'I wish for nothing from mankind except to be left in peace.' The crown prince's death brought Elizabeth and Franz Joseph together in grief, and, even though they were apart for months at a time, they corresponded daily. In one of his last letters to her, Franz Joseph poignantly wrote:

> *Happiness is hardly the right word for us, we should be satisfied with a little peace, a good understanding between us and fewer misfortunes . . .*

He did not get his wish. In September 1898 Elizabeth was stabbed in the heart by an Italian anarchist as she boarded a ferry on Lake Geneva. Luigi Lucheni had travelled to Geneva to assassinate the duke of Orleans but couldn't find him. Hearing that empress was in the vicinity he took his chance, saying afterwards: 'I wanted to kill a royal, it didn't matter which one.'

As Elizabeth lay dying, a doctor forced a sugar lump soaked in brandy between her lips, an ironic final touch for a woman who today would have been diagnosed as suffering from an eating disorder. Always destined to play the tragic heroine, a few days earlier she had confided to her companion, Countess Sztaray, that she felt 'a vast longing to lie in a good large coffin and simply find rest, nothing but rest'.

~

**Dr John Harvey Kellogg** (1852–1943) had a simple slogan: 'Eat what the monkey eats, simple food and not too much of it'. His advice went against the grain for large numbers of his fellow Americans who were then, as now, fond of red meat and white bread. Concerned with the dangers of constipation and a 'slow colon', Kellogg advised that healthy people should give themselves enemas at least three times each week. He published over fifty books, many of them alerting the public to the dire consequences of masturbation – or 'self-pollution' as he called it – lest it make them idle, spotty, depressed and, in the case of boys, stunt their height. At 5′4″, perhaps he knew something he wasn't telling. Although Kellogg and his wife Ella fostered forty-two children and adopted seven of them, they never had sex. On his wedding night, he sat up into the small hours working on one of his most successful books, *Plain Facts for Old and Young*, a treatise on healthy living based on the suppression of sexual urges. Kellogg was a virgin when he died aged almost ninety-two.

As a young man John Harvey was chosen by Ellen G. White, the founder of Seventh Day Adventism, to help run the Western Health Reform Institute in Battle Creek, Michigan which she had founded in 1866. Recognising Kellogg as energetic and a fast learner, she subsidised him to study medicine in New York. One of her beliefs was that vegetarianism was part of the path to enlightenment. Studying at Bellevue Hospital, Kellogg had a strict breakfast regime of seven water biscuits and an apple, with the weekly luxury of a coconut and very occasionally some oatmeal or potatoes. However, he struggled to buy healthy grains and cereals that were easy to prepare and, returning fully qualified to Battle Creek in 1876, he set out to develop simple foods that opened up the bowels at least three times a day. From these experiments emerged Granola and, in due course, the world's most popular breakfast cereal, Kellogg's cornflakes.

Battle Creek's three principles were exercise, diet and purging the body of impurities. But Kellogg was also a skilled surgeon, performing over 20,000 operations during his career – as many as twenty-five a day at his peak – and he was still operating at the age of eighty-eight. Trained as a gynaecologist, he also specialised in removing haemorrhoids. Patients on the table received a cleansing enema of lukewarm water and to reduce post-operative shock their beds were packed with warm sandbags. Kellogg also sprinkled lactose on their wounds to prevent infection. Although he kept his patients confined to bed immediately after surgery, he believed in exercise to aid recovery, sometimes stimulating their muscles with painless electric shocks.

John Harvey Kellogg's younger brother William began as his assistant, but was to go on to found the family cereal empire, originally called the Battle Creek Toasted Cornflake Company. Although John Harvey recognised that the sanatorium needed to function as a business, he didn't like the idea of using his methods for commercial gain. William was more practical and – crucially – was willing to add sugar to the cornflakes to make them more palatable to a wider market. The Kellogg brothers fell out over this and didn't speak to one another for the last thirty years of their lives. While William became a wealthy man, John Harvey ploughed his salary back into running the sanatorium and endowing hospital beds in India and China. The royalties from his books were used to feed and clothe his enormous brood of foster children.

As well as abstaining from red meat, John Harvey Kellogg advocated fresh air and the consumption of nuts, even writing a paper entitled 'Nuts may Save the Race'. He was an early proponent of yoghurt and tofu and, long before Jane Fonda was born, a believer in exercising to music in order to relieve boredom. Columbia Records issued a set of five phonograph records to accompany his booklet on exercise. Kellogg also dabbled in eugenics (improving human health and intelligence by selective breeding) and was a founder of the 'Race Betterment Foundation'.

Many of Kellogg's theories, once thought to be outlandish, have since been vindicated. He was one of the first doctors to campaign against smoking. He argued that cow's milk was unsuitable for invalids, that salt should not be added to food, and he was one of the first to state that a diet high in animal fats and dairy products was ultimately unhealthy. He also recognised that vegetable oils were preferable to lard, suet and butter. His system of 'Biologic Living' was aimed at promoting 'good digestion, sound sleep, a clear head, a placid mind and joy to be alive'. Part of that system involved sleeping outdoors 'watching the squirrels gambolling' and relying on fruit, nuts and berries for sustenance, a simple life that Kellogg said would allow people 'to listen to the music of the spheres'. He applied his theories to his own life, getting by on four hours sleep a night, and staying fit and healthy until he succumbed to pneumonia at ninety-one.

~

The founder of another, even more successful, American business dynasty also paid close attention to diet and exercise. At the age of seventy-five **Henry Ford** (1863–1947) could still do handstands. In his late fifties he impressed friends by leaping into the air and kicking a cigar off the mantelpiece. He attributed his physical fitness to avoiding anything that might poison his body. Like Kellogg, he saw white bread as a major enemy and sternly warned his friends and associates against it. He always drank his water warm, believing that the body wasted energy heating it up if it were drunk cold. He never took sugar because he thought the sharp edges on the crystals were like pieces of glass that could damage internal organs, until it was pointed out to him that the crystals dissolve when wet.

For a time in the 1920s Ford tried eating only wheat – which he held to be a miracle food. His doctor told him he was starving to death and this was demonstrated by experimenting with pigs fed only on wheat. When they almost died, Henry was persuaded to vary his diet. In 1926 he decided that carrots were a magical cure-all and devised a meal made up of fourteen different carrot recipes. In 1927 he announced that pigs, cows and chickens would soon be 'redundant' as he was working on a biscuit made of wheat germ, oatmeal, pecan and olive oil that would be sufficient for all human dietary needs. The 'wonderfood' biscuit never went into mass production but that didn't stop Ford's relentless dietary experimentation. No one was spared. Businessmen and friends invited to lunch at Ford's mansion near Detroit were faced with what Ford called 'roadside greens', including stewed burdock and soybean-bread sandwiches with a filling of milkweed.

This attitude to food reveals much about Ford's attitude to life in general. For him, control was of paramount importance. In *Brave New World* (1932) the state religion is called 'Fordism': Aldous Huxley saw that Ford's working methods were as much to do with social manipulation as economic freedom. Ford's mission in life was to make the process of making things more efficient. He thought that the key to human happiness was productivity, and that anything that interfered with it – war, organised religion, financiers, trade unions, bad diet – was to be resisted.

It was an insight that changed the world. What we now call the consumer society was practically invented by Henry Ford: the idea that we 'consume' goods in the same way we consume food was entirely new. The first recorded use of the word 'consumer' in this way was in a Sears Roebuck catalogue of 1896. Ford found his metier aged fifteen, when he discovered that he had a gift for taking watches apart and putting them back together again. By the age of thirty he was chief engineer for the Edison Illuminating Company in Detroit. Ford idolised Edison and worked hard in the temple of electricity but, with typical single-mindedness and self-belief, in his spare time he was developing an entirely different source of power: the petrol engine. In 1896 he unveiled his crude first 'horseless carriage'. It was called the Quadricycle because it used four bicycle wheels and was driven by a chain. In an uncharacteristic example of poor planning, the finished version was too large to get out of the workshop and Ford had to improvise a larger doorway using an axe. But Edison was impressed and urged him on:

*We do not know what electricity can do, but I take for granted that it cannot do everything. Keep on with your engine. If you can get what you are after, I can see a great future.*

Two years later Ford left to set up his own business. In 1903 he personally broke the world land-speed record in a car called the '999', reaching 91 miles per hour on the frozen surface of Lake St Clair near Detroit. Impressive though this was, the 'motor car' was easily dismissed as a plaything for the well off, expensive to make and to buy. But Ford had other ideas. His invention of the assembly line simplified the manufacturing process, keeping costs down and radically reducing production times. But the real stroke of genius was to keep prices down too. Every worker was a potential customer and the profits would come from volume. It worked. In 1908 the first Model 'T' Fords began rolling off the line, priced at $825 dollars. By 1914 the price had fallen to $360 (equivalent to a very affordable $7,000 or £4,500 at today's prices). By 1918 half the cars in America were Model Ts and when production finally stopped a decade later, 15 million had been produced – more than any other car except for the Volkswagen Beetle.

Ford had managed this through some bold innovations, all of them designed to centralise control. The eight-hour shift allowed three sets of workers to keep the production line running twenty-four hours a day. In 1913 the introduction of the first-ever conveyor-belt-driven 'moving production line' reduced the time it took to produce the car's chassis from six hours to just ninety minutes. At the same time, a network of Ford dealerships was established, which not only made the dealers themselves wealthy, it also meant Ford cars were visible in every American city, helping to create yet more demand. At the other end of the supply chain, Ford looked to buy – or form strategic alliances with – the companies producing parts, glass and rubber, to improve consistency of delivery and drive production costs down further. This was to become the template for the modern manufacturing corporation and Ford did it all without accountants. He didn't like employing people who weren't directly involved in making or managing: in his lifetime, the Ford Motor Company was never audited.

Ford's other major innovation was to do with staff. In 1914 he introduced a minimum wage of $5 a day, a huge leap from the previous rate of $2.34. It was an instant success, attracting thousands of highly motivated workers to Detroit and ending the high staff turnover problem overnight. But there were conditions. To qualify for the minimum wage meant conforming to Ford's social vision: no heavy drinking, no smoking, no divorce, no union talk. He set up a Social Department under the ex-boxer and tough guy Harry Bennett. Bennett had a team of fifty investigators gathering information about the personal lives of the workforce. Anyone who failed to meet the standards of the Ford Motor Company forfeited their right to the minimum wage. Bennett also made sure union activity was disrupted at every turn, employing thugs and ex-criminals under the guise of a crime rehabilitation programme. He was the ultimate fixer and he enjoyed Ford's complete trust, picking his boss up and dropping him home every day for over twenty years. Once, when a newspaper suggested to him that he would paint the sky black if Ford asked him to, he replied:

*I might have a little trouble arranging that one but you'd see 100,000 workers coming through the plant gates with dark glasses on tomorrow.*

The Social Department hints at the darker side to Ford's character. He was an autocrat who couldn't bear dissent. Bennett himself captured this perfectly. Practically the first thing Ford said to him was, 'Harry, never try to outguess me.' 'You mean never try to understand you?' replied Bennett. 'That's close enough.' Those that tried to defy him, including his own son Edsel and his grandson Henry Ford II, found themselves overruled or expelled. This ruthlessness was one of the reasons that Hitler kept a life-sized picture of Ford next to his desk. (He would later claim that the Ford Service Department inspired him to set up the Gestapo, just as the Model T had influenced the Volkswagen Beetle.) And this wasn't all that Hitler had in common with Ford. In the 1920s, he was the proprietor of the *Dearborn Enquirer*, a newspaper that had published a series of anti-Semitic tracts including the notorious (and fake) 'The Protocols of the Learned Elders of Zion'. Ford later disowned the paper and claimed he was unaware of its racist content, but all the evidence points to these apologies as window dressing. Even in his final weeks he was still grumbling about Jewish bankers having caused the Second World War.

In June 1916 the *Chicago Tribune* published an article head-lined 'Ford is an Anarchist' which claimed, incorrectly, that the company was refusing to pay employees called up by the National Guard. Ford sued and the paper was found guilty, but fined only six cents – the amount the jury thought covered the damage Ford and his company had suffered. During the trial, Ford had been cross-examined in the witness box and this had revealed some strange gaps in his general knowledge. It emerged that he thought the American Revolution had taken place in 1812 and he couldn't define words and phrases like 'ballyhoo' and 'chilli con carne'. He thought that the traitor Benedict Arnold was a writer. It was in defence of his ignorance that he made his often misquoted reply 'History is bunk'. What he actually said was: 'History is bunk as it is taught in schools . . .'

What distinguishes Ford from most modern CEOs is that his vision went far beyond business. He was a Utopian, convinced that technology properly managed would lead to a world without war, turning it into one happy global version of the Ford company. This helps explain his obsession with diet and personal morality – and the apparent paradox that the man whose wealth was built on the internal combustion engine was a committed environmentalist. His estate at Fair Lane near Detroit was powered by hydroelectric power from his own dam on the Rouge River. To control mosquitoes organically, he built hundreds of bathouses in the grounds and, while building works were going on, he paid local boys to catch squirrels so that they wouldn't be killed when trees were felled.

As a teenager, Ford had given up hunting after shooting a meadowlark. As he and his two companions retrieved the dead bird, Ford exclaimed 'Well I'm through. When three big ablebodied men with guns will pick on a little bird like this, I've fired my last shot.' For the rest of his life, he was a pacifist: he wouldn't even let his son Edsel play with toy guns.

In many ways, Ford never left the farm where he was born. He loved nature and enjoyed camping, going on regular excursions with a group of wealthy friends who called themselves 'The Vagabonds'. They included his former mentor Thomas Edison, the tyre magnate Harvey Firestone and the naturalist John Burroughs, known affectionately as 'the Grand Old Man of Nature'. In 1921 they were joined for a night by the then president, Warren Harding. According to John Burroughs, the campers would 'cheerfully endure wet, cold, smoke, mosquitoes, black flies and sleepless nights, just to touch naked reality once more'. It was a pretty relaxed form of 'roughing it', though: each man had his own personal tent, with mosquito nets and a separate dining marquee.

On an even folksier note, Ford helped rejuvenate traditional American fiddle-playing. He had his own $75,000 instrument (a Stradivarius, naturally) but no natural talent, and he made himself cross by continually failing to play and dance a jig at the same time. To make up for it, he hired an elderly fiddler called Mellie Dunham to record traditional tunes and funded the Henry Ford Gold Cup for fiddling. The publicity generated was huge. Fiddling underwent a national revival and remains an essential part of country music to this day.

Perhaps it was inevitable that a farm boy turned technologist would end up finding a way to combine the two disciplines. In the 1930s he saw his chance: a new branch of science called 'chemurgy', which sought to find new uses for agricultural raw materials in industry. Ford became so interested that the Ford Motor Company began using soybeans as an ingredient of its gear-knobs and car-horn buttons and, in 1934, he formed the Farm Chemurgic Council, with a national conference at Dearborn, Michigan to which George Washington Carver (1864–1943) was invited.

Carver was a legendary figure. A former slave, in 1896 (the debut year of the Quadricycle and the word 'consumer') he had been appointed by the great educator Booker T. Washington (a former slave himself) to be the director of Agricultural Research at Tuskegee Normal and Industrial Institute for Negroes. His aim was to help black farmers improve their crops by means of crop rotation and by finding alternatives to cotton, which depleted the soil. It was Carver's championing of soybeans that drew him to Ford's attention, but it was peanuts that assured his immortality. Largely due to him, over the next fifty years, peanuts became one of the dominant crops in the whole of the South.

Initially, there wasn't much call for peanuts so Carver set about exploring the possibilities for by-products. His ceaseless experiments produced some 300 peanut derivatives, including: evaporated peanut beverage, cheese, ink, dyes, soap, medicinal oils and cosmetics, metal polish, plastic, instant coffee, meat tenderiser, shaving cream, talcum powder, wood stains, shoe polish, peanut oil shampoo and various cooking sauces, earning himself the nickname, 'The Peanut Man'. He may well have invented peanut butter but he never patented it. He believed food products were a gift from God and therefore belonged to everyone.

Some weeks after going to Dearborn, Carver sent Henry Ford a recipe for a gravy substitute made using soybean oil, adding a note to Mrs Ford:

> *Please watch the digestive tract of Mr. Ford for a few days after he has eaten the gelatinised pig's feet. Notice how his face will fill up. To clear the skin, remove wrinkles etc, try massaging with pure, refined peanut oil.*

The same month, Carver wrote again to Clara Ford saying: 'I want to help Mr Ford prove his startling statement that we can live directly from the products of the soil.' Their collaboration culminated in 1942 in an idea that was decades ahead of its time: a plastic car-body made from soybeans that weighed 30 per cent less than the standard steel model and ran on grain alcohol.

Sadly, the war intervened and the first-ever eco-car never went into production.

Ford's last years were dominated by paranoia and speculation on the afterlife. These were brought into sharp focus when his son Edsel died of cancer, aged only forty-nine, in 1943. Ford became convinced that the government were planning to oust him and, fearful of assassination attempts, had all his chauffeurs armed. In fact, it was simply ill health that cut short his tenure and his grandson Henry Ford II replaced him in 1945. Some say his final decline was caused by a stroke that struck him down as he watched uncut footage from the infamous Nazi concentration camp at Majdanek in Poland.

Ford had become a firm believer in reincarnation, inspired by one of the few books he admitted to having read: *A Short View of Great Questions* (1899) by Orlando Jay Smith. The book's contention that our experiences in life are never wasted struck a chord. Henry Ford hated waste.

> *Religion offered nothing to the point. Even work could not give me complete satisfaction. Work is futile if we cannot utilise the experience we collect in one life in the next.*

He decided that, because he was born in 1863 – the date of the Battle of Gettysburg – he was the reincarnation of a soldier who had died there.

By the end of his life, Ford had amassed a fortune that would today be worth $188 billion. Reincarnation gave him a plausible reason for the magnitude of his success and for his sureness of touch. He'd been round the block many times before. In 1928, he explained it to a reporter from the *San Francisco Examiner*:

*Genius is experience. Some seem to think that it is a gift or talent, but it is the fruit of long experience in many lives. Some are older souls than others, and so they know more. The discovery of reincarnation put my mind at ease. If you preserve a record of this conversation, write it so that it puts men's minds at ease. I would like to communicate to others the calmness that the long view of life gives to us.*

The other way Henry Ford put his mind at rest was by making sure everything was neat and tidy. He was very keen on keeping records. When his wife Clara died three years after him, in 1950, staff found that many of the fifty-six rooms at his house, Fair Lane, were crammed with his papers, notebooks and receipts – even letters Edsel Ford had written to Father Christmas as a small boy. He had thrown nothing away in over sixty years. The collection became the basis of the Ford archives which number more than 10 million documents.

～

Henry Ford's entrepreneurial flair, his enormous wealth and his attempts to control every aspect of his life, pale into insignificance however compared to the life and career of another billionaire, **Howard Hughes** (1905–76).

When Hughes died in 1976, he was the second richest man in the United States after J. Paul Getty. His father had made a fortune by patenting (in 1909) the rotary drill bit that was to revolutionise the oil industry. By 2000, the Hughes Tool Company still had an astonishing 40 per cent share of the world drill-bit market. Hughes used his inherited wealth to build an empire that included not just oil but mining, aviation, armaments, films and property, including many of the hotels and casinos in Las Vegas. When he sold his controlling shares in the airline TWA in 1966, he was presented with the largest cheque that had ever been made out to an individual – for $566,000,000. On his death a decade later, he left around the same amount – though unravelling the details of his investments and legacies took another fifteen years. This sounds like the classic American dream but whatever else his vast wealth did for Howard Hughes, it never made him happy.

From about 1950, he became increasingly reclusive, disabled by obsessive-compulsive disorder and anorexia. The last twenty years of his life were spent being looked after by a small team of loyal aides and doctors, an inner circle that either protected him from outsiders or, depending on your perspective, colluded to imprison him within his neuroses. Many of them were Mormons, whom Hughes trusted despite not being a member of their church. He died in an air ambulance en route to a Texas hospital from Acapulco, emaciated, unwashed, and pumped full of painkillers and sedatives. In a life that had more drama than anything he ever produced in Hollywood, his eating habits particularly stand out. They became a series of increasingly bizarre personal rituals, outward symbols of his inner distress.

It had all started very differently. As a young man, Hughes had declared:

> *I intend to be the greatest golfer in the world, the finest film producer in Hollywood, the greatest pilot in the world, and the richest man in the world.*

He came very close to achieving all these ambitions (although he never bettered a handicap of two in golf). Even if he hadn't moved into film, he would be remembered for his achievements as a pilot. Just as Henry Ford had tested the possibilities of the automobile by becoming a racing driver, Hughes taught himself to understand the new science of aeronautics from inside the cockpit. Flying a Lockheed Super Electra in 1938 he broke the world air-speed record, as well as the records for the fastest flights across America and for round the world (91 hours 14 minutes in 1938). In 1939, his flying career was recognised by the award of the Congressional gold medal. It is typical of Hughes that he never bothered to collect it: years later, President Truman finally sent it to him by post.

If flying was Hughes's amateur passion, he managed to turn it to good use in his professional career as a movie producer. His first successful film was *Hell's Angels* (1930), an epic tale of First World War fighter pilots. Budgeted at $3.8 million, at the time it was the most expensive film ever made, in no small part due to Hughes's perfectionism. He sent buyers to Europe to find as many First World War aeroplanes as possible for the film and shipped eighty-seven of them to America. He choreographed many of the dog-fight scenes and, when the stunt pilots all refused to fly the dangerous final scene, he did it himself, crashing the plane but escaping with minor injuries – and the shots he wanted. Three other stunt pilots died during the making of the film.

Handsome, daring and rich, Hughes's roll-call of lovers matched that of any of the leading men he cast. Jean Harlow, Katherine Hepburn, Rita Hayworth, Bette Davis, Ginger Rogers, Kathryn Grayson, Ava Gardner and Lana Turner were all charmed by his good looks and generosity. Hepburn in particular was smitten by his bravery, packing him turkey and cheese sandwiches for his round-the-world flight in 1938, while on another occasion he let her steer his private plane under 59th Street bridge on a night flight across Manhattan. He was also rumoured to have had affairs with Cary Grant, Randolph Scott and numerous other 'pretty boy' stars.

Throughout the 1930s and early 1940s, Hughes appeared to be fulfilling all his youthful ambitions. But even then, ominous signs were perceptible. His colleagues complained of unreasonable requests, violent mood swings and a fixation with tiny details. Obsessed with Jane Russell's breasts in his 1943 movie *The Outlaw*, he designed and built a cantilevered, steel-reinforced bra to show them off to their full advantage (though Russell later claimed she never actually wore it). More troubling, in 1941 he was diagnosed with syphilis (probably contracted from Lana Turner) and he started to agonise over the possibility of 'catching germs' from other people. After being given penicillin for the infection, he instructed his housekeeper to put almost all of his clothing into laundry bags and seal them with padlocks, after which they were to be thrown on to the lawn and burned. The syphilis caused an angry red rash to erupt on Hughes's hands and his doctor told him not to shake hands with anyone until the antibiotics had cleared it up. His fixation with not touching anything dirty was about to take root.

In December 1947 he suffered a total breakdown. Telling his staff that he wanted to watch some movies, he disappeared into a nearby studio's screening room and didn't emerge for four months, refusing to speak or be spoken to, only communicating with his staff via notes scrawled on a yellow pad and living entirely on chocolate bars and milk.

He reappeared in the spring of 1948, but he was never the

same again. He stopped cutting his hair and nails, saved all his urine in glass bottles and preserved any of his stools that he considered 'worthy'. He ate only room-service meals, instructing that his sandwiches be cut in precise triangles, that no tomato should be sliced thicker than a quarter of an inch, and that his lettuce should be shredded 'on the bias'. He kept a ruler in the room to measure any peas he ordered, sending back any that were 'too big'. Hughes never really regained equilibrium. From now on he gradually disappeared from his own life.

By the time he married his third wife, the actress Jean Peters, in 1957, his fear of germs had reached a new level of intensity. He was getting through a dozen boxes of tissues a day, using them to pick things up and to isolate him from anything he sat on. Even tins of food had to be scrubbed and disinfected and the contents removed very slowly, so that they did not brush against the sides of the can and become contaminated. When he and Jean stayed at a hotel in Nassau, he refused to let housekeeping staff into their room, instead simply moving to another one once it was too dirty. They remained married for fourteen years but, at times, Peters was a virtual prisoner, forced to write Hughes a letter whenever she wanted permission to leave their hotel. One of the less attractive aspects of their marriage was that she was kept awake at night by the clicking of his gigantic toenails, which he refused to cut. To enable her to get a good night's sleep, he first slipped tissue paper between his toes, and then asked engineers at the Hughes Aircraft Company to build him a set of callipers with metal ridges in the foot plate that would hold his nails apart. Mr and Mrs Hughes had to have separate fridges so that he didn't catch germs from her, and for the same reason she wasn't allowed to touch the knobs on the TV. They divorced in 1971, though they hadn't lived together for over a decade. When she remarried, Hughes bought the houses either side of her new marital home, and two others across the street, just so he could keep an eye on her.

Hughes died without friends or family, his sordid decline eked out in hotel rooms, the windows shrouded with blackout material. Often he would sit naked, a hotel napkin covering his genitals, watching movies over and over again. He was rumoured to have watched *Ice Station Zebra*, the 1968 Alistair MacLean spy thriller starring Rock Hudson, more than 150 times. No one knows what it was in the film that piqued his interest. When Hughes was chronically constipated and dehydrated in his final months, his assistant John Holmes would arrive every three days to deliver brown-paper bags containing almond Hershey bars, homogenised milk and unsalted pecan nuts to his bedside. These had to be handed over in silence, the bag held out at 45 degrees so that Hughes could reach inside and remove the items individually with a clean paper tissue for each one. According to one biographer, Richard Hack, the chocolate was 'cut into half-inch squares, each square chewed individually and completely, followed by a swallow of milk'. Hughes weighed less than 7 stones when he died. His appearance was so changed through neglect and malnutrition that the FBI had to resort to fingerprints to identify him.

As falls from grace go, Hughes's has a mythic quality to it. Few men have ever enjoyed so much money and fame; few have ended in such a complete rejection of the world. What was it that first sent Hughes over the edge in 1947? There are clues in his childhood: his mother, Allene, was always worried about germs, sending news clippings to the supervisor of young Howard's summer camp advising caution when allowing so many boys to mix together because of the dangers of spreading polio. His grandmother Mimi was also fearful of dirt and refused to have any built-in cupboards in the house because they could not be moved outdoors to be 'disinfected' by sunlight. And both his parents had died suddenly when Hughes was in his late teens.

But there were two other specific events that took place just before his breakdown that may have contributed more directly to it. In July 1946 he was the pilot on the test flight of a spy-plane called the XF-11 when mechanical failure brought the plane down on the edge of Beverly Hills. It collided with three houses and then exploded. Hughes was severely injured, puncturing a lung, breaking six ribs and his collarbone and suffering extensive cuts and burns. The morphine used to treat a serious burn to his hand probably started his dependency on prescription drugs and he remained in constant pain for the rest of his life.

The second setback involved Hughes's contribution to the war effort. Concerned at the loss of American troops and equipment through U-boat action in the Atlantic, he had secured the government contract to build a huge transport seaplane, big enough to carry 750 troops and two tanks. The eight-engined H-4 Hercules, or 'Spruce Goose', was the largest plane then built and remains the largest wooden aeroplane in history. Though the Spruce Goose's size has since been beaten by the Russian Antonov An-225, its wingspan of 320 feet is still a world record. Like many of Hughes's schemes, it went wildly over budget and was never delivered, the contract being cancelled amid accusations of bribery. The prototype flew only once, in November 1947, a journey of about a mile at an altitude of 70 feet. Hughes was at the controls. The collapse of this project was a huge blow to his pride (and his pocket) and he kept the plane in a hangar in perfect condition at a cost of $1,000,000 a year until his death in 1976. He was not a man who was used to failure. As he reminded a reporter: 'I'm not a paranoid deranged millionaire. Goddamit, I'm a billionaire.' Two weeks later, he withdrew to his screening room and began his long descent into oblivion.

~

Howard Hughes's descent into culinary lunacy feels a long way removed from the dietary eccentricities of Helena de Noailles or John Harvey Kellogg, or the weight-watching routines of Empress Elizabeth. Today when we call someone a glutton, we mean they eat too much. Of the lives in this chapter, only George Fordyce fits that description. But the original meaning of gluttony was much more subtle. The great medieval moralist St Thomas Aquinas defined it as the sin of 'inordinate desire': as well as eating too much, he thought eating too soon, eating too eagerly, eating too expensively and eating too fussily were all equally wrong. And we're talking to an expert here. St Tom himself was so fat he had to have a semi-circle cut out of his dining table to accommodate his stomach. But where food is concerned we should not be too hasty in our judgments. As G. K. Chesterton said: 'There is more simplicity in the man who eats caviar on impulse than in the man who eats grape-nuts on principle.'

# CHAPTER SIX

# Grin and Bear It

*Without fear and illness, I could never have accomplished all I have.*
EDVARD MUNCH

Ambition, fame, sex, gluttony: all these have the capacity to transform our lives for better or worse and, as we have seen, the struggle to control them can be the making of us. But there are some traumatic events over which we can have no possible control: the loss of a limb, the onset of blindness, an attack of mental illness. The human race fights a running battle against disease and injury. Most people who have ever lived (perhaps as many as 45 billion) died of malaria; plague and smallpox have killed more human beings than all the wars and natural disasters put together. Even in affluent Britain and America today, one in ten adults are registered disabled: over the age of fifty, this rises to one in two. A quarter of Americans suffer from some form of neurotic, psychotic or addictive disorder, and the commonest illness treated by doctors in Britain is depression. Whether we find comfort in religion, consolation in philosophy, or simply adopt a stiff-upper lip, learning how to deal with sudden physical misfortune is something we all, sooner or later, have to deal with.

Posterity hasn't been kind to **Pieter Stuyvesant (1612–72)**, the last Dutch governor of what we now call New York. Ask an American what they know about him and they will probably tell you he had a wooden leg. The football team at New York's Stuyvesant High School are still called 'the Peg-leggers' and grumpy, stubborn Peg-Leg Pete is seen as, at best, a bit-part player in the long drama of the nation, an irrelevant prologue before the main act gets under way. In Washington Irving's satirical *Knickerbocker's History of New York* (1809), Stuyvesant is described as 'a tough, sturdy, valiant, weather-beaten, mettle-some, obstinate, leathern-sided, lion-hearted, generous-spirited old governor'. By 1938 this rather admiring portrait had given way to the repressive proto-Fascist of the musical *Knickerbocker's Holiday* by Kurt Weill and Maxwell Anderson. In the one number from the show that's become a classic, Stuyvesant's character gets to sing the bittersweet 'September Song'.

Stuyvesant's real life was more bitter than sweet. He came from Friesland in the flat northlands of the Netherlands, an area of devout peasants and grim-faced ultra-conformity. His father was a minister in the Dutch Reformed Church and Pieter's obvious career path was to follow him there. But the young Stuyvesant rebelled, choosing to study philosophy rather than theology and getting himself kicked out of university for sleeping with his landlord's daughter. He immediately joined the Dutch West India Company as a clerk, rising quickly through the ranks, until he was appointed the director of the Caribbean colony of Curaçao in 1642, just before his thirtieth birthday.

Stuyvesant was ambitious, single minded and charismatic, gathering a string of acolytes around him. The most dedicated of these was John Farret, a fellow West India Company employee and an accomplished painter and poet. For many years, the two men enjoyed a diverting correspondence conducted entirely in verse. Farret hero-worshipped Stuyvesant, referring to him as 'Excellency' and 'My Stuyvesant' and calling Stuyvesant's own rather clunky verses 'godlike'. These letters (which only came to light in the 1920s) have a faint flavour of homoeroticism about them, though there is no suggestion of any sexual liaison. They put a fresh slant on Stuyvesant's dour and crusty image, rather like discovering Oliver Cromwell had a camp Cavalier pen pal.

Stuyvesant was two years into his Caribbean appointment when, during an ill-advised expedition to recapture the island of St Martin from the Spanish, his leg was blown off. He was flamboyantly planting the Dutch flag on a rampart that his troops had thrown up on the beach when a cannon ball fired from the island's fort shattered his right shin. That he lived to tell the tale indicates his considerable resilience. Dutch doctors were the most advanced in Europe and ingenious in devising new techniques of amputation, but none of them were easy or pleasant. Speed was of the essence. Fat and muscle had to be cut away to create a skin flap, and the bone sawn through as quickly as possible. Some surgeons could manage the whole procedure in less than a minute, but the survival rate was less than one in three.

Whoever saved Stuyvesant did an excellent job, but the patient was delirious for several weeks afterwards. He got back to his desk as soon as he could, his first act being a letter of apology to the directors of the company, regretting that his attack 'did not succeed so well as had hoped, no small impediment having been the loss of my right leg, it being removed by a rough ball'. He then dashed off a poetical note to Farret who responded with his own attempt, 'On the Off-Shot Leg of the Noble, Brave Heer Stuyvesant, Before the Island of St Marten'. Even by Farret's fulsome standards, the poem hit new heights of Stuyvesant idolatry: 'The bullet hits his leg; the rebound touches my heart...'

Despite his determination to carry on as normal, the heat of the tropics meant Stuyvesant's wound began to fester and he was reluctantly forced to return home to recuperate properly. His nursemaid was the plain but good-hearted spinster, Judith Bayard, three years his senior and his brother-in-law's sister. When he announced his intention to marry her, Farret goaded him by suggesting the marriage would never be consummated because Stuyvesant wasn't up to the job. Stuyvesant's verse in response was defiant and the couple went on to have a pair of sons.

Once better, Stuyvesant reported for duty at the West India Company's offices in Amsterdam. He had an expensive state-of-the-art wooden leg, and a cheap spare one for emergencies. It was a scene from a seventeenth-century version of *The Terminator* – the wounded soldier returns, older, wiser, more focused, his false limb glinting with the silver nails used to reinforce it. Here was the complete company man. The directors were impressed. They gave Stuyvesant a new mission: to impose order on the unruly colony of New Netherland on the east coast of North America.

As director-general of the settlement, based in the capital, New Amsterdam, Stuyvesant diligently looked after the Company's interests for the best part of sixteen years, He was a shrewd negotiator: tough, uncompromising and fair, holding off threats from the Swedes and the Native Americans and even managing for a while to get the New Englanders to accept Dutch sovereignty. In the end though, it all came to nothing. And, as it is the victors who decide what history gets taught in school, very few people today have heard of New Netherland, and if they've heard of Pieter Stuyvesant at all, they know only that he was

Dutch and had a wooden leg. This is most unfair.

New Netherland was a colony of over 10,000 people. Unlike most of Puritan New England, it wasn't founded on religious grounds. It was primarily a trading centre, infused with the liberal outlook that made the Netherlands the financial and intellectual powerhouse of the seventeenth century. As a result, it was a melting pot of nationalities and mixed marriages. New Amsterdam was to become New York, but its heart – and tongue – remains Dutch. Many words we consider uniquely American are in fact adopted from Dutch: 'boss' for master, cookies, coleslaw, even Santa Claus. It was the Dutch who erected the defensive wall that became 'Wall' Street; Stuyvesant's farm or 'bouwerie' is now The Bowery, one of the city's most famous thoroughfares; even Broadway (built by Stuyvesant) is merely the English pronunciation of *Breede weg*. The homesteads of New Amsterdam – Nieuw Haarlem, Breukelen, Greenwyck, Bronck's Plantation, Jonker's Plantation – all survive in the names of modern New York's boroughs: Harlem, Brooklyn, Greenwich, the Bronx, and Yonkers.

This last was originally a sawmill on the Hudson River, named after its owner Jonkheer Van Der Donck. Adriaen Van Der Donck was a young lawyer and landowner and Jonkheer was his honorific title (it means 'Young Gentleman', roughly equivalent to The Hon. in English). He had studied at the University of Leiden, where complete religious freedom and lack of censorship were the order of the day, and he was steeped in the new learning of Galileo, Descartes and Spinoza. Arriving in America in 1641, he had immediately fallen in love with the country: the landscape, plants, animals and most of all, the languages and customs of the local Mohican and Mohawk tribes.

Recognising early on the importance of beavers to the fledging economy he kept them himself as pets and studied every aspect of their life cycle. He saw New Netherland as a place of almost endless possibility, where laws and governance could be founded on the principles of peace and co-operation between peoples. In the passion he brought to his task of recording and mapping the colony, one can detect the first glimmering of the ideas that led to America's independence over a century later.

Stuyvesant's predecessor as director-general, Willem Kleft, had been very unpopular with the colonists. Against van der Donck's peaceful principles, he had started a bloody Indian war that drained the colony's resources and made outlying areas dangerous. Van der Donck used his oratorical skills to oppose Kleft and lobby for his replacement. When Stuyvesant arrived in 1647, van der Donck was appointed 'President of the Commonality', effectively Stuyvesant's deputy. The two men at first got on well, but the new director-general was easier to admire than to like. Unlike Adriaen Van Der Donck, he was a deeply conservative man who had no time for anything other than the iron laws of God and their earthly manifestation, the Dutch West India Company. He was an autocrat, referring to his fellow citizens as 'subjects' or 'his children' and winning arguments, not by subtle legal niceties, but by shouting, swearing and stamping his wooden leg on the floor. The pain caused made him increasingly difficult to deal with. Intractable differences both of character and political aspiration made the relationship with his deputy untenable. Van der Donck was stripped of public office. In quick succession, he lost his job, his right to practise law and his life. In a tragic irony, he was murdered in an Indian raid.

What Stuyvesant lost was the colony. Ten years after van der

Donck's death, the Second Anglo-Dutch War broke out and four English warships sailed up the Hudson. The Dutch knew they had no chance: the West India Company either couldn't or wouldn't send troops to defend the colony properly. The battle-weary Stuyvesant stood bravely at his post as New Netherland's leading citizens – including his son – pleaded with him to give in. 'I would much rather be carried out dead,' he replied. When finally forced to accept the inevitable, he did so proudly, stumping out of Fort Amsterdam in full uniform with his Dutch troops behind him.

It's hard not to feel sorry for him. Without his cussedness and intelligence, the colony might have fallen to the English much sooner. When it did, it was well established enough for most of the colonists – including Stuyvesant and his family – to segue peacefully into life as New Yorkers. Little is known of Pieter Stuyvesant's private life, but he did have one passion, inspired by his years in Curaçao. He collected tropical birds and by the time of his death in 1672 had several large aviaries full of them. It's an odd thought that this tight-lipped old moralist, with his black-and-white view of the world, saw out his days surrounded by loud squawks and splashes of brilliant colour, on the farm that would one day become famous as the street of bums and drunks.

~

It's impossible to tell how much the loss of his leg changed Stuyvesant's life. One of the central tenets of the modern approach to disability is that no one should be limited or defined by it. Stuyvesant, in his stoical Dutch way, would have assented to that. The career of another one-legged military man makes a dramatic contrast. **General Antonio de López de Santa Anna**

(1794–1876) holds the unique distinction of being the only person to become head of the same nation state on eleven separate occasions, once for less than a fortnight. From 1833 to 1855, Mexico was unstable even by Mexican standards: the presidency changed hands thirty-six times. To carve out a political career in these unpromising conditions, Santa Anna had to use anything he could to gather popular support, including the shameless exploitation of his missing appendage.

He was born into a respected Mexican Spanish family in the port of Veracruz and his initial loyalty was to the Spanish crown. He was an outstanding soldier but also a keen gambler, and as a young officer he was often in debt. During his first tour of duty in Texas he appropriated money from regimental funds, got caught and was sent back to headquarters in Veracruz as punishment. This allowed him to indulge his other passion, women. His military duties were not demanding and he soon acquired a reputation for whoring and for dalliances with other men's wives.

The first wife of his own was only fourteen when he married her. Too busy fighting to make the ceremony, he deputised his prospective father-in -law to stand in for him. His bride brought a dowry large enough for Santa Anna to buy a country estate but, not long afterwards, he made a personal appearance at another marriage ceremony in Texas, having persuaded one of his soldiers to dress up as a priest so he could bed a young woman who had agreed to sleep with him – but only if he married her.

This flexible ruthlessness was to serve Santa Anna well in politics. At various points in his long career others claimed him as a liberal and a conservative, a monarchist and a republican, a liberator and a despot. In fact, he was a pragmatist. Political ideology didn't excite him: what mattered was to be on the winning side. His first major defection was in 1821. Now a colonel, Santa Anna was part of the Spanish force sent to crush the uprising of Agustín de Iturbide. Seeing that the tide was about to turn in the rebels' favour, Santa Anna switched sides. Iturbide promoted him to the rank of brigadier general, and crowned himself Mexico's first constitutional emperor. But the two men didn't get on. According to one (entirely believable) rumour Iturbide didn't like Santa Anna flirting with his sixty-year-old sister. Santa Anna was once more sent back home to Veracruz, but this time as the state Governor.

He lost no time in securing himself a luxurious hacienda and large tracts of land, while imposing punitive taxes on the port's citizens. He became so unpopular that the self-styled Emperor had to recall him to the capital. This was a mistake. Santa Anna's antennae told him the wind was changing once more: he joined forces with the liberals to overthrow Iturbide and establish a republic under a new president, Vicente Guerrero. He later remarked:

*I did not know what a republic was myself, but the more I tried to reason with the people, the louder they cried, 'Viva La Republica!' so we all went off in search of one.*

In 1829 his moment of glory arrived. In Spain's last attempt to re-take their colony, 3,000 Spanish troops landed at Tampico on the Gulf of Mexico. Santa Anna, with half as many men, penned in the invaders for six weeks until lack of supplies and yellow fever forced them to surrender. Single-handedly, he had saved the Republic and become a national hero. He 'modestly' retired to his hacienda in Veracruz 'until his country needed him'. He didn't have to wait long. In 1833 he was elected president for the first time.

Rather as with his wedding, Santa Anna didn't feel the need to govern in person, staying at home on his ranch and delegating power to his vice-president, Valentín Farías. Unfortunately, Farías was a *genuine* liberal and within a couple of years his reforms had enraged the Catholic Church and disgusted the landed gentry – of which Santa Anna was a prominent member. Alarmed by the sudden intrusion of politics into his life, Santa Anna acted decisively, sacking Farías, suspending the new Constitution, and imposing a central dictatorship. This provoked several Mexican states, including Texas, to declare their independence. Mexico was at war yet again.

It was the Texan campaign that made Santa Anna famous outside Mexico. On 6 March 1836, after a twelve-day siege, his 1,500-strong force took the small garrison known as the Alamo. Hugely outnumbered, the Texans resisted bravely, but Santa Anna offered no quarter, ordering the execution of all who surrendered. The brutality of his troops that day probably changed the course of the war and certainly ensured his reputation in America as a sadistic tyrant. Even after the garrison had capitulated, Mexican soldiers continued to shoot and bayonet the corpses, which were then heaped into an unceremonious pile and burnt. As well as the folk heroes Jim Bowie and Davy Crockett, another 250 Texans were slaughtered. Only women and children and two slaves were spared. They were turned loose to spread panic through the rest of the state. Three weeks later, Santa Anna excelled himself by ordering the massacre at Goliad when 342 unarmed Texan prisoners-of-war were shot by Mexican troops, the survivors being clubbed, stabbed or trampled to death by cavalry.

Once news of these atrocities leaked out, the Texan army was inundated with volunteers. Led by General Sam Houston, they got their revenge by ambushing Santa Anna's army at San Jacinto while it was enjoying its siesta. Falling on the enemy with the now legendary cry 'Remember the Alamo!', they killed over half the drowsy Mexicans in eighteen minutes. Santa Anna escaped but was captured the next day. Having ditched his fancy uniform he was identified by the fact that he was the only prisoner wearing silk underwear, hardly standard issue for a Mexican infantryman. Forced to sign a humiliating peace treaty to save his own life, he was disowned by his government and exiled to the United States. Texas became an independent republic with Houston as its president.

In 1837 Santa Anna crept home to lick his wounds. But history intervened again. The French fleet arrived to blockade Veracruz, ostensibly in support of an extremely angry French pastry-cook called Monsieur Remontel. He had written to Louis-Philippe I complaining bitterly of the chaos that reigned in Mexico City, which was having a deleterious effect on his pastry business. Like a Hispanic King Arthur, Santa Anna charged into the fray. In Mexico's hour of need, he would once more save his fatherland from foreign domination. The government had no choice but to back him.

He won the 'Pastry War', but lost his leg in the process. A cannonball killed his horse and pulverised his ankle. As he lay waiting for the surgeon he piled on the pathos in a letter to the latest Mexican President, Anastasio Bustamente:

*I ask of the government that my body may be buried in these very sand dunes, so that my comrades in arms know that this is the line of battle I leave marked for them: that from today onward, the Mexicans' most unjust enemies may not dare place the filthy soles of their feet on our territory. All Mexicans, forgetting my political errors, do not deny me the only title I wish to donate to my children: that of having been a Good Mexican.*

He didn't die, but the leg was amputated rather inexpertly: the surgeons left a nub of bone protruding too far and had to over-stretch the skin to cover the stump. For the rest of his life Santa Anna suffered pain and inflammation, and sometimes the skin would split and bleed. But it was a propaganda weapon his rivals could do nothing to match: his missing leg was the living embodiment of Mexican independence and sacrifice. In May 1839 he was elected president for the second time.

His second administration was even more oppressive than his first, so he played the leg card. At political rallies, and to inspire his troops, he waved his wooden limb above his head, confirming his status as a war hero. In 1841 he had his original leg cere-moniously disinterred from its last resting place in Veracruz, taken to the capital under escort in a glass casket, and reburied with full military honours in a mausoleum in the cemetery of Santa Paula. It wasn't enough to stem the tide of resentment. In 1844 a rampaging mob smashed his statue, rushed into the cemetery and dug up the casket containing the revered limb. It was carried through the streets to cries of 'Death to the cripple!' Shortly afterwards Santa Anna was deposed and exiled to Cuba.

A year later he was back. The United States, keen to expand and consolidate its southern territories, had declared war on Mexico. Santa Anna wrote to the Mexican government offering his services with the solemn promise that he would not pursue the presidency. The long-suffering Farías, president once more, reluctantly agreed. What he didn't know was that Santa Anna had been in secret talks with the US government, offering to sell them large parts of Mexico if he ever returned to power. By early 1846 Santa Anna had returned to the place he loved best, at the head of the Mexican army. Never one to do anything by halves, he decided to renege on both promises simultaneously, seizing the Presidency and turning his army on the invading Americans. But Santa Anna was outmanoeuvred by the US forces and outgunned by their heavy artillery, losing six straight battles in a row. The Mexican-American War ended in disaster for Mexico and humiliation for Santa Anna, culminating in the fall of Mexico City in September 1847 and the loss of more than half of Mexico's northern territory. On 2 February 1848 the Mexican states of Utah, California, New Mexico, Arizona, Nevada and half of Colorado joined Texas as part of the USA. Apart from those who fell in battle, deaths from secondary infection and disease on both sides claimed over 50,000 lives. Santa Anna went into exile again, this time in Jamaica.

His leg had also had a bad war. In the battle of Cerro Gordo in 1847 the Americans overran the Mexicans so quickly that Santa Anna was forced to leave his half-eaten chicken dinner and both wooden legs behind. The legs were 'taken prisoner' by two members of the 4th Illinois Infantry. The fancy one, made of cork and leather, was the work of Charles Bartlett, a New York cabinetmaker. It had cost $1,300 at the time (worth about $35,000 today), and had an articulated foot that moved on ball bearings. After the war, it was exhibited at state fairs for a dime a peek before finding its way to the Illinois State Military Museum in Springfield. The simpler (spare) peg-leg was used as a baseball bat by General Abner Doubleday and can now be seen at the

Oglesby Mansion Museum in Decatur, Georgia

That ought to be the end of the Santa Anna story but it isn't. He operated on a purely mythological level in the minds of his countrymen and, though he had just lost half the country, was invited back, this time by the conservatives. In 1853 he was sworn in as president for his eleventh and final term. Dispensing with even the pretence of democracy, he appointed himself dictator for life, insisting on the official title, His Serene Highness. His Napoleonic fantasy was complete. Writing to a former ally he made his position quite clear:

> *For a hundred years to come, my people will not be fit for liberty. They do not know what it is, unenlightened as they are, and under the influence of a Catholic clergy, a despotism is the proper government for them, but there is no reason why it should not be a wise and virtuous one.*

Unfortunately, Santa Anna was incapable of being either wise or virtuous. Back in power, he sold another chunk of territory to the Americans so they could build a railway, making sure that some of its $15 million price tag found its way into his pockets. Even his conservative allies finally decided he was a liability and, in 1855, he was deposed for good, exiled to Cuba and tried and convicted in his absence for corruption.

The late 1860s found him living in exile on Staten Island in New York. Here, inadvertently, he made his most significant and lasting contribution to world history. He had become friendly with an American inventor, Thomas Adams. Adams was intrigued by the General's habit of chewing chicle, the gum from the evergreen *Manilkara* tree, something Mexicans had been doing since the times of the Mayan Empire. Adams hoped to make it into a cheap rubber substitute and bought a ton of chicle from Santa Anna, just in case. He failed to make rubber, but discovered that, by adding sugar, he had a terrific new confectionery product: chewing gum. In 1871, he launched it as 'Adams New York No. 1'. His company later merged with Wrigley's. In 2006 the chewing-gum giant had a turnover of $4.6 billion and a 63 per cent global market share.

Santa Anna didn't make a peseta from his role as father of American chewing. In 1874 he was finally allowed back into Mexico. In the two decades since he had left, the country had been plunged into civil war and had had an Austrian puppet emperor imposed on them by the French. Now the liberals were back in power. President Benito Juárez was the first indigenous Amerindian (and the first civilian) to govern Mexico. He ignored Santa Anna's return: there was to be no re-entry to political life for him this time. The 'Napoleon of the West' died, almost blind and penniless, stripped of property and honours, in Mexico City in 1876. His wooden leg remains in exile. Several attempts to return it have foundered: the last received a frosty response from a historian at the National Museum in Mexico. Santa Anna, he said, was a theatrical opportunist who only looked out for himself: 'Returning the leg wouldn't mean much. We do not want the leg returned.'

Did the loss of a leg profoundly alter the course of Santa Anna's life? Probably not. Was it a defining moment? Without doubt. The lost limb was the symbol of his self-appointed role as saviour of his country, a kind of visual proof of his canonisation. At the same time, as with Stuyvesant, it became a national joke. Santa Anna's life, with its vanity, cruelty and lack of integrity, nonetheless has a compelling quality: rather as if Casanova had put his energy into politics instead of sex. Though the immortal national hero status he lusted after was ultimately denied him, how many people have ever inspired a sea shanty?

> *O! Santianna had a wooden leg*
> *Heave away, Santianna!*
> *He used it for a cribbage peg*
> *All on the plains of Mexico*
>
> *O! Santianna's day is o'er,*
> *Heave away, Santianna!*
> *Santianna will fight no more.*
> *All on the plains of Mexico!*

~

There are no songs dedicated to the 'surprising Corpulency' of **Daniel Lambert** (1770–1809), but for a while his name was the universal cliché for anything big. London was 'the Daniel Lambert of cities' and any especially erudite scholar, the 'Daniel Lambert of learning'. There have been heavier men since – but not many, and none as fondly remembered. Perhaps for this reason he has kept an honourable mention in the *Guinness Book of Records*. When he died, aged thirty-nine, he weighed almost 53 stones (335 kg) and his waist was 9' 4" (284 cm) in circumference. In today's terms that would give him a Body Mass Index of 104 – three times the level at which obesity kicks in. Quite how he got so large was as much a puzzle to him as to others. He didn't eat to excess and drank only water. He just kept getting bigger.

Obesity is not a modern phenomenon, although it has become a modern obsession. Today, in Britain and America, one in four adults is obese and the costs (in terms of healthcare and lost earning potential) runs into hundreds of billions. Cheap food has meant that, for the first time in history, the bottom 20 per cent of earners are, on average, more obese than the top 20 per cent . The diet industry in the US alone is valued at $60 billion per annum, more than the global turnover of Microsoft and McDonald's combined. This double hysteria – overeating then trying to lose weight again – is a long way from rural Leicestershire in the late eighteenth century.

Lambert came from a cheerful lower-middle-class family. None of the rest of his relatives was in the least remarkable, either in size or achievement. His father was keeper of the Leicester County 'bridewell', or house of correction. Bridewells got their name from the original Bridewell in the city of London, first a royal palace, then a hospital and finally a prison. They were run by local magistrates and were used to keep the streets clear of vagrants, idlers and minor offenders. Keepers were salaried but were allowed to supplement their income by hiring out inmates as a source of cheap local labour. Lambert's institution had eight rooms, three for men and five for women (it wasn't considered appropriate for women to share a room).

Daniel grew up living the active, outdoor life of a Leicestershire countryman. He was a passionate devotee of cock-fighting and hare-coursing, rode with the hunt and taught children to swim in the River Soar. He matured quickly, reaching almost six feet tall in his teens. He was also extremely strong; said to be able to carry huge cartwheels and quarter-ton weights and swim with two men clinging to his back. Once Lambert's dog attacked a dancing bear that was due to perform in the town. The bear had retaliated and, to encourage some sport, its handlers removed its muzzle. When they refused Lambert's request to restrain the bear, he felled it with a single blow to the jaw and rescued his dog.

When Lambert's father retired, Daniel took over the running of the prison. He was well liked by his charges, working hard to improve their living conditions and ensure all of them were treated fairly; there are even reports of inmates crying with gratitude for his kindness as they left. The only problem with the job was that it didn't involve much more than sitting on his seat in the street outside the prison. He became a popular character in Leicester, puffing on a pipe of tobacco, striking up conversations with people as they passed or swapping tips about breeding fighting cocks and greyhounds. It was this sudden transition to a sedentary life that Lambert blamed for his rapid weight gain, but it's probable he suffered from a metabolic disorder. Within two years he weighed 32 stones and was too big to find a horse that would carry his weight. Even simple physical tasks started to exhaust him: it was easier to sit and watch the world go by. In 1803 a prison inspector noted Lambert's 'constitutional propensity to ease . . . He is spoken of as a humane, benevolent man but I thought him a very improper person to be the Keeper of a prison.'

Then, in 1805, the Leicester magistrates decided to close the correction house and set the inmates to forced labour instead. Lambert was awarded a one-off annuity of £50 as a thank-you, but this wasn't enough for him to live on (it would be worth about £4,000 today). He was now thirty-five years old and his weight had crept up to 50 stone, making it impossible for him to find work. He couldn't even squeeze into a standard-sized coach to visit the races. By the end of the year, out of money and deprived by his immense size of the hobbies he loved, Lambert found himself practically housebound. Things weren't helped by a string of visitors wanting to see if the rumours of Leicester's 'Human Colossus' were true. One pushy man from Nottingham pressed for admission on the grounds that he had a particular favour to ask. Lambert eventually let him in only for the man to ask the pedigree of a local mare, information readily available from the owner. Lambert, who had by now developed a smart line in witty put downs, answered, 'Oh! If that's all, she was got by Impertinence out of Curiosity.'

Annoying as these visitations were, they helped him conceive a plan. In early 1806, he surprised everyone by renting a house on Piccadilly in London. He announced his arrival with a flurry of handbills and newspaper adverts: for the price on one shilling, the gentlefolk of London would be able to enjoy an audience with 'the Heaviest Man in Britain'. Lambert had decided that, as his condition prevented him from working, he would turn people's nosiness into an income. He had strict rules: politeness was an absolute pre-requisite, and gentlemen were ejected if they refused to remove their hats. He did what he could to defuse the invasiveness of some people's questions with humour. When a young beau accosted him by peering through the fashionable device of a quizzing glass (a monocle on a long stick) and asking what he most disliked, he retorted, 'To be bored by a quizzing glass.' A woman who asked him how much his enormous red coat cost was told, with a twinkle, 'If you think it proper to make the present of a new coat, you will then know exactly what it costs, madam.' With rudeness, he operated a zero-tolerance policy: a man who accused him of paying too much attention to the lady guests was threatened with immediate defenestration. His 'act', was simply to tell amusing stories, discuss the news of the day, and pick over in detail the qualities of particular horses or packs of hounds. He did brisk business on the side, selling his own lines of pedigree pointers and spaniels. His pet terrier was so admired he was once offered a hundred guineas for it – equivalent to over £8,000 today – but he refused, pleading that it was his closest and most loyal companion. A visit to Lambert became a must for every fashionable Londoner and some afternoons as many as 400 people would pass through his house. *The Times* wrote admiringly:

> *To find a man of his uncommon dimensions possessing great information, manners the most affable and pleasing, and a perfect ease and facility in conversation, exceeded our expectations, high as they had been raised. The female spectators were greater in proportion than those of the other sex, and not a few of them have been heard to declare, how much they admired his manly and intelligent countenance.*

For all his handsome profile and his witty conversation, there is no record of Lambert ever having had a romantic attachment. He was not, by this point in his life, built for love:

> *When sitting he appears to be a stupendous mass of flesh, for his thighs are so covered by his belly that nothing but his knees are to be seen, while the flesh of his legs, which resemble pillows, projects in such a manner as to nearly bury his feet.*

One of his regular visitors was the celebrated Polish dwarf, Count Joseph Borulawski, whose 'entertainment' Lambert remembered visiting in Birmingham when he was an able-bodied apprentice, twenty years earlier. Standing to show the count his full bulk, the tiny visitor grasped one of his calves (by then over three feet in circumference) and exclaimed, '*Ah mein Gott*! Pure flesh and blood. I feel de warm. No deception! I am pleased: for I did hear it was deception.' In turn, Lambert asked if his (normal-sized) wife was still alive. 'No she is dead,' the midget replied. 'I am not very sorry, for when I affronted her, she put me on the mantel-shelf for punishment.'

Lambert returned to Leicester later that year wealthy and famous. Through his excellent manners and his cheerfulness, he had turned the nightmare of his condition to good account. Most important of all, he had done it on his own terms, escaping the horrors of the freak show. Even allowing for a more tolerant attitude to fatness than in our own diet-obsessed times, Lambert was considered an astonishing phenomenon, in the words of the *Morning Post*, 'the acme of mortal hugeness'. But perhaps because of his dignity and his utter lack of self-pity, he became a symbol of British pride. Rather like a champion bull, his size and good nature showed off the best of the national character. In a cartoon of April 1806 a gargantuan Lambert is shown taunting the amazed (and tiny) Napoleon:

*I am a true born Englishman from the county of Leicester – a quiet mind and good constitution nourished by the good air of Britain makes every Englishman thrive.*

In another, Napoleon eats a small bowl of soup while Lambert feasts on a round of roast beef, with a bowl of mustard, a whole loaf and a foaming pot of stout. No further caption was needed. Here was John Bull in all his splendour.

Over the next two years, Lambert toured the country in a specially reinforced coach to exhibit himself in provincial cities such as Birmingham, Cambridge and York, as well as twice returning to London. But the constant travelling took a toll on his health and he started to make plans for his retirement. In September 1809, he returned to Stamford in Lincolnshire for what would be his last residency. He loved the Stamford race meeting and in the times when he was merely huge rather than vast, he had enjoyed laying bets in the town's many pubs that, given a small head start, he could win a race from one end of Stamford to the other. The town was a maze of narrow alleys, and he knew that, once he got ahead of people, he could literally block their passage and they would never be able to get past him.

As he could no longer climb stairs, he had taken a room on the ground floor of the Wagon & Horses inn and sent a droll note to the *Stamford Mercury* asking them to send someone to take an order for printed handbills announcing his arrival: 'As the mountain could not wait on Mahomet, Mahomet would go to the mountain.' The printer came and though Lambert complained of being tired, he seemed full of enthusiasm for his appointments the next day. The following morning he was about to shave when he complained to the landlord that he was finding breathing difficult. Ten minutes later he was dead. There was no autopsy but the likelihood is that he suffered a massive blood clot to his lungs. Two days later he was buried, the *Mercury* commenting that 'his remains had been kept quite as long as was prudent'.

Burying Lambert was a feat of engineering. It took 112 feet of elm wood to construct his gargantuan square coffin and the entire wall of his hotel room had to be dismantled to get him out. The coffin was fitted with axles and wheeled slowly down towards the church, where a huge crowd had gathered. It took twenty men half an hour to lower Daniel Lambert into the grave. His friends paid for a memorial that carried this affectionate epitaph:

*In Remembrance of that PRODIGY in NATURE DANIEL LAMBERT a native of LEICESTER who was possessed of an exalted and convivial Mind and, in personal Greatness had no COMPETITOR*

It is a fitting tribute to a decent man. The famous Leicestershire horse-trainer Dick Christian remarked that Lambert 'was a cheery man in company but shyish of being looked at'. By pure force of character he had overcome his shyness, and the shame and discomfort of his size, to become a national hero. Today, the local tourist office proudly bills him as 'Leicester's largest son'.

~

The relaxed jollity that Daniel Lambert managed throughout his short life would elude **Florence Nightingale (1820–1910)** until the very end of hers. Most people now have an inkling that the 'ministering angel' or 'Lady with the lamp' image hides a more complex reality, but it still comes as a shock to learn that she spent more than half her life not as a nurse but as an invalid, much of it bedridden in her Mayfair flat.

The precise nature of this illness has been the cause of much speculation. She did her best to keep up appearances and would, on most days, get washed and dressed before retiring to the bed again, ready to receive a maximum of one visitor a day, if strictly necessary. But she also kept herself manically busy. Perpetually armed with a pen and writing paper, she produced books, papers and a stream of correspondence with her family and famous friends, starting her working day as early as 5 a.m. In her life, she wrote more than 14,000 letters, although many of the most personal ones she marked 'Private. Burn.' Most of what we now associate her with – the foundation of modern nursing practice and improved standards of hygiene – were products of her years in bed rather than her brief stay in the Crimea. In the century since her death, biographers and historians have variously accused her of malingering, of strategic invalidism in order to manipulate others, of hypochondria and even neurotic lesbianism. More charitably, she has also been retrospectively diagnosed with post-traumatic stress disorder, manic depression, schizophrenia (because she claimed to hear God's voice) and chronic fatigue syndrome.

The medical evidence all points to the fact that she was properly ill. Her physical symptoms are consistent with the bacterial infection we now call brucellosis (then known as Crimea or Mediterranean fever), which she probably picked up by drinking unpasteurised milk while working in the military hospital during the war. Without treatment it leads to long-term health problems, consistent with those that Florence Nightingale experienced in later life. From 1861–8 she was especially unwell, and had to be carried from room to room. Her own descriptions of her symptoms are terse but telling. In 1863 she complained of 'over pressure of the brain'; in 1865, it was 'rheumatism of the spine and right elbow'. That year she also experienced 'great breathlessness,' and in 1866 'spasms of the lungs'. By 1867, she was 'bereft of an ounce of strength' and, in 1868, 'felt as if the top of my head was blown off'. In 1879, she complained of 'rapid palpitations' and 'ninety hours without sleep'.

But these physiological symptoms, though undoubtedly real, masked a strong psychological component. Her compulsive attitude to work and desire to hide from the world were the outward expression of an inner turmoil that stretched back deep into her childhood. Florence's early life was apparently happy and balanced. Her parents were kind and loving and the family was well off, with houses in Derbyshire, Hampshire and London. Her parent's home was part of a lively intellectual scene that encompassed theologians, social reformers, historians and artists. The Nightingales were Unitarians, liberal Christians who believed in a single, beneficent God, but also in science and progress. William Nightingale had named his younger daughter Florence after the city of her birth, establishing it for the first time as a popular name for girls. Until then it had been a boy's name. Her sister, born a year earlier in Naples, got saddled with Parthenope, the Greek name for that city, which (so far at least) has not caught on to the same extent. William undertook the education of his two daughters himself, and it was apparent from the start that Florence was academically exceptional: brilliant at languages, arts and sciences. This, however, was to prove a constant source of tension in her life. For much of it, she was by far the brightest person in any room and she knew it. 'I must overcome my desire to shine in company,' she wrote in her diary while still a teenager. She was also attractive. The novelist Mrs. Gaskell described her as: 'tall, willowy in figure, [with] thick shortish rich brown hair, a delicate complexion, and grey eyes that are generally pensive but could be the merriest'. Her profile in *The Times* makes her sound almost too perfect, 'a young lady of singular endowments . . . her attainments are extraordinary'.

Florence Nightingale didn't have the horrors of poverty, neglect or abuse to contend with, yet she was plagued by fits of depression and suicidal self-loathing – a typical diary entry reads 'In my thirty-first year, I see nothing desirable but death'. The source of her unhappiness was her deep sense of being at odds with the stultifying social requirements and hypocrisy of the world she had grown up in. Far from the stiff-collared, sharp-tongued martinet of popular legend, the young Florence was like the heroine of a Mrs Gaskell or George Eliot novel: fiercely bright, passionate, and headstrong. She was desperate to be loved, but couldn't bear the idea of falling into the same polite, bourgeois trap as her parents:

> *It is not surprising that husbands and wives seem so little part of one another. It is surprising that there is so much love as there is. For there is no food for it. What does it live upon – what nourishes it? Husbands and wives never seem to have anything to say to one another. What do they talk about? Not about any great religious, social, political questions or feelings. They talk about who shall come to dinner, who is to live in this lodge and who in that, about the improvement of the place, or when they shall go to London . . . But any real communion between husband and wife – any descending into the depths of their being, and drawing out thence what they find and comparing it – do we ever dream of such a thing? Yes, we may dream of it during the season of 'passion,' but we shall not find it afterwards. We even expect it to go off, and lay our account that it will. If the husband has, by chance, gone into the depths of his being, and found there anything unorthodox, he, oftenest, conceals it carefully from his wife, – he is afraid of 'unsettling her opinions'.*

This passage is from a book called *Cassandra*, written when she was in her early thirties but, on the advice of her learned male friends, never published. At various times a novel, a philosophical dialogue between two sisters and a heartfelt polemic, it is the most complete statement of her belief that only work make would sense of her life. It is one of the great feminist texts of the nineteenth century, intellectually and emotionally intelligent but so raw that later writers found hard it to swallow. Virginia Woolf acknowledged its influence but thought it 'a shriek of nervous agony'.

The more of Florence Nightingale's work one reads, the more one senses that, had she been born a man, she might have become a great moral philosopher like John Stuart Mill or a respected historian like Thomas Carlyle (both of whom admired her writing). Instead, she grew up in a household where men idly theorised and women wasted their lives 'looking at prints, doing worsted work and reading little books'. Acutely conscious as a child of the suffering of the Victorian poor, from the age of six she set her mind on 'a profession, a trade, a necessary occupation, something to fill and employ all my faculties'. Only this could liberate her 'from the accumulation of nervous energy which has had nothing to do during the day' and which makes women feel 'every night, when they go to bed, as if they are going mad.'

At the age of sixteen Florence had a religious experience in which 'God had called her to his service'. This didn't mean fiddling around doing charity work at her local church: it meant using her hands and brain to right the wrongs of the world. She asked her parents if they would support her intention to go into nursing. They were horrified and refused. In fact, her mother Fanny fainted at the shock of what her youngest daughter was suggesting. 'We are ducks,' she later lamented 'who have hatched a wild swan.' So Florence continued to live at home and tried to escape the glacial atmosphere in the house by plunging herself into a study of mysticism. Over the next decade, she would develop her own theology, which she outlined in another book that was destined to remain unpublished, *Suggestions for Thought to the Searchers after Truth among the Artizans of England*. Her studies took her far beyond the shores of Christianity – one wonders how many other English women in the 1850s would ever conceive of writing to a friend: 'You must go to Mahometanism, to Buddhism, to the East, to the Sufis & Fakirs, to Pantheism, for the right growth of mysticism.' At the same time, she dutifully fulfilled her social obligations and entertained a string of enthusiastic suitors.

Her most persistent male admirer was Richard Monckton Milnes, a literary patron and minor poet, who was also the MP for Pontefract. He was a good friend of Tennyson's, the first biographer of John Keats, and the man who introduced the work of Ralph Waldo Emerson to Britain. On the face of it, he was the perfect match for Florence: clever, well connected and wealthy. He obviously thought himself the right man for the job: he patiently paid court to her for nine years. She was also clearly tempted by him:

> *I have an intellectual nature which requires satisfaction, and that would find it in him. I have a passional nature which requires satisfaction, and that would find it in him. I have a moral, an active nature which requires satisfaction, and that would not find it in his life. Sometimes I think I will satisfy my passional nature at all events, because that will at least secure me from the evil of dreaming. But would it? I could be satisfied to spend a life with him in combining our different powers in some great object. I could not satisfy this nature by spending a life with him in making society and arranging domestic things.*

By early 1849 Mr Monckton Milnes decided he needed a definite answer. She said no. Her parents were furious and Florence tortured herself with remorse:

*I know that if I were to see him again . . . the very thought of doing so quite overcomes me. I know that since I refused him not one day has passed without my thinking of him, that life is desolate without his sympathy.*

By the end of the year, she was in a state of near mental collapse and friends of the family offered to take her on a trip through Greece and Egypt. 1850 was her thirtieth year and she was determined to make it a turning point:

*To-day I am 30 — the age Christ began his mission. Now no more childish things. No more love. No more marriage. Now Lord let me think only of Thy Will, what Thou wiliest me to do.*

But her diary of the year is anything but a peaceful acceptance of God's will. She was obviously still being assailed by 'the evil of dreaming':

*March 15:* God has delivered me from the greatest offence and the constant murder of all my thoughts.
*March 21:* Left the boat ringing our hands. Such a delicious hour in the gardens of Heliopolis – where Plato walked and Moses prayed. Undisturbed by my great enemy.
*June 7:* But this long moral death, this failure of all attempts to cure. I think I have never been so bad as this last week.
*June 12:* To Megara! Alas it matters little where I go – sold as I am to the enemy – Whether in London or Athens, it is all alike to me.
*June 17:* After a sleepless night physically and morally ill and

broken down, a slave – glad to leave Athens. I have no wish on earth but sleep.

*June 18:* I had no wish, no enemy, I longed but for sleep. My enemy is too strong for me, everything has been tried. All, all is vain.

*June 21:* Two delightful days at Corfu. My enemy let me go. I lived again, in both body and mind. Oh! today, how lovely it was, how poetic – and I was free

*June 29:* Four long days of absolute slavery.

*June 30:* I cannot write a letter, can do nothing.

*July 1:* I lay in bed at night and called upon God to save me. My soul spoke to His & I was comforted.

These enigmatic entries read very like the tortured spiritual travails of the Christian mystics she had studied: St Teresa of Avila or St John of the Cross. Like them, she often refers to God as her 'husband'. There is more here than just religious ecstasy. No one can be fully sure what the 'dreaming' that so disturbed her at night was, but it seems most likely to have been sexual fantasy, possibly even masturbation. In rejecting Milnes, she was rejecting marriage itself, and, by extension, sex. She makes it plain that she was physically attracted to Milnes and we will never know what passed between them privately. He was certainly not a sexual innocent: after he died it was revealed that he had one of the largest collections of erotic literature ever assembled, with a particular fondness for the works of the Marquis de Sade. Her embrace of mysticism, of marriage with God, may well have offered her a way of sublimating some of this energy. But by the end of the year, she was convinced that the solution to her 'dreaming' was to keep her hands and her mind busy.

In 1851 she went to Kaiserswerth Hospital in Germany to take a basic three-month course in nursing with the Institute for Protestant Deaconesses. This was a revelation to her: 'The nursing there was nil, the hygiene horrible,' she later wrote, '...But never have I met with a higher tone, a purer devotion than there. There was no neglect.' She followed this with a stint with the Sisters of Mercy near Paris, but on her return home, plunged into another depression in which she hardly ever stirred from her bed. The family doctor persuaded her parents that moving her out of the house would be good for Florence's 'nerves' and in 1853 she was appointed superintendent of the Institution for Sick Gentlewomen in Distressed Circumstances at Harley Street in London. An outbreak of cholera in nearby Soho allowed her to demonstrate for the first time her flair for administration and unflappability under pressure as she helped local hospitals manage the huge flood of patients.

Towards the end of 1853 Britain became embroiled in the Crimea, siding with France to support Turkey against Russia. Newspaper reports alerted the British public to the poor standards of care given to the troops evacuated from the Crimean peninsula to Scutari in Turkey. Sidney Herbert, a close friend of Florence's, was appointed Secretary of State for War and asked her if she would lead a party of British nurses to the war zone. In November 1854 she arrived at the Barrack Hospital with thirty-eight nurses and proceeded to re-organise it from top to bottom. Fresh air, cleanliness, good diet and exercise were her principles, and in the midst of the chaos and the stench, her nurses were impeccably turned out and records were kept with a military precision. Florence led from the front, covering four miles each evening walking through the wards, helping injured soldiers to write letters home and checking on their welfare. Although she was always more of a nursing theoretician than an actual swiller-out of bed-pans or bandager of wounds, these nocturnal walks are what gave rise to her legend among the troops and the public back home.

Her first few months at Scutari were disastrous. Death-rates at the hospital soared and even nurses and doctors succumbed to disease. The death-rate only began to drop when the sewerage system had been overhauled and the source of infection was removed. Nightingale didn't make this connection herself until the war had ended. She returned to London in 1856 a heroine and, despite being traumatised and ill, threw all her energy behind getting a Royal Commission on army health established. She met Queen Victoria and Prince Albert to press her case. Afterwards the Queen remarked 'What a head! If only we could have her at the War Office.' Her efforts paid off and Sidney Herbert was appointed to chair the Commission.

In 1858 Florence submitted her evidence to the Commission in the form of an 830-page report, *Notes on Matters Affecting the Health, Efficiency, and Hospital Administration of the British Army*. Appended to it was what she called her 'coxcomb' of statistical diagrams, devised with the help of William Farr, head of the General Registry Office. This included her famous 'polar area diagram', a kind of pie chart which has since become a standard of statistical graphics. What the figures and diagrams showed came as a profound shock. During the first awful winter of the war, soldiers had been three times more likely to die in Scutari than they had been in the basic field hospitals at the front. What had killed most of the soldiers in the Crimea wasn't their wounds, but infections caused by poor sanitary conditions on the wards. Scutari, as one historian put it, was more of a death camp than a hospital. Florence was mortified. If she had overhauled the sewerage and general hygiene sooner, thousands of soldiers' lives might have been saved. All the hand-holding and ward-walking had been beside the point. In an agony of trepidation she put forward her report, fully expecting 'the Lady of the Lamp' to be exposed as a fraud: 'The lamp shows me only my utter shipwreck.' The report was never published. Although its conclusions framed British policy on hospital hygiene and nursing practice for generations to come, the government decided that to present the full weight of the evidence would be too damaging to national morale. This was too late to save Florence. The stress of preparing the figures, the weight of personal blame she felt, and the symptoms of her worsening brucellosis led to a physical collapse and she came close to death. At the age of thirty-seven she took to her bed and never really emerged again.

Nonetheless, her fame and her influence grew steadily. From her bed in Mayfair, insulated from the disruptions of her family, she directed the course of health, hygiene and sanitation all over the world. A public collection in her name raised £45,000 and was used to set up the Nightingale School of Nursing at St Thomas's Hospital in London. She became the first woman to be made a Fellow of the Royal Statistical Society (her experience in Scutari had taught her that 'statistics were the measure of God's purpose'). In 1860 she published *Notes on Nursing: What It Is, and What It Is Not,* a book that made her 'fresh air and cleanliness' gospel available to everyone. Although she rarely ventured out, she corresponded with many of the most famous people of her time, including Mrs Gaskell, General Gordon (of Khartoum), William Gladstone and Harriet Beecher Stowe. As far as romantic entanglements went, the closest she came to that was a long and witty correspondence with Benjamin Jowett, the Master of Balliol College in Oxford, who became her spiritual confessor, encouraging her to write the last in her now tall pile of unpublished books, *Notes from Devotional Authors of the Middle Ages*, a history of mysticism. He called her 'Florence the First, Empress of Scavengers, Queen of Nurses, Reverend Mother Superior of the British Army, Governess of the Governor of India'. She responded with: 'Maid of all dirty work rather, or, the Nuisances Removal Act, that's me.' As Lytton Strachey remarked, 'She remained an invalid, but an invalid of a curious character – an invalid who was too weak to walk downstairs and who worked far harder than most Cabinet Ministers.'

Against all odds, Florence Nightingale outlived the misery of her condition. She died in her sleep at the age of ninety, shortly after becoming the first woman to receive the Order of Merit. In the last two decades of her life, she had mellowed. The intellectual arrogance, the not-suffering-fools-gladly impatience and the perfectionism that had driven her faded, and she became an indulgent, eccentric old lady, devoted to her cats. Animals had always been a solace to her and she had often recommended the healing power of pets to her patients. For a while she had shared her life with a small owl she had found while visiting the ruins of the Parthenon in 1850. A fledgling, it was being tormented by some Greek boys after falling from its nest. Florence gave them a farthing and kept the owl, which she named Athena. It lived in a bag in her coat-pocket during the day and flew around the house at night. But cats were her constant companions during the long years spent in bed. She owned more than sixty over the years, including Quiz, Muff, Dr Pusey and Bismarck. As enigmatic, self-contained and sedentary as a cat herself, you can see why she liked them:

# Grin and Bear It

*I learned the lesson of life from a little kitten, one of two. The old cat comes in and says, 'What are you doing here, I want my missus to myself.' The bigger kitten runs away. The little one stands her ground, and when the old enemy comes near, kisses his nose and makes the peace. That is the lesson of life: kiss your enemy's nose while standing your ground.*

~

Few people have stood their ground like Florence Nightingale. She once boasted she had never been 'swayed by a personal consideration.' Her body may have let her down, but she always knew her own mind. The Portuguese writer **Fernando Pessoa** (1888–1935) suffered from an entirely different affliction. He had a hundred different minds to choose from. Like Florence Nightingale he was a depressive who died a virgin. He was also an alcoholic hypochondriac who died of liver failure at forty-seven. He had published almost nothing. The problem with Pessoa, though, is, who exactly was 'he'?

After Pessoa died, a wooden trunk was discovered containing more than 25,000 handwritten sheets of his work, much of it still unsorted to this day. The archive contains both poetry and prose, everything from horoscopes to detective stories. The contents established him as one of the great poets of the twentieth century, or maybe several of the great poets – the work was written by Pessoa's hand but under more than a hundred different names – not mere pseudonyms but individual literary identities who wrote in consistently different styles. Pessoa said that the names were not synonyms but 'heteronyms'. He described his alter egos as 'non-existent acquaintances'.

Pessoa began creating heteronyms aged six, writing letters to himself in French from 'Le Chevalier de Pas'. His best-known creations are Alberto Caeiro (1889–1915), whom he described as 'an ingenious unlettered man who lived in the country and died of TB', and Ricardo Reis, a doctor who wrote classical odes. There was also Alvaro de Campos – a monocle-wearing existentialist and naval engineer who liked writing in free verse. Caeiro, Reis and de Campos even wrote about each other's work, dissecting it and being critical when needed. Some of the minor heteronyms were exotic, like the Baron of Tieve, a suicidal aristocrat, or Jean Seul de Méluret, a French essayist with an interest in dancing girls. Only one of Pessoa's heteronyms was a woman – Maria José, a tubercular hunchback with crippled legs who pined after a handsome metalworker who passed by her apartment every day.

Pessoa's best-known identity is Bernardo Soares who wrote most of *The Book of Disquiet*, a remarkable sprawling biography that reads, in part, like a diary and was published long after Pessoa's death. In his letters, Pessoa referred to the book as 'a pathological production' and a 'factless autobiography'. At the beginning of the book he wrote, 'These are my confessions, and if in them I say nothing, it is because I have nothing to say.' Soares's personality, said Pessoa, 'is not my own, but it doesn't differ from it, but is a mere mutilation of it'. He said Soares 'appears when I am tired and sleepy, when my inhibitions are slightly suspended; that prose is a constant daydreaming'. This might sound more like fun than misfortune, but that would be to miss the quiet desperation of much of Pessoa's life, a pain he numbed with drink. It also assumes that he was in control of his heteronyms, which it seems he wasn't. That is what makes him so fascinating. As far as we can tell he wasn't suffering from a psychological condition like schizophrenia or multiple personality disorder, but his 'possession' was so extreme and complete that it chips away at our stable notions of 'self' and 'personality'. In his influential essay, 'Tradition and the Individual Talent', another great poet, T. S. Eliot, makes a very pertinent observation:

> *Poetry is not a turning loose of emotion, but an escape from emotion; it is not the expression of personality, but an escape from personality. But, of course, only those who have personality and emotions know what it means to want to escape from these things.*

What was Pessoa escaping from?

He had spent much of his childhood in South Africa: his stepfather was the Portuguese consul in Durban. As a result, he became bilingual in Portuguese and English from the age of seven. His father had died from tuberculosis two years earlier (the year before Fernando created his first heteronym), and the following year he lost his younger brother too. His mother and stepfather soon produced two half-sisters and two half-brothers, but the rapid disappearance of his original family left Fernando feeling isolated and rejected.

At school in Durban he excelled, winning poetry prizes and creating his own 'newspaper' in which he wrote all the stories and drew all the illustrations under the name Alexander Search. By the time he was fourteen he was sending riddles to a newspaper in Lisbon under the pseudonym 'Dr Pancrácio' (Dr Simpleton). When his mother took the family back to Portugal in 1902 he sent newspaper articles in the opposite direction – to a Durban newspaper written under the name 'Tagus' or signed with the initials J. G. H. C. or as Charles Robert Anon.

When Pessoa's grandmother died in 1907 she left him some money. He used this to set up a small printing company called 'Ibis', but it soon failed. Few anecdotes survive about him, but his half-brother Joao said that Fernando used to embarrass the family by staggering along the street, swinging on lamp-posts pretending to be drunk. Standing on one leg he would shout out 'I am an ibis'. It's fairly tame behaviour for a twentieth-century poet, but in the staid confines of Lisbon society it probably seemed extreme. Later on, Pessoa didn't need to pretend to be drunk, as alcohol increasingly took over his life.

Pessoa's rejection of self is fascinating, especially as, of all ironies, *pessóa* means 'person' in Portuguese. (His name should properly be spelt Pessóa but he removed the accent over the 'o' because it felt more cosmopolitan.) Outside his immediate family Pessoa seems to have had no close friendships. He eked out a living as a translator, working for businesses that needed to conduct relationships with English speakers, and kept himself to himself in a set of small, furnished rooms in the old city of Lisbon. 'Bernardo Soares' explained:

> *The idea of any social obligation – going to a funeral, discussing an office matter with someone, going to the station to wait for someone I know or don't know – the mere idea disturbs a whole day's thoughts.*

When he was thirty-two he formed an attachment with a young woman of nineteen named Ophelia Queiroz. There was probably no physical side to the relationship, he just wrote to her under different heteronyms for nine months and then broke it off. Almost a decade later, he made contact with Ophelia again but once more stopped communicating suddenly and refused to answer her letters. He also wrote to the English occultist Aleister Crowley, assisting him fake his own suicide when he visited Lisbon in 1930. Crowley must have found him beguiling. Pessoa would be gripped by what he called 'automatic writing' where he transcribed communications from the Other Side. He also received messages from his dead uncle, from the English philosopher Henry More (1614–87), from an inscrutable entity called 'Wardour' and occasionally from Count Alessandro di Cagliostro (q.v.). Some of these spirits rather sensibly urged Pessoa to stop masturbating and encouraged him to lose his virginity. He ignored their advice. Pessoa himself ridiculed the idea that actual spirits were getting in touch with him, but said he liked the fact that he could ask them for advice. They provided him with the social contact he couldn't get from real people. For Pessoa, the only true reality was the one he (or, in this case, Soares again) created for himself:

> *The experience of life teaches nothing, just as history teaches nothing. True experience consists in restricting our contact with reality and increasing our analysis of that contact. In that way our sensibility extends and deepens itself, because everything is within us; all we have to do is look for it and know how to look for it.*

Pessoa was twenty-six when he was first seriously 'possessed' by one of his heteronyms. He was standing beside a chest of drawers when he was overcome by the urge to write poetry. Standing upright at the chest he pumped out thirty poems in quick succession, entitling the collection 'The Keeper of Sheep' and signing it 'Albert Caeiro'. He compared the experience to being in a trance, saying 'my master had appeared inside me'.

The literary critic Cyril Connolly once said that Pessoa 'hived off separate personalities like swarms of bees', but these were only apparent on the page: they were never shared with anyone else. Pessoa was a loner. He dined in the same restaurant every day for thirty years.

> *If after I die, they want to write my biography,*
> *There is nothing more simple.*
> *There are only two dates: my day of birth, day of death.*
> *Between one and the other all the days are mine.*

Eerily, it was Alvaro de Campos (the monocle-wearing existentialist) who said, 'Fernando Pessoa, strictly speaking, didn't exist.' The man called 'person', with over a hundred different personalities, spent almost his entire life denying his own existence.

Like so many bright children denied proper affection from their parents, Pessoa read his way out of the lonely realities that surrounded him. The bustling pages of Dickens were a particular favourite:

> *There are children who really suffer because they weren't able to live in real life with Mister Pickwick and could not shake hands with Mister Wardle. I am one of them. I have wept real tears over that novel, for not having lived in that time, with those people, real people.*

Again this is not Fernando Pessoa but 'Bernardo Soares'. Pessoa read the novels but Soares wrote about them. When reading any of Pessoa's authors, the constant danger is to mistake the mask for the man. Though Soares wrote 'I will never write a page that will reveal me or reveal anything else', Pessoa actually revealed a great deal. He is a unique writer – one who can be uniquely described as 'multiply unique' – because he delivers so many different styles, so many ideas, such a rich mix of insights and possibilities. It's almost as if he created his own self-referential literary tradition as both inspiration and company. His own life might have been sad, short and tragic, but every bit as much as Florence Nightingale or Daniel Lambert, he – or rather his team –turned his misfortune into something of lasting value:

*If a man only writes well when drunk, I would tell him: Get drunk. And if he said to me that his liver suffers because of that, I would answer: What is your liver? It's a dead thing that lives as long as you do, while the poems you write live forever.*

~

If Fernando Pessoa had more selves than he could handle, the English writer **Dawn Langley Simmons** (1937–2000) had only one, but she had two different bodies. In a life that veered wildly between vaudeville and Greek tragedy, she began her life as Gordon Langley Hall, the illegitimate son of Vita Sackville-West's chauffeur. Later, she was adopted by the English character actress, Margaret Rutherford and had one of the first sex change operations performed in America. In 1969 she broke another taboo by marrying her black butler in Charleston, South Carolina, the first legal mixed-race marriage in the state. As one of her obituaries commented: 'It is a measure of the ascending scale of prejudice that, of all her transgressions, it was her crossing of the racial divide that most shocked her Southern neighbours.'

Dawn Simmons was born either with both male and female genitalia, or –as she always insisted – with female genitalia that an adrenal abnormality had caused to look male. In any event, although she always felt female, her family brought her up to be a boy called Gordon. 'He' was raised by his grandmother Nelly Hall Ticehurst and spent the holidays at Sissinghurst, home of Vita Sackville-West and Harold Nicolson. As a small boy their son, the writer and publisher Nigel Nicolson, played with Gordon, known to everyone as 'Dinky'. Sackville-West was famously the inspiration for Virginia Woolf's novel *Orlando* (1928), in which a boy is transformed into a beautiful woman. Simmons would later write in her autobiography: 'Had she lived a little longer, Vita would have been intrigued to know that the child "Dinky", as she called me, would become a real-life Orlando.'

Gordon started writing early, having his first poem published at the age of four and his first interview – conducted sitting in Mae West's lap – appearing in the *Sussex Express* when she was nine. In 1953, his grandmother died and he emigrated to Canada, becoming a teacher on an Ojibwa native reservation. Despite having had periods through 'her' teens and 'his' voice not having broken, Gordon still at this stage appeared male, and wore a crew cut. He turned his experiences with the Ojibwa into a best-seller, *Me Papoose Sitter*, published in 1955, and soon after moved to New York, where he worked as a journalist and society biographer writing critically acclaimed lives of Mrs. Abraham Lincoln, Princess Margaret and Jackie Kennedy. Witty, eccentric and ostentatious, Gordon made friends across a very broad swathe of New York society, from fellow writers like Carson McCullers, to actresses like Joan Crawford and sportsmen like the boxer Sugar Ray Robinson. A distant relative, the wealthy painter Isabel Whitney, took to him at once and invited him to live with her in West 10th Street mansion. Here Gordon met

Margaret Rutherford, the matronly actress still best remembered as Madam Arcati, the medium in the 1945 film of Noël Coward's *Blithe Spirit*. Rutherford had come hoping to be cast in the role of the grandmother in the proposed film of *Me Papoose Sitter*, but was immediately smitten by the person of Gordon himself. She described him as 'a child . . . with large brown eyes inherited from some long dead Andalusian ancestor . . . a large green and red Amazon parrot named Marilyn on his shoulder.' When Isabel Whitney died of leukemia in 1962, Margaret Rutherford and her husband legally adopted Gordon. He was twenty-five.

Whitney left Gordon her house and $2 million estate. He used the proceeds to buy a faded 1840s pink stucco mansion in the gay neighbourhood of Charleston in South Carolina. Gordon displayed impeccable interior décor sense, filling the house with Chippendale and early American furniture and transforming the garden with designs sent over by Vita Sackville-West. He was regarded as a fixture in Charleston high society: an eligible, if undeniably camp, bachelor. He once threw a coming-out party for two of his dogs, where the pooches were displayed on velvet cushions, dressed in chenille, long gloves and pearls.

Then, in 1968, it all changed. Gordon checked himself into the brand new Gender Identity Clinic at Johns Hopkins University in Baltimore and underwent corrective genital surgery and a course in counselling. One of the psychiatric reports noted with a hint of foreboding that, despite her high intelligence, as far as men were concerned the newly female Dawn had 'the mind of a fourteen-year-old girl'. So it was to prove. She returned to Charleston as Dawn Pepita Hall, sporting 'a Dippity-Do hairstyle – a dowdy doppelganger of Jackie Kennedy' according to one neighbour – and within a very few months announced her engagement to a black motor mechanic, butler, and aspiring sculptor, John-Paul Simmons. 'His black hand touched my white one; it was as simple as that,' she wrote in her autobiography.

Charleston was outraged. Bomb threats meant the ceremony had to take place in their front parlour, and *Newsweek* claimed the event had 'shaken the Confederacy'. It certainly didn't shock Margaret Rutherford. She told *Time* magazine, 'I am delighted that Gordon has become a woman, and I am delighted that Dawn is to marry a man of another race, and I am delighted that Dawn is to marry a man of a lower station, but I understand the man is a Baptist!' She offered practical support, too, leaning on the then Archbishop of Canterbury, Geoffrey Fisher (with the help of her friend Tony Benn) to organise a second, English, ceremony in Hastings.

In Charleston, things went from bad to worse. The crate containing the couple's wedding presents, sent over from England, was deliberately set on fire in the street. The local police chief arrived personally to serve Simmons a ticket, claiming that the smouldering remains of the blaze (which his own men had swept into the street) were obstructing the highway. The couple's dogs were poisoned; they were shot at on the street for walking hand in hand; there were rumours of a Mafia contract taken out on Dawn's life. The birth of her daughter, Natasha, in 1972 was the final straw. Charleston denounced it as a stunt, but Margaret Rutherford was able to produce a Harley Street surgeon to confirm that Dawn Langley Simmons had a fully functioning womb. Shortly afterwards, the baby was attacked by an intruder who proceeded to rape Dawn and left her with a broken nose and severely injured arm. The Simmons's decided enough was enough and moved to Catskill, New York.

By then, however, their marriage had turned sour. John-Paul was drinking heavily. She claimed he was also beating her and selling her possessions to buy whisky. In 1974 he left her for another woman 'who had shot and killed her first husband', but soon afterwards was committed to a mental institution suffering from schizophrenia. Dawn divorced him, but continued to look after him until her death in 2000.

In 1981, when Dawn was still living as Gordon in Hudson, New York, working as a teacher in Catholic school, he/she was commissioned to write a biography of his/her adoptive mother, Margaret Rutherford. Her own autobiography *Dawn: A Charleston Legend* followed in 1995. Both were well received and widely reviewed. Dawn's final years were spent back in Charleston, with Natasha and her three granddaughters, to whom she was a proud and devoted granny. The city that had once tried to ruin her now happily accommodated her as a much loved, if slightly whacky, local celebrity.

After Dawn's autobiography was published in 1995, Nigel Nicolson wrote a moving piece about her in the *Spectator*. 'I have maligned her in the past, mocked her strange fate and refused to meet her,' he wrote. 'She had asked me for help in arranging an English marriage, and when she called on me, I hid.' He had even refused to meet her when he visited Charleston. It was only when he saw her interviewed on television and saw pictures of his own mother on her wall that he relented. 'For the first time, I was touched'. He added that, in spite of his unkind behaviour towards her, 'there is not a word of reproach for me in her book. Like everything else about Dinky, it is gallant, resilient and unfailingly generous.'

The unlikely and optimistic story of Dawn Langley Simmons

concludes this catalogue of men and women assailed by bizarre and unlooked for misfortune.

~

As we have seen, such disaster may not bring self-knowledge (Santa Anna), victory (Stuyvesant), love (Florence Nightingale), longevity (Lambert) or happiness (Pessoa) but (the appalling Santa Anna apart) it always produced a change for the better, giving each of them an assured place in history.

The Swiss psychologist Carl Jung believed that difficulties were necessary for health. They offer potential for change, most particularly a change of attitude. The Stoics of ancient Athens based a whole school of philosophy on this idea, but it is the German philosopher, Wilhelm von Humboldt (whose only misfortune was to have an even more brilliant and famous brother), who expressed it most succinctly:

> *I am more and more convinced that our happiness or un-happiness depends far more on the way we meet the events of life, than on the nature of those events themselves.*

# CHAPTER SEVEN

# The Monkey-keepers

*Cats and monkeys, monkeys and cats – all human life is there.*

HENRY JAMES

Unlike cats, monkeys demand active husbandry, deep pockets and endless patience. No one keeps a monkey by accident. More people than you might imagine have taken the job on. As well as the eight mentioned below, other notable monkey keepers include Peter the Great, Lord Byron, Alexander von Humboldt, Francis Galton, Meher Baba and Michael Jackson.

As Queen Victoria remarked after being introduced to Jenny the orang utan at London Zoo, monkeys and apes are 'frightfully and painfully and disagreeably human'. Monkeys are bonsai people: they remind us of ourselves.

The long and controversial career of **Oliver Cromwell** (1599–1658) almost didn't happen. His parents were regular visitors to Hinchingbrooke, the country estate of his grandfather, Henry, and it was there, shortly after Oliver was born, that he was abducted by grandpa's pet monkey. The creature grabbed the baby from his crib and made for the roof. Servants rushed to bring mattresses into the courtyard to soften his fall if the animal dropped him, but for several minutes the monkey ignored them, hopping from ridge to ridge with young Oliver clamped under his hairy arm. The assembled company at last enticed the beast down and the future Lord Protector of England was returned unharmed. There is no record of how they did it – though modern monkey-handlers recommend that a dish of jam usually does the trick.

As far as we know, Cromwell never kept a pet monkey himself – it would have been rather surprising if he had – but in the frontispiece of a 1664 satirical cookbook, purporting to be by his wife, Elizabeth, she appears with a monkey on her shoulder. The illustration portrays her as a plain-looking frump and the anonymous author refers to her throughout as 'Joan' (the stock name for a scullery maid), mockingly remarking that Whitehall had been turned into a dairy and that her 'sordid frugality and thrifty baseness' was 'a hundred times fitter for a barn than a palace'. The monkey on her shoulder is there to make a monkey out of Mrs Cromwell, letting everyone know she is a jumped-up country bumpkin and reminding readers of the old proverb, 'the higher the monkey climbs, the more your can see of its arse'.

~

For several centuries, monkeys had been the favoured pet of queens: 'Joan' Cromwell's monkey also implies that she was 'aping' her royal betters. Monkeys that appear in portraits of actual queens are coded symbols for lust, childish exuberance, bad decision-making or a weakness for the occult. All these qualities were brought together in the most famous of all monkey-owning queens, **Catherine de' Medici** (1519–89). Also known as 'The Black Queen', 'Madame La Serpente' and 'The Maggot from Italy's Tomb', she was the most powerful woman in Europe for over forty years.

Catherine was the great-granddaughter of Lorenzo the Magnificent, the man who bankrolled the Florentine Renaissance, but she didn't have an easy start in life. As a merchant's daughter, she was technically a commoner and, within weeks of her birth, an orphan too. Things looked up a little in 1523, when her cousin was elected Pope Clement VII. Aged only four, she became a bargaining chip in the endless marital poker game of European royal politics. Then, in 1527, the Medicis were overthrown in Florence. Catherine was taken hostage and imprisoned in a series of convents.

By the time she was twelve, she had been made to ride through the streets on a donkey jeered by an angry crowd and survived a planned attempt on her life which would have seen her lowered naked in a basket outside the city wall in an attempt to trick members of her own family to shoot at her. (They were besieging 'their' city at the time.) When Florence surrendered, Catherine was summoned to Rome by her papal cousin, who greeted her with tears in his eyes. Within months, he had wangled her engagement to Henry, Duke of Orleans, second in line to the French throne. Pope Clement was delighted. With the usual Medici gift for understatement, he proudly announced 'the greatest match in the world'.

Henry's father, Francis I, was also pleased and very keen to help. On the couple's wedding night in 1533 he stayed in their bedchamber until he was sure 'each had shown valour in the joust'. Despite this promising start, it was ten years before Catherine bore Henry a child. That she survived as his wife bears testimony to her strength of will and shrewd political instincts.

It certainly wasn't her looks that did it. Although she was said to have 'delicate features', she was short with a 'too large mouth' and the trademark bulging eyes of the Medici. Despite her trim figure and a beauty regime that involved applying a daily face mask of pigeon dung, the Venetian ambassador was moved to say that she looked good 'only when her face is veiled'. Yet she had a definite sense of style, shocking the French court with her racy two-inch-high heels and her steel corsets, made by her husband's armourer and the secret of her 13-inch waist. She was a game girl, too – she hunted enthusiastically until she was well into her sixties and introduced riding side-saddle to the French (thus showing off her shapely calves, one of her few visual strong points).

Catherine's other fashionable innovations were broccoli, artichokes, cauliflower and the fork. She also pioneered the wearing of perfume, hair-dye and underwear and, despite never touching alcohol, was an enthusiastic early adopter of tobacco. She was an avid collector, garlanding her palaces with imported china, minerals, dolls, stuffed crocodiles and a host of live pets, including her favourite, a long-tailed monkey from the Indies. She fussed over it continually, calling it her lucky talisman.*

Catherine set a new European standard for opulent parties, masques and balls. Her entertainments, which deployed the finest artists, dancers, architects and musicians of the day, were known as '*les magnificences*'. One highly effective novelty was her 'flying squadron', a group of eighty ladies-in-waiting whose services added spice and intrigue to the conduct of international diplomacy. At one memorable magnificence in 1577, they served

---

* It's possible that she inherited the monkey from her father-in-law: a long-tailed monkey appears in a miniature portrait of Francis I and his courtiers.

supper topless. These ladies also established the new fashion of not shaving or plucking their pubic hair: on Catherine's strict orders (bald pubes might mean pox). Her rival, the straight-laced Jeanne, Protestant Queen of Navarre, wrote of Catherine's court: 'I knew it was bad, I find it even worse than I feared. Here women make advances to men rather than the other way around.'

During her barren years, Catherine's position as queen was under constant threat, particularly when Henry proved his virility by fathering a child with a servant. Roused by this, he took Catherine's famously beautiful cousin, Diane de Poitiers, as a mistress. Catherine refused to give up trying to conceive, down-ing large draughts of mule's urine, wearing stags' antlers and dressings of cow dung, and consulting her friend Nostradamus for advice. She even bored a hole in the floor of her husband's bedchamber so she could stand underneath to spy on Henry and Diane and pick up any practical tips. Some historians credit the royal physician, Jean Fernel, with the decisive breakthrough. He had noticed some 'irregularities' in the couple's organs of generation and suggested a way to solve the problem. Whatever it was, after her first child was born, Catherine had no further trouble conceiving. She produced nine more children, seven of whom survived into adulthood. Three of her sons became kings of France and two of her daughters married kings. She outlived all but two of them.

Her sole aim through her years as consort, and then as the guiding power through the reigns of her three sons, was to keep the Valois dynasty of her husband in the ascendant. To do so, she had to navigate her way through the French Wars of Religion, which threatened to tear the country apart between 1562 and 1598, by shrewdly playing off Catholic against Huguenot. In defence of political stability she was capable, when necessary, of acts of startling viciousness, even towards her own children. On discovering that her teenage daughter Marguerite was sleeping with the son of her archrival, the Duke of Guise, she dragged her out of bed, ripping her nightclothes and pulling out handfuls of her hair. Later, when Marguerite was caught again (this time being unfaithful to her husband, King Henry of Navarre) Catherine had the lover executed, cut Marguerite out of her will and never spoke to her again.

Catherine's last months were plagued by bouts of gout and colic (she was always a big eater and once nearly died after consuming a vat of chicken-gizzard stew). After her death, a chronicler observed that 'no more notice was taken of her than of a dead goat'. Her bones were later thrown into a pit by the Revolutionary mob. Her lavish buildings have mostly been destroyed. Even her power-broking and intrigue didn't outlast her. Just eight months after her passing, 300 years of Valois rule ended with the murder of her son, Henry III. Her long-suffering son-in-law, Marguerite's husband, became Henry IV of France, founding the Bourbon dynasty. Despite having suffered serial humiliation at the hands of both Medici ladies, he was surprisingly generous about his former mother-in-law, commending her 'wise conduct' and commenting, 'I am surprised that she never did worse.' Perhaps the best epitaph for Catherine's ambiguous legacy comes from a contemporary who wisely chose to remain anonymous: 'She had too much wit for a woman, and too little honesty for a queen.'

If part of the appeal of monkeys for royalty was their rarity and peculiar miniature-human quality, it shouldn't come as any surprise that real miniature humans also found themselves at court.

Catherine de' Medici practically farmed her troupe of dwarfs, keeping them dressed in finery and making sure they had a whole retinue of servants to look after them. She even arranged inter-dwarf marriages and encouraged them to breed. The strange fascination that dwarf sex exerted is another link with monkeys: both were seen as helpless victims of animal lust. Getting monkeys and dwarfs to play together was even more fun. Here's an account of a wrestling match between a dwarf and a monkey, arranged for the entertainment of Cosimo I de' Medici not long after he became Duke of Florence in 1537:

> *The dwarf had two injuries, one in the shoulder and the other in the arm, while the monkey was left with his legs crippled. The monkey eventually gave up and begged the dwarf for mercy. The dwarf, however, didn't understand the monkey's language and having seized the monkey by the legs from behind kept beating his head on the ground. If My Lord the Duke hadn't stepped in, the dwarf would have gone on to kill him. The dwarf fought naked, having nothing to protect him except a pair of undershorts that covered his private parts. Suffice it to say that the dwarf was the victor and he won ten scudi in gold.*

Cosimo's great-granddaughter, Henrietta Maria, Charles I of England's queen, was another monkey and dwarf enthusiast. Her court favourite was the most celebrated of all English 'little people', Sir Jeffrey Hudson (1619–82), keeper of the royal monkey.

Jeffrey Hudson was born in Oakham, Rutland. He was the son of a bull-baiting butcher 'of lusty stature' and no one could understand why he was so small. Local theories ranged from his mother choking on a gherkin while pregnant to dark rumours about his parents keeping him in a box. Actually, he suffered from growth-hormone deficiency, caused by a misfiring pituitary gland.

At the age of eight he had reached only 18 inches in height. His father, sensing an opportunity for betterment, took him to his employer, the Duke of Buckingham. The duchess, Katherine, was entranced. Her husband was the King's 'favourite' at the time and very probably his lover, too. This did not please the queen, so the duchess decided to present Jeffrey to her as a gift: a peace-offering from one wronged wife to another. She arranged for the little man to arrive at court inside a cold venison pie. Jeffrey then leapt out, bowed and marched up and down the table in a full suit of armour. He was an instant hit. The queen invited him to enter her service, gave him a servant of his own, and put him in charge of her pet monkey, Pug.

Jeffrey soon found his niche as a court entertainer, making friends with a 7½-foot-tall porter called William Evans. They developed an act together where Evans would pull a loaf of bread out of one pocket and Hudson out of the other and proceed to make a sandwich. The two were often seen together in public and a number of London pubs were named in their honour. Together with a later arrival, Thomas Parr, who claimed to be 151 years old, they were known as the 'Three Wonders of the Age.'

Jeffrey was more than just a curiosity: he was bright and audacious enough to act as a diplomat for the Stuart court. At the age of eleven, he was part of an embassy sent to France to bring back a midwife for the pregnant Queen Henrietta Maria. The ambassadors were granted an audience by Marie de' Medici, the queen's mother, who was so taken with Jeffrey that she presented him with £2,000 worth of jewellery. This was an enormous sum of money. Jeffrey's father, by comparison, probably earned around £10 a year as a butcher.

In the 1620s and 1630s, the French coastal town of Dunkirk was an independent Flemish state and a notorious pirate base. It was these 'Dunkirkers' who intercepted the royal ship on its way back across the Channel, stealing Jeffrey's newly acquired jewels and kidnapping all the members of the party. The group were a little too 'hot' for the pirates, though, and they were quickly released. The incident inspired a mock epic, *Jeffreidos* (1638) by William Davenant, which featured an unnerving assault on the dwarfish hero by a hungry turkey-cock.

As he grew older, Jeffrey began to excite attention from the ladies. Paintings show him to be attractive and properly proportioned (if small) with large blue eyes and a mane of blond curls. He was fond of boasting that, as a young man, he had slept with at least fifteen court lovelies and in 1641 he was the master of ceremonies at the 'bedding' ceremony following Charles's daughter Mary's wedding to William of Orange. As she was just nine years old, 'consummation' only required the royal couple to touch bare legs. However, much to the puzzlement of the Dutchman, she had been sewn into her nightdress – until Sir Jeffrey sauntered in, wielding a pair of shears.

During the Civil War, Jeffrey commanded of a troop of horse in the king's army, after which he always referred to himself as Captain Jeffrey Hudson. When the war was lost, he accompanied the queen to her court-in-exile in France. In this more informal atmosphere, Jeffrey found himself subjected to teasing by the cavaliers. To nip this in the bud, he issued a challenge to the brother of William Crofts, the captain of the queen's guard, and a duel was arranged. Croft made the fatal error of turning up with a water pistol. Jeffrey wasn't amused. He had used his idle hours well and was an accomplished marksman. He shot Croft clean through the forehead. The queen managed to get his death-sentence commuted to exile, so Jeffrey set off back for England. With singular bad luck, he once again fell victim to pirates – this time the rather more serious Barbary corsairs from North Africa – who sold him into slavery in Algiers. He remained there for the next twenty-five years.

No one is quite sure how or by whom Jeffrey was ransomed and returned to England but, in the intervening years, he had more than doubled in height: a growth spurt he put down to the trauma of being repeatedly buggered by his Turkish captors.

At just under four foot, he was decidedly tall for a working dwarf so he returned to Rutland. For a while he sat at home, like a real-life hobbit, smoking and drinking ale and telling tales of his exploits, but in 1678, poor and bored, he decided to move back down to London to see if the new king would employ him. It was unlucky timing. London was in the grip of the Popish Plot organised by his fellow Rutlander, Titus Oates. As a well-known Catholic and royalist, Jeffrey, even in his new taller incarnation, was instantly recognisable so he found himself thrown into the Gatehouse prison. Later released, he received a small honorarium from the king for services rendered (though never specified), but it wasn't enough to save him from penury. Captain Jeffrey Hudson, whom the playwright Thomas Heywood had called 'the prettiest, neatest, and well-proportioned small man that Nature bred', died in obscurity, his small body buried in a secret grave reserved for Catholic paupers.

～

Poverty also stalked the life of another famous monkey owner, **Rembrandt Van Rijn** (1606–69). Rembrandt was an almost exact contemporary of Jeffrey Hudson and like the Englishman enjoyed the fruits of fame while still young. But unlike the randy little courtier he had earned his pre-eminence through hard work. He toiled through his teens, denying himself the 'the normal pleasures of young men' although he was fully aware of what he was missing. 'I love those decadent wenches who do so trouble my dreams,' he later confessed.

By the time Rembrandt arrived in Amsterdam in 1630, he was ready for success, money and love. All three came quickly. In less than two years he had painted forty-six portraits of the great and the good of his adopted city, making himself wealthy in the process. Merchants, lawyers, local dignitaries and their wives fought one another for the chance to sit for him. At the age of twenty-six Rembrandt was, as the film-maker Peter Greenaway put it, 'a cross between Mick Jagger and Bill Gates': young, successful, good at business and full of swagger. Like Raphael, Leonardo and Michelangelo before him, he signed his work with his first name, which is what we still call him. In 1633 he added a 'd' to his signature, where previously he had just been 'Rembrant'. No one knows why, but it obviously mattered to him because he kept it for the rest of his career.*

In the same year, he met and married Saskia van Ulenborch, the daughter of an extremely affluent Amsterdam family. As well

---

* His contemporaries found it difficult to agree on how to spell his name – probably because his fame spread by word of mouth. Here are some of the many versions recorded: Rhembrant, Rheinbrand, Reijnbrand, haerbrant, Rimbrantt, Rembrand, Remblant, Reijnbrant, Rembrando, Rheimbrand, Rijnbrandt, Rimbrandt, Rem Brant, Reijmbrant, Renbrant, Reynbrant, Rymbrandt, Rheinbrandt, Rhijnbrandt, Reimbrant, Rhinbrant, Rinebrant, Rynbrant, Rijnbrant, Reinbrand, Rimbram, Rhinbrand, Rhimbrant.

as being attractive and fond of the high life, Saskia was an excellent financial manager and the couple were soon able to move into an expensive house in the Jewish quarter, which Rembrandt filled with the artworks and exotic bric-a-brac he loved to collect. As well as the amazing torrent of his own work – there are over 2,300 paintings, sketches and etchings that we know about – Rembrandt was also a gifted teacher; at least fifty of his pupils went on to establish themselves as working artists.

The Van Rijns' apparently unbeatable marriage of art and commerce was not to last long. Saskia gave birth to four children in as many years, but only one, Titus, survived beyond a few weeks. She herself succumbed to tuberculosis shortly afterwards. Without his wife's business acumen, Rembrandt's mania for collecting meant that his debts begin to pile up. He didn't appear to care, working even harder, producing a string of masterpieces: portraits, biblical scenes, self-portraits and large commissions, the grandest of which was *The Night Watch* (1642). The painting should really be called *The Company of Captain Frans Banning Cocq and Lieutenant Willem van Ruytenburgh*. It was a group commission from eighteen merchants who were also a part-time civic guard. The payment terms were simple: the more money each man put in, the more prominently Rembrandt would paint him. Unfortunately, like many of Rembrandt's best works, it suffered from poor attempts at conservation, with thick layers of varnish being ladled all over it, darkening the scene to such an extent that, when Sir Joshua Reynolds saw it a century-and-a-half later, he referred to it as 'The Night Watch' and the name stuck. As modern restoration has shown, it's actually set in broad daylight.

Stories about Rembrandt always seem to come back to

money. His greed was legendary: his students would paint coins on the floor and see how long it took before he stooped to pick them up. Others described how his clothes resembled filthy rags: he used them to wipe his brushes and 'other things of a similar nature'. If he didn't waste money on clothes, Saskia's relatives were painfully conscious of his other extravagances. They made sure that, if he remarried, he would inherit none of her estate. So, though he became the lover of Titus's nursemaid, the malodorous Geertje Dircx, he refused to marry her. When, seven years later, he turned his amorous attentions to his buxom young housekeeper, Hendrickje Stoffels, Geertje sued him for breach of promise. He won the case but Geertje was awarded a lifetime annuity of 200 guilders a year, a sum the near-bankrupt Rembrandt couldn't afford. He responded by getting her committed to a workhouse for moral delinquency and promiscuity.

Financially, things went from bad to worse. In the early 1650s, the Dutch economy, weakened by the Anglo-Dutch war, suffered a severe credit crunch. A Rembrandt portrait was expensive in both time and money: a subject might have to sit for three months and the artist refused to court fashion by using the cheaper, gaudy colours pioneered by the Flemish school of Anthony van Dyck. The commissions dried up.

In a last-ditch attempt to save his home, Rembrandt transferred the deeds to his fifteen-year-old son. As soon as his creditors learned of this, they panicked and called in his debts. In July 1656 he was forced to apply for a *cessio bonorum*. This spared him the shame of bankruptcy, but required that all his possessions be sold to pay his debts. Years of collecting fell under the hammer –a giant's helmet, a plaster cast of a negro's head, crossbows, thirteen bamboo wind instruments, a sculpture of a child urinating, the skins of a lion and lioness and scores of paintings. His art collection was so huge that the Artist's Guild worried that the market would be swamped. They used their influence to speed up the sale; Rembrandt only raised a paltry 600 guilders and was forced to move to a small rented house in a poor part of the city.

Virtually bankrupt, Rembrandt's housekeeper/lover and his son concocted a scheme to keep him solvent. They started an art business, buying and selling paintings under their own names, but employing Rembrandt as an 'assistant'. The man who was once Amsterdam's most popular artist was now an employee of his own staff. More tragedy followed. Plague claimed Hendrickje in 1662 and Titus in 1668. Rembrandt died the following year, 'without a friend or a guilder, or even a good piece of herring'. He was buried in an unmarked grave.

In the years after Saskia's death, his favourite companion had been his pet monkey, Puck, and their closeness reveals the side to Rembrandt that we now most appreciate. He cared little for money, as such. He liked what it bought but not what it did to people. He egged on the swanks and grandees who trooped into his studio to dress opulently, making themselves look even more ridiculous and vain. Rembrandt preferred to paint life in the raw: people urinating, wrinkled faces, dimpled thighs. Even in his biblical pictures, like the *The Preaching of Saint John*, he couldn't resist painting a pair of copulating dogs in the foreground. When Puck died, Rembrandt was heartbroken. Just as he had painted his beloved Saskia as she lay dying, he commemorated Puck's memory by painting his corpse into the portrait of a family he was working on. The paterfamilias protested and threatened to withdraw the commission unless

Rembrandt removed the offending item. Rembrandt refused, sacrificed the cash and kept the painting, monkey included. Sadly, this masterpiece of simian portraiture has long been lost.

~

Another painter with a penchant for self-portraits and monkeys was the moustachioed, mono-browed Mexican Frida Kahlo (1907–54). She is often called a Surrealist but she never felt comfortable with the label, referring to André Breton and his gang as 'coo-coo lunatic sons of bitches'. 'I never painted dreams,' she wrote, 'I painted my own reality.' From the age of six, when she first contracted polio, this reality was more or less defined by pain.

On 17 November 1925, when she was only eighteen, Frida was travelling home from school on a bus when a tram hit it broadside on. She broke her back, pelvis, collarbone, ribs and right leg (in eleven places) and dislocated a foot and a shoulder. A piece of metal handrail also pierced her vagina. Although she was expected to die, after more than a year prostrate in bed, she recovered. Her father, a photographer (and an artist himself) rigged up a mirror and various contraptions over her bed so that she could see and draw objects in the room. It was this that led Frida to become an artist. In the remainder of her life, she underwent thirty-five surgical operations (as well as several abortions and miscarriages) and her art almost always revolved about her body, her pain and her suffering, sometimes in shockingly realistic detail.

As if the physical pain wasn't enough, Frida also managed to fall in love with one of Mexico's most flamboyant and difficult men, the Marxist mural painter Diego Rivera. He was twenty-one years her senior (and twice her size) when they married in 1929, and, while it was definitely a love match, it had more ups and downs than the most lurid Mexican soap opera. For all his talent and chutzpah, Diego had a violent temper and was compulsively unfaithful to Frida – even with her own sister Cristina. He happily concurred with his doctor's diagnosis that he was 'unfit for monogamy' and it was said that, for American women visiting Mexico, sleeping with Diego Rivera was as important a part of the tourist itinerary as visiting the Aztec city of Tenochtitlan.

Not that Frida was any slouch in this regard. She, too, had numerous affairs, both with men and women – most famously with Leon Trotsky, a liaison that started in 1937 while he and his wife Natalia were staying as houseguests of the Riveras. Frida called Trotsky her Piochitas or 'little goat', because of his beard. Later, she tired of *el viejo* ('the old man') and broke off the affair, much to his disappointment. Trotsky's ice-pick-wielding assassin, Ramón Mercader, was invited over to dinner at the Riveras shortly before his arrest for murder. Frida and Diego remained staunch communists and supporters of the Soviet Union all their lives, and Frida hung photographs of Stalin, Lenin, Marx, Engels and Mao at the foot of her bed.

Their political views didn't stop them enjoying themselves (or employing a team of servants). Supper at the Riveras' was a riot of conversation, wine and tequila with guests ranging from the president of Mexico to Nelson Rockefeller and George Gershwin. Though regularly encased in a steel-and-plaster corset to support her back, Frida dressed flamboyantly in the traditional dress of Tehuantapec (an area in southern Mexico she had never actually visited): vibrant floral prints in bright yellows, blues and reds. She never appeared in public without make-up, but adamantly refused to remove her trademark moustache, often using a pencil to make it darker. A lover of gossip and dirty jokes, she had little time for the abstract theorising of the European art houses:

> *I would rather sit on the floor in the market of Toluca and sell tortillas, than to have anything to do with these 'artistic' bitches of Paris. They sit for hours in cafés warming their precious behinds, and talk without stopping about 'culture', 'art' 'revolution' and so on, thinking themselves the gods of the world, dreaming the most fantastic nonsense, and poisoning the air with theories that never come true.*

Even allowing for her own extra-marital dalliances, the strain of living with Diego became too much for Frida. She found his constant philandering deeply wounding. 'I have suffered two grave accidents in my life,' she wrote, 'one in which a streetcar ran me over; the other accident is Diego.' For a while, they tried living in separate houses linked by a footbridge. This didn't work and when Diego suggested a divorce in 1939 Frida accepted. She started drinking heavily, cut her hair short and began wearing men's clothes. They were re-married within a year, largely at the suggestion of her doctor who was worried about Frida's mental health. Diego described the deal they came to in his auto-biography:

> *For her part, she asked for certain conditions: that she would provide for herself financially from the proceeds of her own work; that I would pay for one half of our household expenses – no more; and that we would have no sexual intercourse. In explaining this last stipulation, she said that, with the images of all the other women flashing through her mind, she couldn't*

*possibly make love to me, for a psychological barrier would spring up as soon as I made advances.*

They never had children: Frida's physical condition made it impossible. But she was desperately maternal: she even kept one of her aborted foetuses in a jar by her bedside. Her child substitutes were her pet monkeys, on whom she lavished her affection, particularly the spider monkey, Don Fulang Chang. Her beautiful self-portrait, *Fulang Chang and I* (1937), was bought for $1 million by Frida Kahlo's no. 1 fan, Madonna, in 1988. Monkeys appear in several of her other paintings. Instead of their usual symbolic baggage of lasciviousness or stupidity, Frida's monkeys represent natural grace and childlike mischief. They kept her company during Diego's long absences along with the rest of her menagerie –Granizo the deer, Bonito the parrot, a miniature hairless dog called Señor Xolotl and an eagle by the name of Gertrude Caca Blanca.

Frida's work was not widely recognised while she was alive. Her commercial breakthrough came in 1938, when she accompanied Diego on a tour of the USA (or 'Gringolandia' as she called it). She held her first solo exhibition in New York and her first significant sale was to the Hollywood tough-guy actor Edward G. Robinson, who bought four paintings for $200 each. In 1939 Frida went to Paris, becoming the first twentieth-century Mexican artist to have a work purchased by the Louvre. Only one Mexican show was organised in her lifetime, and that didn't take place until 1953. Forbidden to attend by her doctors, Frida had herself transported to the gallery, still in bed, on a lorry, and was wheeled triumphantly into the party.

Shortly afterwards, her health began to deteriorate sharply, the decline being exacerbated by her drinking and over-use of sleeping pills. In August of that year her damaged right leg was amputated because of gangrene. A year later she was dead, seemingly of pneumonia, though some friends believed she may have taken an overdose. A few days before she died, she wrote in her diary: 'I hope the exit is joyful – and I hope never to come back.'

Since then, she has never been away. Frida Kahlo is a one-woman international industry: feted by feminist critics, her mono-browed, moustachioed visage is used to sell exhibitions, prints, tote bags, mouse mats and watches all over the world. In 2001, she became the first Hispanic woman to feature on a US postage stamp – surely the only America-loathing, unrepentant Stalinist to have been so honoured. None of this would have surprised Diego. In comparison to Frida's work, his own socialist realist murals now look rather old-fashioned and politically naive. For all his many sins, Diego understood better than anyone the quality of his wife's astonishing paintings:

*I recommend her to you, not as a husband but as an enthusiastic admirer of her work, acid and tender, hard as steel and delicate and fine as a butterfly's wing, loveable as a beautiful smile, and profound and cruel as the bitterness of life.*

~

Cruelty and bitterness are more or less the whole story of Jiang Qing (pronounced 'jang ching'), **Madame Mao** (1914–91), wife of Chairman Mao, poster-girl for the Cultural Revolution and one of the infamous Gang of Four. So far, we have had monkeys as intimate companions, substitute children, artists' muses and living embodiments of royal wealth and privilege. Madame Mao's monkey was far more sinister. Hers was the monkey as henchman and accomplice in crime.

Jiang Qing was born Li Jinhai, one of eight names she bore during her life. Her youth in Shandong province in eastern China was tarnished by poverty and neglect. She later blamed her persistent ill health on the fact that she spent most of her childhood hungry. Her mother was a concubine with little love to spare for her pretty daughter, but she didn't subject her to the grisly ritual of foot-binding either. Jiang's father was a violent and abusive alcoholic who drove mother and daughter out of the family home, though not before Jiang had demonstrated her fighting spirit, attacking him and biting him viciously on his arms. At the age of fourteen, after being expelled from school for spitting at a teacher, she ran away to Beijing and became an actress.

The details of this part of her life are hazy, not least because she rigorously repressed any mention of them when she came to power, but it seems she married and separated at least twice, became a communist and was at some point arrested for terrorism. Her enemies always alleged she slept with her captors to ensure her escape. Under the stage name Lan Ping ('Blue Apple'), she landed some major roles, including Nora in Ibsen's *A Doll's House*, whose self-discovery and rejection of men seemed to resonate with the young actress's own experience. Jiang developed a love for Hollywood films, copied Garbo in her dress, and wore make-up and high heels. She was also spiteful and had a long memory. Decades after being beaten to a leading role by a girl called Wang Ying (who went on to become a famous actress and performed at the White House for the Roosevelts) Jiang had her arrested and imprisoned, making sure she died in jail.

In 1937 she forsook the stage and volunteered for the revolution, at that time based in the Yunnan caves, the endpoint of the Long March, deep in central China. She soon made herself known to Mao, sitting in the front row of his lectures. Mao, in turn, came to see her perform in an opera organised for his troops. Appearing backstage after the show, he placed his coat round her shoulders. The next day, Jiang visited the Leader to return his coat and ended up staying the night.

The relationship was not a popular one with the communist high command. Mao was technically still married to a senior party official and Jiang's past was a heady mix of sex, deceit and Western-style debauchery. She seemed an unnecessarily controversial addition to the Great Leader's burgeoning cult, especially when rumours circulated that one of Jiang's former lovers had tried to commit suicide by swallowing a bottle of surgical spirit and crushed match-heads. This didn't bother Mao. He cut a deal with the Party where he got to keep Jiang as his partner on condition that she would not be acknowledged publicly as his wife or hold any political office for twenty years.

The marriage does not seem to have been a particularly happy one. Mao soon lost interest in Jiang sexually (at twenty-three she was a little old for his taste: he had an insatiable preference for teenage virgins). At the same time, he saw that she was fanatically loyal and ruthless enough to be useful to him. As she later commented: 'Whoever Chairman Mao asked me to bite, I bit.' So it was that, in 1963, when the twenty-year 'ban' had passed, Mao chose Jiang to head up his Ministry of Culture.

These were the years of her greatest influence. As the 'Great Flag-carrier of the Proletarian Culture' she oversaw the Cultural Revolution, totally suppressing all traditional cultural activities and organising mass rallies in which her enemies were humiliated and physically abused by the infamous Red Guards. She drew up the 'Kill Culture' manifesto and in 1966 took over as head of the 'Revolution Small Group' responsible for ensuring that the only books, paintings and films available in China were for propaganda purposes. Jiang herself had a hand in producing the handful of films available. The Revolution Small Group even banned the piano, denouncing it as the most dangerous of all Western instruments.

In her heyday, Jiang – or Madame Mao, as the Western media dubbed her – behaved like the Chairman's empress-in-waiting: an unsavoury combination of paranoia, excess and hypochondria. She made sure that people who knew about her past were imprisoned or killed. While Chinese peasants struggled in appalling poverty, she would instruct warships to cruise up and down rivers so she could practise her hobby of photography, and roads were built specifically for her to visit beauty spots. Though the masses were fed a bland diet of Maoist propaganda, she busily imported Western films (*The Sound of Music* was her favourite).

Life with Madame was a nightmare. Her rooms had to be kept an exact 21.5 °C in winter and exactly 26 °C in summer. She had an intense fear of strangers and of unexpected sounds, and lived in constant terror of assassination. Servants were jailed for phantom indiscretions. Her nerves were so bad she took three lots of sleeping pills every night, ordering her staff to remove all birds and cicadas from around her house so they wouldn't disturb her. Servants had to walk with arms aloft and legs apart in case she heard their clothes rustling. At one point, she heard of a technique for promoting youth and vigour that involved transfusions of the blood from healthy young men. She put dozens of guards through a physical check-up before choosing the best for her 'new programme'. Fortunately for them, Mao got wind of her plans and put a stop to them – on health grounds: she might be opening herself to infection.

In this grotesque atmosphere, where even her only child's nurse was thrown into prison and tortured for attempting to poison her mistress (Jiang had succumbed to a nasty bout of diarrhoea), the role of her pet monkey is clear. It was absolutely loyal, never answered back and yet was capable of capricious acts of violence. Like Mrs Coulter's sinister golden monkey-daemon in Philip Pullman's *His Dark Materials* trilogy, Jiang's monkey was her constant companion, dressed in silk and fed the finest food. She took particular pleasure in setting it on people as they strolled through her orchid garden in Canton, laughing at their discomfort as it leapt onto their heads and shoulders and savagely punishing anyone who didn't make a fuss of the beast. Men, she once remarked, contributed nothing more to history than 'a drop of sperm'. Monkeys seemed preferable by far as companions.

For all her delusions of grandeur, it seems unlikely that Mao ever seriously considered this spoiled, borderline psychotic as his successor. He had used her remorselessly to engineer a culture of fear but, towards the end of his life, she was reduced to asking his girlfriends to put in a good word for her. Within weeks of Chairman Mao's death in 1976, Madame Mao and the rest of the Gang of Four were arrested in a bloodless coup. Her trial in 1980 was televised each night and attracted huge audiences. She was convicted of 'counter-revolutionary crimes' and sentenced to death, although this was later commuted to life imprisonment. Jiang hanged herself in a hospital bathroom in 1991.

Her passing went unmourned: even her daughter refused to write to the authorities and request her release (this occasioned one of Jiang's last outbursts, throwing a watermelon on the ground and accusing her daughter of being 'heartless'). As the living personification of the brutal persecutions and mayhem of the Cultural Revolution, almost no one in China has ever been more despised. Mao himself captured her self-inflicted isolation: 'Few people suit her taste – only one: she herself.' The fate of her monkey is not recorded.

~

The high-water mark for the monkey as domestic pet was reached in Victorian England. The spoils of empire included a regular stream of outlandish wildlife arriving to swell the households of the moneyed classes, and monkeys, despite (or maybe because of) Darwin's efforts, became must-have accessories. Patterson's 1888 *Notes on Pet Monkeys and How to Manage Them* captures the mood:

> *Where a fancier is not addicted to balancing the matter of pet-purchase and pet-keeping upon the snap of his purse, a series of monkeys, in a properly-arranged domicile, not only affords himself considerable interest and entertainment, but gives unlimited fun to a large circle of ever-ready-to-be-amused acquaintances.*

One of the most complete accounts of monkey stewardship is to be found in the work of **Frank Buckland** (1826–80), the David Bellamy of the mid-nineteenth century. He was the son of the dean of Westminster, William Buckland (1784–1856), the man who made geology and palaeontology respectable academic disciplines and was the first to describe a dinosaur, twenty years before the word 'dinosaur' itself was coined. (Buckland called his find 'the Great Fossil Lizard of Stonesfield'.)

The Bucklands' domestic arrangements were idiosyncratic even by Victorian standards. Part museum, part zoological garden, live and dead animals jostled for space with geological samples. Owls and jackdaws flew free, snakes and toads were scattered through the rooms in cages and the children were allowed to ride their ponies inside the house. Raised in this atmosphere, it is hardly surprising that young Frank decided his vocation was to become 'a high priest of nature and a benefactor of mankind'. Even at the age of four, asked to identify an ancient fossil by his father, he piped up at once: 'they are the vertebway of an icthyosawus'. At university, he impressed his peers by climbing into the fountain of Christ Church, Oxford, and riding astride first a large turtle and then an ailing crocodile.

Both of these were destined for the table. Zoophagy, the eating of unusual animals, was another passion Frank Buckland shared with his father. The dean set the bar high; he claimed to have eaten through the whole of creation from mouse to bison. Hedgehog, rat, puppy, potted ostrich, tortoise and pickled horse tongue were regulars on the menu at home, with roast or battered mouse a house speciality. John Ruskin was an eager dinner guest:

> *I have always regretted a day of unlucky engagement on which I missed a delicate toast of mice; and remembered, with delight, being waited upon one hot summer morning by two graceful and polite little Carolina lizards, who kept off the flies.*

Buckland senior confessed himself gastronomically defeated on only two occasions – by boiled mole and a ragout of bluebottles.

Young Frank pushed it even further, making pies from rhinos ('like very tough beef'), frying earwigs ('horribly bitter'), stewing the head of a porpoise ('like broiled lamp wick') and consuming chops from a panther that had been buried for several days ('not very good'). He did favourably surprise guests, though, with his accidentally roasted giraffe (the happy result of a zoo fire), raw sea slugs and kangaroo ham (at least, until he told his guests what they were eating). There was a serious purpose to his hobby. In 1859, Frank founded the Society for the Acclimatization of Animals to the United Kingdom, which set out to import exotic species as alternative, high yielding food sources. We owe the contemporary fashion for farming ostrich, water buffalo and bison to Frank Buckland's manic enthusiasm.

The most bizarre comestible that ever found its way into a Buckland stomach was the heart of Louis XIV. Although the consumption of this withered and leathery object is often attributed to Frank, the only first-hand account occurs in the autobiography of the English raconteur and travel writer Augustus Hare (1834–1903). He makes it clear that William was the one guilty of royal cardiophagy:

> *Talk of strange relics led to mention of the heart of a French King preserved at Nuneham in a silver casket. Dr. Buckland, whilst looking at it, exclaimed, 'I have eaten many strange things, but have never eaten the heart of a king before,' and, before anyone could hinder him, he had gobbled it up, and the precious relic was lost for ever.*

Not that this proves it actually happened, and certainly the various colourful embroideries to the tale – that it was sautéed and roasted; that it was served with a side helping of French beans; that Buckland considered its flavour would have been improved with a gravy made from marmoset's blood; that he ate it for Christmas dinner – really don't stand up to scrutiny. But the incident may explain Charles Darwin's 'strong prejudice' towards the older Buckland. He disliked his 'coarse joking manner' and 'undignified buffoonery'. The Bucklands, in turn, both rejected Darwin's theory of evolution, maintaining a creationist line despite having been personally responsible for putting back the geological age of the earth by millions of years.

Eccentricity and good humour characterised the son's life every bit as much as his father's. Frank shared his rooms at Christ Church with marmots, guinea pigs, a chameleon, several snakes, a jackal, an eagle, his monkey, Jacko, and a bear called Tiglath-Pileser, named after an ancient Assyrian king. After the bear made several appearances in a scholar's cap and gown at college drinks parties, the dean of Christ Church gave Frank the ultimatum to remove either 'Tig' or himself from the college. The bear was duly rusticated; the expulsion of Jacko and the increasingly bad-tempered eagle followed in quick succession.

Frank graduated in medicine and in 1854 became assistant surgeon to the 2nd Life Guards. He served with the regiment for ten years but failed to gain promotion, probably because his real interests lay elsewhere, writing racy, readable accounts of his adventures for *The Field* magazine. The many reminiscences of Frank at this time make him seem thoroughly likeable: he was a 4½-foot tall, barrel-chested, cigar-smoking, ginger-haired ball of energy, the self-appointed curator of all that was odd, grotesque or inexplicable. He was also a walking zoo. Wherever he appeared, he might be expected to produce a writhing ball of slow worms from inside his coat or a matchbox full of baby toads.

Once, arriving at Southampton docks, he was charged 5 shillings for trying to smuggle his monkey onto a train. The clerk insisted on treating it as a dog, and issuing it with a dog ticket. Buckland rallied by producing a tortoise from his pocket. 'Perhaps you'll call that a dog, too?' he asked. 'No,' said the clerk, 'we make no charge for them, they're insects.'

As well as curiosities of natural history, Frank wrote up reports of mummies preserved in guano, fossilised mermaids, singing Siamese twins, unnaturally fat babies, impossibly tiny babies, the 'Human Frog' (who could smoke underwater) and the man who walked on his head. His journalism is marked by a very un-Victorian sense of sympathy for his subjects. Observing the poor mummified corpse of Julia Pastrana, the Mexican bearded lady, he wrote:

> *Her features were simply hideous on account of the profusion of hair growing on her forehead, and her black beard; but her figure was exceedingly good and graceful, and her tiny foot and well-turned ankle,* bien chaussée, *perfection itself.*

Unlike his father the Dean, Frank Buckland can't be counted a great scientist, but he was certainly a great populariser of science: in his endless enthusiasm for the new and hitherto unnoticed he often reads like a one-man *Fortean Times*.

In 1867 his life changed. A Royal Commission appointed him Inspector of Salmon Fisheries. This was a proper grown-up job and within a very short time, Buckland had made himself into the UK's 'Mr Salmon', mastering all the intricacies of his subject, pioneering new techniques and technology for fish hatcheries and using used his great charm and energy to lead the first nationwide campaign against river pollution. He wasn't exactly an ecologist but he did commission first-hand research into the effect of ocean temperatures on the shoaling of fish and the importance of net mesh-size in keeping fish stocks at optimum levels. He was also single-handedly responsible for the stocking of the rivers and lakes of India, Australia and New Zealand with salmon and trout. This proved a rather more successful venture than his earlier scheme to manufacture shoes and gloves from the skin of rats.

Home life for the Bucklands always involved at least two monkeys. Frank's study, where the monkeys lived, was called the 'Monkey Room' and no writer has better captured the topsy-turvy madness of keeping them as pets. He considered them much superior to all other animals in terms of intelligence: 'almost fit to go up for a competitive examination,' as he put it. The monkeys graced all the Bucklands' social occasions, with outfits to match: Frank particularly liked them in green velvet dresses, trimmed with gold lace. He described them as some-times having the appearance of well-behaved children (his only child, Frank Junior, died aged five); sometimes like snoozing club bores (they loved a fire and had a taste for port and grog; one of them even smoked a pipe); but mostly they were the source of barely containable chaos. He describes his favourite pair, Tiny and 'the Hag' – West African guenon monkeys – launching themselves around the house 'with the velocity of a swallow'. The Hag took an irrational dislike to Mrs Buckland's sister and 'very nearly had the dress off her back'. Food was stolen, visitors tweaked, ornaments shattered, other pets terrorised. Given ten minutes in a bedroom by themselves, wrote Frank, 'the bill will rival that for the Abyssinian expedition'. Their vast cheek pouches swelled with booty (Frank estimated that the Hag could secrete twenty acid drops in each pouch). One afternoon he got them to disgorge 'a steel thimble, my own gold finger ring, a pair of pearl sleeve links, a farthing, a button, a shilling and a bit of sweet-stuff'.

But Buckland was not averse to a little anarchy:

*Although my monkeys do considerable mischief, yet I let them do it. I am amply rewarded by their funny and affectionate ways...nothing whatever would induce me to part with them. My monkeys love me, and I love my monkeys.*

With the Hag, in particular, he developed a close understanding. 'I could tell from her look what she wanted; and I am pretty sure she could read my thoughts in her own way.' There are, as he said, 'monkeys and monkeys; no two are alike'. She was his constant companion for twelve years and 'if ever an animal thought, it was the old Hag'.

Unlike many of his contemporaries, Buckland didn't senti- mentalise his relationship with animals; after all, this was the same man who had enjoyed roasting field mice while still a schoolboy. But he had a close affinity for monkeys that bordered on the inspirational: 'Many an idea I have had looking into the dear Hag's brilliant eyes.' Perhaps this explains why, given all the roasted, boiled, stewed, puréed animals he had consumed over the years, there is no record of Frank Buckland ever eating a monkey.

~

Should you be tempted to keep a monkey yourself, consider this last cautionary tale. **King Alexander I of Greece** (1893–1920) of the house of Schleswig-Holstein-Sonderburg-Glucksburg was the second son of King Constantine I, and first cousin to our own

Duke of Edinburgh. As he looked unlikely ever to become king, Alexander lived his role as crown prince to the full: going up to Oxford, playing inordinate amounts of football and tennis and driving racing cars as fast he could. He was an extremely popular and agreeable young man, though somewhat accident-prone. In 1917 he narrowly averted death in a train bombing. On other occasions, he broke a leg while 'practising jumping' and was seriously injured in a car crash after swerving to avoid a stray goat.

His accession to the throne in 1917 came about as a result of his father opting to keep Greece neutral during the First World War (they were, after all, a mostly German family). The Allies couldn't be doing with this and the governments of the UK, France and Russia issued an ultimatum: either Constantine left the country with his pro-German eldest son, or the alliance would recognise the revolutionary Eleuthérios Venizélos as the legal ruler of Greece. This left Alexander in the rather irregular position of inheriting the Greek crown while the two rightful heirs were still alive. Shortly after Alexander's coronation, Venizélos became prime minister of Greece in any case. He dominated the new king and, though there were reports of clashes, in reality Alexander I was the puppet of the new democratic government.

Not that the regime had long to enjoy his services. Three years into his reign his dog (not very tactfully named Fritz) was attacked by two of his father's pet monkeys. In defending the dog, Alexander received a severe mauling from the monkeys and died shortly afterwards of blood-poisoning.

It is perhaps the only example of a simian-led coup in modern European history but its effects were far reaching. Constantine regained the throne and plunged Greece into a disastrous war with Turkey, the effects of which are still felt today. As Churchill observed: 'A monkey bite cost the death of 250,000 people.' In 1922, the Greek monarchy fell and the royal family was sent permanently into exile. One of their number was Prince Philip Schleswig-Holstein-Sonderburg-Glucksburg, later Philip Mountbatten, born the year before on the dining-room table of the Villa Mon Repos, the family home in Corfu. He was carried off to safety in an orange crate.

~

As any of the subjects of this chapter could have told you, when you keep a monkey you take on their dark feral side as well as their capacity for friendship, intimacy and joy. Older cultures dealt with this dual nature by according them divine status. The ancient Egyptians worshipped monkeys as cleverer than their own children. They believed that baboon-headed Thoth, their god of wisdom and creativity, was the inventor of writing. India had the noble and ingenious Monkey God, Hanuman, and in medieval China, Sun Wukong, the Monkey King, was powerful enough to cover more than 30,000 miles in a single somersault.

Human beings, apes and monkeys all spring from the same evolutionary source. Some of us have tails, some do not, but it often seems that we have more in common than a common ancestor. It's tempting to wonder, as Descartes did, whether monkeys might be a lot wiser than they're letting on. That actually, our older cousins are perfectly capable of talking, but are smart enough not to do so in front of us, in case they get asked to do some work.

# CHAPTER EIGHT

# Who Do You Think You Are?

*Who in the world am I? Ah, that's the great puzzle.*

LEWIS CARROLL

Many of us daydream about what it would be like to be someone else, but actually passing yourself off as a different person takes a lot more time and trouble. **Titus Oates (1649–1705)** had good reason to make the attempt.

He was a ghastly child. Sickly, with a permanently runny nose and dribbling mouth, he suffered from convulsions and, as he grew older, walked with a pronounced limp and developed an irritating voice, halfway between a bark and whine. His face was startlingly ugly, bright red in colour and with almost no chin, so that his face appeared to be an extension of his corpulent neck. His character was no more appealing than his appearance. He was dim-witted, dull and a habitual liar: nobody liked him, not even his own father. After being expelled from school for cheating his teacher out of his tuition fees, he went up to Cambridge where he was thrown out of one college for stupidity and sent down from a second one for laziness. Leaving without a degree, he just pretended he had one anyway. This enabled him to get a licence to preach from the bishop of London and, in

March 1673, he was installed as the vicar of Bobbing in Kent. So began a fantasy life that would be responsible for one of the most absurd and tragic episodes in British history.

Oates's father, Samuel, was the son of a Church of England clergyman. As a young man, he had left the church to become a radical Baptist preacher and chaplain in Cromwell's New Model Army but, by the time Titus was born, he had swung round again and converted back to Anglicanism. This rather flexible relationship with Christian belief was about the only character trait he passed on to his son.

Oates was no more popular as a parish priest than he had been at school or university. A heavy drinker, he was rude and foul-mouthed to his flock and lasted less than two years before they arranged to get rid of him. Returning to the family home in Hastings, he stood in as curate to his father but decided he would rather have the local schoolmaster's job. So he accused him of sodomy. This blatant lie was quickly uncovered and, to escape a court appearance for perjury, Oates decamped to London and set out to sea as a naval chaplain.

It was on board the *Adventure* bound for Tangier, that Oates claimed he first heard rumours of the 'Popish Plot' to assassinate Charles II, but his maritime career was cut short when he was discovered performing homosexual acts, or 'Italian love', as it was then more delicately known. Sodomy was a hanging offence; it was only the fact that he was a clergyman that saved his skin.

Undaunted by his narrow escape, Oates bluffed his way into becoming chaplain to the Earl of Norwich. Within a few months, he was sacked for being generally unsuitable and constantly inebriated. His career options rapidly narrowing, he decided to try his luck as a Catholic. Pulling the wool over the eyes of an eccentric (and possibly insane) priest called Father Berry he was received into the Church of Rome in March 1677. Shortly afterwards he met Father Richard Strange, head of the English Jesuits. There is strong evidence that Strange became Oates's lover at this stage – it would be hard to explain why else he would bother with such an unattractive addition to the order.

Strange arranged for Oates to study with the Jesuits at Valladolid under the pseudonym Titus Ambrosius. Once again, it didn't last long. The Spanish booted him out when they realised he had no grasp whatever of Latin. Oates returned to England, boasting of a divinity degree from the University of Salamanca (which, of course, he had never even visited). Encouraged by Strange to try elsewhere, he enrolled in another Jesuit seminary in France under another false name: Samson Lucy. Here, his engaging personal habits – drinking, smoking, swearing and lying – made him so unpopular that a fellow seminarian attacked him with a frying pan. In a pattern that was by now tediously familiar, he was expelled and returned to London empty-handed. What fleeting attraction Catholicism had exerted over him had gone. Now all he wanted was revenge on the Roman Church – and the Jesuits in particular – that had so snubbed him.

He didn't have to wait long. An elderly friend of his father's, Dr Israel Tongue, a virulent anti-Catholic, proposed producing some pamphlets using Oates's first-hand 'knowledge' to expose the so-called 'Jesuit menace'. Together they hatched what purported to be an undercover report on the Church of Rome's plans to assassinate Charles II and replace him with his Catholic brother, James. It was a lie from top to tail: a half-digested string of rumours, myths and suppositions that the two men attempted to craft into a coherent story. It used every emotive device it could muster: a Europe-wide conspiracy at the highest level, private armies being amassed, secret cabals convened in London taverns, large injections of finance from treacherous Catholic families, even a special weapon that fired silver bullets, which would be used to do the deed while the King was out walking.

Charles II did this every day, regular as clockwork. He had even bought a piece of land so he could take his daily 'constitutional walk' from Hyde Park to St James's without leaving royal soil. Then called Upper St James's Park (now Green Park), it is how Constitution Hill got its name. On 13 August 1678, the King was intercepted on his customary stroll and handed a copy of Tongue and Oates's ramblings. The document listed the names of nearly one hundred 'plotters', most of them Jesuit priests. Every slight that the twenty-nine-year-old Oates had ever suffered had been poured into one lurid, win-or-bust piece of deception. Charles was unimpressed and inclined to ignore it, putting the matter into the hands of his first minister, the Earl of Danby. His brother James felt differently. He was outraged by the implications and publicly demanded an investigation.

With the 'plot' now out in the open, Oates took the initiative. Before a magistrate called Sir Edmund Godfrey, he swore on oath that his allegations were true. He was an energetic but far from convincing liar. His evidence was confused and contradictory. He made forty-three separate charges, naming the names of prominent English Catholics in a more or less random list. Godfrey was sceptical, but Oates was summoned to appear before the Privy Council. Shrewdly cross-examined by the king himself, Oates warmed to his theme. He increased the number of charges to eighty-one – throwing in Samuel Pepys and the Archbishop of

Dublin for good measure – and then produced his trump card. It was a letter from Edward Coleman, a genuinely fanatical Catholic and secretary to James's wife, Mary of Modena, Duchess of York, written to Father La Chaise, personal confessor to King Louis XIV of France. Barely had this shocking revelation become the subject of heated debate in every tavern and coffee-house in London when, a few days later, the body of Sir Edmund Geoffrey was found on Primrose Hill, strangled and impaled on his own sword. The Privy Council jumped to the conclusion that papists were to blame and gave Oates *carte blanche* to crush the plot. He couldn't believe his luck. As one contemporary observed: 'His greatest pleasure was to speed hither and thither accompanied by soldiers, enjoying complete power to imprison those he chose.' He even took the chance to settle a score by arresting his old headmaster, whom he hadn't forgiven for expelling him as a boy.

Samuel Pepys was seized and sent to the Tower of London. After the jury took just fifteen minutes to reach their verdict, Edward Coleman was hanged, drawn and quartered and thirty-four other people – including several Catholic priests and the Archbishop of Armagh – were executed for treason. Public panic set in: anyone even remotely suspected of being Catholic was driven out of London and not allowed back within a ten-mile radius. The House of Commons was searched for gunpowder and there were rumours of a French invasion on the isle of Purbeck in Dorset. By the end of 1678 Parliament had passed the second Test Act ruling that only Protestants could sit in the Houses of Parliament. Anyone in public office had to swear allegiance to the Crown and take an oath of 'supremacy' confirming that the monarch was supreme head of the Church of England. Many people – including the King – doubted the truth of Oates's allegations, but he was rewarded with an apartment in Whitehall, an annual allowance of £1,200 and his own coat of arms.

Gradually, though, public opinion began to turn. No 'great plot' materialised. Serious contradictions in Oates's evidence began to emerge and the judges started to find in favour of those he had accused. In 1681 he was thrown out of his grace-and-favour lodgings. In 1684 he was arrested at a city coffee house, tried for defamation, fined £100,000, and thrown into prison for calling the King's brother James a traitor. Worse was to come when James came to the throne, intent on revenging his fellow Catholics that Oates's lies had condemned to death. The one-time saviour of the English monarchy was now vilified in pamphlets as a 'Buggering, Brazen-faced, Lanthorn-jawed, Tallow-chapt Leviathan'. He was re-tried, this time for perjury, sentenced to life imprisonment, stripped of his clerical status and forced to endure a public flogging. He received over a thousand lashes while being dragged behind a cart from Aldgate to Tyburn, a distance of more than three miles. To rub salt in the wound, he had to appear five times a year in different parts of London, spending a whole day in the stocks being pelted with eggs and kitchen slops.

Notwithstanding his horrific injuries from the flogging and regular beatings from his gaolers, Oates survived and, with the accession of William of Orange in 1688, he was free once more. Undeterred by his experiences, and his powers of persuasion still intact, he got a job as a royal spy, the new king paying him an allowance to keep an eye on possible French Jacobite plotters. In 1693, hideous though he was, Oates married a wealthy young widow and, despite the sniggering about his homosexuality, the couple went on to have a daughter. Somehow, he got yet another job as a minister, this time as a Baptist. It was no more successful than any of his other clerical posts. One of his parishioners, Heather Parker, disliked him so much that, on her deathbed, she expressly asked that he be barred from attending her funeral. When the day came, Oates's response was to occupy the pulpit and preach an interminable and irrelevant sermon to delay the ceremony, causing a riot in the church, and being thrown out, yet again, by his own congregation.

It was to be his last expulsion, but not his last appearance in court. In 1702 he was fined at Westminster for hitting a woman over the head with his walking stick. She had confronted him about his sermons criticising the Church of England and accusing Charles II of being a closet papist. A man in his mid-fifties hitting a woman is particularly pathetic. Prison had not improved his manners or diminished his insolent self-regard. He was what he always had been, an insecure coward and a bully. His delusional fantasies had signed the death warrant of thirty-five entirely innocent men, changed the law of the land and disrupted the lives of thousands of English Catholics. He spent his last years in obscurity writing religious tracts that nobody read and haunting the Westminster law courts as a spectator. He never tired of complicated, self-justifying stories.

~

If Titus Oates had any redeeming features, history does not record them. The same cannot be said of **Alessandro, Count Cagliostro** (1743–95). He too was a liar and a charlatan, but he became a genuine celebrity all over late eighteenth-century Europe. Magician, Freemason, alchemist, forger, spiritualist and healer, he inspired both Goethe's *Faust* and Mozart's *The Magic Flute*. It's hard to think of another historical figure whose story also links Pope Pius IV, Marie Antoinette, Catherine the Great, Casanova and William Blake.

Born Giuseppe Balsamo in one of the poorest parts of Sicily, he lost his father while still a child. His mother couldn't afford to educate him so, at the age of fifteen, with the help of relatives, he was sent to a nearby monastery. The Fatebenefratelli, or 'Do-Good Brothers', were Augustinian monks famed for their network of hospitals. Medicine and chemistry were well taught and Giuseppe was a gifted pupil, spending his free time in the library, poring over books of occult lore. But he was still a Sicilian street brat at heart and – rather like Oates – foul-mouthed, belligerent, and lazy. During mealtime readings of the lives of the saints, he swapped their names for those of notorious Palermo prostitutes. The monks rapidly tired of these games and let him go. Bright and unscrupulous, he settled into a life of petty crime and soon became a gang leader. Using what he'd learned in the monastery, he was also able to pose as a convincing alchemist. In this guise he persuaded a goldsmith called Marano that he had sold his soul to the devil and could locate a cave in the mountains stuffed full of gold, but that first he would need 60 ounces of the precious metal to perform some expensive preliminary magic. The venal and credulous Marano fetched the money and, at midnight, set out for the hills where he was promptly ambushed by six of Giuseppe's accomplices dressed as devils armed with pitchforks and, according to the terrified merchant, blowing blue and red flames. They beat and robbed him and left him for dead. Giuseppe pocketed his share of the cash and left Palermo, never to return.

The attention to detail is impressive. The costumes weren't strictly necessary for the robbery, but they gave life to a tale that was told and re-told and which always left Marano looking a fool. This imaginative approach to crime – with the victims appearing to deserve their come-uppance – was to become Giuseppe's trademark.

Arriving at Messina on the other side of the island, he lodged with his well-to-do uncle, Joseph Cagliostro, before swiftly making off with some of his money and his surname. As Giuseppe Cagliostro, he set out on a series of escapades in Egypt and Turkey in the company of a mysterious adept called Althotas, an alchemist who spoke several Eastern languages. To fund their travels, they hawked a chemical formula devised by the old magician that supposedly transformed rough fibres of hemp so they appeared to be silk. These could be sold on to merchants at a profit, a rather more practical alchemy than turning base metal into gold.

By 1765 he was in Malta, in the service of the secretive Knights Hospitaller, Europe's richest and most powerful charitable institution. The Grand Master was himself an alchemist and Giuseppe's training as an apothecary came in handy: he ground medicine during the day and concocted his own potions in the evenings. After three years, he decided it was safe to return to Italy and, in 1768, surfaced in Rome, carrying letters of recommendation from the Grand Master himself. These secured him the patronage of Cardinal Orsini, whose secretary he became. Rome had a thriving Sicilian community: sharp-witted, resourceful immigrants keen to make money, from whom Giuseppe learned how to forge paintings and antiquities and sell them to tourists. At the same time, he put his medical skills to good use, presenting himself as a physician and pedalling the fruits of his Maltese experiments: an Elixir of Life that was said to delay the ageing process.

Not long after he arrived, he fell in love with and married a fourteen-year-old Roman girl from a poor family called Lorenza Serafina Feliciani. She was both heart-stoppingly beautiful and more than a match for her husband in cunning. Without her, Giuseppe Balsamo might never have promoted himself to the giddy heights of Count Alessandro di Cagliostro. They were a brilliant team – he was handsome, charismatic and ruthless; she was prepared to do anything to achieve a life of luxury and privilege. Giuseppe used her charms to entrap wealthy men whom he could then blackmail. On meeting the consummate con man, the Marquis of Agliata, he went even further, trading his wife's sexual favours in return for instruction in how to forge official documents. Soon he could produce letters of credit, wills, army commissions, even titles. A string of new identities followed. Styling themselves 'the Colonel and Mrs Pelligrini', they met Casanova. He was captivated by them but warned them to be careful: forgery was a risky business and carried the death penalty. He needn't have worried: Rome was already becoming too small and the Inquisition too suspicious. The Pelligrinis disappeared and the Count and Countess di Cagliostro took Europe by storm.

Over the next two decades, they lived and worked in France, England, Portugal, Spain, Germany, Russia and Poland. In Germany they met another great impostor, the Count de Saint Germain, who made a decent living by claiming to be 2,000 years old. As ever, Cagliostro listened and learned. In Strasbourg, he encountered the fashionable theory of animal magnetism and incorporated it into his act. In London, the chance discovery of an old manuscript inspired him to revive the ancient Egyptian Order of Masons, publicising it as a return to the authentic roots of freemasonry. Renting a house in Sloane Street, he billed himself as the 'Grand Coptha'. Serafina was the Grand Priestess, able to transfer the eternal spirit simply by breathing on a person's cheek. The Order not only admitted women to the Lodge, it held elaborate ceremonies in which participants of both sexes wore nothing but diaphanous robes. Acolytes were taught the names of seven secret angels to ease their path to earthly riches and immortality. Polite London society was mesmerised and subscriptions poured in.

The basic business plan was the same wherever they went. Arriving in a city, they rented grand and luxurious rooms and announced the establishment of a brand new school of medicine and philosophy. The services they offered wove together Masonry, alchemy, animal magnetism and Giuseppe's trusty elixir of life – with an unmistakeable background throb of sex. Cagliostro led the healing and the rituals; the Countess sat looking ravishing and offering a direct connection to the spirit world, like some elegant piece of mystical wireless technology. As one Parisian chronicler remarked:

> *There was hardly a fine lady in Paris who would not sup with the shade of Lucretius; a military officer who would not discuss war with Caesar, Hannibal or Alexander; or an advocate or counsellor who would not argue legal points with Cicero.*

Premium services such as the elixir and the spirit consultations had to be paid for, but the healing was free and open to all. This was a brilliant marketing ploy: once the news spread, the sick and the poor queued up at the premises, adding philanthropy to the Cagliostros burgeoning reputation. What's more, the treatments seemed to work. In Strasbourg more than 15,000 people claimed they had been cured; in Bordeaux the crowd greeting their arrival was so vast the local militia had to be deployed; and in Lyon Cagliostro-fever led to the building of a vast new Masonic temple to house his 'Egyptian Rite'.

As is the way with fads, the excitement soon faded. Most of the cures came from the placebo effect, from people's own belief in the magical powers on offer. Once that started to waver, the success rate dwindled and Cagliostro was forced to make even more extreme claims: that he could travel in time; he had been with Christ at the wedding at Cana; he could make himself invisible. When business started to fall off, it was time to move on.

This served them well for several years and they amassed quite a fortune. Then things started to go seriously awry. Cagliostro's attempt to seduce Catherine the Great with a love potion was a hopeless failure. She declared him a fraud and a menace and had him thrown out of Russia. In London a team of tricksters, intent on relieving him of his alchemical formulae, took advantage of his ignorance of English law and summonsed him for debt. Much of the money he had made inducting men and women into his Egyptian Order went to bribe his way out of debtor's prison. In France, his friend Cardinal de Rohan became embroiled in the 'Affair of the Diamond Necklace' implicating Marie Antoinette. Without a shred of evidence, Cagliostro was thrown into the Bastille. Even there he left a lasting impression: graffiti he scrawled on his cell wall was said to have predicted the Bastille would be 'pulled down' in 1789.

Ejected from France, almost bankrupt and tired of their rootless and increasingly hazardous travels, Serafina persuaded Cagliostro to return to Rome. It was a terrible mistake. The Inquisition had Freemasonry in its sights and the great illusionist was caught trying to recruit two papal spies into his Egyptian

Order. To save herself, Serafina testified against him. Cagliostro received a death-sentence but, after an audience with the Pope, this was commuted to life imprisonment. The unique life of Giuseppe Balsamo, Count di Cagliostro ended in a stone box high up in the fortress of San Leo, near Urbino. For four years, his only connection with the outside world was through a tiny trapdoor. Tormented by his captors, starving and louse-ridden, he gradually lost this mind and died of a stroke in 1795. As a heretic, he was refused the last rites and buried in the grounds of the castle in an unmarked grave. So many people refused to believe the news that Napoleon was forced to commission an official report: detailing beyond doubt that Cagliostro – inventor of the elixir of life – really was dead.

Some years earlier, Johann Wolfgang von Goethe (1749–1832) had visited Sicily, fascinated by rumours that Cagliostro wasn't really a count at all, but a jumped-up guttersnipe from Palermo. He tracked down Cagliostro's mother, who was living with her daughter and two grandchildren crammed into a one-room apartment. Rather touchingly, they were thrilled to hear that their Giuseppe had done so well for himself, but disappointed that he hadn't thought to help them. Goethe later sent them some money but the visit proved far more valuable for him. The idea of a man whose life is based on a lie and who claims to possess supernatural powers found its niche in history many years later in his great play *Faust*. Cagliostro's journey from poverty, to fame and riches, to penury and disgrace has an undeniably mythic quality. Even today, some people make claims for him as a great seer, with the courage and energy to do what few of us manage: to dream up a better life for himself and then to live it. Just as Oates had exploited people by playing on their nameless fears of impending doom, Cagliostro tapped into the common sense that there is more to life than meets the eye; that what happens to us is driven by unseen forces. It may be that he succeeded because people wanted to believe him.

~

Cagliostro never admitted his humble origins and most impostors never do. Some are unveiled by others; some move through a succession of disguises; very few unmask themselves. One who did is **George Psalmanazar** (1679–1763) who first appeared in England in 1704, feted as a Prince of Formosa, the first from his remote land (modern-day Taiwan) ever to visit Europe. It was the culmination of several years roaming the Continent trying on personalities. The first of these was as an Irish pilgrim on his way to Rome – the pilgrim's cloak gave him the right to beg for money – but people's knowledge of Ireland proved to be annoyingly widespread, so he developed a new persona: that of a 'heathen' from Japan, fond of swearing and eating heavily spiced raw meat and sleeping upright in a chair. In Germany, he enlisted as a mercenary, using his leisure to methodically build up corroborative evidence of his new identity: a 'Japanese' alphabet of twenty characters that read from right to left; the rules of 'his' language and pagan religion; and a calendar of twenty months. By the time he reached the Netherlands in 1701, he had adjusted his point of origin to the even more obscure Formosa and called himself Psalmanazar, a name he had borrowed from the biblical Assyrian king Shalamaneser, adding the foregoing 'P' for a natty alien flourish.

In Holland he met an ambitious young Scottish army chaplain called Alexander Innes. One of the legacies of the anti-Catholic paranoia that Oates had left in his wake was a deep antipathy to the Jesuits. They were believed to run a secret international spy ring, designed to undermine Protestantism and make converts at every turn. Psalmanazar said he had been tricked into leaving his homeland by a Jesuit in disguise, which had left him with a strong aversion to Catholicism. Whether or not Innes believed him, he at once saw a chance for professional advancement. Here was a potentially high-profile convert in the opposite direction. Now all that was needed was for him to be received into the Church of England. The plan worked. The Bishop of London was thrilled by the heathen-turned-Anglican and proudly introduced him to the great and the good of London society. Not only was Innes lavishly praised for having brought about the conversion, he also retained the lucrative rights to Psalmanazar's public appearances, exhibiting him as a glamorous 'royal' to a paying audience.

Given that even educated English people of the time knew next to nothing about the Far East (and even less about the island of Formosa) Psalmanazar was able to get away with some madly outlandish claims. Its capital Xternetsa, he revealed, was presided over by the Emperor Meriaandanoo and men went naked except for a decorative plate of silver or gold covering their sexual organs. Though now reformed, he himself had once been a cannibal, because in Formosa it was legal to eat adulterous wives. Men did not generally marry until they reached fifty, but thereafter did so as often as possible because a supply of baby boys was in constant demand as live sacrifices to their god, who appeared sometimes as an elephant, sometimes as an ox. Psalmanazar wore a snake around his neck because, he explained, that was how Formosans kept cool. Within a year he had produced a book that became an immediate best-seller. *A Historical and Geographical Description of Formosa, an Island subject to the Emperor of Japan*, painted elaborate pictures of Formosan life, language and culture. It was ingenious, sensational and entirely bogus.

Some were dubious from the beginning. Psalmanazar went head to head with Jean de Fontenay, a Jesuit who had actually spent time in Formosa, who asked him why his skin was so fair. He responded by saying that Formosan royalty lived underground. He was invited to speak to members of the Royal Society, where the astronomer Edmund Halley challenged him vigorously. Halley inquired if sunlight ever shone directly down the chimneys of Formosan houses. Since the island was near the equator it was logical that at certain times of year it would do so, but Psalmanazar said it didn't. Then, sensing a trap, he added, 'Formosan chimneys are almost always built at crooked angles and containing bends.'

By 1707 the Formosan craze was over. Psalmanazar's attempts to capitalise on his fame by marketing a brand of lacquer which he called 'white Formosan work' failed to catch on and, after brief stints painting ladies' fans and working as a clerk to an army regiment, he decided to devote himself to writing. In 1717 he confessed to his friends that the whole thing had been a fraud. It's a testament to his true character that he wasn't ostracised. Far from it: the 'pretended Formosan' settled quite easily into life as a jobbing member of Grub Street. Already fluent in Latin, he learnt Hebrew and his contributions to several large encyclopaedias were praised for the accuracy of their research, particularly when describing the customs and culture of ancient peoples. He even produced a corrective article on Formosa, this time basing it on fact. The young Dr Johnson counted him a close friend: enthusiastically stating that his company was 'preferable to almost anyone else'. When Boswell asked him if he ever mentioned

Formosa, Johnson replied he was 'afraid even to mention China' and, as for opposing so learned and devout a man: 'I should as soon think of contradicting a Bishop!'

Psalmanazar's final act of contrition was to write his memoirs. Published after his death, they throw light on his unfathomable decisions to construct and then de-construct his Formosan identity. Though he never reveals his true name – and no one has ever been able to do so since – he does say that he was born into a poor family in southern France, was educated by Jesuits, and that his father left home when he was young. Psalmanazar's troubles began when he was sacked as a tutor to a rich family for refusing the sexual advances of the mistress of the house. His 'prodigious' gift for languages offered a way out and a chance to earn a living as someone else. Fastening on Formosa afforded him 'a vast scope to a fertile fancy to work upon.' In another age, with his talent for fine-grained invention, he might have made a superb fantasy novelist.

Unlike Oates and Cagliostro, Psalmanazar was, in the end, a truthful man. He underwent a religious experience after reading William Law's *A Serious Call to a Devout and Holy Life* (1728), an eighteenth-century self-help manual that also changed the life of his friend Dr Johnson. Law's mystical work advised surrender to God on the grounds that God's wisdom is beyond rational enquiry. This new philosophical outlook, coupled with a deep absorption in his scholarship, somehow released Psalmanazar, enabling him to come to terms with what he called the 'vile and romantic account' that had briefly made him famous. He re-invented himself as a pious and respected English man of letters, his last and happiest persona. But there is in the memoirs, written in his eighties, still a mischievous twinkle in his eye: 'I never met with, nor heard of any one, that ever guessed right, or any thing near it, with regard to my native country.' His last secret – who he really was – he took with him to his grave.

~

Almost half a century later, another example of self-appointed foreign royalty came to light in the West Country in the exotic persona of **Princess Caraboo** (1791–1864).

In April 1817 a beautiful young woman in a turban knocked at the door of a cobbler in the village of Almondsbury in Gloucestershire, not far from Bristol. She spoke an unintelligible language, but gestured that she needed a place to sleep. Unsure what to do, the cobbler's wife took her to Mr Hill, the overseer of the poor. He would normally have locked her up as a vagabond but instead chose to escort her to the manor house to seek advice from the local bigwig, Samuel Worrall, the county magistrate and town clerk of Bristol. Worrall's manservant (who was Greek and spoke several European languages) could make no sense of her either, so it was arranged for her to spend the night at the village inn. There, she insisted on sleeping on the floor rather than a bed, and, on seeing a picture of a pineapple on the wall, said the word 'ananas'. Offered a cup of tea, she covered her eyes and muttered what seemed to be a prayer before drinking it.

The next day she was taken back to the manor house for a second interview. Samuel Worrall's American wife Elizabeth took a liking to her, showing her some furniture decorated with Chinese scenes and coaxing her into revealing her name was 'Caraboo'. But the Greek manservant was suspicious and Worrall himself – known as 'Devil' Worrall and a notorious drunkard – irritably intervened and declared she was a beggar and must be sent to Bristol to be tried for vagrancy. During her brief incarceration there, a Portuguese sailor was found who claimed to understand her language. He explained that she was from an island called Javasu. Her mother had been killed in a war against the Boogoos (who were cannibals), and she had been kidnapped by pirates (killing one of them in the process). She had escaped by leaping from the pirate ship as it passed through the Bristol Channel and swum ashore. What's more, she was a princess.

This rather altered things for 'Devil' Worrall. He had been trying to publicise his struggling private bank and was most accommodating when his wife insisted the 'princess' be brought back to Knole Park as an honoured guest. She stayed with them through the summer, delighting throngs of visitors. She showed off her fencing and archery skills, swam naked in the lake, performed a war dance involving a gong, prepared a spicy chicken curry and prayed to 'Allah Tallah' from the treetops. The Worralls' Greek manservant brooded in the background. Once, he woke her in the middle of the night yelling 'Fire!' but the Princess showed no sign of alarm. A written sample of Princess Caraboo's native language found its way to Oxford University where linguists gave their opinion that it was as a fake, so Mr Worrall invited the learned Dr Wilkinson from Bath to settle the matter once and for all. Wilkinson, who lectured on everything from electricity to washable wallpaper, immediately brushed all doubts aside. The incisions on the back of her head could only be the work of oriental surgeons and her language was, of course, Rejang, a dialect of Sumatra.

A delighted Worrall encouraged Dr Wilkinson to publish his findings in full in the local paper, and this proved to be the Princess's undoing. Mrs Neale, a landlady from Bristol, identified her as a former lodger who had entertained the household by reciting a made-up language. When confronted with the news, the Princess broke down and confessed the truth to Mrs Worrall: she was really Mary Baker, a cobbler's daughter from Titheridge in Devon.

The Worralls (and the ludicrous Dr Wilkinson) became a laughing-stock, but they decided that punishing the girl would only make things worse. It would be less embarrassing if she just disappeared, so they put her aboard a ship sailing for Philadelphia. Worrall's bank collapsed soon afterwards, forcing him to resign as Town Clerk. For a few months Mary made theatrical appearances in America and wrote letters to Mrs Worrall, keeping her up-to-date with her progress as a minor celebrity. By the year's end the letters stopped coming. Nothing more was heard of her until 'Princess Caraboo' suddenly re-appeared in Bond Street in London. Later she toured other European countries, but the shows were not a success and she returned to Bristol where she got married (oddly enough, to a man called Baker) and gave birth to a daughter.

The details of her life before she became Princess Caraboo are sadly typical of many poor women of her time. She had contracted rheumatic fever as a child after which, her father said, she had 'never been right in head'. Worn out by spells as a farm labourer and a domestic maid, but always a tomboy, she left home at nineteen and set off on the road, living rough. Half-starved and depressed, she tried to hang herself, but stopped at the last minute, afraid of committing a mortal sin. When she reached London she was seriously ill – the scars of the back of her head that Dr Wilkinson had found were in fact the result of a clumsy operation in a poor-house hospital.

Mary had many other adventures during her five- or six-year

absence from the West Country. She was briefly admitted to Magdalen hospital, a home for fallen women, but was asked to leave when it became clear she hadn't ever actually worked as a prostitute. When asked why she had come there in the first place, she said simply that she'd liked the look of the brown dresses and straw hats the inmates wore. Once, walking over Salisbury plain, disguised as a man for safety, she was captured and imprisoned by a band of highwaymen. On another occasion, she became pregnant, identifying the father as an Exeter bricklayer called John Baker, or else a Frenchman she had met in a bookshop. The child didn't live long and Mary was on her way once more. She fell in step with a group of Romanies, who may have inspired her to invent her 'Javasu' language, and worked as a cook for a Jewish family, whose religious rituals possibly provided material for her own arcane incantations.

Just before appearing from nowhere as Princess Caraboo, she was sacked as a children's nanny by a Mr and Mrs Starling of Islington, for frightening the young Starlings with hair-raising tales of being born in the 'East Indies'. Mrs Starling declared her anecdotes so wild she could 'not even begin to recollect a quarter of the girl's vagaries'. Mary had also set fire to two beds in a week.

A contemporary account of Princess Caraboo's life noted her remarkable ability to maintain her story in the face of repeated questioning and called her performance 'an instance of consummate art and duplicity'. On arriving in Bristol from London, Mary noticed the Breton beggar girls, and copied their dress by adopting a turban. She pretended to be French, but when questioned by a French official, she said she was Spanish. When the inevitable Spaniard was produced she improvised her own 'lingo' out of her own head.

It now seems clear that her great deception began only to avoid being locked up for the night for vagrancy. Finding herself believed by so many of the good folk of Almondsbury, the temptation to avoid, by any means, a return to her degrading and aimless past must have been impossible to resist. What she lacked in formal education she more than made up for in imagination, quick thinking and an excellent memory. The local gentry were content to go along with her fantasy rather than betray their own ignorance and, when 'experts' on foreign countries were called in to question her, the Princess invariably kept a judicious but enigmatic silence. But she listened carefully, squirreling away their overheard conversations to use later. As with Psalmanazar, celebrity changed and calmed her. The adulation of her many admirers seemed to assuage the restlessness and suicidal urges of her youth. She did not find riches with her fame, but maybe she found herself and, with that, the contentment that had eluded her for so long.

For the last thirty years of her life Mary lived a genteel existence, quietly supplying leeches to Bristol Infirmary. Her past only occasionally rose up to embarrass her when local children called out 'Caraboo!' She fell dead in the street on Christmas Eve 1864, and was buried in an unmarked grave. Her daughter, also called Mary, carried on the leech business, living alone in a house full of cats, where she died in a fire in 1900.

～

Take away the pretensions to royal blood, and Princess Caraboo's story is echoed a generation later in the adventures of **Louis de Rougemont (1847–1921)**. He came to public notice via a series of fantastical articles published in London's *Wide World* magazine, in which he recalled his thirty years in the wilds of Papua New Guinea and the Australian Outback.

His story went like this. Originally Swiss, he had been shipwrecked in 1864 en route to northern Australia on a Singaporean pearling boat. Rescued by his dog Bruno, who dragged him from the depths by his long hair and then towed him ashore by his tail, he spent two years on an uninhabited island, keeping fit by doing gymnastics on the sand and taking rides on the backs of turtles. He steered the turtles by poking his left or right toe into the appropriate eye according to which direction he wanted to travel and then ate them, using their blood to nourish the corn he planted in their upturned shells. Liberated by some passing natives in a canoe, he went back to their village where he married an Aboriginal tribeswoman called Yamba and was treated as a god. He was given the name 'Winnimah' (meaning 'lightning') because he could shoot down birds in mid-flight with his bow and arrow. He would lead the tribe into battle against other villages, wearing stilts and dressed as a wizard. At sea he was a fearless sailor, once killing a whale single-handed and on another occasion wrestling a crocodile.

De Rougemont's articles did not go unchallenged. Like Psalmanazar, he received a public grilling, in his case by members of the Royal Geographical Society. They were unimpressed by his inability to show them where he had been on any map, and by his sparse grasp of any of the native languages he had supposedly learnt in the wild. In due course, an investigation by the *Daily Chronicle* revealed that De Rougemont's real name was Henry Louis Grin, and that he had a wife and seven children in Australia. He had run away from his responsibilities after various hare-brained inventions failed to sell, including an automated potato digger that didn't work, and a diving suit that drowned the first man who tried it. He had augmented his knowledge of northern Australia with research in the reading room at the British Library. Exposed by the press, De Rougemont (or Grin) turned it to his advantage, touring South Africa in 1899 as 'The Greatest Liar on Earth', though a similar tour to Australia didn't go down at all well and he was booed offstage.

In 1906 he appeared in the huge aquarium at the London Hippodrome where he successfully demonstrated his turtle-riding skills, but his last business venture (producing an apparently inedible substitute for meat) came to nothing during the First World War.

After that, De Rougemont lived, according to his obituary in the *New York Times,* in 'a simple style' in London as 'Louis Redmond', until his death in a workhouse hospital in 1921.

Compared to Cagliostro, his career as an impostor was fleeting. The world had moved on since the days of Psalmanazar and Princess Caraboo. Rationality was the order of the day. Modern communications offered fewer places to hide, and science had learned much with the passing of the years. Though De Rougemont was a plausible liar and armed with in-depth research, he couldn't resist pushing things too far. His claims of encountering flying wombats were never likely to survive expert scrutiny.

~

One who did survive expert scrutiny, unsuspected, and for an entire lifetime, was **James Barry** (1792–1865). Even without the concealment at its heart, Barry's life would rank as extraordinary. Graduating as a doctor at thirteen, he joined the army and was appointed assistant surgeon before his fifteenth birthday. His first posting was to Cape Town, where he became personal physician to the Governor, Sir Charles Somerset. In 1826 he found fame as the first British doctor to perform a successful caesarean section. Slightly built, and just above five feet tall, James Barry was also famous for his sharp tongue and quick temper, challenging several men to duels (though he never killed anyone). After tours of duty in Mauritius and Jamaica, he was posted to St Helena as resident surgeon. Here his argumentative streak led to a court-martial for 'conduct unbecoming' and, although he was exonerated, he was sent home to England. In 1851 he was appointed deputy inspector-general of hospitals in Corfu, where his innovations in the hygiene and diet of patients set new standards that were to inspire Florence Nightingale. Barry was considered too senior to serve in the Crimea, but he nevertheless visited it and met the Lady with the Lamp, giving her the worst dressing down of her life. She was later to write: 'I should say [he] was the most hardened creature I ever met throughout the army.' After many more medical reforms and other successes, Barry was retired (against his wishes), settling in Marylebone, London, where he died of diarrhoea during an epidemic in 1865.

He had left strict instructions that his body was to be left in the clothes he died in and sewn up in a sheet before his burial. Although the senior doctor had already examined him and signed his death certificate, as his corpse was being laid out, a female attendant noticed something unusual. It was the body of a woman – and one that had, at some point, borne a child. The funeral at St Paul's went ahead regardless and Barry was buried (as a man) in Kensal Green cemetery, but the scandalous news soon leaked out. Some said Barry was a hermaphrodite, others that she was a woman; many refused to believe any such thing. But as there was no post-mortem, no definitive judgement could be made and the army decided to lock Barry's records away for a century.

Thanks to some heroic research in the 1950s by the historian Isobel Rae, we now know that James Barry was born Margaret Ann Bulkley, the daughter of a Cork grocer. She had started dressing as a boy from the age of ten. Her mother, Mary-Ann, was the sister of a real James Barry, a professor of painting at the Royal Academy. The family fell on hard times after Margaret's father was gaoled for debt in 1803, so her mother and some influential friends of her uncle James conspired to smuggle her into medical school.

The disappearance of Margaret Bulkley and the appearance of James Barry were carefully orchestrated. Mrs Bulkley and 'James' travelled up to Edinburgh posing as aunt and nephew, and the new 'James Barry' enrolled at university. To protect the secret, they cut themselves off from friends and family. Only the conspirators knew who they were. From then on, Margaret always wore an overcoat and lied about her age to avoid questions about her smooth chin and high voice. Her graduation in 1812, though no one suspected it at the time, made her the first woman to qualify as a doctor in Britain.

As for the question of her baby, it seems likely that it was conceived as a result of her relationship with Lord Charles Somerset, governor of the Cape Colony. Their close friendship had given rise to rumours of a gay affair at the time, and Barry made an unexplained excursion to Mauritius for several months where it is possible she gave birth. No record of the fate of the child has survived and her mother, of course, never even so much hinted at its existence.

It's barely credible that such a successful and public individual managed to conceal the secret of her sex for more than sixty years. The pressure to keep up appearances must have been extraordinary, and her aggressive demeanour part of that front. Once dismissed as a transvestite, or some sort of inter-sexual freak, neither description does justice to this astonishing person. Man enough to flirt with women, and feminine enough to give birth to her lover's child, James Barry must rank as the most successful impostor of all time.

~

A single change of identity was enough to last Margaret Bulkley for a lifetime, but **Ignácz Trebitsch Lincoln (1879–1943)** seems to have suffered from multiple personality disorder. He was variously an actor, arms dealer, post-office worker, oil speculator, British Liberal MP, vicar and German spy. His spiritual loyalties were even looser than those of Titus Oates, veering from Judaism to Presbyterianism, working as an Anglican missionary and finally ending up as a Buddhist monk. Like Oates, he combined a desperate desire for recognition with a breathtaking dishonesty. Unlike Oates, he was also highly intelligent and immensely likeable.

Ignácz Trebitsch was born in the small town of Paks in central Hungary, one of at least fourteen children. The scant attention he received no doubt explains much of his future behaviour. In 1895, his family moved to Budapest and the sixteen-year-old Trebitsch enrolled at the Royal Hungarian Academy of Dramatic Art. He lied to get in and dropped out after a year. Falsehood and inability to stick to one course were to be the hallmarks of his career. At eighteen, pursued by the police for stealing a gold watch, Trebitsch fled abroad. He spent almost no time in his homeland again. As his biographer Bernard Wasserstein put it: 'Travel for Trebitsch was not a source of amusement or of intellectual enrichment; it was a disease.'

In London, he met the Reverend Lypshytz of the Society for the Promotion of Christianity among the Jews. Trebitsch had been raised as an Orthodox Jew and was woefully short of cash, so he knew at once what to do. The prospect of a regular income as a Presbyterian missionary was easily enough to induce him to convert to Christianity. Sent to Montreal in Canada, he squandered large amounts of the society's money without denting the religious persuasion of anyone. In 1901 he married Margarethe Kahlor, the daughter of a German sea captain, and brought her back to England where she had four sons and he spent her inheritance. He served briefly an Anglican curate in Appledore in Kent – just 40 miles from Bobbing where the Rev. Oates had enraged his flock – adding the word 'Lincoln' to his name by deed poll to make himself sound more English. It was one of over a dozen names he was to use in his career.

In 1904 I. T. T. Lincoln, as he now styled himself, failed the exams for the priesthood and started casting around for gainful employment. His eye fell on Benjamin Seebohm Rowntree, Quaker philanthropist, Liberal grandee and confectionery magnate. Expertly charming his way into Rowntree's affections, Trebitsch Lincoln got himself appointed as his research assistant for a book he was planning on poverty in Belgium. The work involved frequent visits to the Continent and the linguistically gifted Trebitsch was ideal. He set to the task with alacrity, using Rowntree's name, money and access to British embassies around Europe to live life to the full, and supplementing his already generous income (or so he later claimed) by moonlighting as a German double agent.

The innocent Rowntree was impressed by his energy and it occurred to him he was just the sort of person Britain needed as an MP. He used his influence with the Liberal Party to take him on as candidate for the safe Conservative seat of Darlington: the only Hungarian citizen ever to be formally adopted by a major British political party. Hurriedly securing British naturalisation, Mr Ignatius Lincoln stood in the general election of January 1910. Endorsed by his fellow Liberals Churchill and Lloyd George, and delivering his speeches in a thick Hungarian accent, he ridiculed his opponent's trade policy by claiming it was forcing Germans to eat their own dogs. To everybody's amazement, he won. Though only by the slender margin of twenty-nine votes, it was an astounding achievement: the sitting Unionist MP was Herbert Pike Pease, a prominent local figure whose family had founded the Stockton and Darlington railway and who basically owned the town. Lincoln's victory earned him a cartoon in *Punch*. He took his seat in the House but, as MPs were unpaid at the time, he was soon in considerable debt. When a second general election was called in December, he stood down, pleading insolvency.

This freed him up to concentrate on a more straightforward career as a fraudster. With financial backing from the unsuspecting Rowntree, he floated a series of public corporations to exploit oil wells in central Europe, raising large amounts of investment on the stock market, not repaying borrowed money and ruining the shareholders in the companies he started, all of which collapsed. Desperate, he resorted to forgery to obtain further loans, but by 1914 he was bankrupt again.

When the First World War broke out, Trebitsch Lincoln, as a former Austro-Hungarian citizen with a German wife, found himself in an awkward situation. He was also fearful of arrest, lest his forgeries be discovered. Never one to take the easy option, he decided he would become a spy – ideally as a double agent in a neutral country.

He didn't mind who took him on. He offered his services to the British first, but they ignored him. He then went to Holland and tried the Germans. The Germans were dubious, but decided to give him a go. So he returned to England and promptly offered to sell German secret codes (that he didn't have) to the British. While he was getting nowhere with them, his past caught up with him (as he had feared it would) and he had to leave in a hurry for the United States to avoid arrest for fraud. Here he sold his story to the papers: the British MP turned German master-spy.

Infuriated by his antics, the British government sought his extradition and Trebitsch was arrested by the Americans and packed off back to London. While in prison awaiting trial, he was given a job in the censor's office at Mount Pleasant Sorting Office, reading mail written in German. He was taken there and back each day in a prison van. Making friends with his guards, on the way home one evening, he somehow persuaded them it would be a good idea if they all stopped off for a drink. So, while the guards went to the bar, Trebitsch went to the toilet and escaped out of the window.

He went on the run, making his way back to the States and supporting himself by writing yet more brazen (and largely fictitious) accounts of his spying career for the newspapers. The British, after much difficulty and a series of fiascos involving the US Federal police and the Pinkerton detective agency, managed to track him down and extradite him a second time. He stood trial and was sentenced to three years for fraud, which he served in Parkhurst on the Isle of Wight. In 1919, having done his time, he was stripped of his British citizenship and deported to mainland Europe.

He headed for Germany, where the extreme right-wing journalist Wolfgang Kapp and a cadre of anti-Semitic former German army officers were plotting the overthrow of the Weimar Republic. Trebitsch, with his effortless ability to get on with absolutely anybody, was appointed press officer to the group, in which capacity he met the young Hitler. With his fellow Nazi Dietrich Eckart, Hitler had flown to Berlin intending to join the coup. But on catching sight of Trebitsch's distinctly Jewish physiognomy, so the tale goes, the deal was off. 'Come on Adolf,' said Eckart. 'We have no further business here.' Another version casts Trebitsch in an even more pivotal historic role: it is said that he saved Hitler's life by bundling him on to a plane as he was about to be arrested.

The putsch took place in 1920, when Kapp and 6,000 German naval commandos under General Walther von Lüttwitz marched on Berlin. The occupation was short-lived (the rebels were brought down in less than a week by a general strike) but, for a brief glorious moment, Mr Ignatius Lincoln was Minister of Information – the only former British MP ever to serve as a member of a German government. The revolt having failed, Trebitsch went south and took refuge in Munich, the heartland of fascism. Here he devoted himself to Byzantine intrigues with extreme right-wingers in Austria, Czechoslovakia and Hungary. In Budapest he became involved with a loose alliance of rabid monarchists and fervent anti-communists known as 'White International'. Many of its members were so murderously anti-semitic that they preferred to avoid delegation and personally kill Jews themselves, but Trebitsch, as ever, charmed them all. After which, true to form, he betrayed them: selling their secret plans to the Czechoslovak government. Because of his reputation, no one but the Czechs believed that the (for once) genuine documents were actually genuine. Trebitsch then set off for Italy to campaign for the Fascists but they didn't trust him an inch and threw him out. As a deportee from the USA, Britain, Austria and Italy, he was becoming quite famous: *Time* magazine called him 'the man no country wanted'.

Trebitsch didn't care. He chose a country where no one had ever heard of him and went there: China. Calling himself Puk Kusati, he dabbled in forged passports and worked for three different warlords as an arms-dealer, dashing off a few pieces of anti-British propaganda in his spare time. Then in 1925, after a revelatory epiphany, Trebitsch Lincoln surprised everyone by suddenly converting to Buddhism and becoming a monk. As Chao Kung, he was an assiduous student, meditating for six years and rising to the high rank of Bodhisattva. He had his shaven head branded with the twelve circular symbols from the Buddhist wheel of life and became the first Westerner to found his own Buddhist monastery in the East. But old habits die hard: on entering the sacred portal, initiates were required to hand over their worldly goods to Abbot Chao Kung, and he passed the evenings seducing nuns. His Shanghai monastery would be the closest thing he had to a settled base for the rest of his life. In 1931 he published an autobiography in which, despite having written an earlier book entitled *Revelations of an International Spy*, he denied ever having had any involvement in espionage. He wrote only of his newfound passion for Buddhism and his vision for world peace.

The outbreak of the Second World War spurred the old Trebitsch back into action once more. The city of Shanghai was also the base of the Far Eastern section of the Gestapo. Trebitsch contacted the bureau chief, Joseph Meisinger, the 'Butcher of Warsaw' who had ordered the execution of thousands of Jews. Like many an anti-Semite before him, Meisinger was completely taken in by Chao Kung/Trebitsch. Under the guise of a peace mission, Chao Kung offered to deliver every Buddhist in the East to the German/Japanese cause. His price was a face-to-face meeting with Hitler, where he would prove his power by conjuring three Tibetan sages out of thin air. Incredibly, both Rudolf Hess and von Ribbentrop enthusiastically endorsed this plan, which only foundered when Hess flew to Scotland in 1941. Two phials of sacred Tibetan liquid were found in his plane. Shortly after that, Chao Kung did something entirely out of character: he wrote to Hitler denouncing the Holocaust. It was to prove his death warrant. When the Japanese invaded Shanghai in October 1943, he was summarily arrested. He died a few days later from 'a stomach complaint', poisoned on the instructions of the Nazi high command.

What are we to make of Trebitsch Lincoln? The very least one can say of him is that he never wasted a day. The range of people he persuaded to trust him is amazing– Yorkshiremen, Nazis, Buddhists: none of them are exactly noted for their gullibility. Like Cagliostro, he seems to have had an almost magical talent to impress and inspire people that he himself wasn't fully able to control. And it is just possible that his final religious conversion – to Tibetan Buddhism – marked some sort of genuine spiritual homecoming.

In 1925, the year of his mystical experience, he had tried to return to England to see his twenty-three-year-old son, John, who was awaiting execution for murder. John Lincoln was a British soldier who had bludgeoned a travelling salesman to death while drunkenly trying to burgle his house. Despite a petition with over 50,000 signatures asking for the hanging to be delayed so that Trebitsch could visit his son for the last time, the authorities went ahead as planned. They even refused him a temporary entry visa to go to the funeral. When informed of John's death as he waited for a boat at The Hague, he broke down and wept, exclaiming in despair: 'My sins have been visited on my son!'

~

No one reads Trebitsch Lincoln's books these days, but it is curious to discover that the author of the twentieth-century's best-selling books on Tibetan Buddhism was yet another impostor: **Tuesday Lobsang Rampa** (1910–1981) He rocketed to fame in 1956 with the publication of *The Third Eye*, a riveting account of growing up in Tibet. Despite having been rejected as an obvious hoax by several publishers and receiving horrendous reviews (only the *Times* charitably called it 'almost a work of art'), it became a massive international best-seller. The publishers, Secker & Warburg, admitted that they too had had doubts about its authenticity, but thought it would make a good read anyway. They prefaced it with a statement saying that many of the author's stories were 'inevitably hard to corroborate'. On one occasion, to test his veracity, Lobsang Rampa's editor at Secker & Warburg read out some phonetic Tibetan to him to which he didn't react. When he was told that he had just failed to understand a single word of his 'own language', Lobsang Rampa threw himself on to the floor, apparently writhing in agony. His excuse was that that he had been horrifically tortured by the Japanese during the war and had blocked out all knowledge of Tibetan through self-hypnotism.

In fact, he had done no such thing. Tuesday Lobsang Rampa was Cyril Henry Hoskin, a plumber's son from Devon. There was a stark contrast between his actual character and his literary alter ego: Hoskin had never been outside England and didn't even have a passport. Exposed by the *Daily Mail* in 1958, based on information acquired by a private detective in the pay of Heinrich Harrer (author of the classic travelogue *Seven Years in Tibet*), Hoskin was unrepentant. He explained that the spirit of a Tibetan monk had possessed him after he fell out of a tree in his garden in London while trying to photograph an owl.

Some of Tuesday Lobsang Rampa's disclosures must stretch the credulity of even the most devoted fan. He claimed to have had a splinter inserted into his pineal gland in Tibet, which had activated his 'Third Eye'. The operation took place when he – or the monk who possessed him – was eight, he said, and was accompanied by a slight 'scrunch' as the splinter went into his skull and a 'blinding flash'. He learned from the monk who carried out the procedure that this would enable him to 'see people as they are, and not as they pretend to be'. Whether this, or some other gift, was responsible, 'Lobsang Rampa' went on to produce another eighteen books. In *Doctor from Lhasa*, he tells how he learned to fly a plane, was captured by the Japanese during the Second World War, spent time in concentration camps as the official medical officer, and was one of very few people to survive the atomic bomb dropped on Hiroshima. In *The Rampa Story*, he describes journeying through Europe and the USA, enduring further capture and torture, before transmigrating into the body of Cyril Henry Hoskin. His first name, 'Tuesday', marked the day of the week on which his 'reincarnation' took place. Nor did he restrict himself to mere terrestrial travel, recounting a visit to Venus aboard a space ship and meeting two aliens – helpfully named 'the Tall One' and 'the Broad One'. His fifth book, *Living with the Lama,* he admitted, was not Lopsang Rampa's work at all: he had taken dictation from Mrs Fifi Greywhiskers, his Siamese cat.

To avoid continual public ridicule, Hoskin left England in the early 1960s, settling first in Ireland and then Calgary in Canada. When he died in 1981, he left much of his fortune to his beloved cats. His Lobsang Rampa series had sold more than four million books, and they continue to sell.

Hoskin insisted to the end that he really was 'Lobsang Rampa' inside, and the books have an undeniable energy to them. But they are complete fakes, as little to do with real Buddhism or life in Tibet as Psalmanazar's book was with Formosa. Like Cagliostro's elixir of life, they are a beguiling attempt to give people what they want – versions of a strange, mystical East, where ancient sages hold all the universe's secrets, where the laws of time and space don't hold, and where the tawdriness of the modern world – of life under the kitchen sink – holds no sway.

~

It's safe to assume that when eighteen-year-old **Archibald Belaney** (1888–1938) left Hastings in Sussex for the wide-open spaces of Canada, he had no plans to become an impostor. Like so many of the other people in this chapter, his early life was marked by rejection and abandonment. His father was a drunken wastrel, leaving his mother for a new life in America when Archie was only thirteen, and dying some years later in a bar-room brawl. His mother, Kitty, had already taken herself off to London, leaving Archie to be raised by his two viciously disciplinarian aunts. He grew up a self-absorbed child, playing at Red Indians alone in the nearby woods and keeping a menagerie in his room, with a strong distaste for authority and the petty snobbishness of English suburban life. After attending Hastings grammar school, he managed a short stint in a timber yard before being sacked for detonating a home-made bomb in the works chimney. In exasperation, his aunts allowed him to pursue his dream of moving to Canada to study farming.

Archie at once fell in love with the wild, unspoilt Canadian outback. He also fell in love with, and married, a Native American woman, Angele Egwuna, an Ojibwa from northern Ontario. His affinity for the land, and for its indigenous peoples, took firm root and, gradually, Belaney began to abandon his English background. He worked as a trapper and guide and soon took to using an Indian name – Washaquonasin, translated into English as Grey Owl, or 'Walks-in-the-Dark'. But, dogged by the shadow of his past, in 1912, like his own father before him, he left Angele and their two little daughters, Agnes and Flora, and moved in with Marie Girard with whom he had a son, Johnny. At the same time, he buffed up his biography. He was now the son of a Scottish father and a half-Apache mother, born in Mexico but since accepted as an honorary Ojibwa.

On the outbreak of the First World War, Belaney joined the Canadian Black Watch: as an Indian. He earned the respect of his comrades for his exceptional marksmanship and knife-throwing skills, and for his uncanny ability to move undetected across no-man's-land. He became a sniper, but was wounded badly in his foot. After it developed gangrene, he was sent back to England to recuperate. There, in 1917, he met and married his old Hastings sweetheart Ivy Holmes. The marriage lasted for five years till Ivy found out about Angele and divorced him for bigamy. Belaney, by then honourably discharged from the army and with a disability pension, headed back to Canada and the great outdoors. He made no attempt to contact Marie Girard, or his first wife Angele Egwuna (although he never divorced her).

By 1925 he was living with Gertrude Bernard, a beautiful Iroquois woman eighteen years his junior, whom he renamed Anahareo. It was Anahareo who seems to have put the idea into Archie's head that killing animals for money wasn't a good thing. With her encouragement, he began instead to write for the Canadian press about life in the wilderness. By the early 1930s, he had become a naturalist for the Canadian National Parks service. The couple lived in a cabin on a lake in central Saskatchewan with Rawhide and Jellyroll, their two adopted beavers, whose lodge took up almost half the cabin.

During this period Grey Owl became famous as the first environmentalist activist to achieve an international following. A sequence of books about his life with Anahareo followed and, in 1935, at the request of his publisher, Lovat Dickson, the Canadian who ran Macmillan in London, he began a high-profile lecture tour of England. Dressed in full Indian headdress and buckskin, Grey Owl was dubbed the modern Hiawatha. The tour was a huge commercial success but the workload put a strain on his relationship with Anahareo. In 1936 she moved out with their small daughter, Shirley Dawn, while Grey Owl entered into another bigamous marriage with a medical assistant called Yvonne Perrier. At their wedding in Montreal, he used the name Archie MacNeil, to fit in with his supposed Scottish heritage.

A second international lecture tour saw him mobbed by

crowds wherever he went. He was invited to Buckingham Palace to meet the young Princesses, Elizabeth and Margaret, and gave a royal command performance, attended by the young Richard and David Attenborough, both of whom later said that the experience had a significant influence on their careers. (Sir David was captivated by the naturalism, and, over sixty years later, Lord Richard was to make a movie of Grey Owl's life.) Though now a celebrity on both sides of the Atlantic, Grey Owl's triumph was short lived. After an intense schedule of over two hundred lectures, he returned to his cabin in Canada in 1938 suffering from exhaustion and died of pneumonia shortly afterwards.

Within weeks of his death, newspapers began to unearth Grey Owl's true identity. It wasn't an edifying picture. The latter-day Hiawatha was an English bigamist who had dyed his hair and his skin to appear more authentic. He had walked out on at least four women, fathering children by three of them. Several native Canadians had clearly been aware of his true identity – or at least his racial origins – but it seems they kept quiet about it: he was such a fine ambassador for their way of life and the land they wanted to protect. Anahareo, the woman to whom he had been closest, always maintained she had never doubted his story. The initial shock was hard for his friends to take. Lovat Dickson, who at first valiantly tried to defend Grey Owl's reputation, was forced to concede that he, too, had been fooled: 'We had been duped,' he wrote in *Wilderness Man*, his definitive biography of Belaney. 'There was no Arcadia.' Grey Owl's books stopped selling and the conservationist causes he had championed fell out of favour.

But when the dust had settled, people began to reassess his reputation. In 1940 Anahareo published a remarkably positive autobiography, reminding Grey Owl's huge fan base just how much good he had done. He had cared nothing for money; he had used his fame only to help raise awareness of the threatened habitats of his friends: the beavers, eagles and bears.

Did Grey Owl's deception really matter? There is something magnificent in his refusal to conform to modern life. And his achievements, at least, were real: he lived an authentic life among native Canadians, his knowledge of their lore and culture second to none. Most of all, his work as a conservationist changed the thinking of an entire generation:

> *The voice from the forests momentarily released us from some spell. In contrast to Hitler's screaming, ranting voice and in contrast to the remorseless clanking of modern technology, Grey Wolf's words evoked an unforgettable charm, lighting in our minds the vision of a cool, quiet place, where men and animals live in love and trust together.*

No one captures the double life of the impostor better than Archie Belaney. On the one hand, an abandoned child, seeking refuge in the company of animals and dreaming of being a 'Red Indian', growing into a man unable to form a stable relationship with a woman; a loner who drank too much and was capable of acts of cruelty, 'almost a madman' on occasions. On the other hand, the powerful and admirable hero, the first eco-warrior, whose books and talks offered a new and genuine connection with nature. You can see how two such complex characters inhabiting a single body might easily drive a man to an early grave. But, to produce a human being as singular as Grey Owl, perhaps you can't have one without the other.

~

The label 'impostor' is invariably meant as an insult, and when contemplating the character of a Titus Oates or a Ignácz Trebitsch Lincoln, or Lobsang Rampa's claim's to be transcribing the thoughts of his Siamese, seems well deserved. But it is not easy to judge all impostors so harshly. Surely we all feel a sneaking admiration for the survival strategies of a Cagliostro or a Mary Baker, or a straightforward respect for the heroism of a James Barry? And when Archie Delaney tells us, 'My heart is Indian', we know he is pointing to an inner transformation that is more complex than simple lying. Impostors unsettle us because they remind us how fragile our own identities can be, and how much of our time is spent fulfilling the expectations of others. As the essayist William Hazlitt observed in his *Notes of a Journey through France and Italy* (1826): 'Man is a make-believe animal – he is never so truly himself as when he is acting a part.'

# CHAPTER NINE

# Once You're Dead, You're Made for Life

*One may see the small value God has for riches*
*by the people He gives them to.*

ALEXANDER POPE

We could all use a bit more cash. As Spike Milligan put it, 'All I ask is a chance to *prove* money can't make me happy.' Even Oscar Wilde ruefully admitted that it is 'better to have a permanent income than to be fascinating'. There are many ways to become rich – noble birth, fame, genius, hard work, good luck – but getting wealth is no guarantee of keeping it. Someone in the world today goes bankrupt every four seconds and history is littered with extraordinary men and women who at first carried all before them but went to the grave unable to pay their own funeral expenses. Mozart, Rembrandt and Napoleon all died without a penny to their names – although Napoleon simply ignored the technicalities, bequeathing millions of imaginary francs in his will. The father of printing, Johannes Gutenberg, was ruined by his own investor; Georges Méliès, the Frenchman who invented the cinema, was reduced to selling toys in a Paris railway station; Frank X. McNamara, creator of the first commercial credit card in 1949 and named by *Life* magazine as one of the most influential Americans of the twentieth century, died broke aged forty; and Billy Crapo Durant, founder of General Motors, ended up running a bowling alley.

~

For almost a hundred years after her death, **Emma Hamilton** (1765–1815), Nelson's celebrated mistress, was airbrushed from the official record. She had tarnished the reputation of England's most glorious hero, something the establishment could not possibly tolerate: even her own daughter refused to acknowledge her as her mother. From the most unpromising beginnings, she had risen to become not only wealthy, but the most famous and glamorous woman of her age – only to lose it all in a mess of drink, debt and bitter disappointment.

Emy Lyons was born in a hovel in Ness, a miserable coal-mining hamlet in the Wirral peninsula in Cheshire. Her father, Henry, was a violent, heavy-drinking blacksmith who died within a month of her birth. During a drunken argument with her mother, he fell – or was pushed – fatally and Mary Lyons fled with her baby back to Hawarden in North Wales where her family lived. The house, already full to overflowing, stank permanently of dung. The family horse provided the fuel they were too poor to buy. Emy slept with her mother on a straw pallet and as the youngest, and a girl, was always the last to be fed. She probably owed her life to the fact that Mary was having an affair with an unidentified man of means – probably a high-ranking servant at the local stately home – who would slip her food and money. As a result, Emma grew up tall, strong and with lustrous black hair and a clear complexion.

Mother and daughter were very close and, although neither of them had ever been to school, they were both highly intelligent

317

and resourceful. Throughout Emma's golden years, her mother was always there in the background, acting as her confidante and personal assistant. When she left the claustrophobia of Hawarden to follow her lover to London, she took Emy with her and found her a suitable position in the capital. Though only twelve, Emy began work as a nursemaid to the children of a respectable doctor's family in Blackfriars. It was here that she met Jane Powell, an aspiring actress, and the two became close friends. Then as now, the lure of the West End was strong and, when Emy was sacked for staying out all night in Covent Garden, she turned her back on domestic service to pursue a career in the theatre. Starting on the lowest rung, as a maid to a wardrobe mistress in Drury Lane, she soon found something altogether more to her liking.

Late eighteenth-century London was the largest sex-resort in the world. In the square half-mile of St James's alone there were 900 full-blown brothels and 850 lesser knocking-shops providing 'entertainment for gentlemen'. Even in this broad-minded neighbourhood, Dr James Graham's 'Temple of Health' caused something of a stir. He was an unqualified, charismatic Scottish con man who, though remarkably enlightened on social issues such as slavery and women's education and a vegetarian to boot, knew that the serious money was in sex. The centrepiece of his business was the 'Celestial Bed' – a huge ornate couch raised up on eight brass pillars, that looked (and sounded) like an unholy cross between a Greek temple and the orgasm-inducing 'Excessive Machine' in Roger Vadim's 1968 film *Barbarella*. It was a giant conception device. James Graham believed having healthy children was a patriotic duty, and what he promised was not just bedsprings, but offspring. Under a dome swirling with fragrant vapours and live doves, customers were surrounded by forty crystal pillars, mirrors offering a view from every possible angle, a frieze of erotic scenes, and pipes sparking with mysterious 'electrical energy', which were connected to 500 magnets underneath the mattress. The bed, which could be tilted to reach the perfect angle for entry, delivered mild doses of 'electrical fire' designed to promote 'superior ecstasy' in a woman, which guaranteed conception. It also incorporated an organ whose tunes reached a crescendo in time to the occupant's exertions. It cost £50 a night (about £3,500 in today's money) and was patronised by some of the great men of the day, including the Prince of Wales and the noted parliamentarians Charles James Fox and John Wilkes. The whole experience kicked off with a seductive live show of scantily clad goddesses, who danced suggestively around the bed. One of them was young Emma Lyons, whose striking, straight-nosed classical profile was to make her a star.

Despite all the publicity, Graham proved to be a poor businessman. After running out of money he became a born-again Christian, convinced that human health (and God) were best served by fasting and 'earth bathing'. He delivered public sermons in Charing Cross, buried up to his neck in a vat of soil. Emma moved on to Madame Kelly's, the most prestigious whore-house in St James's, where her erotic dancing bewitched the MP for Portsmouth and notorious brothel-frequenter, Sir Harry Featherstonehaugh. Sir Harry bought her freedom and installed her as his mistress in a cottage near his huge country estate, Uppark in Sussex. Still only fifteen, Emma worked as a maid during the day and danced naked on the table for his friends in the evening. It was one of these friends, the Hon. Charles Greville, MP for Warwick, who stepped in after the oafish and intolerant Featherstonehaugh threw her out when, to her horror, she found she was with child. Greville was mesmerised by Emma and offered to take her on as his permanent mistress, as long as she refused to see other men. Pregnant and destitute, she leapt at the chance. She moved into his London house in Paddington as 'Emma Hart' and was joined by her mother, who now called herself 'Mrs Cadogan'. The baby – a girl, also called Emma –was hurriedly fostered and her existence kept a secret.

This domestic arrangement worked well for a while, but Greville couldn't help showing off Emma's beauty to others. A connoisseur of painting and sculpture, he arranged for her to pose as an artist's model. Her loveliness and poise so enchanted his friend, the rising portrait painter George Romney, that he became obsessed, producing over sixty paintings of her in various poses until her image was famous all over Britain. She is still, in fact, the most painted Englishwoman of all time. But Emma was not only pretty: she was spirited, bright and altogether delightful. Greville's plans to keep her as his private mistress were swept away by the arrival of a social sensation, whose exquisite good looks were matched by a direct and witty sensuality. Emma Hart was soon lusted over by gentlemen from London to Leeds.

This was a disaster for Greville. He was not a wealthy man – he had started hiring Emma out as a model for pocket money – and he needed to find a wife with a substantial dowry. That wasn't going to happen with Emma hogging the limelight on every social occasion. She had become particularly matey with Greville's uncle, Sir William Hamilton, the British ambassador to Naples, whom she called 'Pliny' because of his passion for antiquities, and he called her the 'fair tea-maker of Edgware Row' in return. Greville hatched a plan to transfer his mistress to his uncle in return for his wiping out a considerable debt. Telling Emma she was to visit Sir William for a holiday, he packed her off to Naples and several months later wrote making it clear he didn't want her back. She was devastated, writing him a stream of angry and imploring letters until, once more, she succumbed to pragmatism. Life in Naples, after all, was civilised and glamorous and she was feted for her beauty wherever she went. Sir William was sweet natured and devoted; his household was renowned for its lavish hospitality and aristocratic good taste. She soon became his mistress and then in 1791, much to the surprise of his friends, his wife.

'Am I Emma Hamilton? It seems nearly impossible!' The pauper-turned-prostitute, who still spoke with a pronounced northern accent, was now the wife of an ambassador. Hamilton, thirty-four years her senior, was delighted. 'It has often been remarked that a reformed rake makes a good husband. Why not vice versa?' Emma became both a favourite of Queen Maria Carolina of Naples (the sister of Marie Antoinette), and a fixture in the highest echelons of Neapolitan society. She had reached the very top of the social ladder, mixing with royalty and many of the great artists and thinkers of the day. This stirred Emma's ambition: she wasn't content merely to fulfil her role as hostess and dutiful wife. She was a performer at heart and wanted to create something new, something only she could do. She succeeded beyond her wildest dreams. Calling on her experience as a model for George Romney and Sir Joshua Reynolds, she developed what she called her 'Attitudes', a series of evolving tableaux in which she transformed herself into great women from history. With Sir William providing a narrative and accompanied by music, she began her performances draped in Indian shawls, gradually divesting herself till she was revealed in only a figure-hugging 'chemise of white muslin, her fine black hair flowing in ringlets over her shoulders'. Ariadne would merge into Medea, Medea into Cleopatra, and so on. For some it was little more than a classy striptease; for others, it was as if the history of Western painting had come to life. In his *Italian Journey* Goethe writes of being captivated by this 'young English girl . . . with a beautiful face and perfect figure'.

> *The spectator can hardly believe his eyes. He sees what thousands of artists would have liked to express realised before him in movements and surprising transformations, standing, kneeling, sitting, reclining, serious, sad, playful, ecstatic, contrite, alluring, threatening, anxious, one pose follows another without a break . . . As a performance it's like nothing you ever saw before in your life.*

Lady Hamilton's 'Attitudes' caused a sensation. The grace and presence that had distinguished her from the other tarts capering around the Celestial Bed in London's red-light district propelled her to international stardom. She became one of Europe's most popular tourist attractions, inspiring copycat performances all over the continent. Even her critics were impressed: the society diarist Mrs St George noted how 'graceful and beautiful' Emma's costumes were, though she couldn't help adding caustically, 'her usual dress is tasteless, loaded, vulgar and unbecoming'. Vulgar or not, back in London, Lady Hamilton fever took hold. Her trademark white crepe and satin dresses were all the rage. *The Times* bemoaned the padded bosoms that went with them, blustering that they had 'lowered the character of many young ladies'. People were at once fascinated and appalled and the gossip-mongers and caricaturists had a field day. But, for Emma Hamilton, it had only just begun.

She met Horatio Nelson by chance in 1793. He was forty, already renowned for his leadership and tactical flair, but not yet a commander of the fleet. Europe, still reeling from the shock of the French Revolution, was on the brink of war. Captain Nelson had been sent to recruit troops from King Ferdinand IV of Naples to reinforce the port of Toulon, then held by the British but threatened by a French force that included a young artillery-man called Napoleon Bonaparte. Nelson hit it off splendidly with the Hamiltons and Emma flirted with him as she did with everyone else. But a definite impression was made on both sides.

They weren't to meet again for five years. By then, Emma had grown seriously porky. In 1796 Sir Gilbert Elliott, the Viceroy of Corsica, remarked: 'Her person is nothing short of monstrous for its enormity, and is growing every day.' The famous hostess, Lady Elgin was crisper: 'She is indeed a Whapper!' A Swedish diplomat was distinctly undiplomatic: 'She is the fattest woman I've ever laid eyes on, but with the most beautiful head.'

When Nelson returned to Naples in 1798, he was a hero. His victory at the Battle of the Nile had saved the city from a French invasion. Emma wrote to him in breathless anticipation:

> *I walk and tread in the air with pride, feeling I was born in the same land with the victor Nelson . . . For God's sake come to Naples soon . . . My dress from head to foot is alla Nelson . . . Even my shawl is in Blue with gold anchors all over. My earrings are Nelson's anchors; in short, we are be-Nelsoned all over.*

The 'be-Nelsoning' grew ever more fervent as the victor approached and the outpouring of joy as his ship entered harbour was close to hysterical. Nelson's travails had aged him visibly; one eye was damaged beyond repair and he was suffering from the effects of a head injury. If Nelson noticed that Emma was plumper than he remembered, he never mentioned it. She assumed the role of his nurse, Sir William threw him parties and the three of them quickly became inseparable. So began a *ménage à trois* (they preferred the more sophisticated Latin, *tria juncta in uno*) that would last until Sir William's death in 1803.

By the end of the 1798 King Ferdinand's Neapolitan army had disintegrated in the face of French aggression and Nelson was charged with escorting the royal family and their friends to safety in Sicily. On the way, they sailed into the worst storm Nelson could remember. He was amazed by Emma's courage, in contrast to the complete panic of his other distinguished passengers. As Sir William prepared to shoot himself rather than drown, Emma gently tended the king's young son, who had gone into convulsions and later died in her arms. By the time they reached Palermo, the flirtation had become a torrid affair. Emma and Nelson dropped all pretence of decorum, entering into a nonstop round of drinking, gambling and late-night partying that only ended with Nelson's recall to London.

By early 1800 Emma was pregnant with his child and Nelson had formally separated from his wife, Fanny, leaving her to fend for herself in Norfolk. He bought Merton Place, a ramshackle property on the outskirts of Wimbledon, and Emma started doing it up. She designed it as a home fit for a hero – as well as a hero's mistress, a hero's mistress's husband and a hero's mistress's mother. Emma's taste wouldn't have looked out of place in *Hello* magazine. The effect was a cross between one of those celebrity footballers' mansions in Alderley Edge and the National Maritime Museum:

*The whole house, staircase and all, are covered with nothing but pictures of her and him, of all sizes and sorts, and representations of his naval actions, coats of arms, pieces of plate in his honour.*

The vulgarity and brazenness of it all provided an unprecedented feast for the popular press. Everything was avidly dissected in minute detail. In January 1801, Emma gave birth to twins, but only one survived. To avoid any doubt over the girl's origins, the proud parents named her Horatia. Then, in a half-hearted attempt at discretion, they added the surname Thompson, the *nom de plume* used by Nelson in his secret correspondence with Emma. Polite society was shocked: 'She leads him about like a keeper with a bear,' commented one affronted hostess. Even Nelson's closest friends were traumatised. Sir Gilbert Elliot, now Lord Minto, wrote angrily:

*Nothing shall ever induce me to give the smallest countenance to Lady Hamilton . . . She is high in looks, but more immense than ever. She goes on cramming Nelson with trowelfuls of flattery, which he goes on taking as quietly as a child does pap. The love she makes to him is not only ridiculous, but disgusting.*

Nelson and Emma were oblivious, busy making the most of their brief moments together. As she wrote to a friend:

*I love him, I adore him, my mind and soul is now transported with the thought of that blessed ecstatic moment when I shall see him, embrace him . . . I must sin on and love him more than ever. It is a crime worth going to Hell for.*

Eventually, even the gentle, indulgent Sir William lost patience. By the end of 1802, he was warning Emma that he might have to consider a separation if things continued as they were. But, in the spring of the following year, he died, much as he had recently lived, in his wife's arms, holding Nelson's hand. More or less at once, the war with France demanded Nelson's attention again and he was on the high seas when little Emma, his second daughter, was born. She lived only a few days and her grief-stricken mother had to pay double for the undertaker to keep the details out of the press. The loneliness and the long separations from Nelson began to tell on Emma. She took to drinking heavily again, and gambling, and the debts soon mounted up. Nelson knew nothing of all this. He was fired by his love for her. 'If there were more Emmas,' he wrote, 'there would be more Nelsons.'

In September 1805, after barely a month's leave, the newly created Viscount Nelson left home for the last time. Five weeks later, he fell at Trafalgar in the midst of his greatest victory. Already the most famous man in England, the deluge of public grief at his death was like nothing the country had ever seen. Emma retired to bed for three weeks, utterly bereft, but the powers-that-be had done with her and took their revenge. Ignoring Nelson's specific requests in his will and on his death-bed for the nation to 'look after Lady Hamilton' and to allow her to sing at his funeral, Emma wasn't even invited to the ceremony.

Worse was to come. Emma had inherited Merton Place and a small annual income for its upkeep but, already spending more than she earned, she felt duty-bound to continue decorating it obsessively. Pursued by creditors, blackmailed by family members and former servants, shunned by many of Nelson's friends, the facade of wealth quickly began to crumble. Within three years of the Admiral's death, she owed £15,000: more than £1 million at today's value. The house went up for sale but the market was at its worst point in a generation and buyers were put off by the bizarre nautical decor.

On 14 January 1809, Emma's mother died. Apart from being an emotional body-blow, the funeral costs stretched her credit to breaking point. Then her private correspondence with Nelson was stolen and published, destroying the last vestiges of support from public opinion. A few remaining friends rallied round with gifts, loans and advice but it was never enough. In 1813 she was arrested and taken to the King's Bench Debtors' Prison in Southwark. Granted parole to live in nearby lodgings, Emma and Horatia escaped to France. They arrived in Calais in August 1814, with just £50 to their names. They found a shabby two-room apartment in the centre of town where Emma went back to bed and methodically drank herself to death. Horatia, then just thirteen, was smuggled back to England dressed as a boy and fostered by a family in Burnham Market in Norfolk, barely a mile from where her father had been born. She lived out the rest of her life uneventfully, marrying the handsome local vicar and raising a large family. The children's mysterious grandmother was never mentioned.

Emma was not without her faults, but she didn't deserve the vilification and neglect she endured after Nelson's death – nor after her own. Doing her best to survive a succession of self-regarding lovers, she was no mere gold-digger. By the time she met Nelson, Emma was already famous and the intensity and depth of their relationship went far beyond sexual intoxication. Nelson had lost his mother young. Emma, increasingly maternal in shape, was warm, witty, and endlessly adoring. She filled the emotional hole his mother's death had left and gave him the solid platform he needed. A happy Nelson was an unbeatable naval commander, as the nation came to realise. They made a contented and generous couple and, if their infatuation seemed desperate at times, it should be remembered that, in the seven years of their relationship, they only spent two and a half years together.

Emma Hamilton's reputation has recovered considerably since the Victorians. During the Second World War, Churchill calculated that the morale-boosting film *Lady Hamilton* (1942), starring Laurence Olivier and Vivien Leigh, was worth four divisions. And, although she died in penury, Emma Hamilton was a remarkable woman. As the *Morning Post* obituary reminded its readers at the time: 'Few women, who have attracted the notice of the world at large, have led a life of more freedom'.

~

If Emma Hamilton was destroyed by love and war, **Dr John Dee** (1527–1609) was reduced to poverty by magic. One of the most brilliant men of his age, he would have called himself a philosopher, mathematician, astronomer and seeker after truth. History remembers him as the archetypal magician, the model for countless fictional characters from Prospero in *The Tempest* to Dumbledore in Harry Potter. And he certainly looked the part.

> *He had a very faire cleare rosie complexion; a long beard as white as milke. He was tall and slender; a very handsome man . . . He wore a black gowne like an Artist's gown, with hanging sleeves and a slitt.*

The seventeenth-century diarist John Aubrey got this description from an old woman who knew Dr Dee in his final years. Add this to the personal possessions he left behind – conjuring table, crystal ball, gold amulet, obsidian mirror – and it's easy to see how he got his reputation. But just because John Dee looked like a wizard, it doesn't necessarily mean he was one.

Today we would call him a scientist, though the word 'science' didn't exist then, and didn't appear in anything like its modern meaning until 1725. In the sixteenth century, those who sought to identify the rules of nature were called 'natural philosophers'. Like Pythagoras, John Dee believed that the universe was written in the language of mathematics (which he called 'a ravishing persuasion'). His most important 'scientific' legacy was to edit and introduce (in 1570) the first English translation of the most successful textbook ever written, Euclid's *Elements*.

Dee was a Neo-Platonist. He thought that everything – both matter and spirit – was interconnected and that the physical world was merely the external manifestation of an intangible realm of 'forms', in which all real chairs, for example, emanate from the Idea of a Chair. Dee called these ideal forms the 'pure verities' and he thought that if the laws by which they operate could be found, a universal religion, uniting all people in a single faith, would follow.

For Dee and many of his contemporaries, scientific enquiry, pure and applied mathematics, philosophy and what we would call 'magic' were all aspects of same search for truth. Like modern physicists, Dee was looking for a Theory of Everything: something that made sense of all the observable facts. For men of his age, alchemy (forerunner of chemistry) and astrology (indistinguishable in Renaissance times from astronomy) were just as 'scientific' as geometry. And before pointing out the 'obvious flaw' that these things aren't 'true', remember that it was men like

Dee, probing the unknown in search of invisible forces, who laid the groundwork for Newton and Faraday, without whom we would have no understanding of gravity or electricity.

The challenge, then as now, was how to fund a life of pure research. Dee lived in an age of superstition and paranoia. He was a devout Protestant at a time when the Catholic Counter-Reformation in Europe was at its height and the fledgling Church of England still in turmoil. Any new ideas might easily be denounced as witchcraft or blasphemy and punished by imprisonment or death. Royal patronage was essential and young Dee was luckily well placed to take advantage of this. His father was a cloth merchant and 'gentlemen sewer' at the court of Henry VIII, so Dee was educated well, at Chelmsford grammar school and St John's College, Cambridge. He performed brilliantly, especially in mathematics and Greek, establishing the work pattern he would maintain throughout his life: eighteen hours of study, four hours for sleep and two set aside for meals. It was at university that he was first, quite absurdly, accused of witchcraft. For a production of Aristophanes' comedy *Peace* he had built an impressively realistic giant mechanical beetle that carried one of the actors up to the 'heavens' in the Great Hall at Trinity College, terrifying some of the more unsophisticated members of the audience. Dee cleared his name but left Cambridge in disgust, determined to pursue his studies abroad.

From 1548 to 1551, Dee built a reputation as one of Europe's leading scholars. His lectures on Euclid in Paris attracted large and appreciative audiences. He met the Danish astronomer Tycho Brahe, who told him of the revolutionary theories of Copernicus, and he became close friends with the cartographer Gerard Mercator, working with him to develop a new set of tools for making accurate maps. He also began to collect books; this would remain a lifelong passion. Dee amassed over 4,000 volumes, the largest library of any kind in Europe, and twenty times as many books as held at Cambridge University. The breadth of his interests is astonishing. From magic to mathematics, subjects included the church in Armenia, botany, chastity, demonology, dreams, earthquakes, Etruria, falconry, games, gymnastics, horticulture, Islam, logic, marriage, mythology, the nobility, oils, pharmacology, rhetoric, saints, surveying, tides, veterinary science, weather, women and zoology.

Dee was offered the job of scholar-in-residence at several European courts but turned them all down to return to England as the teenage King Edward VI's special advisor on 'philosophical' (i.e. scientific) matters. This came with an annual pension of 100 crowns and guaranteed him lucrative additional work tutoring the sons of senior courtiers such as the Duke of Northumberland. This was the perfect outcome for Dee, providing financial security to enable him to continue his studies, and a position at the centre of things with a chance to put his theories into practice. This happy state of affairs lasted just two years. The accession of the Catholic Queen Mary brought a wholesale purging of the court's inner circle and in 1555 Dee was arrested and charged with casting horoscopes for the queen's sister Princess Elizabeth and 'conspiring by enchantment' to subvert the queen herself. His main accuser was George Ferrers, once a rival stage-designer and no doubt jealous of Dee's talent. Soon after Dee's arrest, one of the Ferrers children dropped down dead and another was struck blind. This hardly helped Dr Dee's reputation as a practitioner of the dark arts, but he defended himself eloquently and Edmund Bonner, Bishop of

London, cleared him of heresy. Dee was released and, eager to prove himself a scholar not a sorcerer, made a detailed proposal to the Queen for establishing a national library, gathering together all the books and manuscripts scattered during her father's dissolution of the monasteries. It was a bold and ambitious plan and would have turned England into the research powerhouse of Europe. Mary listened politely but declined.

Meanwhile Dee's father, Rowland, had lost his position at court and all his assets had been stripped, leaving his son without an inheritance. Dee returned to Europe where his services as an astrologer could be charged at a much higher premium than in England. At the same time, he discovered the works of the hermetic philosopher Cornelius Agrippa, which quickened his interest in alchemy. When Mary died in 1558, Queen Elizabeth offered him his old job back, though at a substantially lower rate of pay, which caused Dee great annoyance. He came back all the same, becoming one of her most trusted advisors, and even casting the horoscope to select the date for her coronation.

Over the next decade Dee made many practical contributions to public life. He was the first person to apply geometry to navigation and trained many of the great navigators of the age both to read maps and to make them. He also prepared the intellectual and legal case for Britain's expansion into the New World, coming up with justifications that stretched back into the mythical past, in particular the supposed discovery of North America by the Welsh Prince Madog in 1170. He was the first person to use the phrase the 'British Empire', and the first to suggest a voyage to map the Northwest Passage that was believed to link the Atlantic and the Pacific. And he became a spy for the Queen, going on secret missions to Europe and communicating by means of elaborate codes of his own devising. He signed his letters to her '007'. Dee was also summoned to the royal presence whenever something out of the ordinary occurred; on one occasion he was asked to comment on a wax effigy stuck with pig bristles that was found in Lincoln's Inn Fields, and on another he was asked to explain a 'blazing star' that had appeared in the sky. His job under these circumstances was always to come up with plausible explanations that reduced rather than encouraged superstitious speculation.

We know very little of Dee's personal life until 1577, when he started to keep a diary. It is one of the many paradoxes running through Dee's life that the very scrupulousness that made him such a good scientist also furnished the evidence that was to damn his reputation. The diary is meticulous. From it we know that he was married for the second or (possibly) third time in 1578, to Jane Fromonds, a lady-in-waiting at Elizabeth's court. He was fifty-one and she was twenty-three and she bore him eight children. The couple seem to have been devoted, in Dee's case almost to the point of mania. The diary contains detailed, cryptic records of her periods, carefully logging not only when they occurred but also how heavy they were, whether the 'show' was 'small' or 'abundant'. He also noted down when they had sex, giving not just the date, but also the time. But much more damaging is the revelation in the diary of Dee's developing fixation with 'angelic communication'.

In 1578 Dee's beloved mother died, bequeathing him her house in Mortlake. He was an only child and they had lived under the same roof for most of his life. Perhaps as a result of this loss, and inspired by a sequence of strange and powerful dreams, he became entranced by the ethereal otherworld. Using his 'scrying' mirror of polished black obsidian, rumoured to be an Aztec treasure stolen by the conquistador Hernán Cortés himself, he attempted to make contact with the spirits. Nothing materialised. 'I know I can not see, nor scry,' he confessed to his diary. A crystal he had tracked down from a collector of curiosities in Glastonbury seemed to provide tantalising glimpses, but he struggled to 'see' anything at all. So in 1582 he began using the services of a medium called Edward Talbott. Talbott was an unprepossessing man from Lancashire who always wore a cowl over his head to hide the fact that his ears had been cut off for counterfeiting. He had a basic grounding in alchemy from his time as an apothecary's assistant and claimed to have the gift of divination. Almost at once, Talbott was able to summon up richly detailed visions for Dee. Most of them came via an 'angel' called 'Madimi' who spoke a language called Enochian. According to Dee, she was 'a spiritual creature, a pretty girl of seven to nine years of age, half angel and half elfin'. For Dee, there was nothing 'occult' or un-Christian about these proceedings; indeed, he prepared for each session with prayer and fasting. He was delighted with the results and the two men formed a partnership, Talbott renaming himself Kelley to shroud his chequered past.

In the meantime, Dee continued at court as a successful practical scientist. In 1583 he devised a scheme to bring the English calendar into line with the astronomical one. It was even more accurate than the one Pope Gregory XIII had recently imposed on the rest of Europe, and the neatness of Dee's maths was widely admired, but the Archbishop of Canterbury blocked it: he saw it as capitulation to Rome. Later that year, the Queen introduced Dee and Kelley to Prince Albrecht Łaski, a visiting

Polish diplomat. He was keenly interested in the occult and invited them to bring their 'philosophical experiments' to his country. Encouraged by the positive endorsement of their spirit guides, Dee, Kelley and their families set off for Poland.

Over the next six years, the two Englishmen practised astrology, alchemical experiments and spiritual divination in the grand palaces of Europe. The King of Poland and the eccentric Holy Roman Emperor Rudolf II (an ardent alchemist himself) were enthusiastic patrons. Dee and Kelley finally settled at the court of Count Rosenberg in Bohemia. Here, their waif-like angelic interlocutor Madimi suddenly evolved into Uriel, a full-breasted siren. She instructed Kelley that no further progress towards mystical enlightenment would be made until the two men shared everything, particularly their wives. Dee's diary records his distress, not least because Jane had always professed to dislike Kelley, but he allowed the matrimonial exchange to take place as instructed. Soon afterwards the spirit conversations ceased, the partnership broke up and the Dees returned to England in 1588.

At first sight, it looks as if Kelley manipulated the whole thing. By playing on the spiritual ambitions of the elderly Dee, he had his way with his partner's pretty young wife and then managed to be rid of them both. Certainly he got rich quite quickly after Dee left; for ten years he conned European monarchs into believing he could manufacture gold at will. In recognition of his work, he was even made a baron by Rudolf II. Eventually, however, the lack of any actual gold became something of an issue, and he died in 1589 attempting to climb out of a tower where the Emperor had imprisoned him. But Dee's diary tells a different story. Five weeks after what he calls his 'Covenant' with Kelley, Jane found she was pregnant. When the baby was born, the Dees and the Kelleys were reunited at the christening and the child named Theodore – 'beloved of God'. Far from falling out, Dee and Kelley continued to correspond and Dee's diary records his great sorrow on hearing of Kelley's death. If that were not sufficient evidence, the Dees named their next daughter Madimi.

Meanwhile, on their return to Mortlake, the Dees found their house had been ransacked: many books and instruments had been stolen and a maid had used a collection of Dee's scientific papers to line pie tins. The queen's enthusiasm for Dee had cooled, doubtless fanned by gossip from the Continent, and the best position she could offer him was the wardenship of Christ's College, a religious institution in Manchester. Not only was his income much reduced, but he found his authority with the Fellows undermined by constant mutterings about his being a conjuror. In 1603 Elizabeth died, and was replaced by James I, a man famously averse to witchcraft in all its forms. The following year Dee wrote to him professing his loyalty and reassuring him that 'none of all the great number of the very strange and frivolous fables or histories reported and told of me are true'. The king didn't even bother to reply.

The next year, plague swept though Manchester, pitilessly claiming the lives of Jane Dee, Theodore, Madimi and all of John Dee's younger children. He returned sorrowfully to Mortlake with his surviving daughter Katherine. For the next four years, until his death aged eighty-two, he lived in desperate poverty, selling his books one by one in order to eat. His only solace was to get back in touch with the angelic domain through a new medium called Bartholomew Hickman. It was at this point, at the very end of his life, that Goody Faldo of Mortlake (the old lady who described Dee to John Aubrey) met him when she was a young girl and fixed him forever as the white-bearded, black-gowned sage of legend. She told Aubrey he was the model for Ben Jonson's *The Alchemist* but also sweetly said of him: 'He was a great peacemaker; if any of the neighbours fell out, he would never let them alone till he had made them friends.' Her final verdict was simple: 'A mighty good man he was.'

Posterity is a fickle thing. Had John Dee's diary and his book of spirit conversations, *A True & Faithful Relation of What Passed for Many Yeers between Dr. John Dee and Some Spirits*, not been discovered and published by an enterprising bookseller in 1659, it is possible he would have been mainly remembered as a pioneering scientist alongside his close contemporary Sir Francis Bacon. He might have been discussed as the man who used geometry to map the globe, or as the greatest book-collector of his age, rather than the wife-swapper who talked to angels, the inspiration for the esoteric excesses of generations of self-styled magicians and occultists.

❧

One such occultist, also a brilliant scientist, was born almost 400 years later. **Jack Parsons** (1914–52), the maverick pioneer of American rocket technology, invoked Satan for the first time when he was only thirteen. He was born in Los Angeles on 2 October 1914, on the exact date that the Jehovah's Witnesses had predicted the Apocalypse. Named 'Marvel' by his father, Captain Marvel Whiteside Parsons of the US Army, his mother always called him John or Jack. She had caught his father having an affair while she was pregnant and he played very little further role in the boy's upbringing. Jack had a lonely childhood. His only real friend was Edward Forman, who shared his obsession with fireworks, science fiction and the arcane. Together they pored over old books of incantations, enacting spells to jinx older boys who bullied them at school.

Jack and Edward dropped out of high school to join the Hercules Powder Company, a Californian armaments manufacturer. Jack's unique talents as a self-taught explosives chemist soon got him a job with the 'suicide squad', a bunch of rocket-obsessed misfits at Caltech's Guggenheim Aeronautical Laboratory. By the outbreak of the Second World War this had evolved into the Jet Propulsion Laboratory, backed by substantial military funding. Wernher von Braun later said it was not himself but Parsons who was the real father of the US space programme. Still only in his mid-twenties, Jack created solid fuels that would be used in the Apollo space missions, and liquid binders later employed in the propulsion of Polaris missiles. He was regularly called as an explosives expert at courtroom trials. In the meantime, still fascinated by the black arts, before each experiment he would invoke the spirit of Pan, the horned pagan god of fertility.

When Parsons was twenty-eight, he and Forman and four colleagues formed their own rocket corporation, Aerojet Engineering. Parsons left after the war, selling his shares for just $11,000. Aerojet is still a major player in the industry, making the propulsion units on NASA's space shuttle. Had Parsons kept his shares, he would have been a multimillionaire in less than a decade. Instead, he used the proceeds to start a Laundromat chain, which failed.

Parsons was never good with money and he was even less adept at managing his personal life. His relationship with his mother was intense and very probably incestuous. He was extremely good-looking, tall and promiscuous, working his way through the secretarial pool at Aerojet, even though he had a physiological disorder that caused him to sweat profusely. He dealt with the resultant chronic body odour by dousing himself liberally in strong-smelling cologne. Opinions about Jack were divided, to some he was the office clown, 'a delightful screwball'; to others he was dangerous, possibly even psychotic.

It was this darker side of his character that led him to fall in with the OTO (Ordo Templi Orientis), the so-called Templars of the East, a Masonic-style organisation under the leadership of the mesmeric necromancer, Aleister Crowley. Variously known as the Beast, 666, Frater Perdurabo and Master Therion, Crowley claimed to be the reincarnation of John Dee, among many others. He had taken over the English-speaking arm of the order in 1912, when he discovered they already practised some of the ancient Hindu 'sex magick' rituals he was keen to revive. The essence of Crowley's philosophy was the notion of *thelema*, translated as 'do what thou wilt'. In his *magnum opus, The Book of the Law* (1925), he is at pains to point out that the 'wilt' in question does not refer to mere egotistical will-power, but to the dictates of the true or inner soul. According to Crowley, thelemic practice or 'magick' (the 'k' is important to differentiate it from stage magic) was a path to spiritual development, not sensual indulgence. Having said that, for the philosophy to flourish participants needed to 'de-condition' themselves from restrictive social inhibitions to allow the subconscious mind to express itself – essentially by having prodigious quantities of wild, abandoned sex.

Crowley had come to California in the early years of the war. He was almost seventy, broke and addicted to heroin, dependent on the generosity of wealthy young acolytes like Parsons, who embraced Crowley's teachings whole-heartedly. In 1941 Jack and his wife Helen joined the Agape Lodge of the Order. The master of the lodge was an expatriate Englishmen, Wilfred Smith, another legendary womaniser. He wrote to Crowley full of excitement about his new recruit: 'I think I have at long last a really excellent man . . . He has an excellent mind and much better intellect than myself.' Crowley agreed, and within a year he had installed Parsons himself as lodge-master.

In 1942 Jack's father died, leaving him a large house in one of the wealthiest suburbs in Pasadena. He and Helen moved in and turned it into a centre for lodge activities, much to the annoyance of the neighbours. Parsons loved to play classical music at a very high volume and throw noisy parties. He would place advertisements in local newspapers offering rooms to 'Bohemian types', adding the requirement, 'Must not believe in God.' Police were called to the home on a number of occasions to investigate allegations of backyard rituals and sex orgies, but Parsons always managed to talk them down, reminding them of his place in the community as an eminent rocket scientist.

As they became more deeply involved in the cult, Jack and Helen agreed to divorce. She was having an affair with the former lodge-master Wilfred Smith, and Jack had taken up with Helen's eighteen-year-old sister Sara, whom he renamed 'Betty'. Jack encouraged Betty to take other lovers, as he did himself, claiming that, as 'superhumans', they were above petty jealousy. One of Betty's lovers was a young science-fiction writer called L. Ron Hubbard, who later went on to found the most successful alternative religion of all, Scientology. By early 1946 Ron Hubbard had moved in with Parsons and been fully initiated into the order. Parsons enlisted his help in enacting the most extreme of Crowley's rituals, the birth of a 'magickal child' or 'Thelemic

Messiah', who would usher in a new apocalyptic age. First, using the 'Enochian' language recorded by John Dee and Edward Kelley, they had to summon up Babalon, the Goddess of Pleasure, so that she would incarnate before them as 'the Scarlet Woman'. Over eleven nights Parsons invoked the goddess by masturbating furiously ('manipulating his magickal wand') as Hubbard performed the role of scribe, recording the ritual in precise detail. A day after its completion, Marjorie Cameron, a beautiful redheaded artist, appeared on Parson's doorstep. 'I have found my elemental,' Jack wrote exultantly to Crowley. He renamed her 'Candida' (meaning 'white' or 'pure'), she was initiated into the Order and agreed to help Cameron produce his 'moonchild'. They married soon after.

Meanwhile, Betty and L. Ron Hubbard talked Parsons into setting up a joint venture, Allied Enterprises, into which all three would pool their earnings. Parsons had already sunk most of his money into the lodge but put what was left – about $12,000 – into the new company. Hubbard invested $1,200 and promptly disappeared to Miami with Betty where he used all the Allied Ventures capital to buy a pair of yachts. Jack, with nothing in his bank account, had to take a job at a petrol station to pay for food. When he eventually tracked the couple down in Florida, they swiftly absconded on one of the boats. Furious, Parsons summoned up a storm (or so he claimed) at sea which forced them to return to port.

Jack sued Hubbard, but only got part of his money back. He returned to Pasadena, resigned from the OTO and broke with Crowley. Crowley was indifferent. He had regarded Parsons's and Hubbard's Babalon ritual as ridiculous and wrote to a friend despairing of the 'idiocy of these goats'. Parsons seemed equally disillusioned:

*Now it came to pass even as BABALON told me, for after receiving Her Book I fell away from Magick, and put away Her Book and all pertaining thereto. And I was stripped of my fortune (the sum of about $50,000) and my house, and all I Possessed. Then for a period of two years I worked in the world, recouping my fortune somewhat. But that was also taken from me, and my reputation, and my good name in my worldly work, that was in science.*

The last sentence refers to his investigation by the FBI where he was under suspicion, not only for occult activities, but also for associating with known communist sympathisers. This cost him his government clearance, which meant he could no longer work on official rocket projects. Financially ruined and pushed to the edge, he contemplated suicide but then, with Candida's support, he decided he was ready to go beyond even Crowley. He took the Oath of the Abyss and declared himself the Antichrist.

This sounds ludicrously overdramatic, but Parsons's idea of the Apocalypse was different from the one in the Bible. In fact, it reads more like a vision of the counter-cultural movements that would sweep America in the 1960s.

*An end to the pretense and lying hypocrisy of Christianity. An end to the servile virtues, and superstitious restrictions. An end to the slave morality. An end to prudery and shame, to guilt and sin, for these are of the only evil under the sun, that is fear. An end to all authority that is not based on courage and manhood, to the authority of lying priests, conniving judges, blackmailing police, and an end to the servile flattery and cajolery of mobs, the coronations of mediocrities, the ascension of dolts.*

Jack Parsons, 'the James Dean of the Occult', never got to see his satanic Utopia. By early 1952 he had begun to manufacture bootleg explosives at home. He and Candida planned to move down to Mexico to create one that was 'more powerful than anything yet invented'. Before they left, on 17 June 1952, Parsons, sweaty-palmed as ever, accidentally dropped a phial of the extremely volatile compound known as fulminate of mercury. The explosion blew off his entire right forearm, broke his other arm and both legs, and ripped a hole in his jaw. It was heard over a mile away. Parsons died an hour later protesting: 'I wasn't done.' Shortly after hearing the news, his mother committed suicide.

Marjorie 'Candida' Cameron went on to become a successful painter and actress in avant-garde films. She is sometimes cited as the inspiration behind the Eagles song 'Hotel California'. In recognition of his work on the space programme, Parsons had a crater named after him on the moon – on the dark side, naturally.

～

In 1946 Parsons, a great believer in UFOs, claimed to have met a Venusian in the Mohave Desert. Venusians were very much in fashion at the time and it was only a couple of years since the death of the Serbian engineer **Nikola Tesla** (1856–1943), whom some believed had been sent from Venus to modernise earthly technology. Tesla was one of the great innovators of the modern age, often so far ahead of his time that he might as well have been from another planet. Honoured as 'the man who invented the twentieth century' and nicknamed 'the patron saint of electricity' for developing the alternating current system that underpins all today's electrical networks, he held over 700 patents in his lifetime, for innovations in electro-magnetics, robotics, remote control, radar, ballistics and nuclear physics. He invented the Tesla Coil, which gave us radio, X-ray tubes and fluorescent light. Some of his ideas were so advanced that science has still not caught up with them and his almost 'extraterrestrial' gifts as a scientist were matched by a strange and otherworldly personality. If John Dee and Jack Parsons fall into the category of madly brilliant eccentrics, Nikola Tesla is in a class of his own.

Were he born today he would be diagnosed as being on the autistic spectrum, with a severe case of obsessive-compulsive disorder. But those labels weren't available in the mid-nineteenth century. Mental illness was put down to 'nerves' or 'hysteria', and real oddities were either tolerated or committed to the asylum. Tesla's peculiarities meant that the scientific community would never truly come to accept him, nor did he receive either the acclaim or the financial rewards his work should have commanded.

He was born into a Serbian family in Smiljan, then part of Austro-Hungary, now in Croatia: it was his proud boast to be both Serbian *and* Croatian. The fourth of five children, he recalled his early years as exceptionally happy, growing up in the country surrounded by farm animals. Later in life he would tell how it was witnessing the sparks generated by stroking the family cat that made him want to understand what electricity was. 'Eighty years have gone by since,' he wrote, 'and I still ask the same question, unable to answer it.' The Teslas were a clever family, blessed with exceptional memories, and Tesla's father, Milutin, a Serbian Orthodox priest and poet, devised mental exercises to keep his children's minds supple and alert. He had an impressive library of books but said it wouldn't matter if he lost them because he had memorised the classics by heart. Tesla's mother Đuka was barely able to read, but could recite thousands

344

of verses of Serb sagas and long passages from the Bible. Her needlework was famously intricate – using only her fingers, Tesla claimed, she could tie three knots in an eyelash. She also improvised ingenious labour saving devices, even constructing her own mechanical eggbeater. 'I must trace to my mother's influence,' Tesla wrote, 'whatever inventiveness I possess.'

The great tragedy of Tesla's youth was the death of his older brother, Dane, in a riding accident. Nikola was only five, but he had vivid nightmares about it for the rest of his childhood. A conscientious, sensitive boy, he felt his parents' grief keenly and, no matter how hard he worked, was conscious that he could never make up for the loss of his brilliant sibling. Dane and Nikola shared at least one outstanding talent: the ability to visualise things in precise, three-dimensional detail. Vivid images of memorable or traumatic events would return to Tesla at any time of night or day, often accompanied by flashes of light, and refuse to disappear. 'Sometimes they would remain fixed in space even though I pushed my hand through them,' he recalled. Though distressing for a child, this pictorial clarity would be very useful to him as an inventor.

Young Nikola was hopelessly accident-prone and had several brushes with death. He fell headlong into a kettle of boiling milk, nearly drowned after swimming under a raft, was almost swept over a waterfall at one of the nearby dams, and suffered serious bouts of both malaria and cholera. These shocks provoked a general sense that the world was out to get him, and worsened the long list of obsessions he suffered from:

> *I would not touch the hair of other people except, perhaps, at the*
> *point of a revolver. I would get a fever by looking at a peach and*

*if a piece of camphor was anywhere in the house it caused me the keenest discomfort. I counted the steps in my walks and calculated the cubical contents of my soup plates, coffee cups and pieces of food, otherwise my meal was unenjoyable. All repeated acts or operations I performed had to be divisible by three and if I missed I felt impelled to do it all over again even if it took hours.*

At nineteen Tesla went to study electrical engineering at the Austrian Polytechnic in Graz. He was an astonishing student, able to solve mathematical problems almost before his teachers had finished writing the formulae on the blackboard. In his spare time, he taught himself five languages, committed large chunks of Goethe and Shakespeare to memory and ploughed his way through the complete works of Voltaire: 'I learned, to my dismay, that there were close on one hundred large volumes in small print which that monster had written while drinking seventy-two cups of black coffee per diem.' Like John Dee, he set himself a punishing work schedule, studying for up to twenty hours a day and sleeping less than three hours a night. He also indulged in more traditional student pursuits: drinking, smoking, gambling to excess and, briefly, falling in love with a girl called Anna. This period of his life came to an abrupt end when he lost all the money his father had sent him for his studies in a card game. Deeply ashamed at what he had done, he gave up gambling and smoking for good and forswore all further contact with women.

While at Graz, Tesla encountered the Gramme dynamo, the cutting edge of electrical engineering at the time. It was a dual-purpose machine that when supplied with mechanical energy generated electricity, and when supplied with electrical energy could be used as a motor to drive things. Tesla was enchanted by it but puzzled by its constant sparking. The basic principle of generating electricity by 'induction' – introducing a rotating wire into a magnetic field – had first been described by Michael Faraday forty years earlier. The electricity Faraday had produced was called 'alternating current', because it continually switched direction as the electrons in the rotating wire swept past first the north and then the south pole of the magnet. In order to produce 'useful' electricity, this alternating current had to be converted into 'direct' current, similar to the electricity produced by a battery, where the electrons all flow in one direction, from the positive to the negative terminal. To achieve this, a switch, called a commutator, short-circuited the generator at each half-spin, so that the current continued its flow in the same direction. This shorting was what caused the dynamo to spark. Tesla thought this an overly complex, even clumsy solution. Why not find a way of harnessing the alternating current, he asked? His professors laughed at him, pointing out that would be tantamount to producing a perpetual motion machine. Early attempts to produce motors with alternating current had been dismal failures.

Tesla never completed his degree. In 1881 he moved to Budapest and found work as a telephone engineer. This suited him much better than academia, and it was during this time that he came up with his first invention, a kind of early loudspeaker. Towards the middle of that year, Tesla began to suffer from a peculiar condition: a multiple sensory overload where sunlight blinded him, the ticking of a watch sounded like the blows of a hammer, vibrations from traffic made him lose his balance and his pulse spiked and plummeted wildly. His doctors were baffled and at one point thought they would lose him, but then it stopped, as suddenly as it had started. Soon afterwards, walking in the park as he was convalescing, and reciting a passage from Goethe's *Faust* to a friend, he had an epiphany:

> *As I uttered these inspiring words the idea came like a flash of lightning and in an instant the truth was revealed. I drew with a stick in the sand the diagram shown six years later in my address before the American Institute of Engineers. The images were wonderfully sharp and clear and had the solidity of metal.*

What he had seen that afternoon was to change the world. It was a detailed vision of the electrical Holy Grail, the alternating current motor. His solution was brilliantly simple: to rotate the magnetic field as well as the coil. And, instead of a single circuit, to have two, but each timed differently, so that, like the firing of pistons in a combustion engine, when one was down the other would be up, and the forward momentum of the motor would be maintained. No sparks, no loud vibrations – and the motor's motion was reversible. Tesla had literally 'seen' the future. But his vision went even deeper. His recent illness had made him sensitive both to light and to vibration. Now he saw the connection between the two. Alternating current produced a frequency, a wave, as the electrons whizzed backwards and forwards. It was a relatively low-frequency wave, but light was also a wave, a vibration, though at a far higher frequency. Suddenly the whole universe was revealed as a vast symphony of electrical vibration. And, if his alternating current could be transformed into useable power, what might be achieved if he harnessed the potential of those higher frequencies? Exploring the implications of this insight would dominate the rest of his life.

In 1884 the twenty-eight-year-old Tesla turned up at Thomas Edison's office in New York with four cents and some Serbian poems in his pocket. He had spent the previous two years working for Edison's company in Paris, and built his first alternating current (AC) motor there in his spare time. Now he was ready to share it with the world. He handed over a letter from his employer in Paris, Charles Batchelor. Addressed to Edison, it said, simply: 'I know two great men and you are one of them; the other is this young man.'

Edison wasn't interested in Tesla's ideas about AC power; he was building direct current (DC) generators. These were proven to work and his customers liked them. It was Tesla himself who intrigued him. He was an exotic figure: 6′4″ tall, a cultured, poetry-loving European, always immaculately dressed in morning coat, spats and gloves. Edison was a shambolic mess of a man who cut his own hair and wore the same food-spattered black clothing every day. About the only thing they had in common was the capacity to survive on virtually no sleep. Tesla's spooky ability to know the answer to mathematical problems halfway through the question and to conjure phantom engineering diagrams from thin air were in marked contrast to Edison's '99 per cent perspiration' approach. As Tesla would later remark: 'If Edison had a needle to find in a haystack, he would proceed at once with the diligence of the bee to examine straw after straw until he found the object of his search.' But Edison was a shrewd judge of people and had had plenty of practice in turning their ideas into his own money. He hired Tesla for the miserly sum of $18 a week, promising a $50,000 bonus if the young Serb could find a way to make the company's temperamental DC generator system more efficient.

Tesla set to the task with his customary application. At first, he was in awe of his new boss. When Edison told him he ate

Welsh rarebit every day to increase his IQ, Tesla took the joke to heart and ate barely anything else for weeks. He found Edison's sense of humour a lot less amusing when, almost a year later, having solved the problem of the DC generator, Edison refused to pay his bonus: 'When you become a full-fledged American you will appreciate an American joke.' He offered him a raise to $25 per week instead. It was a mistake Edison would live to regret. Tesla was incandescent with rage and resigned, spending the next year earning his living as a labourer (ironically at one point digging ditches for Edison's expanding network of DC cables) and working on his inventions at night.

By early 1887 Tesla had saved enough money to register seven patents covering the full range of AC generators, transformers, transmission lines, motors and lighting. These were awarded unopposed and would become the most valuable patents registered since the telephone. At a stroke, they solved the thorny problem of long-range power distribution. Direct current required a generator to be located within a mile of where the electricity was being used and was inconveniently inflexible: electricity from the same DC generator couldn't be used to run machines requiring different voltages. To increase the voltage in a direct current circuit meant also increasing the amperage, which meant thicker copper wire and greater loss of energy through heat. With Tesla's AC solution, power could be generated at a low voltage, then, using a simple device called a transformer, it could be 'stepped up' for transmission and 'stepped down' again at the customer's house or business premises. Taking the analogy of a water pipe – the higher the pressure (voltage) the further and faster the same amount of water (electrical energy) will travel, but the hose attachments (transformers) will determine how that water is used at the other end. The elegant simplicity of Tesla's system attracted the attention of Pittsburgh industrialist George Westinghouse. He hired Tesla, purchased his patents for $60,000, and agreed to pay him royalties of $2.50 for every horsepower of AC electricity sold.

Whether or not Edison saw the writing on the wall, he knew that Tesla and Westinghouse had to be stopped. His war machine rumbled into action. His line of attack was that AC was dangerous. While direct current was 'like a river flowing peacefully to the sea', he alleged, alternating current was 'a torrent rushing violently over a precipice'. To make his point in the most brutal way, he began using AC to electrocute animals in public. Twenty-four dogs (bought from local children for 25 cents each), two calves, a horse and Topsy – a zoo elephant that had killed its keeper – were all 'Westinghoused'. Scenting blood, Edison developed the electric chair, secretly acquiring three Tesla generators to make it happen. The first person to die by legal electrocution was messily dispatched using AC at Auburn, New York, in 1890. 'They could have done better using an axe,' commented Westinghouse drily. But Tesla and Westinghouse got their revenge by underbidding Edison for the contract to light the Chicago World's Fair in 1893, the world's first major 'All-Electric' event. Thanks to Tesla's AC system, Westinghouse could quote a price that was less than half of Edison's, because so much less copper wire was needed. Edison retaliated by refusing to supply them with Edison light bulbs, but the game was up. Twenty-seven million people visited the Fair and, from that moment on, 80 per cent of all electrical devices bought in the US were AC. In 1898 the final nail was hammered into DC's coffin when Westinghouse and Tesla built the world's first hydroelectric plant, harnessing the power of

Niagara Falls to generate alternating current and piping it the 17 miles to their new power station in Buffalo, New York.

Tesla had used the money Westinghouse had paid him for his patents to set up a lab in West Houston Street in New York City and the 1890s were a decade of creative overdrive for him. He discovered X-rays three years before Wilhelm Roentgen and was the first to point out their biological risks. He devised the first radio-wave transmitter two years before Marconi and he invented and patented radio control, demonstrating the first radio-controlled boat in Madison Square Garden in 1898. Having mastered the transmission of AC by wire, by the end of the decade he was sending it through space *without* wires. Showing unexpected talents as a showman, he would enthral and horrify audiences at public demonstrations by running hundreds of thousands of volts through his own body, lighting electric bulbs from a distance while flames shot from his head and his hands sparked. In 1899 he moved his lab to Colorado Springs to unveil his *pièce de résistance*. This, he believed, of all of his inventions, would prove the 'most important and valuable to future generations'. It was a massive 'magnifying transmitter' able to send radio waves and electricity through the air over long distances. At 51 feet in diameter it could generate 4 million volts, and light 200 lamps, without wires, from 25 miles away. Even more astounding, he used it to make artificial lightning, generating electrical flashes over 130 feet long. In 1900 the banker J. P. Morgan agreed to invest $150,000 in an even bigger wireless transmitter, the Wardenclyffe Tower in Long Island. Tesla's plan was global: to unite telephone and telegraph systems in a single wireless network, transmitting pictures and text from one side of the globe to the other in minutes, and delivering mail between special terminals, using electronic messaging. He had, in effect, envisioned the World Wide Web a hundred years early, not only with universal wi-fi, but one where computers could operate without batteries and would never need to be plugged in.

Tesla was forty-four at this point and almost exactly halfway through his life, when, at the peak of his fame and influence, things began to unravel. In 1903 Morgan pulled out of Wardenclyffe, claiming Tesla had sold it to him as a radio transmitter, and betraying a complete lack of understanding of the potential of Tesla's vision. In 1904 the US Patent Office incorrectly awarded Marconi the patent for radio, even though Marconi's work had all been achieved after Tesla, actually using Tesla's own patented instruments. The insult was made worse by the award of the Nobel Prize to Marconi in 1909; just as Roentgen had been awarded his in 1901. Tesla never received one. By 1905 he had run out of funds and was forced to close his lab. Two years later George Westinghouse was almost wiped out by a stock-market crash and by the long and expensive turf war with Edison. In desperation, he asked Tesla's permission to amend their contract. In one of the noblest gestures in modern business, Tesla released Westinghouse completely, saying:

> *You have been my friend, you believed in me when others had no faith; you were brave enough to go ahead . . . when others lacked courage; you supported me when even your own engineers lacked vision . . . you have stood by me as a friend . . . Here is your contract, and here is my contract. I will tear both of them to pieces, and you will no longer have any troubles from my royalties. Is that sufficient?'*

Westinghouse paid Tesla a one-off fee of $216,000. At that

time, the value of Tesla's royalty stood at more than $12 million, enough to make him one of the richest men in the world at that time. If he had kept that royalty until today, even if no more electricity had been generated than the relatively tiny amount that existed in 1890, he would now be worth $40 billion. In 1914, however, the outbreak of the First World War cut off the remaining income he had been earning from his European patents and, two years later, he was forced to file for bankruptcy. He never recovered financially, living out the last ten years of his life in room 3327 of the Hotel New Yorker, his bills settled by his friends.

This falling apart of his financial affairs was matched by increasingly unstable personal behaviour. His fetish for cleanliness grew to Howard Hughes-like proportions. He went to great lengths to avoid shaking hands, placing his own behind his back when meeting people. At the dining table, he asked that each item of silverware be heat-sterilised before being brought to him. He would then pick up each item with a napkin, clean it with another napkin, and then drop both napkins onto the floor (he got through fifteen napkins a meal on average). If a fly landed on his table, he had to move to another seat and make an entirely fresh start. He gradually abandoned the two-steaks-a-night supper he had once enjoyed, becoming a vegetarian and eating exactly the same food in the same restaurant every night: warm milk, bread, and a concoction made from a dozen vegetables. But he continued to dress nattily. (In 1910 he had announced to a secretary that he was the best-dressed man on Fifth Avenue and intended to maintain that standard.) He wouldn't go out without his grey suede gloves, which he wore for a week and then discarded. He bought a new red or black tie each week and would only wear white silk shirts. Collars and handkerchiefs were only used once and he developed an aversion to jewellery. He could not sit near a woman who was wearing pearls. Most poetic of all, he was sure the hours he'd spent thinking were draining the colour from his eyes.

His work became similarly unhinged. He claimed to be getting radio messages from Mars and Venus. He talked about using electricity to control the weather. He proposed a form of eugenics leading to women becoming dominant, so that human society would more closely resemble that of the honeybee. In his late seventies, he announced he was working on a device with which to end all wars, a weapon that

> *would send concentrated beams of particles through the free air, of such tremendous energy that they will bring down a fleet of 10,000 enemy airplanes at a distance of 200 miles from a defending nation's border and will cause armies to drop dead in their tracks.*

Inevitably, the media dubbed this Tesla's 'Death Ray', and it confirmed his passage in the public mind from revered genius to mad scientist.

He died in 1943 aged eighty-six, heavily in debt, alone in his hotel room. In 1944 the US courts finally found in his favour and confirmed that it was Tesla and not Marconi who was the inventor of radio. Much has been done since to restore his reputation, but Edison and Marconi are still the names everyone remembers. Tesla, like Dee and Parsons and even poor Emma Hamilton, was too absorbed in his own passions to be bothered with mere accountancy. He lived with the burden and the joy of having glimpsed a much deeper reality than most people ever see, and that sense of his special destiny never deserted him. Marriage was not for him, not because he was homosexual or afraid of women, but because nothing could be allowed to interfere with his mission: 'I have planned to devote my whole life to my work and for that reason I am denied the love and companionship of a good woman; and more, too.'

Weeks before his death, he had a final feminine visitation. He had befriended a pigeon that came every day to his windowsill in room 3327. She had become his favourite, 'a beautiful bird, pure white with light grey tips on its wings'. He had always loved birds, but this one 'he loved as a man loves a woman . . . She understood me and I understood her.'

> *Then one night as I was lying in my bed in the dark, solving problems, as usual, she flew in through the open window and stood on my desk. I knew she wanted me; she wanted to tell me something important so I got up and went to her. As I looked at her I knew she wanted to tell me – she was dying. And then, as I got her message, there came a light from her eyes – powerful beams of light. It was a real light, a powerful, dazzling, blinding light, a light more intense than I had ever produced by the most powerful lamps in my laboratory.*
>
> *When that pigeon died, something went out of my life. Up to that time I knew with a certainty that I would complete my work, no matter how ambitious my program, but when that something went out of my life I knew my life's work was finished.*

~

In 1881, two years after Tesla's world-changing vision of the revolutionary alternating current motor in a park in Budapest, the revolutionary political philosopher **Karl Marx** (1818–83) died penniless in London. Marx would have had no truck with Tesla's mysticism, but history was to unite the life's work of both men in 1920, when the Marxist regime of the Soviet Union took the momentous decision to transform their vast country by electrification. Lenin believed the success of the revolution was entirely dependent on the rapid roll-out of new technology; his favourite slogan was 'Communism is socialism plus electrification of the whole country.' In 1948, when George Orwell wanted to personify the evil of the Soviet system in *Animal Farm*, he had the animals build an electrified windmill.

Marx's journey to penury was less tortured than Tesla's: as an asylum-seeker and infrequently employed freelance journalist, he never had much money to lose. He wasn't a 'worker' in the way it is usually meant in Marxist mythology. A friend once teased him that she couldn't imagine him living happily in a communist state as it might mean getting his hands dirty. 'Neither can I,' he agreed, 'These times will come, but we must be away by then.' Even his adoring mother complained: 'I wish you would *make* some capital instead of just writing about it.' Luckily for him, he found a benefactor (and true friend) in Friedrich Engels – fox-hunting mill-owner by day, radical socialist by night – who looked after him, as a recent biographer puts it, 'like a substitute mother, sending him pocket money, fussing over his health and reminding him to study'. Marx may not have been a manganese miner or a tractor driver, but he certainly worked hard: his collected writings come to over a hundred volumes and would spawn a political ideology that, at its height, controlled half the world's population.

Karl Marx was born into a German Jewish family, the scion of one of the most famous lines of rabbis in all of European history, but his father, Heinrich, was a successful lawyer, the first non-religious Marx in generations. When Prussia banned Jews from practising law, he cheerfully converted to Protestantism, holding it to be the most progressive of all religions. Young Karl was baptised a Christian at six years old. He had a happy childhood and was a precocious student. He was also a hothead, known for picking fights in taverns. While reading law at the University of Bonn, he lived student life to full, running up huge debts and taking part in a duel. His father rapidly transferred him to the more academic environment of Berlin, where Karl switched to philosophy and history, graduating with a thesis comparing Epicurus and Democritus, whose anti-religious materialism he found attractive. His first job was as editor of the radical *Rheinische Zeitung* in Cologne but, after the paper was suppressed, he went to Paris, the nineteenth-century's drop-in centre for European revolutionaries. Here, in 1844, he met Engels, with whom he at once formed a close personal and professional bond. Engels was already calling himself a 'communist' and it was his recently published *The Condition of the Working Class in England* that first drew Marx's attention to the plight of the industrial workforce and convinced him, too, to embrace communism. He began writing for *Vorwärts*, the most radical newspaper in Europe, run by a secret society called the League of the Just. When, in 1845, the paper heartily praised an assassination attempt on the King of Prussia, the French authorities ordered Marx, along with many others, to leave Paris. He went to Brussels and renounced his Prussian citizenship. From then on, he was officially classed as stateless.

In 1849 Marx moved to London, where he lived in various degrees of acute poverty for the rest of his days. He came with his wife, Jenny von Westphalen, a Prussian baron's daughter (Marx was rather proud of having married a beautiful society girl). She called him her 'little wild boar' after the bristly hair that sprouted all over his body, as well as by his family nickname 'the Moor' from the huge mane and beard framing his face and his swarthy complexion. Marx's health was a source of continual anguish. He suffered from liver trouble, rheumatism, shingles, ulcers, insomnia, bronchitis, laryngitis, pleurisy and, above all, gigantic boils on his backside, which meant that he had to pen most of *Das Kapital*, his colossal masterpiece, standing up. Engels always said he could tell the passages that had been written under the worst pain. Marx responded 'At all events, I hope the bourgeoisie will remember the carbuncles until their dying day. What a swine they are!' Like another stateless émigré, Sigmund Freud, he was addicted to cigars. In the later years of poverty, though, he was constantly pawning his clothes and furniture to feed his family. He adored his six children, of whom only three made it through childhood. The brutish, bullying intellectual, prone to getting into fights in the pub, was an absolute pussycat at home, with his offspring riding on his back, pulling his hair and being indulged with endless pets – three dogs, two cats and two birds. At bedtime he would read to them from his favourite novel, *Don Quixote* by Cervantes.

The Marxs were always delighted when Engels knocked on the door of their house in Kentish Town, not least because they lived in constant fear of the bailiffs. The family affectionately called him 'General' or 'General Staff'. As well as bringing money, he loved to entertain the household with ribald songs. Sometimes 'Staff' and 'the Moor' did duets, each singing one song's lyrics to another's tune. In 1868 they played a parlour game where Marx's daughter Jenny got both men to fill in her 'confessions' album. The contrast between them is revealing. Under 'Your favourite maxim', Marx put *'nihil humani a me alienum puto'* ('I think nothing human is alien to me') while Engels put 'not to have any'; under 'Your favourite motto' Marx had *'de omnibus dubitandum'* ('doubt everything'), while Engels preferred the splendid 'Take it easy.'

Marx spent thirty-four years in the reading room of the British Museum. After hours, he addressed small political meetings (where his lisp and heavy accent made him a rather underwhelming speaker) and then got drunk on beer at Jack Straw's Castle on Hampstead Heath, the highest pub in London. Out on the town, he would sign his name in hotel registers as 'Mr Charles Marx, private gentleman of London'. On one occasion, he and his fellow socialists Edgar Bauer and Wilhelm Liebknecht set out to drink a beer in every pub from Oxford Street to the Hampstead Road. There were eighteen pubs on that route: by the end, they were so inebriated that they decided to throw paving stones at gas lights, narrowly escaping arrest. Unsurprisingly, Marx was never granted British citizenship. A police report of 1874 declared that 'he is the notorious German agitator, the head of the International Society and an advocate of communistic principles. This man has not been loyal to the King.' More intimately, a Prussian spy who had seen his family life at first-hand concluded: 'Washing, grooming and changing his linen are things he does rarely, and he likes to get drunk'.

Engels and Marx conceived their history of capitalism, *Das Kapital,* in the late 1840s but the first volume wasn't completed until 1867, well behind schedule. Marx died before he could finish parts two and three. These had been written with the help of his daughter Eleanor (known as 'Tussy'), who later played an important role in the early British Labour movement, and were completed and published posthumously by Engels. Marx, suffering from a swollen liver, lost his wife in 1881 and his eldest daughter Jenny within a year. He died, heart-broken and destitute, only two months later. Only eleven mourners attended his burial at Highgate cemetery, at which Engels delivered the funeral address. Although exasperated at times by Marx's endless grumbling about his troubles and constant demands for money, Engels was his first and greatest admirer: 'I simply cannot understand', he wrote in 1881, 'how anyone can be envious of genius; it's something so very special that we who have not got it know it to be unattainable right from the start.'

Engels' short speech to the little knot of people gathered at Highgate Cemetery on that Saturday in 1883 began: 'On the 14th of March, at a quarter to three in the afternoon, the greatest living thinker ceased to think.' It ended: 'His name will endure through the ages, and so also will his work.' He compared Marx to Darwin, saying that just as one discovered 'the law of development of organic nature', so the other discovered 'the law of development of human history'. With the benefit of hindsight, surveying the wreckage of communism, it's tempting to be dismissive. But though Marx the man, with his boils and his beer, the revolutionary who never led a revolution, the historian of capital who couldn't organise his own finances, is long gone, his analysis is arguably more relevant than ever. Globalisation, rapacious corporations, the decline of high culture, the triumph of consumerism: it's all there in Marx. Almost no one today calls himself a Marxist (as Engels pointed out, neither did Marx), but we have all taken on board his ideas. In a British radio poll in

2005 shock result, a voted him the nation's favourite thinker. Perhaps he did not, after all, discover the hidden laws of history, but his work – and his life – show that you can't make sense of human existence without first understanding its economics.

~

It's astonishing to think that the people who gave us electricity, space travel, and communism made no money from their endeavours, but there are plenty of innovators – equally eccentric, equally influential – who did and who still do. Fame and lasting importance are not commodities to be bought and sold and there is no correlation between money (or the lack of it) and the value of a human life. More money, or better management of money, would not have saved Nelson from a sniper's bullet. John Dee didn't seek enlightenment to turn a profit, nor did Tesla conceive of a world network of wireless energy in order to monetise the intellectual property rights.

There is something oddly liberating about those who die with nothing. The French writer André Maurois captures it beautifully:

> *If men could regard the events of their own lives with more open minds, they would frequently discover that they did not really desire the things they failed to obtain.*

# CHAPTER TEN

# Is That All There Is?

*We have no reliable guarantee that the afterlife will be any less*
*exasperating than this one, have we?*

NOËL COWARD

Death lies in wait for each of us, the full stop at the end of our story. All our strivings, our achievements, our catastrophes; the struggles with ourselves, our families and our bodies are suddenly, mysteriously, over. It is the one unavoidable fact of our lives, yet most of us prefer to ignore it. Half the adults in Britain have not even made a will.

One of the oddest things about our attitude to death is that most of us still don't think it is the end. In the International Social Survey Programme completed at the end of the last millennium, almost 80 per cent of Americans claimed to believe in life after death. In Britain the figure was 56 per cent, and this was the same or higher in most European nations. Quite what form this life will take is unclear – in Ireland and Portugal more people believed in the existence of heaven than in life after death itself, which seems illogical– but despite the best efforts of militant atheists, the afterlife is an idea, however sketchy, that many of us refuse to let go.

This may have less to do with organised religion than the fact that most people, at some point in their lives, undergo a form of inexplicable experience that has traditionally been labelled 'spiritual' or 'religious'. These altered states, whether induced by drugs or meditation, intense emotional trauma or illness, all point us back to the mystery of consciousness itself. We don't know where consciousness comes from, how it works or why it appears to stop. The question of where 'we' go once our bodies cease to function continues to intrigue us. Here are five lives dominated by the question: what happens us to when we die?

~

**St Cuthbert** (634–87) is the most famous saint of northern England. As well as having the gift of holy visions, he was a hermit, healer and bishop of Lindisfarne. Most of what we know about him comes from the Venerable Bede (673–735), a fellow Northumbrian monk and author of the first major work of English history, the *Ecclesiastical History of the English People* (731). Bede's *Life and Miracles of St Cuthbert* was written in 721, only thirty-four years after the saint had died. It includes many first-hand accounts by people who had known Cuthbert well. Though studded with improbable mystic occurrences, it has a historical immediacy that the lives of many other medieval saints lack.

Cuthbert was a shepherd boy in the far north of the kingdom of Northumbria, near Dunbar. He walked with a limp, thanks to a painful tumour on his knee. All attempts to cure it failed and his condition grew so bad he was unable to walk. One day, as Cuthbert sat disconsolately outside his hut, a horseman pulled up beside him. He was dressed from head-to-toe in white. He examined the knee and instructed the boy to apply a poultice of wheat flour and milk. Cuthbert followed his instructions and was cured immediately. Only after the horseman had gone, did he realise the stranger had been an angel. Deeply affected by this, Cuthbert returned to his work. He became increasingly devout. When five monks were swept out to sea while salmon fishing, he knelt on the shore, surrounded by people weeping and blaming the disaster on their sinful nature, and calmly prayed for a change of wind. To everyone's amazement, the wind obeyed and the monks were saved. Soon after this, aged sixteen, he was watching over his sheep one night on the hillside, when he saw the soul of St Aidan, the Irish monk and founder of the abbey at Lindisfarne, being carried up to heaven by angels. He didn't know who Aidan was at that stage (and he certainly didn't know that Aidan had died at that moment) but he knew he was a great man and wanted to follow him. The next day he abandoned his flock and became a novice at Melrose Abbey in the Scottish Borders. Many years later, he would succeed St Aidan as Abbot of Lindisfarne.

Cuthbert was destined to become famous for his piety and for his miraculous gifts. Rather than spend time in the monastery, he chose to be an itinerant missionary, preaching and healing among the remote villages and hill farms of northern Britain. He founded a chapel at Dull in Perthshire and built a monastic cell in Fife, which eventually became the monastery out of which the University of St Andrews was founded in 1413. Like St Francis of Assisi, Cuthbert loved nature and had a particular affinity for wild animals. On one occasion, after spending the night up to his waist praying in the icy North Sea, he was visited by two otters, which first breathed on his frozen feet to warm them and then dried them off by tousling them with their furry backs. Another time, an eagle saved him from starvation by bringing him a fish, which he insisted on sharing with the kindly bird.

In 669 his wanderings came to an end when the Abbot of Melrose sent him on a special mission to Lindisfarne. He was given the task of persuading the monks there to accept the authority of Rome, as ordered by the Synod of Whitby in 664. The Synod was a major turning-point in the early history of the British church. It marked the end of independent Celtic Christianity, a loosely administered, missionary-based religion, introduced into Ireland by St Patrick in the fifth century and taken to Scotland and northern England by St Columba. Theologically, the Synod had concerned itself with technical matters such as the date of Easter and whether or not monks should shave their heads into a tonsure (a Roman custom symbolising the 'Crown of Thorns'). Politically, however, it was about Rome imposing a central set of rules. Many British monastic institutions, (including Lindisfarne, which had been founded in the Celtic tradition) were resistant to the changes.

Cuthbert was the perfect man to make them see the light. He had all the credibility that came from wandering the wilds as a missionary in the Celtic mode, but was also a pious and obedient member of a Benedictine monastery, committed to the authority of Rome. His time at Lindisfarne was stressful – Bede writes of him being 'worn down by bitter insults' – but he managed to win his brothers over by praying harder and longer than anyone else. And his piety was matched by a sunny temperament, which meant he never held a grudge or returned an insult. He gave the credit for his behaviour to the Holy Spirit, working within him and giving him 'the strength to smile at the attacks from without'. Once, having stayed up for several nights in a row praying, he had finally fallen asleep when a novice woke him up again on a trivial matter. He waved away the apologies saying: 'No one can displease me by waking me out of my sleep, but, on the contrary, it gives me pleasure; for, by rousing me from inactivity, he enables me to do or think of something useful.'

Having persuaded the monks to submit to Rome, Cuthbert withdrew from the daily life of the community and retired to an isolated cell where he spent his days in constant prayer and meditation. In 676 a vision commanded him to leave Lindisfarne altogether and become a hermit on the inhospitable island of Inner Farne, two miles off the Northumbrian coast. It was a life of extreme austerity: just him and the elements and thousands of pairs of guillemots, puffins, and eider ducks. With his own hands, out of stone, he built a two-roomed house surrounded by a high wall. This meant he could spend much of his time praying outdoors, 'with only the sky to look at, so that eyes and thoughts might be kept from wandering and inspired to seek for higher things.' He was soon inundated by visits from pilgrims. News of the 'Wonder Worker of Britain' had spread and there was a constant stream of visitors asking for healing and counselling. As Bede describes it: 'Not one left unconsoled. No one had to carry back the burdens he came with.' In return, Cuthbert asked only that his uninvited guests respect the local animals, and he absolutely forbade the hunting of all nesting birds: probably the world's first piece of wildlife conservation legislation. In his honour, the locals still call eider ducks 'Cuddy ducks' there today.

As the years passed, Cuthbert grew ever more isolated. He withdrew further into his sanctuary, communicating with the outside world through a small window and only emerging to have his feet washed by fellow monks on Maundy Thursday, in remembrance of Christ doing the same before the Last Supper. It was the one time in the whole year he removed his leather boots, and the monks noticed that his shins bore long calluses caused by the endless hours of kneeling in prayer.

In 684 Cuthbert was elected Bishop of Lindisfarne. After almost a decade as a hermit, he was reluctant to accept. Only after a personal visit by Ecgfrith, King of Northumbria, was he persuaded to leave his refuge. For two years, he threw himself back into missionary work: travelling all over the diocese, preaching the virtues of frugality and prayer, healing the sick, performing the occasional miracle and taking 'delight in preserving the rigours of the monastery amidst the pomp of the world'. By the end of 686 he'd had enough. A premonition of his impending death led him to return to Inner Farne and prepare for the end.

In the last year of Cuthbert's life, a monk called Herefrith visited him on his island and was taken aback by the level of his self-denial. The saint showed him his weekly rations, which consisted in their entirety of five onions. St Cuthbert told him: 'Whenever my mouth was parched or burned with excessive hunger or thirst I refreshed and cooled myself with these.' Only one of the onions had been touched. Cuthbert had successfully managed to fight off the devils of luxurious sensuality – though he confessed that 'my assailants have never tempted me so sorely as they have during the past five days'. He died quietly, stretching his arms upwards and commending his soul to God. The monks who were with him lighted two beacons, telling their brothers over the water at Lindisfarne that their beloved bishop had passed away.

Cuthbert was fifty-three years old. He had always wanted to be buried where he lay, by his little stone house on his lonely island, near his friends the otters, eagles and seabirds but, shortly before he died, he gave the monks permission to bury him at Lindisfarne. His grave became the site of a miraculous cure. A boy, possessed by demonic fits, was brought to the holy place. The monks located the spot where the water used to wash Cuthbert's body had been poured into the ground and gave the boy some of the soil to eat. At once the demons left him and the boy was calmed.

The monks decided to honour the saint by building him a proper shrine. In 698, eleven years after he had died, his coffin was disinterred and opened for the first time. The miraculous discovery was made that his body had not decayed: not only that, but his limbs were flexible and his clothing had not faded. Those who saw his body reported that he appeared to be not dead but sleeping, a sure sign of sainthood. The new Abbot, Eadfrith, commissioned a copy of the Gospels to be made in Cuthbert's honour. The Lindisfarne Gospels are regarded as the supreme fusion of Anglo-Saxon and Celtic religious art.

The years that followed were precarious ones for the monastery. Viking raids began in earnest in 793 and a major attack in 875 prompted the monks to shift Cuthbert's coffin and his gospels to the mainland. For more than a century, they were venerated at the parish church of Chester-le-Street, a small town eight miles inland from Sunderland. In 995 further Danish raids forced a move further south to Ripon Abbey. During the journey, the cart carrying St Cuthbert's coffin became stuck in the mud. The monks prayed for help and the saint appeared to them in person, asking to be buried at somewhere called 'Dunholme'. Shortly afterwards, by pure chance, they overheard a milkmaid mention the name as the place where she had lost her cow. She led them to a steep, rocky peninsula on a bend in the River Wear and the monks laid the saint to rest. This was the origin of the city of Durham.

By the eleventh century, the tomb of St Cuthbert had become the most popular pilgrim destination in northern England. The sacrist (or keeper) of the shrine was one Elfrid Westoue. He opened the saint's coffin regularly to trim his hair and nails with a pair of silver scissors and travelled up and down the north scooping up the relics of other local saints and placing them in bags in St Cuthbert's tomb for safe keeping. One of the bags contained the remains of the saint's biographer, the Venerable Bede. In 1020 Elfrid had shamelessly stolen his skeleton from the monks at Jarrow. In 1027 the Viking king Cnut, on his way back from a pilgrimage to Rome, paid reverence to the saint, covering the last six miles of the journey in his bare feet.

In 1069 William the Conqueror began his bloody suppression of the North. As he worked his way up from York, burning every house and murdering every person in his path, the monks at Durham hurriedly tried to move Cuthbert's coffin back to Lindisfarne. Caught out by the tide, they were intercepted by King William, who commanded them open the casket. No sooner had he done so than he was seized by a violent fever. Taking this as a sign of the saint's displeasure, he countermanded his order and left Durham, never to return. The monks put Cuthbert back where he'd come from.

In 1104, more than 400 years after Cuthbert's death, the magnificent new cathedral at Durham (begun in 1093) was ready to receive his remains. The decision was taken that his body should be inspected once more. They found the saint lying on his side as if in a deep sleep, accompanied by 'an odour of the sweetest fragrance'. Next to him was a tiny, exquisitely lettered version of St John's gospel, the oldest known leather-bound book to have survived in Britain. Any spare space was taken up with the linen bags parked there by Elfrid, in which were found the relics of eight local saints and the bones of Bede. (Bede wasn't a saint in those days, although he had been declared Venerable in 836. He had to wait until 1899 before being canonised by Pope Leo XIII, who made up for the oversight by appointing him a 'Doctor of the Church', the only native of Great Britain ever to be so honoured.) On the outside of the coffin was a painting, later identified as the first recorded representation of the Virgin and Child in Western art. At some point over the years, an unknown artist of Anglo-Saxon Northumbria had been keeping the flame of Western civilisation alight.

To authenticate the evidence, the coffin and its contents were examined by a gathering of forty-seven senior clerics. The Abbot of Sées in northern France even went as far as touching the corpse, moving its arms and legs about and tweaking its ears to show that rigor mortis had still not set in. The miracle was confirmed and, for the next 400 years, Cuthbert's corpse lay undisturbed.

In 1534, as part of Henry VIII's reforms of the Church of England, the Church Commissioners were instructed to destroy Cuthbert's tomb, removing any treasures that might have been buried with him. Opening it up, they took out his golden staff and other jewellery but once again, to their amazement, they found St Cuthbert 'fresh, safe and not consumed' and sporting what looked like a fortnight's growth of beard. The monks were then allowed to rebury his physical remains – and those of his eight saintly companions – in the floor of the cathedral, where the shrine had once stood.

Somewhere along the line, a legend grew up that Cuthbert hated women, so none were allowed to approach his tomb too closely. Given his regular and apparently cordial dealings with female abbesses during his lifetime, this feels like an unjustified slur invented by misogynistic monks. A second legend was that, at some point in the late seventeenth century, his body had been stolen and replaced. In 1827 the Dean and Chapter decided to see if they could locate the body under the cathedral floor. After a long search they eventually came across a coffin whose exterior closely resembled the one described in the 1104 account. They lifted the lid. Inside, wrapped in five layers of silk, was an ordinary skeleton, an ivory comb, a portable silver altar and, lying on the skeleton's ribcage, a beautiful square Anglo-Saxon gold cross, inlaid with garnet, which has now become the emblem of Durham University.

In 1899 – 1,212 years after Cuthbert had died and the year Bede finally got his sainthood and his doctorate – the coffin was opened for the last time and medical tests were made on Cuthbert's bones. These matched the known details of his life – such as they were – and they suggested that the body had been mummified for a long period after death. More recent scholarship has speculated that the combination of Cuthbert's emaciated state at the time of his death and the high sand-and-salt content in the Lindisfarne soil might well have resulted in mummification. In any event, his legend started a trend and there are now more than a hundred Christian saints who have been reported as 'incorrupt' at some time after burial, although few have endured such a busy posthumous schedule as Cuthbert.

～

In 1835 the remains of an expatriate Englishwoman were exhumed from the cemetery in the hamlet of Watervliet in upstate

New York. In this case, the reason for the exhumation wasn't to see if the corpse was 'incorrupt', but to check that it was there at all. **Ann Lee** (1736–84), known to her followers as 'Mother Ann', or 'Ann the Word', was the leader of the Shaker movement in North America. Her personality was so dominant that even though she was a woman many of her followers believed she was the resurrected Christ and simply refused to accept that she could ever die.

Ann Lee was born in Toad Lane, Manchester. The illiterate daughter of a blacksmith, she came from a large, poor family who sent her out to work as a velvet-cutter when she was only five years old. The job involved hours of walking backwards and forwards with a special knife, slitting open the tightly woven loops of silk to create a velvet pile. In the course of a day, a velvet-cutter might expect to cover 20 miles. By the age of eighteen Ann was working as a cook at the new Manchester Infirmary. She was a strong, big-boned girl with light chestnut hair and intense blue eyes. Despite her good looks, she conceived a deep hatred of sex from an early age, and most of the visions she witnessed (from her early teens onwards) focused on the depravity of human nature and the evils of sexual lust. As second youngest of eight children she had grown up in a tiny house with her elder siblings, several of whom were co-habiting with their spouses. It may have been this exposure to sexual activity at close quarters and at an early age that was the source of Ann's revulsion. She had such a compelling gift for persuasion, however, that she managed to get her own mother to take up celibacy. This infuriated her father, who threatened Ann with a whip.

Her own marriage confirmed Ann's worst suspicions. She had avoided it until she was twenty-six, when her father forced her to marry one of his employees, Abraham Standerin, a junior blacksmith. He was also illiterate and the couple each signed their marriage certificate with a cross. Ann and Abraham would go on to have eight children in quick succession, though four of them were stillborn and none made it past the age of six.

In the meantime, Ann had joined a fledgling religious sect called The Wardley Society. Started by James and Jane Wardley, two married tailors from Bolton, it was colloquially known as the 'Shaking Quakers' (or 'Shakers' for short). The Wardleys had developed the belief that the soul could only be purified of its lusts by the action of the Holy Spirit – which manifested itself by violently shaking the physical body of the sinner. The greater the sin, the more extreme the shaking – and thus the more noise produced in the supplicant. As a result, Shaker meetings were deafening: they could sometimes be heard several miles away:

*One will fall prostrate on the floor, another on his knees and his head on his hands, on the floor; another will be muttering articulate sounds which neither they nor any body else can understand . . . others will be shooing and hissing evil spirits out of the house; all in different tunes, groaning, jumping, dancing, drumming, singing, laughing, talking and stuttering, shooing and hissing makes a perfect bedlam; this they call the worship.*

Ann's reports of her visions entranced the group and the moral leadership of the sect passed to her from the Wardleys. To be a Shaker meant plain and simple living, common ownership of property and, most important of all, complete rejection of sexual activity – even for married couples. Men and women were expected to live and work apart to avoid the temptations of lust and children were separated from their parents and fostered on other believers. This liberated Shaker women from their roles as wives and mothers and made them the equals of men. The Shaker God was male and female, both father and mother, and not 'a trinity of three men'. Since no one had sex, they rapidly ran out of children to pass the faith on to: Shakerism could only grow by making converts.

By the early 1770s the Manchester Shakers had grown in number to about sixty and their odd behaviour and unsettling social practices made them deeply unpopular with regular churchgoers. Their meetings were disrupted by mobs and they were pelted with dung on the street. Ann was arrested for disturbing the peace and imprisoned in a small stone cell. She later claimed she only survived because another leading Shaker, James Whittaker, fed her a mixture of wine and milk smuggled inside in his clay pipe. While in gaol Ann had her most powerful vision, which she called 'a special manifestation of Divine Light', showing her that the second coming of Christ was imminent.

Ann's imprisonment enhanced her authority and, when she emerged, the other Shakers (including the Wardleys) began to refer to her as their 'Mother in spiritual things'. In 1774 she had a new vision where she saw that she must take the most faithful followers and set up a new community in America. Only nine of the sixty made the voyage: at one point their singing and dancing were so annoying that the other passengers threatened to throw them overboard. However, the weather turned rough, and the captain later claimed it was only the Shakers' faith that kept the vessel afloat. The less faithful Shakers, left behind in Manchester, and without the sustaining intensity of Ann to lead them, rapidly disintegrated.

In her vision, Ann had seen, in precise detail, the place that was destined to be the home of the new community. Once in New York, the tiny Shaker group wasted no time in finding the house that Ann had described and presenting themselves to the family living there. The family listened patiently to Ann's tale of how she had been directed there by an angel and invited the whole group in. The unexpected arrangement worked, perhaps because Abraham brought his skills as a blacksmith and Ann was an excellent housekeeper. As a female journalist reported at the time:

*The women are the ugliest set of females I ever saw gathered together, perhaps their particularly unbecoming dress added to the plainness of their appearance; it seems to be adapted to make them look as ugly as art can possibly devise . . . their petticoats are long and trolloping, and there is nothing to mark the waist. They are, however, most scrupulously clean.*

After two years in New York, the Shakers moved out to the countryside near Albany, where their community began slowly to grow and develop its special character. The centre of their devotions was the meeting-room where they kept at their spiritual labours around the clock, operating a shift system for meals. As one group ate and drank, the other brethren sang and danced in front of them. An eyewitness recorded that, when they were spinning, the women's skirts would become 'full of wind to form a shape like a tea cup bottom up'. There was also a regular programme of intensive exorcisms. One man was spun round off his feet for more than three hours, while all about him there was 'yelling, yawing, snarling, pushing, elbowing, singing, dancing'. The observer concluded that 'the worst drunken club you ever see could not cut up a higher dash of ill behaviour'.

In the middle of it all, though rarely participating in the 'shaking' was Mother Ann herself. She ruled with a rod of iron; making sure that there was no backsliding. Like St Cuthbert she hardly ate at all, scraping the 'driblets' off other people's finished plates, but upbraiding others for not eating enough. She was also obsessive about cleanliness, claiming 'there is no dirt in heaven'. At the merest hint of familiarity between men and women she would regale them with her vivid visions of hell, where molten lead was poured on the genitals of the lustful. After a time, this all proved too much for her husband Abraham. Driven from the marital bed by her spiritual 'moanings and weepings', he one day turned up with a prostitute, saying that either Ann performed her wifely duties or he would have to find someone else who did. She threw him out, declaring he had 'lost all sense of the gospel'. He was never heard of again.

Ann was equally ruthless with her spiritual rivals. The eccentric cult-leader Shadrack Ireland had invented and preached the cult of Perfectionism, the idea that heaven was achievable on earth and that, as a result, he would never die. When the inevitable happened – in 1778 – his followers left him sitting in his chair until the smell became so bad they had no choice but to bury him. Ann, quick to spot an opportunity, castigated him as an agent from hell and converted many of his flock to the Shaker faith. On another occasion, when smoke from a prairie fire in upstate New York blotted out the sun, Ann used it as a powerful recruitment tool: a clear sign that the Last Days were nigh.

As the community settled in, many of the more attractive things we now associate with the Shakers began to take shape. Their aesthetic teaching was as plain as their morality – 'Beauty rests on utility' – and their elegant furniture, buildings and music became renowned. Their early melodies were simple and wordless, but over time these developed into beautiful three part harmonies. By the early twentieth century, over 12,000 Shaker songs had been written, so many that a unique shorthand musical notation was devised to record them all, using letters of the alphabet rather than the familiar notes on staves.

Ironically, given their commitment to pacifism, the Shakers were continually at war with neighbouring communities. When the War of Independence broke out, they were subjected to frequent violence. Ann was accused of being a British spy and a man in disguise. She was arrested, beaten and forced to strip to prove she was telling the truth. In 1782 James Whittaker, from whose pipe Ann had drunk in prison, was whipped by a mob 'till his back was all in a gore of blood and the flesh bruised to a jelly'. Apparently, he sang Shaker songs all the way through his ordeal.

As Ann grew older and her health began to fail, her visions intensified. She paid personal visits to those suffering in hell, imagining herself as 'the woman clothed with the sun' from the Book of Revelation who sprouts the wings 'of a great eagle':

> *I felt the power of God come upon me, which moved my hands up and down like the motion of wings; and soon I felt as if I had wings on both hands . . . and they appeared as bright as gold. And I let my hands go as the power directed, and these wings parted the darkness to where souls lay, in the ditch of hell, & I saw their lost state.*

She reported back to the living relatives of the damned how much their prayers had soothed the torments of those who had died unshriven. This led many of her followers to believe she was indeed the second incarnation of Christ. As one young Shaker wrote: 'Every trew believer believes that Christ has made his second appearance in the world clothed in flesh & blood in the form of a woman by name Ann Lee.'

Ann died of leukaemia at Waterlievt in 1784. She was only forty-eight. Worn out by the frequent confrontations and beatings, she ended her life peacefully, after several weeks of sitting in her rocking chair 'singing in unknown tongues . . . and wholly divested of any attention to material things'. Her passage to the spirit realm was helped on its way by a lively Shaker funeral but, for many years, rumours of her impending return persisted. She herself had never claimed any such thing. Her consistent view was: 'The second appearing of Christ is in His Church.' She never expected the 'personal' return of Christ as 'He' had already turned up in the establishment of the Shaker faith.

By the time Ann's skeletal remains were exhumed fifty-six years later to see if she was actually inside her coffin or not, the Shaker community had over 6,000 members living in nineteen different settlements. This was to be the movement's high-water mark. At the outbreak of the Civil War in 1865, President Lincoln, in recognition of their pacifist views, exempted them from combat, making them history's first official conscientious objectors. But gradually, what many people saw as the big drawback of Shakerism – the insistence on celibacy – led to a slow decline in converts. In 1965 they voted to accept no new members. Today there are only three Shakers left, in the last Shaker settlement at Sabbathday Lake, near New Gloucester in Maine. They have the distinction of being America's smallest religious or ethnic minority.

For all Ann Lee's strangeness, her emphasis on equality for all – particularly women – and a democracy based on social justice and religious tolerance were well ahead of their time. Her view of life after death, like everything else, was bracingly clear: give up sex – the curse that had afflicted humanity since Adam and Eve – and you would be saved. As she had seen Hell and could describe it in detail, who would dare risk not believing her?

~

Another regular visitor to Hell was the English poet and painter, **William Blake** (1757–1827). Unlike Ann Lee's hideous vale of torments, Blake's Hell, though the opposite of Heaven, was its equal – and every bit as necessary:

> *Attraction and Repulsion, Reason and Energy, Love and Hate, are necessary to Human existence. From these contraries spring what the religious call Good & Evil. Good is the passive that obeys Reason. Evil is the active springing from Energy. Good is Heaven. Evil is Hell.*

These insights are from his visionary work, *The Marriage of Heaven and Hell*, published in 1790. Unlike Ann Lee, Blake didn't descend into Hell like an eagle, he sauntered around it like a tourist: 'As I was walking among the fires of hell . . . I collected some of their Proverbs . . .' Just as the proverbs of different countries give a clue to their character, so the Proverbs of Hell would provide a better idea of the place than describing what the locals were wearing, if anything. The bits of 'infernal wisdom' he collected there would have appalled Ann Lee:

> *'The nakedness of woman is the work of God.'*

> *'Sooner murder an infant in its cradle than nurse unacted desires.'*

## Is That All There Is?

*'Damn braces: Bless relaxes.'*

*'The road of excess leads to the palace of wisdom.'*

Blake was a favourite of the Beat poets of the 1950s and the hippy movement of the 1960s. For him, full expression of sexuality – for both men and women – was an essential part of worship. The spirit and flesh were one; Blake had no time for the concept of sin, or for the denial of passion. In his notes on his (now lost) painting, *A Vision of the Last Judgement* (1810) he writes:

> *Men are admitted into Heaven not because they have curbed & govern'd their Passions or have No Passions, but because they have Cultivated their Understandings.*

To Blake, the afterlife was neither remote nor frightening. In a letter to his patron and collaborator (the wealthy and popular writer, William Hayley) in 1800, Blake comforted him on the loss of his young son:

> *I know that our deceased friends are more really with us than when they were apparent to our mortal part. Thirteen years ago I lost a brother, and with his spirit I converse daily and hourly in the spirit, and see him in my remembrance, in the region of my imagination. I hear his advice, and even now write from his dictate.*

Blake's younger brother Robert had died of consumption when he was twenty-five, a loss that affected Blake deeply. In a scene reminiscent of Cuthbert's vision of the death of St Aidan, Blake observed his brother's released spirit ascend through the ceiling 'clapping its hands for joy'. Robert regularly visited Blake in dreams. One such encounter produced a brilliant advance in printing technology. In the eighteenth century, pictures called 'etchings' were printed in the following way: Copper plates were covered with wax. The artist scratched a picture in the wax with a needle and then dipped the whole thing in acid. The acid bit into the exposed metal but left the wax alone. The wax was then removed by applying heat to melt it, and the copper plate was inked. After being wiped to remove excess ink, so there was only ink in the indented lines, the plate was then pressed on to paper, providing a print of the original picture. Robert's idea reversed the process. The artist painted directly on to the copper using varnish. When the plate was dipped in acid, the acid cut away the metal around the acid-resistant varnish, leaving the picture standing out in relief. Dispensing with the wax speeded the whole thing up and painting in varnish gave the artist far more freedom of expression than scratching away in wax. Blake's invention could have made him a great deal of money; instead it brought him only delight and immortality. 'Relief etching' allowed him to 'body forth' the visions of his imagination and create his illuminated books, the striking combinations of poetry and images for which he is now famous.

Today, Blake is known as one of England's most original artists and thinkers, but this was far from the case during his lifetime. He mounted only one exhibition of his work, in 1809. He sold nothing at all and attracted only one review. *The Examiner* dismissed him as 'an unfortunate lunatic' who had published 'a farrago of nonsense, unintelligibleness, and egregious vanity, the wild effusions of a distempered brain'. It was a view widely held. On being shown some of Blake's drawings, George III shouted 'Take them away! Take them away!' Even the poet Wordsworth thought he was mad – although, to be fair, he qualified this by saying 'that there is something in the madness of this man which interests me more than the sanity of Lord Byron or Walter Scott.'

How mad was Blake? It sounds as if he might have had bipolar disorder. He suffered from debilitating fits of gloom alternating with periods of visionary intensity and high productivity. At the age of four he saw God's head leaning in at a window. As an eight-year-old, on Peckham Rye, he saw a tree full of angels. Blake's images have a verve and simplicity that makes them feel both wild and oddly real. Today we think of him as 'imaginative' rather than 'mad'.

In *The Marriage of Heaven and Hell*, Blake dines with the Old Testament prophets Isaiah and Ezekiel. He asks them how they dare assert that God spoke to them. Isaiah answers that he 'saw no God, nor heard any' but that he had perceived 'the infinite in every thing'. The voice of God, continues the prophet, is nothing but 'the voice of honest indignation'.

'Honest indignation' describes Blake to a tee. Short, stocky and ginger, as a small child he had such a temper and hated rules so much that his father didn't dare send him to school. Instead, William was educated at home by his mother and his own reading. 'I have a great desire to know everything,' he once remarked. He had an exceptional gift for languages, teaching himself Latin, Greek and Hebrew as well as some French and Italian. His natural intelligence (and his sudden insights) meant that he never felt intellectually intimidated by anyone. His scribbles in the margins of other people's works are always lively and often very funny. Annotating the rather pompous *Discourses* of the great artist Sir Joshua Reynolds, Blake peppers the pages with exclamations like: 'Villainy!' 'A Fine Jumble!' 'Liar!' but can be generous when he agrees with a passage: 'Well Said Enough!'

In one of his own notebooks, Blake suddenly goes off on a tangent about Jesus' nose:

*I always thought that Jesus Christ was a Snubby . . . I should not have worship'd him if I had thought he had been one of those long spindle nosed rascals.*

What really got Blake's honest indignation going was injustice. No less than the Shakers, he was enraged by the class system, by slavery and by the urban poverty he saw around him in London. The values of his society seemed to him to be upside down. What mattered in England was not

*whether a man had talents & Genius, But whether he is Passive & Polite & a Virtuous Ass & Obedient to Noblemen's Opinions in Art & Sciences. If he is, he is a Good Man. If not, he must be Starved.*

Blake didn't exactly starve, but he certainly struggled to make ends meet. His parents were both in the clothing trade – his mother's first husband had died leaving her a hosiery business in Soho and Blake was born above the shop. He had no desire to join the family firm: he was 'totally destitute of the dexterity of a London shopman'. When he was ten, his parents encouraged his natural love of sketching by sending him to a drawing school in the Strand, where he was nicknamed the 'Little Connoisseur'. As a teenager, he spent hours drawing in Westminster Abbey (where he had more visions of Christ and the Apostles) and set out to be apprenticed as an engraver, a relatively humble profession at the time. While casting around for the right master, his stargazing skills came in handy. He turned down one position flat, declaring: 'I do not like the man's face, it looks as if he will live to be hanged.'

Sure enough, twelve years later, the engraver, William Ryland, was hanged for forgery – the last person ever to be executed at Tyburn.

Blake showed great talent as an engraver and soon received a regular flow of commissions, particularly from booksellers wanting illustrations. By the mid-1780s he had earned enough money to buy his own press. But the business didn't last long. Blake wasn't really interested in money and he lived so much in his own head that deadlines were always a problem. He couldn't bear his clients telling him what to do, and resented the shallow tastes of 'Fashionable fools'. He refused to be pigeon-holed: he didn't care for the Romantic school's obsession with landscape and was equally contemptuous of neoclassical life-drawing, which he described as 'looking more like death, or smelling of mortality'. Blake had honed his technique by relentlessly copying the works of the Renaissance masters – Dürer, Michelangelo and Raphael – but his subject matter came directly from his own luminous daydreams. For him, the visible world was just the outward 'mortal' manifestation of an eternal reality. Where others saw the sun rising as 'a round disk of fire somewhat like a Guinea', Blake saw 'an Innumerable company of the Heavenly host crying, "Holy, Holy, Holy, is the Lord God Almighty."'

Wondrous as all this was, it wasn't exactly commercial. He and his wife Catherine lived from job to job, subsidised by hand-outs from friends, for the whole of their married life. When Blake met Catherine (or Kate, as he always called her) in 1781 – he was recovering from rejection by another woman and was vague and distracted. She, on the other hand, was instantly smitten – so much so that she fainted on being introduced to him, knowing instantly that this was the man she was meant to marry. They were wed within the year.

Catherine was illiterate: like Ann Lee, she signed her wedding contract with an 'X'. She ran the household and made Blake's clothes; he taught her to read and write and she learnt to help him with his engraving and colouring. They had no children but it was a warm and happy marriage. In periods of financial hardship, she would put an empty plate in front of him at mealtimes as a hint, but she supported him through all his mood swings, missed deadlines and aborted grand plans. In forty-five years, they spent less than a fortnight apart.

Not that there weren't tensions. During some of Blake's more fevered raptures, Catherine would sit up at night and keep him company; at others, she would leave him to it. In the long and painful gestation for the most ambitious of his prophetic books, *Jerusalem* (1820), she confessed to one of his fellow artists: 'I have very little of Mr. Blake's company; he is always in Paradise.'

There is a persistent rumour about Blake's marriage that he tried to persuade Catherine to experiment with a more open relationship, perhaps through the introduction of a young unmarried woman as a sexual partner, and that she rejected this tearfully. A strong sexual element runs through all Blake's work and his nonconformist religious background may have instilled in him some radical ideas. London in the 1780s was home to a number of religious groups known as 'antinomians'. The term means, literally, 'lawless' and it was used – usually as a term of abuse – to describe extreme Protestants whose belief in 'justification by faith alone' meant that they were supposedly able to ignore normal morality. His mother had been brought up as a Moravian, the oldest of the Protestant sects, founded in the late fourteenth century in the area of central Europe after which it was named. His father was a follower of Emmanuel Swedenborg

(1688–1772), the Swedish scientist, theologian and mystic. There is some evidence of open marriages being tolerated among both Moravians and Swedenborgians. The recent discovery and publication of Swedenborg's *Spiritual Diary* has inflamed this further. Swedenborg – who was a Moravian for a while – practised an intensely sexual mysticism. He had researched in detail the attainment of spiritual ecstasy by delaying orgasm, as practised by some Kabbalistic Jewish sects and by the Tantric school of Buddhism.

How much Blake was aware of this we shall never know: the more pious-minded of his friends destroyed most of his explicitly erotic drawings and manuscripts after his death. What we do know is that Swedenborg's best known work, *Heaven and Hell* (1758), was a major influence on Blake. One of Blake's engravings shows a female figure whose vulva has been translated into an altar, with an erect penis standing like a holy statue at its centre. This is a visual representation of Swedenborg's idea of sex as a religious sacrament.

Blake was unambiguous on the importance of sex in marriage:

> *Abstinence sows sand all over*
> *The ruddy limbs & flaming hair*
> *But Desire Gratified*
> *Plants fruits of life & beauty there*
> *In a wife I would desire*
> *What in whores is always found*
> *The lineaments of Gratified desire*

One day, Blake's friend Thomas Butts came across Kate and William sitting naked in their summerhouse in Lambeth reading one another *Paradise Lost*. Blake – far from being embarrassed – welcomed him in saying, 'It's only Adam and Eve you know!'

In 1800 William Hayley encouraged the Blakes to move near him at Felpham on the Sussex coast. At first it was a refreshing change ('Felpham is a sweet place for Study, because it is more spiritual than London,' Blake wrote) but it was also wartime. The coast was under threat of a Napoleonic invasion and the towns and villages were full of soldiers. One day, Blake found one of them, John Scolfield, lurking in his garden. His assertive streak and his dislike of authority took hold. Blake accosted the soldier and 'taking him by the elbows' manhandled him down the street. A fight followed, cheered on by a number of Scolfield's comrades, who were drinking in the Fox Inn. When it turned out Blake's gardener had invited Scolfield into the garden, Blake was formally charged with assault and – a much more serious matter – sedition: during the tussle he had yelled 'Damn the king. The soldiers are all slaves!' Given the delicate military situation, a conviction might well have cost Blake his life.

The jury acquitted Blake (the locals didn't like the drunken squaddies any more than he did) but he plunged into a depression. By the time he appeared at Chichester assizes in 1804, he had fallen out with William Hayley and he and Kate had moved away from Felpham. Ironically, it was while he was awaiting trial for treason that Blake penned the Preface to his prophetic poem *Milton* that contains his most famous lines, the hymn we now sing as 'Jerusalem', sometimes called 'England's other national anthem'. Blake had loved to ride across the Sussex downs: ' England's green and pleasant land' was his tribute to the magnificent view from Trundle Hill above Chichester.

Blake died in harness, having spent his last shilling on a pencil to keep working on his illustrations for Dante's *Divine Comedy*. He had been complaining for some time of 'shivering fits & ague' and the 'torment of my stomach'. The most likely cause of death was liver damage resulting from fifty years of inhaling toxic copper fumes as he toiled at his engravings. Catherine was with him, and his very last act was to ask her to pose for him: 'Stay Kate! Keep just as you are – I will draw your portrait – for you have ever been an angel to me.' One of his younger admirers, the painter George Richmond, was there too:

> *He died . . . in a most glorious manner. He said He was going to that Country he had all His life wished to see & expressed Himself Happy, hoping for Salvation through Jesus Christ – Just before he died His Countenance became fair. His eyes Brighten'd and he burst out Singing of the things he saw in Heaven.*

He and Catherine had always enjoyed singing together, both old ballads and his own songs, many of which had the simplicity of Shaker hymns. After his death, Catherine lived off his work and kept in close contact with him, 'consulting Mr Blake' before agreeing to any deal. She herself died four years later, calling out to him 'as if he were only in the next room, to say she was coming to him, and it would not be long now'.

It took most of a century for Blake's reputation to rise to the summit of English art and letters. These days, his *Songs of Innocence & Experience* are recognised as classics and *The Tyger* is the most anthologised English poem of all time. The longer, prophetic poems may be read less often, but the illustrations that accompany them are exhibited all over the world as masterpieces of spiritual art; few people have ever transformed their mystical experiences into such simple and instantly recognisable images. Blake's philosophy also seems to resonate deeply with the modern age. The last line of *The Marriage of Heaven and Hell*, 'For everything that lives is holy', reaches out far beyond a narrow Christian interpretation. It would do very well as the slogan for a contemporary environmental charity. But Blake was never a conventional Christian. As he once remarked, relishing the paradox: 'Jesus is the only God . . . and so am I, and so are you.'

~

Blake's reputation, rather like St Cuthbert's body, had many adventures after his death. In contrast, the posthumous fate of Blake's contemporary, the social philosopher and reformer **Jeremy Bentham** (1748–1832), was planned down to the last detail. The father of utilitarianism (the philosophy of 'the greatest good for greatest number') wanted to do something useful with his mortal remains. Instead of leaving them to moulder in the ground, he chose to put them on permanent public display. In his will, Bentham left his body to his friend Dr. Thomas Southwood Smith with very precise instructions on how to turn it into what he called his 'Auto-Icon'. It is still visible today, preserved in a glass-fronted wooden cabinet at University College, London.

Bentham first toyed with the idea of preserving his own body while in his twenties, when he asked a doctor friend to get him a human head so that he could experiment with drying it in his oven. He explained that he wanted to leave his own body to science 'with the desire that mankind may reap some small benefit by my decease, having had hitherto small opportunities to contribute while living'.

Six decades later, Bentham got his wish. He had specified in his will that his body was to be offered up for public dissection, a useful thing in itself. At that time, because of the doctrine of the resurrection of the flesh (when Christ will supposedly return at the Last Judgement to open the graves of the dead), there was still a Christian taboo against not burying bodies. This meant there was a general shortage of specimens for pathologists to work on.

Before the dissection began, at London's Webb Street School of Anatomy, twenty-eight of Bentham's friends gathered to say farewell. His corpse lay before them in a simple nightshirt. In a scene straight out of Mary Shelley's *Frankenstein* (then just into its second edition), the funeral oration was dramatically accompanied 'with thunder pealing overhead and lightning flashing through the gloom'. Once the eulogy had finished, Dr Southwood Smith made sure, as Bentham's will had specified, 'to ascertain by appropriate experiment that no life remains'. He then carefully stripped the flesh from the bones and placed the internal organs and 'the soft parts' in labelled glass containers 'like wine decanters'. His cleaned bones were then pinned together with copper wire and the skeleton dressed in a suit of Bentham's clothes, padded out with hay, straw and cotton wool. A sachet of lavender and naphthalene was placed in the stomach cavity to discourage moths. Again adhering to the instructions in his will, the body was seated in 'a Chair usually occupied by me when living in the attitude in which I am sitting when engaged in thought'. The whole ensemble was to be enhanced by the presence of Dapple, his favourite walking stick, and topped off with his actual head (well preserved and with a suitable hat on it).

Dr Southwood Smith succeeded in all save the preservation of the head. He later explained:

*I endeavoured to preserve the head untouched, merely drawing away the fluids by placing it under an air pump over sulphuric acid. By this means the head was rendered as hard as the skulls of the New Zealanders; but all expression was of course gone. Seeing this would not do for exhibition, I had a model made in wax by a distinguished French artist.'*

Some of Bentham's own hair was attached to the waxwork head, and (for some years) his actual (poorly mummified) head sat at his feet in the glass cabinet, out of which stared the disconcertingly blue glass eyes he had carried around in his pocket for six months before he died. The final flourish, also specified in the will, was the presentation to his close friends of signet rings containing his portrait in miniature, painted using a brush made from his own hair. He hoped that they would meet regularly on the anniversary of his death and that his 'Auto-Icon' would be wheeled out to join them. His wish was fulfilled and Bentham – dressed since 1939 in new, moth-resistant underwear – still occasionally graces university functions. The mummified head, once a victim of regular undergraduate pranks, is now locked away in storage.

Jeremy Bentham was never in any danger of being described as conventional. The son of a solicitor, he was a child prodigy who began learning Latin at the age of three and by the age of five could play Handel sonatas on his violin. He was physically weedy, described as having a 'dwarfish body coupled with a hawkish mind'. His mother died when he was eleven and his father sent him to study classics at Oxford soon afterwards. The young Bentham was far from impressed: 'I learned nothing,' he concluded. 'We just went to the foolish lectures of tutors to learn something of logical jargon.' At seventeen he entered Lincoln's Inn as a lawyer but the self-serving complexity of English law led him to disparage it as 'the Demon of Chikane'. What really interested him was the flood of Enlightenment ideas crossing the English Channel arguing for the reform of a society based on injustice and privilege. By the time he was twenty he had begun writing about the evolution of society and the rights of man. He described himself as 'eeking and picking his way, getting the better of prejudice and non-sense, making a little bit of discovery here and there'.

Gradually recognised by a small circle of London intellectuals, Bentham's first publication was *A Fragment of Government* (1776), a spirited attack on the English legal system. For some years, he relied on the patronage of members of the aristocracy, especially Lord Shelburne (1737–1805), the Whig Home Secretary and Prime Minister, who frequently invited him as a house guest. In 1792 Bentham's father died and his inheritance allowed him to move into a house in Queen Square Place, Westminster, where he lived for over fifty years. In *An Introduction to the Principles of Morals and Legislation* (1789), he was the first person ever to use the words 'international' and 'monetary' and he defined 'utility' as 'the property in an object which tends to produce pleasure, good or happiness, or to prevent the happening of mischief, pain, evil or unhappiness'.

In recognising the 'utility of things' Bentham's conclusion was that the law should be used to ensure 'the greatest happiness of the greatest number of people'. This was revolutionary stuff: the idea that ordinary people were entitled to happiness struck at the heart of the entrenched rights of the aristocracy, the Crown and the judicial system. In order to define happiness precisely, the ever-practical Bentham devised his own system for calculating it, which he called 'felicific calculus', listing fourteen pleasures and twelve pains – though even his closest allies thought it a bit complicated to apply in real life.

The establishment saw Bentham as deeply dangerous. His 'algebra of utility' seemed to eat like an acid through centuries of accumulated privilege and injustice. He opposed slavery, and both capital and corporal punishment; he believed in equal rights for women, and for animals; he called for the decriminalising of homosexuality; he praised free trade and the freedom of the press; he supported the right to divorce and urged the separation of the church and state. Most of what we now call liberalism can be traced back to Bentham. Many other people – not least William Blake – espoused the very same causes, but utilitarianism provided the legal and philosophical principles upon which liberal democracy would be founded. In his lifetime Bentham was much more influential outside Britain: in 1804 Napoleon transformed the European legal system with his *Code Napoleon*, based on Bentham's ideas.

In Bentham's view, English case law, which was administered by judges, had a poor record in delivering justice. He pointed to the absurdity and viciousness of over 200 separate offences that were punishable by death, including 'breaking and entering by a child under ten' and homosexuality.

As well as intellectual acumen, Bentham's other weapon was his work-rate. He cultivated friendships – by letter, as he disliked meetings – with the great and the good: from Catherine the Great of Russia to Thomas Jefferson and James Madison in the newly independent United States; from Francisco da Miranda, the Latin American revolutionary, to Talleyrand, the French master statesman. His ideas were so admired in France that in 1792 he was made an honorary citizen.

Nor did he confine his work to abstract theory. He designed a prison: the Panopticon ('see-everything') whose revolutionary circular design gave prisoners a reasonable amount of space in their cells, but allowed both gaolers and inmates to be seen from a central viewing area. This allowed one person, the prison warden, to keep an eye on everything that happened. The fact that everyone was under constant surveillance would, Bentham thought, allow the prison to function efficiently and peacefully and make its design applicable to lunatic asylums, schools and hospitals. The Panopticon influenced the layout of penal institutions all over the world, including those at Pentonville in London and Joliet Prison in Illinois. Bentham also made practical suggestions for electoral reform, all later adopted, including universal suffrage and the secret ballot. In *Defence of Usury* (1797) he persuaded his friend Adam Smith to accept the charging of interest on loans. The writer G. K. Chesterton called this 'the very beginning of the modern world'.

Despite his relatively low profile in the Anglo-Saxon world at the time, Bentham could make a serious claim to be the most influential philosopher since Aristotle. And he may yet have more surprises in store for us. As he produced, without fail, fifteen to twenty pages of notes every day, he left an archive of more than 5 million manuscript pages behind him, fewer than half of which have ever been published. The Bentham Project at University College, begun in 1968, is now up to twenty-five volumes.

The regularity and sheer pace of his work life protected Bentham from social engagements, which he avoided as hard as he could. He didn't need company, describing himself as being 'in a state of perpetual and unruffled gaiety'. This, and his personal fortune, meant he could pick and choose the people he associated with. He refused to see the French intellectual and writer Madame de Staël (1766–1817) when she asked to meet him, saying she was nothing more than a 'trumpery magpie'. He once met Doctor Johnson but declared him to be 'a pompous vamper of commonplace morality'. Apart from two early dalliances, he seemed to have no intimate dealings with women, although even at the end of his life, memories of his romantic youth would quickly move him to tears. 'Take me forward, I entreat you, to the future,' he would beg his guests. 'Do not let me go back to the past.' He did occasionally allow friends to dine with him, making lists of conversational topics beforehand. At ten o'clock, he took tea. At eleven, a nightcap of half a glass of Madeira, the only alcohol he ever drank. By twelve, his guests would find themselves unceremoniously ejected. He slept on a hard bed and suffered from bad dreams and loud snoring ('If a Bentham does not snore,' he said, 'he's not legitimate.'). By day his favourite pastime was badminton – then known as 'battledore' where the players simply kept the shuttlecock in the air for the highest number of hits possible. In Bentham's lifetime, a Somerset family set the record, managing 2,117. He was also one of the first 'joggers' startling people by suddenly taking off at high speed while walking in London parks, or in his garden on what he called 'ante-prandial circumgyrations'. He once confessed he couldn't swim or whistle, but 'saw no reason to complain'.

As he got older, his eccentricities multiplied. He kept two walking sticks, named 'Dapple' and 'Dobbin'. On meeting friends he would use one or other of these to tap them on the shoulders, in mock knighthoods. He also had a 'sacred teapot' called 'Dickey' which he referred to as a pet. His (real) pet pig allegedly shared his bed for a time, and he was also fond of cats, in particular a tom-cat called Langhorne that he referred to as 'Sir John' for several years, before redesignating him as a vicar to be addressed as 'The Reverend John Langhorne'. His collection of mice ran wild in his office, destroying manuscripts and terrifying guests. 'I love anything with four legs!' he proclaimed. Bentham's house had once belonged to John Milton, to whom he erected a plaque in the garden calling him the 'Prince of Poets', though he personally found poetry a 'misapplication of time'. 'Prose', he said, 'is when all the lines except the last go on to the margin. Poetry is when some of them fall short of it.' It's hard to know whether he was employing the same dry wit when he wrote to London City Council asking if he could replace the shrubs beside his driveway with mummified corpses, which he said would be 'more aesthetic than flowers'. This idea was developed further in his book *Auto-Icon; or Farther Uses of the Dead to the Living* in which he proposed the wholesale transformation of corpses into varnished garden ornaments. On the basis that this suggestion was unlikely to enhance his reputation, his literary executors delayed its publication until a decade after his death,

Bentham liked a joke, but his writing on the Auto-Icon can't simply be dismissed as either a prank or the onset of dementia. His value as a philosopher was in his unswerving application of the principle of utility. Death, then as now, was a taboo, steeped in fear and religious superstition. Burying corpses and letting them rot in the ground seemed to him wasteful, repugnant and unhygienic. Graveyards had been fearful places to him since childhood. He recalled going through one at night, his heart 'going pit-a-pat al the while, and I fancied I saw a ghost perched on every tombstone'. The Auto-Icon solved both problems at once. It made death useful, offering the safe disposal of corpses, while providing a permanent memorial to the dead person. Bentham's own Auto-Icon at University College is the perfect

Enlightenment object, a triumph for rationalism, materialism and utilitarianism, and a rejection of fear, superstition and the tyranny of the Church. The fact that is also very odd and faintly off-putting somehow seems entirely in character with its inventor:

> *Twenty years after I am dead, I shall be a despot, sitting in my chair with Dapple in my hand, and wearing one of the coats I wear now.*

Bentham's publicly displayed three-dimensional version of the afterlife might not shine with the mystic intensity of Blake's, but starting from opposite ends of the spiritual spectrum, they both ended in the same place. Both had faith in the power of their own imaginations. Both used their imaginations to release themselves from the old myths of heaven and hell that had so tormented Ann Lee and, in the process, both made themselves feel a lot happier about dying.

~

Practical philosophy and mystical visions come together neatly in the life of the American architect, inventor, poet, philosopher, author, teacher, entrepreneur, artist and mathematician, **Richard Buckminster Fuller** (1895–1983). He was also preoccupied with salvation, both individual and collective. 'We are not going to be able to operate our Spaceship Earth successfully, nor for much longer, unless we see it as a whole spaceship and our fate as common. It has to be everybody or nobody,' he wrote in 1969. Like each of the other lives in this chapter, his story is about having a vision and trusting it. 'Faith,' he once remarked 'is much better than belief. Belief is when someone else does the thinking.'

The Fullers had always done their own thinking. They were

New England nonconformists known as Transcendentalists, who rejected religious authority in favour of personal inspiration. Like Blake, the Transcendentalists saw both humanity and nature as manifestations of the Divine. They included amongst their number the philosopher Ralph Waldo Emerson (1803–82), the nature writer, Henry David Thoreau (1817–62) and Fuller's great-aunt, Margaret Fuller (1810–50), author of *Woman in the Nineteenth Century* (1845), the first major feminist work in the United States.

The young 'Bucky,' as he was called, was extremely short-sighted. Until he was fitted with glasses, he refused to believe that the world was not blurry. His father, like so many of the fathers in this book, died at a young age, but his family was well established and wealthy, and so, like four generations of his family before him, Bucky was sent to Harvard. It was here that his long battle with authority began. Halfway through his first year he withdrew his entire college allowance from the bank to romance a Manhattan chorus girl and was promptly expelled. He was readmitted the next year and thrown out a second time for 'irresponsibility and lack of interest'. He would later write:

> *What usually happens in the educational process is that the faculties are dulled, overloaded, stuffed and paralyzed so that by the time most people are mature they have lost their innate capabilities.*

In the end, the man who was to become the greatest architect of his age didn't graduate. The only degrees he ever received were the forty-seven honorary doctorates he was awarded many years later.

After brief stints in a textile mill and a meat-packing company, Fuller joined the navy during the First World War. As a boy in

Maine he had amused himself by making tools out of odds and ends and he put this to good use inventing a winch-like device for rescuing the pilots of navy aeroplanes, who often ended up head down underwater. Thanks to this, he was selected for officer training at the US Naval Academy, where he studied engineering. Leaving the navy to marry his wife Anne in 1917, he started a business with her father making bricks out of wood shavings, his first environmentally aware project. Both the marriage and the business were very successful until 1922, when the Fullers' four-year-old daughter, Alexandra, suddenly died from polio.

This affected Fuller terribly. He was devoted to her, and he and Anne had already nursed her through the 1918 flu epidemic and a serious bout of meningitis. The day before she died she had asked him for a walking cane similar to the one he had always used since he had damaged his knee playing football. He then left the family home on Long Island for an overnight trip to watch Harvard, his old college team, play. When Harvard won, Fuller spent the night carousing with his friends. By the time he rang his wife Anne the following afternoon, Alexandra had fallen into a coma. He rushed back home and, when he arrived, she regained consciousness just long enough to ask if he had got the cane. He had forgotten all about it, and Alexandra died shortly afterwards. Fuller was inconsolable, and his life began to fall apart. He started drinking heavily and neglecting the business. Eventually Anne's father lost patience, bought him out and then sold the company on for a fraction of its potential value. Fuller began an intense affair with a teenage girl. When she ended it, his mental health deteriorated sharply. In 1927, aged thirty-two, he walked to Lake Michigan and stood at the water's edge, contemplating suicide.

At that moment, Richard Buckminster Fuller found himself suspended several feet above the ground, surrounded by sparkling lights. Time seemed to pause and he heard a voice say:

*You do not have the right to eliminate yourself. You do not belong to you. You belong to the Universe. You and all men are here for the sake of other men.*

It was at this point that Fuller realised he had faith – faith in what he called 'the anticipatory intellectual wisdom which we may call God'. This inspired him to conceive his 'lifelong experiment', which was 'to discover what the little, penniless, unknown individual might be able to do effectively on behalf of all humanity that could not be accomplished by great nations, great religions or private enterprise'. Specifically, his mission was to plan the survival of humanity. He started compiling his 'Chronofile', a vast scrapbook that included a daily diary, recording all his ideas, copies of all his incoming and outgoing correspondence, newspaper clippings, notes and sketches, even his dry cleaning bills. In it, he called himself 'Guinea Pig B' (B for Bucky). By the end of his 'lifelong experiment', this 'lab notebook' took up 270 feet of shelving. Fuller claimed, with some justification, that he had the most-documented life of any human being in history.

After his mystical experience, he locked himself away for a whole year to read and think. He emerged convinced that the secret to saving the world was better design. His axiom was 'maximum advantage from minimal energy', a principle he observed throughout the natural world in the structure of plants and animals. He started with housing: he already had some experience in construction and knew that cheap, efficient 'machines for living' (as he called them) were needed all over the world. Ignoring thousands of years of building tradition, he went back to first principles. What if he based house design on the human frame, or a tree, hanging everything off a trunk or backbone – a system that used gravity instead of fighting it? And what if he made it from the lightest materials, like those already being used in aircraft manufacture? The result, prototyped in 1929, was the first entirely self-sufficient, portable house. Looking like an aluminium yurt, it was suspended on a central pole, ran on a diesel generator and recycled its own water so it didn't need plumbing. Plus, it was light enough to be airlifted anywhere it was needed. It was called the *Dymaxion* house – 'dymaxion' from a contraction of 'dynamic', 'maximum', and 'tension'. It slept four, and was priced at $1,500 (about $40,000 today), which meant it could be marketed as 'a house that costs no more than a car'. Although it never went into mass production, it put Fuller's name – and Dymaxion's – on the map.

Over the next two decades, Fuller created Dymaxion cars and Dymaxion bathrooms and, especially, the Dymaxion globe. This was an atlas of the world projected onto an *icosahedron* (a solid geometrical figure with twenty sides, each of which is an equilateral triangle) rather than a sphere. It had no 'up' or 'down', 'south' or 'north' and it could be unfolded into a flat map of the world. Unfolded one way it showed how the world's land masses join together; the other way did the same thing for the oceans. Laid out flat either way, it was a much more accurate representation of the world than traditional atlases but, being composed of twenty triangles, startlingly unfamiliar to look at.

Few of these conceptual innovations made any Fuller money but he persevered, taking part-time jobs to keep his wife (and his second daughter, Allegra) clothed and fed. In order to be taken seriously, he gave up smoking and drinking and started eating carefully. 'I found that if I was talking about my inventions and drinking, people just wrote them off as so much nonsense,' he explained. His diet consisted exclusively of prunes, tea, steak, and Jell-O. He experimented with a technique for sleeping as little as possible, to squeeze more out of his day. 'Dymaxion sleep', as he inevitably called it, involved training himself to take a thirty-second nap at the first sign of tiredness. He tried it for two years, averaging only two hours sleep a day, but had to stop because his colleagues at work couldn't keep up.

Then, in 1948, came the great leap forward that changed it all. Fuller had been teaching at Black Mountain College, a liberal arts foundation in North Carolina that acted as a summer camp for the elite of American avant-garde culture. Other faculty members included the composer John Cage, dancer Merce Cunningham and abstract impressionist painter Willem de Kooning.

Always trying to 'do more with less', Fuller had gone on thinking about the lightest and strongest possible building. The *simplest* way of enclosing space is a regular pyramid, or *tetrahedron*, each side of which is an equilateral triangle. (It is also much stronger than anything with rectangular sides.) The most *efficient* way to enclose space is a sphere, because it uses the least possible surface area of any three-dimensional shape. In the back of his mind was the yurt-shaped roof of his Dymaxion house and the twenty equilateral triangles on the surface of the Dymaxion globe. Then came his 'eureka' moment. What if he built a sphere out of triangular planes? Wouldn't that have the spatial capacity of a sphere and the strength of a pyramid? And so it was that, one summer evening at Black Mountain, Fuller and his students took a pile of wooden slats and built the world's first geodesic dome.

It was an approximation of a sphere made out of triangular planes and then cut it in half – and it was the perfect structure: the largest possible volume of interior space with the least amount of surface area, offering huge savings on materials and cost. The ratios were simple and beautiful: double the dome's diameter, and its footprint on the ground quadrupled while its volume grew eight times larger. It was also extremely stable and, because air could circulate freely inside, up to 30 per cent more efficient to heat than a conventional rectangular building. Fuller called it 'geodesic' because a 'geodesic line' is the shortest distance between any two points on a sphere (from the Greek, *geodaisia*, meaning 'dividing the earth'). Most remarkable of all was this: proportionally speaking, the larger the dome, the cheaper, lighter and stronger it became.

The first commercial application of Fuller's design came in 1953. The Ford Motor Company commissioned a geodesic dome to cover the central courtyard of its Rotunda building in Dearborn, Michigan. The US military followed with a second order and soon the world went dome-crazy. His immediate success turned Buckminster Fuller into a household name and even made him some money. He took out the patent in 1954, but always refused to set up as the exclusive manufacturer. When asked why he said:

> *Whatever I do, once done, I leave it alone. Society comes along in due course and needs what I have done. By then, I'd better be on to something else. It is absolutely fundamental for me to work and design myself out of business.*

There are now over 500,000 geodesic structures across the world, including the Eden Project in Cornwall and the Houston Astrodome in Texas.

Fuller's inspiration for the dome was the way in which the protons, neutrons and electrons of the atom fit together to create matter. In fact, he came to believe that the natural geometry of the whole universe is based on arrays of interlocking tetrahedra. He already had seen how the light-but-strong structure was used all over nature: in the cornea of the eye, in the shape of some viruses, and even in the configuration of the testicles. In 1985 his discovery was to receive the ultimate endorsement when a team of scientists in Houston Texas discovered a new class of carbon molecule ($C_{60}$) shaped exactly like a geodesic sphere. Its discovery won them the Nobel Prize and they named the molecule 'buckminster-fullerene' (or the 'buckyball'). It is the third known form of pure carbon in nature, after diamond and graphite.

More recently, buckminsterfullerene has been found in meteorites that date from the time of the Earth's formation, suggesting that the elements needed for life originated in space – something that Fuller himself had long believed.

The later years of Fuller's life were spent travelling back and forth across the world lecturing and inspiring people, particularly the young. He could talk for ten hours at stretch, without notes, and would wear three watches, reminding him of the time where he was, where he was going, and what it was at home. He was on tour in 1983 when he learned that the cancer his wife was suffering from had worsened. Anne had been in a deep coma for some time when he made it back to her bedside. As he held her hand, Fuller felt her move. 'She is squeezing my hand!' he exclaimed. Still holding her hand, he stood up, and immediately suffered a massive heart attack. He died soon afterwards, 'with an exquisitely happy smile on his face', according to his daughter. Anne, his wife of sixty-seven years, died a few hours later.

Way to go. Fuller's inventions may not yet have transformed our daily lives like Nikola Tesla's or even Bill Gates's. We don't live in Fuller-designed houses or drive Dymaxion cars – and geodesic domes have a tendency to leak. None of this would have troubled Fuller: he wasn't interested in inventions as such. Instead of the dome, he said, 'I could have ended up with a pair of flying slippers.' His designs were merely a by-product of his larger quest: 'My objective was humanity's comprehensive success in the universe.' Fuller's real influence has been in the worldview he has helped to create. Words we now use as standard like 'synergy' and 'holistic' are a direct result of Fuller's work. Every global campaign against poverty, or in favour of sustainability, owes something to Fuller's vision outlined in his book *Operating Manual for Spaceship Earth* (1969) and to his 'doing more with less' mantra. As his friend John Cage wrote, 'His life was so important that it shines almost with the same intensity now that it did when he had it.'

The lives of all the visionaries in this final chapter were changed by something they *could not control*, whether they called it inspiration, the Universe, an 'altered state' or the voice of God. Few of us have visions of anything like the same intensity (and let's face it, given a life like Ann Lee's, few of us would want them) but anyone who has ever been so absorbed in something that they forget where they are, will recognise the phenomenon described by the great Scottish physicist James Clerk Maxwell: 'What is done by what is called myself is, I feel, done by something greater than myself in me.'

This is one of the great mysteries of life and (like most of them) it is also a paradox. If I'm most myself when I'm least aware of myself, then, who, or what, am I? As Buckminster Fuller put it: 'I live on Earth at present, and I don't know what I am. I seem to be a verb, an evolutionary process – an integral function of the universe'.

Standing inside the vaulting lightness of a geodesic dome or admiring the beauty of a Shaker bowl, a Blake engraving or St Cuthbert's shrine in Durham cathedral brings us face to face with another mystery. Where do ideas come from? The lives of all the people in this book have survived because they left behind them something they made: a body of work, an idea, a bundle of stories. We have seen some of common factors that unite those whose achievements were built to last. A few of them are obvious advantages – a positive outlook, a gift for languages, good luck – but the majority – terrible childhoods, parents dying young, being hopeless at school, illness, psychological trauma – look more like distinct drawbacks. The Dead were no better than us – they made mistakes, behaved badly, lost the plot, lost hope, treated each other cruelly – and, as we have seen, they certainly cannot be said to have had better lives. Ultimately, though, whatever they started with, and however badly it sometimes ended, all of our distinguished Dead did something that made a difference – and they did it by making something of themselves. And so can you. As a watchword for living, the old Lebanese proverb cannot be bettered:

*The one who is not dead still has a chance.*

# Further Reading and Acknowledgements

Many of the books listed below acted as sources for the lives in this book. More importantly, they seem to us the perfect places from which to start you own explorations in the Underworld.

All books of this kind are built on the scholarship and insight of others. Some repositories were raided more regularly than any others. At the head of the table stands the completely revised 2004 edition of the *Oxford Dictionary of National Biography* (www.oxforddnb.com), which somehow manages to be both accurate and interesting about 57,000 people's lives. It is a national treasure without parallel. Close behind it comes the *American National Biography* (www.anb.org), and the 1911 edition of *Encyclopaedia Britannica,* the last great encyclopaedia to be written by real people, rather than teams of academics, with entries by Einstein, Ernest Rutherford, Bertrand Russell, Algernon Swinburne and even the anarchist Peter Kropotkin. One of the many excellent things about dead people is that, unlike scientific knowledge or our taste in music, the details of their lives never go out of date. It would be churlish not to mention www.wikipedia.com. For all its unevenness and flaws it is an invaluable tool that will only grow in usefulness the more of us that use it.

Wherever possible we have tried to indicate editions of books that are still in print.

## 1 A BAD START IN LIFE

**Leonardo da Vinci**
Charles Nicholl, *Leonardo da Vinci: The Flights of the Mind* (Allen Lane, 2004)
Leonardo da Vinci, *The Notebooks* (Profile, 2005)

**Sigmund Freud**
Peter Gay, *Freud: A Life in Our Time* (W. W. Norton & Co., 1998)
Sigmund Freud, *The Penguin Freud Reader,* ed. Adam Phillips (Penguin, 2006)

**Isaac Newton**
James Gleick, *Isaac Newton* (Fourth Estate, 2003)
Thomas Levenson, *Newton and the Counterfeiter* (Faber, 2009)

**Oliver Heaviside**
Basil Mahon, *Oliver Heaviside: Maverick Mastermind of Electricity* (Institution of Engineering and Technology, 2009)
Paul J. Nahin, *Oliver Heaviside: The Life, Work and Times of an Electrical Genius of the Victorian Age,* new edn (Johns Hopkins UP, 2002)

**Lord Byron**
Fiona McCarthy, *Byron: Life & Legend* (Faber, 2003)
Ashley Hay, *The Secret: The Strange Marriage of Annabella Milbanke and Lord Byron* (Aurum, 2001)

**Ada Lovelace**
Benjamin Woolley, *The Bride of Science: Romance, Reason and Byron's Daughter* (Macmillan, 1999)

# Further Reading

Betty O'Toole, *Ada, the Enchantress of Numbers: A Selection from the Letters of Lord Byron's Daughter and Her Description of the First Computer* (Pickering & Chatto, 1992)

## Hans Christian Andersen
Jens Andersen, *Hans Christian Andersen* (Duckworth, 2005)
Jackie Wullschlager, *Hans Christian Andersen: The Life of a Storyteller* (Allen Lane, 2000)

## Salvador Dalí
Ian Gibson, *The Shameful Life of Salvador Dalí* (Faber, 1997)
Salvador Dalí, *The Secret Life of Salvador Dalí*, tr. Haakon Chevalier (Dover Publications, 2009)

## 2  HAPPY-GO-LUCKY

## Epicurus
Epicurus, *The Epicurus Reader: Selected Writings and Testimonia*, tr. Brad Inwood and Lloyd P. Gerson (Hackett Publishing Co., 1994)

## Benjamin Franklin
H. W. Brands, *The Life and Times of Benjamin Franklin* (Doubleday, 2000)
Benjamin Franklin, *Autobiography & Other Writings*, ed. Ormand Seavey (Oxford, 1993)

## Edward Jenner
John Baron, *The Life of Edward Jenner* (London, 1827)
Richard B. Fisher, *Edward Jenner 1749–1823* (André Deutsch, 1991)

## Mary Seacole
Jane Robinson, *Mary Seacole: The Charismatic Black Nurse Who Became a Heroine of the Crimea* (Constable & Robinson, 2005)
Mary Seacole, *The Wonderful Adventures of Mrs Seacole in Many Lands*, new edn (Penguin, 2005)

## Moll Cutpurse
Janet Todd and Elizabeth Spearing, *Counterfeit Ladies* (New York University Press, 1994)
R. Sanders, *Newgate Calendar* or *Malefactor's Bloody Register* (London, 1760)

# Further Reading

## Richard Feynman

James Gleick, *Genius: Richard Feynman & Modern Physics* (Little, Brown, 1992)

*Surely You're Joking Mr Feynman!: Adventures of a Curious Character* (W. W. Norton & Co., 1985)

Richard Leighton, *Tuva or Bust!: Richard Feynman's Last Journey* (W. W. Norton & Co., 1991)

## 3 DRIVEN

### Robert Peary

Jean Malaurie, *Ultima Thule: Explorers and Natives in the Polar North* (W. W. Norton & Co., 2003)

Fergus Fleming, *Ninety Degrees North: The Quest for the North Pole* (Granta, 2001)

Josephine Peary, *My Arctic Journal: A Year among Ice-fields and Eskimos,* new edn (Cooper Square Press, 2002)

### Mary Kingsley

Mary H. Kingsley, *Travels in West Africa*, new edn (National Geographic, 2002)

Katherine Frank, *Voyager Out: The Life of Mary Kingsley* (Houghton Mifflin, 1986)

Dea Birkett, *Mary Kingsley: Imperial Adventuress* (Palgrave Macmillan, 1992)

### Alexander von Humboldt

Alexander von Humboldt, *Personal Narrative: Of a Journey to the Equinoctial Regions of the New Continent*, new edn (abridged), tr. Jason Wilson (Penguin, 2006)

N. A. Rupke, *Alexander von Humboldt: A Metabiography* (Chicago UP, 2008)

### Francis Galton

Martin Brookes, *Extreme Measures: The Dark Visions and Bright Ideas of Francis Galton* (Bloomsbury, 2004)

Francis Galton, *Hereditary Genius: An Inquiry into its Laws and Consequences*, new edn (Prometheus, 2005)

### William Morris

Fiona McCarthy, *William Morris* (Faber, 1994)

# Further Reading

William Morris, *News from Nowhere & Other Writings,* new edn (Penguin, 2004)

## 4 TOO MUCH OF A GOOD THING

**Giacomo Casanova**

Giacomo Casanova, *The Story of My Life*, new edn, tr. Stephanie Sartarelli and Sophia Hawkes (Penguin, 2002)

Ian Kelly, *Casanova: Actor, Spy, Lover, Priest* (Hodder, 2008)

**Catherine the Great**

Simon Dixon, *Catherine the Great* (Profile Books, 2009)

Virginia Rounding, *Catherine The Great: Love, Sex and Power* (Hutchinson, 2006)

**Cora Pearl**

Virginia Rounding, *Grandes Horizontales: The Lives and Legends of Four Nineteenth-Century Courtesans,* (Bloomsbury, 2003)

Katie Hickman, *Courtesans,* (HarperCollins, 2003)

Cora Pearl, *The Memoirs of Cora Pearl: The Erotic Reminiscences of a Flamboyant Nineteenth-century Courtesan*, ed. William Blatchford (Granada, 1983)

**H. G. Wells**

H. G. Wells, *H. G. Wells in Love: Postscript to an Experiment in Autobiography* new edn (Faber, 2008)

Norman and Jeanne MacKenzie, *H. G. Wells: A Biography* (Simon & Schuster, 1973)

**Colette**

Judith Thurman, *Secrets of the Flesh: A Life of Colette* (Bloomsbury, 1999)

Colette, *Cheri*, new edn (Vintage, 2001)

**Marie Bonaparte**

Celia Bertin, *Marie Bonaparte: A Life* (Harcourt, 1982)

**Alfred Kinsey**

Jonathan Gathorne-Hardy, *Sex the Measure of All Things: A Life of Alfred C. Kinsey* (Chatto & Windus, 1998)

Kinsey Institute for Sex Research, *Sexual Behaviour in the Human Male*,
    ed. Alfred C. Kinsey (W. B. Saunders, 1948)
Kinsey Institute for Sex Research, *Sexual Behaviour in the Human Female*,
    ed. Alfred. C. Kinsey (W. B. Saunders, 1953)

**Tallulah Bankhead**
Tallulah Bankhead, *My Autobiography* new edn (University Press of
    Mississippi, 2008)
David Bret, *Tallulah Bankhead: A Scandalous Life* (Robson, 1996)


5  MAN CANNOT LIVE BY BREAD ALONE

**Helena Comtesse de Noailles**
Catherine Caufield, *The Emperor of the United States of America & Other
    Magnificent British Eccentrics* (Routledge, 1981)

**George Fordyce**
John Cordy Jeaffreson, *A Book about Doctors* (London, 1860)
Clarke, *The Georgian Era: Memoirs of the Most Eminent Persons, who Have
    Flourished in Great Britain* (London, 1832)

**Elizabeth, Empress of Austria**
Joan Haslip, *The Lonely Empress: Elizabeth of Austria* (Weidenfeld &
    Nicolson, 1965)

**John Harvey Kellogg**
T. Coraghessan Boyle, *The Road to Wellville: A Comedy of the Heart & Other
    Organs* (Little, Brown, 1981)

**Henry Ford**
Steven Watts, *The People's Tycoon: Henry Ford & the American Century*
    (Alfred A. Knopf, 2005)
Henry Ford, *My Life & Work* (NuVision Publications, 2007)

**Howard Hughes**
Howard Hughes, *The Private Diaries, Memos and Letters*, ed. Richard Hack,
    (New Millenium Press, 2001)
Peter Harry Brown and Pat H. Broeske, *Howard Hughes: The Untold Story*
    (Little, Brown, 1996)

413

6 GRIN AND BEAR IT

**Pieter Stuyvesant**
Russell Shorto, *The Island at the Centre of the World* (Doubleday, 2004)

**General Antonio de Santa Anna**
Will Fowler, *Santa Anna of Mexico* (University of Nebraska Press, 2008)

**Daniel Lambert**
Jan Bondeson, *The Pig-faced Lady of Manchester Square & Other Medical Marvels* (Tempus, 2004)

**Florence Nightingale**
Mark Bostridge, *Florence Nightingale: The Woman & her Legend* (Viking, 2008)
Hugh Small, *Florence Nightingale: Avenging Angel* (Constable & Robinson, 1999)
Florence Nightingale, *Florence Nightingale's Suggestions for Thought* (Wilfrid Laurier UP, 2005)

**Fernando Pessoa**
Fernando Pessoa, *The Book of Disquiet* tr. Richard Zenith (Penguin, 2002)
Fernando Pessoa, *The Selected Prose of Fernando Pessoa* tr. Richard Zenith (Grove Atlantic, 2002)

**Dawn Langley Simmons**
Dawn Langley Simmons, *Dawn: A Charleston Legend* (Wyrick & Co. 1995)


7 THE MONKEY-KEEPERS

**Oliver Cromwell**
H. E. Marshall, *Through Great Britain & Ireland with Cromwell* (London, 1912)
Antonia Fraser, *Cromwell, Our Chief of Men* (Weidenfeld & Nicolson, 1997)

**Catherine de' Medici**
Leonie Frieda, *Catherine de' Medici* (Weidenfeld & Nicolson, 2004)

**Sir Jeffrey Hudson**
Nick Page, *Lord Minimus: The Extraordinary Life of Britain's Smallest Man* (St Martin's Press, 2002)

# Further Reading

**Rembrandt van Rijn**
Gary Schwartz, *Rembrandt's Universe* (Thames & Hudson, 2006)
Charles Fowkes *The Life of Rembrandt* (London, 1978)

**Frida Kahlo**
Andrea Kettenmann, *Frida Kahlo, 1907–1954: Pain and Passion* (Taschen, 2000)
Hayden Herrera, *Frida: A Biography of Frida Kahlo* (Harper & Row, 1983)

**Madame Mao**
Jung Chang and Jon Halliday, *Mao: The Unknown Story* (Jonathan Cape, 2005)
Ross Terrill, *Madame Mao: The White-boned Demon* (Stanford UP, 1999)

**Francis Buckland**
G. H. O. Burgess, *Curious Ark: The Curious World of Frank Buckland* (New York, 1967)
Frank Buckland, *Curiosities of Natural History* (London, 1859)
Frank Buckland, *Curious Men* (MacSweeneys, 2008)

**King Alexander I of Greece**
John Van der Kiste, *Kings of the Hellenes: The Greek Kings, 1863–1974* (Alan Sutton, 1994)

8  WHO DO YOU THINK YOU ARE?

**Titus Oates**
John Kenyon, *The Popish Plot* (Heinemann, 1972)

**Count Cagliostro**
Iain McCalman *The Seven Ordeals of Count Cagliostro* (Random House, 2004)
Philippa Faulks and Robert D. L. Cooper, *The Masonic Magician: The Life and Death of Count Cagliostro and his Egyptian Rite* (Watkins, 2008)

**George Psalmanazar**
Michael Keevak, *The Pretended Asian: George Psalmanazar's Eighteenth-century Formosan Hoax* (Wayne State UP, 2001)

# Further Reading

**Princess Caraboo**

Jennifer Raison and Michael Goldie, *Caraboo: The Servant Girl Princess* (Windrush, 1994)

**Louis de Rougemont**

Louis de Rougemont, *The Adventures of Louis de Rougemont* (Dodo Press, 2009)

**James Barry**

Rachel Holmes, *Scanty Particulars: The Life of Dr James Barry* (Viking, 2002)

**Ignácz Trebitsch Lincoln**

Bernard Wasserstein, *The Secret Lives of Trebitsch Lincoln* (Yale, 1988)

**Tuesday Lobsang Rampa**

T. Lobsang Rampa, *The Third Eye* (Random House, 1956)

T. Lobsang Rampa, *Living with the Lama* (Random House, 1964)

Sheelagh Rouse, *Twenty-Five Years with T.Lobsang Rampa* (Lulu.com, 2006)

**Archibald Belaney**

Lovat Dickson, *Wilderness Man: the Amazing True Story of Grey Owl* New Ed. (Pocket Books, 1999)

Armand G. Ruffo, *Grey Owl: The Mystery of Archie Belaney* (Coteau Books, 2003)

9 ONCE YOU'RE DEAD, YOU'RE MADE FOR LIFE

**Emma Hamilton**

Kate Williams, *England's Mistress: The Infamous Life of Emma Hamilton* (Hutchinson, 2006)

Flora Fraser, *Beloved Emma: The Life of Emma, Lady Hamilton* (Weidenfeld & Nicolson, 1986)

**John Dee**

Benjamin Woolley, *The Queen's Conjuror: The Science and Magic of Doctor Dee* (HarperCollins, 2001)

Deborah E. Harkness, *John Dee's Conversations with Angels: Cabala, Alchemy, and the End of Nature* (Cambridge, 2006)

# Further Reading

John Dee, *The Diaries of John Dee*, ed. Edward Fenton (Day Books, 1998)

**Jack Parsons**
John Carter, *Sex and Rockets: The Occult World of Jack Parsons* (Feral House, 2005)
George Pendle, *Strange Angel* (Harcourt, 2005)

**Nikola Tesla**
Marc J. Seifer, *Wizard: The Life & Times of Nikola Tesla* (Citadel Press, 1998)
Robert Lomas, *The Man Who Invented the Twentieth Century* (Headline, 2000)

**Karl Marx**
Francis Wheen, *Karl Marx* (Fourth Estate, 1999)
Karl Marx, *Selected Writings*, ed. David McLellan (Oxford, 2000)

10   IS THAT ALL THERE IS?

**St Cuthbert**
The Venerable Bede, *The Age of Bede*, ed. D. H. Farmer (Penguin, 2004)

**Ann Lee**
Richard Francis, *Ann the Word: The Story of Ann Lee* (Arcade, 2000)

**William Blake**
Peter Ackroyd, *Blake* (Sinclair Stevenson, 1995)
Marsha Keith Schuchard, *Why Mrs Blake Cried* (Century, 2006)
William Blake, *The Poetry & Prose of William Blake*, ed. Geoffrey Keynes (London, 1927)

**Jeremy Bentham**
Jeremy Bentham and John Stuart Mill, *Utilitarianism & Other Essays*, ed. Alan Ryan (Penguin, 2004)
Leslie Stephen, *The Utilitarians* (London, 1900)

**Buckminster Fuller**
R. Buckminster Fuller, *Operating Manual for Spaceship Earth* (Lars Müller Publishers, 2008)
J. Baldwin, *Bucky Works: Buckminster Fuller's Ideas for Today* (J. Wiley & Sons, 1996)

## Acknowledgements

Anyone who would like to offer corrections or get specific sources is welcome to visit the special forum on the QI website: www.qi.com/talk/bookofthedead

~

No QI book could be written without the full collaboration of our crack squad of research elves. For this book, three of them went well beyond the usual call of elven duty. Tim Ecott and James Harkin, as well as providing meticulous research notes on a host of lives, also wrote early drafts of some of the chapters; while Andy Murray, like a demented literary bodysnatcher, produced a constant stream of the freshly researched Dead for our consideration.

Piers Fletcher, Molly Oldfield, Justin Pollard, Mat Coward, Dan Schreiber, Arron Ferster and Will Bowen also added the odd corpse to the pile, as did Xander Cansell and Tibor Fischer. Special thanks must go to Catriona Luke, who raided the obituary cupboards at several large newspapers.

Thomas Edison once wrote, 'Everything comes to him who hustles while he waits.' The team at Faber are the most elegant hustlers in the business, and the most patient. Particular thanks must go to Stephen Page, Julian Loose, Dave Watkins and Judith Gates, and their team of freelances, Paula Turner, Eleanor Rees and Patricia Hymans. Beyond them, Hannah Griffiths, Will Atkinson, Miles Poynton, John Grindrod, Becky Fincham, Jason Cooper, Lisa Baker, Lizzie Jones, Archana Rao and Henry Volans all remind us what an honour is to be published by Faber, particularly in this, its eightieth year. The fact that the book's jacket looks as good as it does is down to three people: Anthony Pye-Jeary and Bob King at DeWynters and Eleanor Crow at Faber.

## Acknowledgements

Our special thanks are due to Sarah Lloyd and Rachael Kerr. This book is dedicated to our children, Harry, Claudia, Caitlin, Stella, George, Hamish and Rory, for reminding us daily that life really is the thing.

# Index

# Index

# Index

# Index

# Index

# Index